Powerful Social Studies

for Elementary Students

Second Edition

Jere Brophy
Janet Alleman

Michigan State University

THOMSON

WADSWORTH

Australia • Brazil • Canada • Mexico • Singapore • Spain
United Kingdom • United States

Powerful Social Studies for Elementary Students, Second Edition
Jere Brophy and Janet Alleman

Publisher/Executive Editor: *Vicki Knight*
Education Editor: *Dan Alpert*
Development Editor: *Tangelique Williams*
Assistant Editor: *Jennifer Keever*
Editorial Assistant: *Ann Lee Richards*
Technology Project Manager: *Amanda Kaufmann*
Marketing Manager: *Terra Schultz*
Marketing Assistant: *Rebecca Weisman*
Marketing Communications Manager: *Tami Strang*
Project Manager, Editorial Production: *Emily Smith*

Creative Director: *Rob Hugel*
Art Director: *Maria Epes*
Print Buyer: *Doreen Suruki*
Permissions Editor: *Kiely Sisk*
Production Service: *Sara Dovre Wudali, Buuji, Inc.*
Copy Editor: *Kristina Rose McComas*
Compositor: *Integra*
Cover Designer: *Patricia McDermond*
Cover Image: boy drawing: *Brand X/Getty Images;* map: *Photodisk Green/Getty Images*
Text and Cover Printer: *Webcom*

Library of Congress Control Number: 2006921377

ISBN-13: 978 0-534-55545-0
ISBN-10: 0-534-55545-4

Thomson Higher Education
10 Davis Drive
Belmont, CA 94002–3098
USA

For more information about our products, contact us at:
Thomson Learning Academic Resource Center
1-800-423-0563

For permission to use material from this text or product, submit a request online at **http://www.thomsonrights.com.**
Any additional questions about permissions can be submitted by e-mail to **thomsonrights @thomson.com.**

For Arlene Pintozzi Brophy and George Trumbull

About the Authors

Jere Brophy is a University Distinguished Professor of Teacher Education at Michigan State University. Author, coauthor, or editor of more than 20 books and 250 scholarly articles, chapters, and technical reports, he is well known for his research on teacher expectations, teacher-student relationships, teacher effects on student achievement, classroom management, student motivation, and, most recently, elementary social studies curriculum and instruction. He was a member of the Task Force on Social Studies Teaching and Learning that prepared the National Council for the Social Studies position statement entitled "A Vision of Powerful Teaching and Learning in the Social Studies: Building Social Understanding and Civic Efficacy."

Janet Alleman is a Professor in the Department of Teacher Education at Michigan State University. She is author and coauthor of a range of publications including *Children's Thinking about Cultural Universals* and a three-volume series entitled *Social Studies Excursions, K–3*. In addition to serving on a host of committees at the state and national levels, she has been a classroom and television teacher, actively working in school settings, and has taught at over a dozen international sites.

Brief Contents

Contents

CHAPTER **3**

What Does Goal-Oriented Instruction Entail? 47

CHAPTER **4**

What Do Selecting and Representing Content Entail? 60

CHAPTER 7

How Can I Teach the Other Social Science Content More Meaningfully? 138

CHAPTER **8**

How Can I Structure Classroom Discourse to Help Students Develop Social Studies Understanding? 171

CHAPTER **9**

How Can I Design, Implement, and Evaluate Instructional Activities? 188

CHAPTER 10

What Are Some Other Strategies for Teaching Social Studies? 209

CHAPTER 11

What Is the Role of Curricular Integration? 229

CHAPTER 12

CHAPTER **13**

How Can the Curriculum Be Expanded and Made More Meaningful through Home–School Connections?   264

CHAPTER **14**

What Social Studies Planning Tools Are Available?   278

CHAPTER 15

What Is the Research Base That Informs Ideas about Powerful Social Studies Teaching? 301

Preface

This book is intended for preservice and inservice elementary teachers and for social studies teacher educators. It offers a perspective on the nature and functions of elementary social studies, then presents principles and illustrative examples designed to help teachers plan social studies instruction that is coherently organized and powerful in producing desired student outcomes. It offers in-depth treatment of selected issues that we consider crucial for teachers to work through if they are to develop powerful social studies programs in their classrooms.

The book is designed to accomplish two primary purposes. First, we seek to help elementary teachers develop a clear sense of social studies as a coherent school subject organized to accomplish social understanding and civic efficacy goals. Teachers need to understand the nature and purposes of social studies in order to plan and teach the subject effectively. Second, we seek to prepare elementary teachers to identify significant social education goals that are appropriate for their students and then use these goals to guide them in selecting content, developing it through classroom discourse, and using it in authentic application activities. To illustrate the applications of our suggested guidelines, the book includes extended examples in the form of detailed plans for topically organized curricular units structured around powerful ideas. In addition, the book addresses issues of assessment, curricular integration, and home–school connections as they apply to social studies teaching, and it suggests ways to encourage classes of students to begin to function as learning communities engaged in the social construction of knowledge.

We begin in Chapter 1 by characterizing the nature of social studies as a school subject organized to support students' progress toward social understanding and civic efficacy goals. We then explore the variation that exists in social studies educators' approaches to the subject, identifying contrasting approaches in terms of their relative emphasis on transmission of the cultural heritage, social science, reflective inquiry, informed social criticism, or personal development. Within this context for thinking about K–12 social studies, we then turn to elementary social studies, first describing the widespread dissatisfaction that has been expressed with its content, then delineating reform suggestions advanced by others, and finally outlining and explaining the rationale for the approach that we develop in this book.

We agree with widespread criticisms that the content of primary-grade social studies is thin and trite and the content of middle-grade social studies is mile-wide but inch-deep. We note that these problems are often blamed on the expanding communities sequence that is commonly used as the organizer for the elementary social studies curriculum. However, we argue that this criticism is misdirected because the problem lies neither with this sequence nor with the unit and lesson topics that typically appear within it but instead with failure to develop the top-ics in ways that support progress toward major goals. If developed as networks of connected content structured around powerful ideas (instead of parades of disconnected facts and subskills), these same topics can provide a solid basis for introducing students to the social world.

We do not view the expanding communities sequence (or any other organiz-ing scheme) as fundamental to the creation of a powerful elementary social stud-ies program. Instead, we view the key to program power as organizing the content around major social education goals and associated big ideas, developed with emphasis on their connections and applications. The rationale for our approach emphasizes teaching elementary students about fundamental aspects of the human condition, studied with attention to how and why it developed through time, how and why it varies across locations and cultures, and what all of this might mean for personal, social, and civic decision making.

In particular, we believe that universal human needs and social experiences (food, clothing, shelter, families, communities, government, transportation, commu-nication, occupations, recreation, etc.) are ideal topics for units intended to introduce children to social studies. These topics represent the most fundamental and universal categories of social experience, and topic-focused curriculum units provide a basis for instruction that primary-grade students can understand and appreciate. This foundation established in the primary grades will carry forward to help students understand and appreciate the historical, geographic, and social science content of the middle grades, especially if this content also is taught with emphasis on major social studies goals and big ideas. Consequently, elementary social studies teaching will be made more powerful by continuing to address most of the same general topics that have been addressed traditionally but doing so in ways that feature more consistent focus on key social studies goals and greater coherence in structuring the teaching around powerful ideas that students can apply in their lives outside of school. This involves shifting the focus of instructional plan-ning from the expanding communities sequencing scheme to the key ideas involved in introducing children to the fundamentals of human social experience.

Our approach will appeal to elementary teachers for three reasons. First, it respects the limitations in elementary students' cognitive capacities and prior knowl-edge, so it avoids advocating premature instruction in abstract concepts. It empha-sizes curricular power and coherence but within the context of developmentally appropriate content and teaching methods. Second, it takes seriously the social understanding and civic efficacy goals of social studies, but it interprets and applies them in ways suited to the needs of elementary-grade children. Third, it avoids ill-considered notions about junking the elementary social studies curriculum and replacing it with a mixture of history, myth, lore, and fable. Instead, it calls for retaining the most important topics that have been emphasized traditionally (for good reason) but teaching about these topics in more coherent and powerful ways. The overall goal is to help students to understand how the social system works; how and why it got to be that way; how it varies across locations and cultures; and what this may mean for personal, social, and civic decision making.

Our book reflects recent classroom research on teaching school subjects for understanding, appreciation, and application. It also reflects recent position statements by the National Council for the Social Studies concerning the purposes and goals of social studies as a school subject and the principles involved in teaching it with coherence and power. Finally, although it deals in depth with fundamental issues, the book casts teachers in the role of key decision makers in planning, implementing, and assessing powerful social studies instruction. It encourages teachers to be proactive in identifying suitable social studies goals for their students, in adapting or supplementing the content, questions, and activities that their textbook series offer, and in exploiting local resources (including the students' home cultures and personal experiences) as sources of content and sites for application of social studies learning. Teachers who study the book thoughtfully will emerge from it with clear conceptions of the nature and purposes of social studies and usable knowledge about how to plan their social studies teaching with social understanding and civic efficacy goals in mind.

Noteworthy Features of the Second Edition

This second edition retains the most enduring and important content from the first edition (although in reshaped form), updates that material to take into account the significant events of the last ten years, and includes several new chapters or expanded sections on topics that were treated only briefly in the first edition. The major reshaping feature concerns the chapter on establishing a learning community within the classroom. Besides adding material on motivating students to learn, we have moved this chapter up to immediately follow the introductory chapter. This places the treatment of classroom management and student motivation prior to the treatment of curriculum and instruction, a sequencing that aligns better with the professional development concerns of most preservice teachers. In addition, we illustrate how learning-community principles can be introduced in the process of beginning the year with a unit on childhood. This will help readers to appreciate the ways that generic management and motivation principles get implemented within particular subject matter contexts, paving the way for the chapters on social studies curriculum and instruction that follow.

Chapters 3 and 4 update chapters from the first edition on goal-oriented planning and on selecting and representing content as networks of connected knowledge structured around powerful ideas. The principles emphasized in these chapters are applied within the context of developing a unit on government. Additional components are added to this model unit later to exemplify application of the principles developed in subsequent chapters. These repeated applications to an ongoing example help readers to see the connections between the different components of a good unit plan.

Chapter 3 also introduces a related feature: a planning tool illustrating unit planning and how each of its components fits into it. The complete planning tool appears in the appendix. You can revisit it after reading each of the chapters on unit components (e.g., goals, content selection and representation, discourse, activities, assessment) as a way to reconnect the content of those chapters to the big picture of unit planning.

A great deal of the content taught in social studies is drawn from the disciplines of history, geography, and the social sciences. This second edition dramatically increases attention to issues and strategies involved in selecting and teaching content drawn from these disciplines. Chapter 5 begins by clarifying our commitment to social studies as a pandisciplinary subject organized to pursue social understanding and civic efficacy goals through holistic study of unit topics, not simply a placeholder for courses in the separate disciplines organized to accomplish more narrow disciplinary goals. Then we turn to history, characterizing its nature as a discipline, places where historical content is typically taught in the elementary grades, findings from research on developments in children's historical knowledge and thinking, issues surrounding historical content and pedagogy, national standards for history teaching, and guidelines for and examples of good history content and activities.

Chapter 6 offers similar coverage of geography and anthropology (grouped together because they share a focus on culture). Chapter 7 addresses the rest of the social sciences (psychology, sociology, economics, and civics/government). The length and composition of our treatment of each of these disciplines varies with the available scholarly literature and the extent of their presence within the elementary social studies curriculum. At minimum, however, our treatments address the nature of the discipline and its representation in elementary social studies, developments in children's knowledge and thinking about content related to the discipline, the National Council for the Social Studies' standards and other national standards (if available) for teaching content drawn from the discipline, and guidelines for effective lessons and activities.

Our first edition focused heavily on Grades K–3, addressing the intermediate grades only in a single chapter on history and geography teaching. Our expanded coverage of the disciplines in this second edition is part of a general expansion of purview to the full K–6 grade range. Although the changes are most obvious in Chapters 5–7, revisions and expansions have been made throughout the text as a whole to make it as useful for teachers in Grades 4–6 as for teachers in Grades K–3.

Chapter 8 expands an earlier chapter on discourse to consider the full range of students' construction of meaning through listening, speaking, reading, and writing experiences. Here and elsewhere, the book emphasizes the importance of planning instruction to connect with students' prior knowledge, both building on valid understandings and addressing misconceptions.

Chapters 9 and 10 focus on instructional activities, expanding coverage from conventional activities to include simulation, role-play, field trips, technology-based learning, and a variety of minds-on and hands-on experiences. These chapters develop appreciation for the unique advantages that alternative activity formats offer but at the same time continue to emphasize that activities are not ends in themselves but vehicles for accomplishing particular curricular goals so that decisions about what activities to include must be made accordingly.

Chapter 11 expands the first edition's chapter on curricular integration to view the topic in the light of recent developments of state standards and benchmarks, as well as to suggest guidelines for selecting and using children's literature and technology resources as instructional materials for social studies. In addition to cautioning readers against unproductive forms of curricular integration, the chapter offers positive guidelines for integrating productively.

Chapter 12 is an expansion of the previous chapter on assessment. In addition to covering portfolio assessment and conferencing in detail, it includes new material on more conventional forms of assessment.

Chapter 13 is a new chapter on home–school connections that emphasizes bringing students' home cultures into the classroom as the ideal way to address diversity and multicultural issues. It also shows how the social studies curriculum can be extended into the home through assignments that engage students in communicating about and constructing understandings of social studies content through interactions with parents and other family members. Unlike conventional homework, these assignments are designed to produce discussions that all participating family members will find enjoyable as well as informative.

Chapter 14 is a new chapter that emphasizes how elementary social studies, more than most other subjects, requires teachers to do a lot of independent planning and decision making in order to create a powerful program. It then introduces the tools available to teachers as they carry out these responsibilities (standards, textbooks and other instructional materials, the Internet, and others), and develops principles for using these tools productively to generate or adapt instruction to meet the needs of one's students.

Chapter 15, also new, looks back at the approach to powerful elementary social studies developed throughout the text and considers it with reference to two potential sets of guidelines for instructional planning: the recent emphasis on high-stakes testing that has culminated in the No Child Left Behind legislation; and the research on effective teaching for understanding, appreciation, and life application that has developed over the last 40 years. The chapter characterizes the former as often counterproductive and the latter as the key to powerful teaching of all of the school subjects (not just social studies). It offers a synthesis of these research findings, organized around twelve principles that comprise a network of powerful ideas within which to subsume most of the principles and strategies recommended in the text as a whole.

In addition to these content features, the second edition includes several pedagogical features that should help readers to understand and apply the principles. First, the chapters end with a Your Turn section in which readers are invited to apply the chapter's principles to a scenario involving planning for teaching on a particular topic. In addition, the chapters also include comments by novice and experienced teachers who communicate in their own words their views on content developed in the chapters and talk about how they implement the principles. The chapters conclude with reflection questions designed to help readers assimilate and apply the major ideas and guidelines, whether through their own independent reflection or through discussions with peers.

Finally, more material from instructional units developed by the authors is included as examples, and mostly integrated into the chapters rather than placed in appendices. Furthermore, as noted previously, material relating to development of a powerful unit on government is introduced in the chapter on planning and elaborated in subsequent units to illustrate the decision making involved in selecting and representing content, scaffolding students' construction of understandings, evaluating learning, and so on.

So far, we have characterized our approach to elementary social studies teaching and summarized the major differences between the first and second editions of this text. As additional orientation to readers, we continue this preface with notes addressed to professors and to students, then conclude it with answers to frequently asked questions.

To the Professor

We have organized the text in a way that makes sense to us, but we encourage you to assign chapters in a different order if that is better suited to your style and organizational scheme. For example, we have placed the chapter on planning (Chapter 14) near the end of the text because it allows us to illustrate how all of the parts represented in earlier chapters fit together in comprehensive unit planning. Also, our experience has been that most preservice teachers are asked to develop units near the end of their social studies course. However, you might want students to read Chapter 14 closer to the beginning of your course as a way to allow them to see how this text frames the big picture.

To the Student

To be successful in using our text, we encourage you to begin by studying the table of contents carefully. Feel free to read any chapter or section before it is assigned. The chapters are arranged in an order that makes sense to us; however, you might have a different organizational scheme. For example, if you want to learn more about NCSS standards early in the course, we encourage you to turn to Chapter 14. If integration comes up in an early discussion as a means of finding time for social studies, skip to Chapter 11 to learn about our perspective.

View the Your Turn sections as opportunities to apply what you are reading and discussing in class. Some of you will be taking a course that uses this text early in your teacher education sequence while others will be using it during student teaching or an internship, or as part of a graduate program. If you have your own classroom, it will be easy to do the activities we suggest. However, it's not the end of the world if you don't have your own students. We recommend that you observe social studies teaching even if it is not a course requirement. Practice doing the exercises, including the design of units, either for hypothetical students or for those in one of the classes you observe. Share your work. Often, classroom teachers will offer you the opportunity to co-teach or serve as guest instructor.

Our hope is that you will apply what you are learning throughout the course. Your engagement with the content and the suggested activities will make the experiences much more memorable.

Frequently Asked Questions

1. **How do you view your textbook?**
   Our book, not unlike any other textbook for students or teachers, is not intended to be a single source. While it might be the only social studies text

they are asked to purchase, we encourage our readers to expand their repertoire of perspectives by locating articles and books referenced at the ends of chapters, searching the Internet, reviewing selections suggested by other professionals, and so on.

2. **What does your text offer teachers in the early grades?**

We are convinced that children have untapped capacity. Our research on children's thinking about cultural universals has been encouraging and eye opening. It suggests, for example, that these are viable topics for young children. Their interest surrounding these topics is high, but they lack networks of connected knowledge and possess lots of misconceptions. Other researchers have found other similar patterns. Knowing about how children think about social studies topics can help teachers both to connect with and build on their accurate prior knowledge and to address their misconceptions.

The text provides K–3 teachers with an expanded and more sophisticated approach to social studies. We promote depth over breadth, the use of a range of activities, strategies, assessments, and out-of-school learning opportunities with an eye always on the goals and big ideas. Examples throughout the book, including the Planning Tool, illustrate this position.

3. **What does this book offer for Grades 4–6 teachers?**

Typically, the curriculum at these levels is overloaded with content that is fractured and factually dense. We promote depth over breadth and emphasize big ideas. We provide lots of examples for making the content more authentic with questions and activities that enable students to connect what they are learning to their lives outside of school and to contemporary society.

We include an explanation, laced with examples, illustrating the importance of balancing and shifting between teaching and learning during the instructional process. While this is obviously necessary in the early grades, we view it as necessary at all levels. We advocate teacher modeling, facilitating, and debriefing opportunities using a host of strategies, assessments, and home assignments, always with an eye on the goals and big ideas.

4. **Why do you provide separate chapters on history and geography/anthropology but cluster all the other social science disciplines within a single chapter?**

The literature is much more highly developed in history, geography, economics, and civics/government than in psychology, anthropology, or sociology (as applied to elementary social studies). Also, some of these areas are emphasized more within the elementary curriculum than others. In any case, we promote a pandisciplinary approach that features holistic study of unit topics. For example, in designing a unit on the community, we would begin with the local community and study its history, its geography within the five themes, past and present economic conditions, its political or governmental structure, and sociological aspects such as roles of community members in their work, as citizens, and so on.

5. **How are you treating multicultural education in this text?**

   We take the term *multicultural* to refer not to a separate topic or set of lessons but to a perspective that pervades all aspects of powerful social studies teaching. It begins with establishing a learning community that celebrates diversity and reaches out to students' families and home cultures. It implies that history will be taught with attention to multiple perspectives on significant events and attention to the stories of people whose histories are often ignored. It assumes teaching about regions, countries, states, and other locations with attention to their cultures along with their geographic and economic characteristics. More generally, it means teaching social studies topics in ways that help students come to understand local and familiar practices within global and multicultural perspectives that "make the strange familiar" and "make the familiar strange." Finally, part of the rationale for our emphasis on human activities related to cultural universals is that this facilitates teaching with a focus on commonalities rather than differences. This promotes empathy and helps redirect children's tendencies toward presentism in thinking about the past and chauvinism in thinking about other cultures.

6. **How is technology treated in your textbook?**

   Throughout our book, we reference websites that fit naturally with the content, and there are sections in the Strategies and Planning chapters that focus on technology. We encourage teachers to use it when it matches the goals and enhances the development of the big ideas within the unit but caution against technology-based activities that lack goal relevance or cost-effectiveness. The guiding principles for selecting, implementing, and evaluating activities emphasized in Chapter 9 apply as much to technology-based activities as to more conventional activities.

7. **Why is there so much more attention given to units than to individual lessons?**

   We are proponents of depth of development of powerful ideas over breadth of coverage. We want to illustrate for the reader the value of networks of connected knowledge structured around powerful ideas that can be learned with understanding and retained in ways that make them accessible for application. In contrast, disconnected bits of information presented as isolated lessons are likely to be learned only through low-level processes such as rote memorization.

8. **What are your views on assessment?**

   We view assessment as an integral part of ongoing teaching and learning. Different forms and times for assessment should be determined by the purpose of the learning situation, the kind of information acquired, and how it will be used to accomplish social studies goals. Learning activities play an important role—they are both curriculum components that need to be assessed as such and mechanisms for eliciting indicators of student learning.

   Currently, teachers are faced with many obligations, responsibilities, and frustrations regarding assessment. To aid with these challenges, we acknowledge, describe, and provide examples to illustrate how state and national standards can inform instructional planning. Chapter 12 features guidelines for designing paper–pencil tools as well as a range of informal measures. Special attention is given to authentic instruments for serving our diverse learners.

9. **How much attention do you give to inquiry?**

We describe inquiry teaching in Chapter 10 and include examples that draw on this approach throughout our book. Inquiry can be effective for introducing new topics, processing information, and constructing/deconstructing knowledge. It also can be valuable for promoting curiosity and engaging learners in the instructional process. The key is for the teacher to "rein in" multiple responses in order to promote understanding of the big ideas and at the same time promote further investigation.

10. **What role does literacy play?**

Literacy is threaded throughout the textbook. While we are well aware that social studies is often justified because of its literacy connections, our intent is to provide a text that emphasizes subject-matter knowledge and uses reading, writing, speaking, and listening for developing that content. We recommend that literacy skills be taught during instruction time allocated for that subject and then used during social studies time in the service of social education goals.

We encourage the use of authentic children's literature, including informational texts, and provide a chapter on integration that sheds further light on issues associated with literacy.

11. **How do you think about social action within the elementary social studies program?**

We view social action as an integral part of the elementary social studies program and an important part of developing citizenship. Social action activities should match the goals and big ideas of the unit and be authentic and appropriate for the grade level.

Social action initiatives also promote self-efficacy. There is nothing more satisfying for a child than feeling s/he is making a difference. Lessons within the shelter and government units and examples described in Chapter 13 focusing on home–school connections illustrate social action possibilities for the elementary grades.

Acknowledgments

We wish to thank the colleagues, students, and teachers who have collaborated with our work and enriched our understanding of social studies. In particular, we want to express our appreciation to Donna Anderson, Ruth Bell, Nancy Bredin, Jan Paul, Laura Docter Thornburg, and Bruce VanSledright.

We also wish to express our appreciation to June Benson, who has been our secretary throughout our collaborations in social studies scholarship and research. June has made enormous contributions to our work, not only by consistently handling manuscript preparation and other normal secretarial tasks with efficiency and good humor, but in addition by producing remarkably complete and accurate transcriptions of our observational field notes and our interviews with teachers and students. She has made our work both easier and better, and we are most grateful for her help.

Finally, we wish to thank the following reviewers for their insightful suggestions: Susan M. Adler, University of Illinois, Urbana–Champaign; Maggie Beddow, California State University, Sacramento; Marsha Daria, Western Connecticut State University; Sherry Field, University of Texas, Austin; Judy Hale McCrary, Jacksonville State University; Jennifer Jakubecy, Mary Washington College; Virginia Johnson, St. Joseph's University; Bruce Larson, Western Washington University; Karon LeCompte, Peabody College of Vanderbilt University; Thomas Lucey, Illinois State University; Lauren McCay, University of Montevallo; Margit McGuire, Seattle University; Angela McNulty, University of Texas, Dallas; Donna Pearson, University of North Dakota; Yolanda Ramirez, University of Texas, Permian Basin; Tracy Rock, University of North Carolina, Charlotte; Thomas Vontz, Rockhurst University; Jane White, University of South Carolina.

CHAPTER 1

ELEMENTARY SOCIAL STUDIES: What is it? What might it become?

Barbara Knighton, Experienced Teacher

Yogi Berra is credited with the saying, "If you don't know where you are going, how will you know when you get there?" To me, that summarizes the importance of this topic. When I first began teaching, I simply taught the activities provided by my school district. I didn't have a clear picture in my head about what I wanted or expected to accomplish with my social studies lessons. My only goal was to do enough to check off social studies on my to-do list for the year. After reading this chapter, I realized that social studies is as important as literacy and math instruction in elementary classrooms.

I started by creating a set of goals and big ideas for my social studies instruction. That way, all my lessons, classroom discussions, and even assessments contribute to meeting those goals. For example, during a discussion about clothing, students were easily distracted by fabric names, stores, or manufacturing techniques. By knowing that my goals centered around why people wear clothing, I was much better prepared to focus student attention on the important information for the day.

"Social studies bears a special responsibility for citizen education." I looked for ways to emphasize citizenship within our classroom and our school. My students and I now have regular class meetings where we discuss both good times and bad and how they as citizens can contribute to a great classroom. I often ask students, "How are you helping our learning or our classroom?" We also look for ways to support our school community. We clean the playground and create snack bags for classes participating in state testing.

"Social studies is an interdisciplinary subject." I searched for ways to connect to other pieces of our curriculum. Social studies is no longer just a thirty-minute part of our day; it is part of our conversations all day long.

One example is students talking about civic and ecological responsibilities and housing developments during our science lesson on insect life cycles.

Overall, my social studies instruction is more powerful than ever before. My students look forward to the lessons and retain information. They independently discuss social studies topics during other parts of the school day. They all have a greater sense of civic responsibility in addition to a well-developed feeling of efficacy and control over how their world works.

Social studies is the hardest thing you could ever ask me to explain. I guess social studies is a class where you learn about different things that happen around the world, and do reports on stuff that happens around the world, or things like that.

(A fifth-grader quoted by Stodolsky, Salk, & Glaessner, 1991, p. 98)

My general approach is to introduce geographic ideas to lay a foundation—create a sense of what geography is that can be built on later. The students also work on self, family, and Michigan awareness (during Michigan Week). Other than that, though, social studies is basically geography. Another part is teaching students to get along with one another and fulfill the student role. My emphasis is on centers and hands-on activities. The room includes a "mystery country of the week" bulletin board that features a map, photos, and artifacts (stamps, coins, flags, etc.) from the mystery country that students can use as clues to guess what the country is by the end of the week. Around the room are posters of international flags and a variety of different types and sizes of flags, globes, and maps. Students each have pretend passports that gradually get filled up as they "visit" each mystery country.

(A first-grade teacher)

My approach follows district policy. The content focuses on map skills, self, families, and communities. There is a unit on Native Americans of the region and on feelings and autobiography (linked with language arts, in which students write their own biographies). The emphasis is on commonalities among people and the acceptance of different cultures in food, shelter, family life, affection, and learning. We also talk about famous Americans throughout the year and discuss current events each morning. Social studies is not what is in books, but what is all around you. You have to be aware of that and share it with the children. I couldn't come in here and teach without doing the news. That is what life is all about and what the children are talking about.

(A second-grade teacher)

Social studies is people in the community, the world, living with each other, working with and learning about each other. Also, a sense of history and how it plays a part in the present and future. Helping students to understand the world, whether at a map or differences in language. It is more than just subject matter in that it needs to be made real to students, something they become actively involved with and can apply to their lives. I have found that if I keep my students involved and thinking, I can make it meaningful to them. For example, some aren't much interested in government or how it influences them, but if you talk about laws that affect them personally, you can make it real to them.

(A third-grade teacher)

Social studies is taught for knowledge and awareness of the society, the world, and its geographical and physical makeup. It's the world that students live in. It's their life. This includes getting along with others that you interact with socially, as well as history (you bring all of your background with you into your social interactions). Another aspect is awareness and acceptance of other cultures. This starts at the grass-roots level—acceptance of one another. Then it can go out to acceptance of different cultures. Also, environmental awareness, not only of geography and land forms but environmentally safe practices and conservation. There is all of the history that I teach too, but that is just part of social studies.

(A fifth-grade teacher)

As these quotations illustrate, there are varying views about social studies and its nature as a school subject. Lacking a clear sense of social education purposes and goals, many teachers are uncertain about how to teach social studies (Thornton, 2005). Often they downgrade its importance in the curriculum or offer fragmented programs because they select activities for convenience or student interest rather than for their value as means of accomplishing clearly formulated social education goals.

Such confusion is readily understandable. The history of social studies has been marked by ongoing debates over the nature, scope, and definition of the field (Armento, 1993; Evans, 2004; Seixas, 2001). Social studies educators disagree both on the general purposes of social studies and on how to accomplish particular goals effectively. Consequently, social studies instructional materials differ considerably, not only in the general kinds of content included (history, geography, etc.) but also in their approach to topics covered in common (which tribes are covered in units on Native Americans, which countries in units on geographical regions, etc.).

Fortunately, however, most competing points of view can be understood as contrasting combinations of a few basic ideas about the purposes and goals of social education. Once you understand these ideas, you can clarify your own position, recognize the thinking behind social studies curriculum guides and instructional materials prepared by others, and, if necessary, adapt them to better serve your students' social studies needs. In this initial chapter, we first describe and critique the major approaches that have been taken to social studies in general and elementary social studies in particular, then explain the position we favor (which is elaborated throughout the rest of the book).

Competing Visions of Social Studies as Citizen Education

The emergence of social studies as an interdisciplinary school subject is often credited to an influential committee report issued by the National Education Association (1916). The report called for incorporating content from previously disconnected courses in history, geography, and civics within a curriculum strand to be called "social studies." Its primary purpose would be social education. Its content would be informed by history, geography, and the social sciences, and would be selected based on its personal meaning and relevance to students and its value in preparing them for citizenship.

This same vision is still emphasized today by leading social studies educators and organizations. For example, the National Council for the Social Studies (NCSS) defined social studies as "the integrated study of the social sciences and humanities to promote civic competence." It added that "the primary purpose of social studies is to help young people develop the ability to make informed and reasoned decisions for the public good as citizens of a culturally diverse, democratic society in an interdependent world" (NCSS, 1994, p. 3).

Elementary social studies (Grades K–6) did in fact develop along the lines envisioned in the 1916 report. The curriculum drew from history, geography, civics, and economics, and later from sociology, anthropology, and psychology. Furthermore, the content was taught as interdisciplinary social studies organized by topic, rather than as school-subject versions of the academic disciplines taught as separate courses. Gradually, the *expanding communities* approach became the dominant framework for structuring the elementary social studies curriculum. Also known as the expanding horizons or the expanding environments approach, this framework begins with the self in kindergarten and then gradually expands the purview to the family and school in first grade, the neighborhood in second grade, the community in third grade, the state and region in fourth grade, the nation in fifth grade, and the hemisphere or world in sixth grade.

Secondary social studies courses (Grades 7–12) also are taught within a social studies curriculum strand that includes responsibility for preparing students for citizenship. However, most secondary courses are school-subject versions of history or one of the social sciences, in which content is addressed primarily within the single discipline rather than through interdisciplinary treatment of topics. There have been exceptions to this general trend: Contemporary ones include courses in law-related education, global education, environmental studies, or conflict resolution. Past exceptions have included mini-courses on a variety of topics and a twelfth-grade Problems of Democracy course intended as a capstone for K–12 citizenship preparation. For the most part, though, secondary social studies courses have featured titles such as U.S. History, Economics, or American Government.

Most social studies educators accept the idea that social studies bears a special responsibility for citizen education, but their visions of the ideal curriculum conflict because they differ in their definitions of citizen education and in their assumptions about how to accomplish it. Some of these disagreements are linked to curricular tensions observable in all school subjects, some reflect issues especially salient to social studies, and some reflect competition for curriculum space among disciplinary and special-interest groups within social studies.

Curricular Tensions That Cut across Subjects

Kliebard (2004) noted that curriculum debates in all school subjects reflect continuing struggles among supporters of four competing ideas about what should be the primary basis for K–12 education. The first group believes that schools should equip students with *knowledge that is lasting, important, and fundamental to the human experience*. This group typically looks to the academic disciplines, both as storehouses of important knowledge and as sources of authority about how this knowledge should be organized and taught. The second group believes that *the natural course of child development* should be the basis for curriculum planning. This group would key the content taught at each grade level to the interests and learning needs associated with its corresponding ages and stages. The third group works backward from its perceptions of *society's needs,* seeking to design schooling to prepare children to fulfill adult roles in the society. Finally, the fourth group seeks to use the schools to *combat social injustice and promote social change*. Consequently, it favors focusing curriculum and instruction around social policy issues. Many past and present curricular debates in social studies can be understood as aspects of the ongoing competition among these four general approaches to K–12 curriculum development.

Competing Approaches to Social Studies

Almost all social studies educators agree that citizen education should be the major focus of social studies, but they differ in their perspectives on citizen education and their descriptions of how it should play out in classrooms. Thus, reasonable people disagree about what is needed to prepare students for responsible citizenship.

Here are five alternatives identified by Martorella (1994):

Social Studies Should Be Taught as:	Citizenship Education Should Consist of:
1. Transmission of the cultural heritage	Transmitting traditional knowledge and values as a framework for making decisions
2. Social science	Mastering social science concepts, generalizations, and processes to build a knowledge base for later learning
3. Reflective inquiry	Employing a process of thinking and learning in which knowledge is derived from what citizens need to know in order to make decisions and solve problems
4. Informed social criticism	Providing opportunities for an examination, critique, and revision of past traditions, existing social practices, and modes of problem solving
5. Personal development	Developing a positive self-concept and a strong sense of personal efficacy

Transmission of the cultural heritage has always been the mainstream approach in the elementary grades. It emphasizes didactic teaching and content that features support for the status quo, emphasis on the development of western civilization, and uncritical celebration of and inculcation in American political values and traditions. Periodically, the transmission approach is challenged by two contrasting reform movements. Calls for one type of change typically come from academic historians and social scientists who want more organization of curricula around conceptual structures drawn from their disciplines, more coverage of disciplinary content, and preservation of the integrity of the separate disciplines in the form of separate courses. The other recurring reform position calls for more emphasis on reflective inquiry. Rooted in the ideas of John Dewey, this approach is associated with inquiry into and discussions of problems and issues that feature critical thinking, values analysis, and decision making.

Some social studies educators call for activities that go beyond those usually emphasized within the five approaches summarized in the table. Berman and LeFarge (1993) encourage lessons to help students develop competence in areas related to cooperation, conflict resolution, and respect for diversity. They believe in providing students with approaches for attacking issues in ways that will make a difference. Hess (2001) suggests that students need to participate in class discussions that focus on the kinds of divisive issues that students routinely face, while Wade (2001) suggests that the most powerful citizenship experiences rest with service learning.

Despite their varying emphases, different approaches contain many commonalities. This is because most of the diversity in social studies is not random or chaotic. Instead, it results from competition among well-understood alternative interpretations of its citizen education mission. To prepare yourself to make good social studies planning decisions, you need to clarify your own priorities concerning social education purposes and goals and their implications for your social studies teaching.

You do not need to select a single perspective. In fact, addressing more than one in a unit often will be most supportive of your goals. We will use Government to illustrate how you might incorporate all five perspectives within your unit.

If an important goal is to develop understanding and appreciation for the contributions of the founders in formulating our core democratic values, the citizenship transmission perspective might be the place to start. If another goal would be to develop an understanding of the three branches of government and how they apply to our lives today, you could draw content from political science and incorporate some of the social science perspective. If a goal would be to develop understanding and appreciation of the voting process and what it means to be an informed voter, the reflective inquiry perspective would be appropriate. If a goal would be to develop understanding and appreciation for rights and responsibilities of citizens in a democracy and you were teaching upper-elementary students, you might include a social criticism component (e.g., by debating the question, "Is there justice for all in America?"). Finally, to foster personal efficacy, you would want to include the personal development perspective (e.g., by developing the idea that government cannot do everything, so responsible citizens should consider volunteering to contribute to society as individuals who make a difference).

We offer these as examples of viable goals reflecting multiple perspectives that might be included in a government unit. Multiple perspectives add interest, balance, and variety, and have the potential for creating powerful social studies learning. The goals you select, along with age appropriateness, should be major determinants of the perspectives you emphasize.

Competition for Curriculum Space among Interest Groups within Social Studies

In addition to continuing competition among alternative positions on social education purposes and goals, current curricular debates reflect renewed competition among the disciplines for curricular "airtime." Organizations representing history, geography, and the social sciences have begun to issue policy statements concerning how their respective disciplines should be taught in K–12 social studies. These statements from disciplinary groups contain helpful summaries of powerful ideas and suggestions about teaching methods and activities. However, they also imply that their respective disciplines ought to be taught much more extensively than they are now. In building a positive case for their discipline, the authors of these statements usually do not address the question of what might be reduced in the curriculum if space for their discipline were to be increased. Sometimes, however, they attack the educational value of rival disciplines, at least as they are currently represented in typical instructional materials.

Advocates of history have been especially prone to attacking other disciplines, which they believe have supplanted history as the core of the social studies curriculum. History-oriented reform proposals call for a return to a social studies curriculum focused primarily on history, supported by geography and civics. Social science content would be included but within history courses. Advocates argue that history is the naturally integrative focal point for social studies instruction because it allows for comprehensive coverage of each topic—not only its historical aspects but also its geographical, civic, cultural, economic, and social aspects. Reform models based on these ideas include the Bradley Commission's (1988) *Building a History Curriculum: Guidelines for Teaching History in Schools* and the curriculum guidelines for history and social science teaching published by the California State Department of Education (1997).

History-centered reform proposals have not been received warmly by social studies leaders and professional organizations. Part of the conflict involves disciplinary turf protection: The social sciences do not want to cede curricular airtime to history. In addition, social scientists argue that their disciplines offer important insights about how the social world functions that all citizens ought to understand and be able to bring to bear in their civic decision making. Some of them also disparage the value of history as a basis for citizen education, arguing that knowledge about the past has limited application to the complexities of the contemporary world (Engle & Ochoa, 1988; Evans, 2004).

Many social studies educators view history-centered proposals as products of a politically conservative philosophy of schooling that emphasizes inculcation over education and embodies an overly traditional knowledge- and values-transmission approach (Cornbleth & Waugh, 1999; Nash, Crabtree, &

Dunn, 1997; Symcox, 2002). They would like to see social studies curricula be more global and multicultural in purview, more critical of traditions, and more focused on current and future issues than on the past.

For the most part, the arguments and curriculum ideas advanced in reform proposals issued by discipline-based organizations and special commissions are focused on the secondary grades. With one important exception, they do not have much to say about elementary social studies, and especially not about the primary grades. The exception involves opposition to the expanding communities sequencing framework, especially in history-centered reform proposals.

The Expanding Communities Framework

Textbook publishers and teachers traditionally have relied on the expanding communities framework for organizing the elementary social studies curriculum. For a time, this framework and the content scope and sequence associated with it was almost universal in U.S. elementary schools, and it still is used in most of them. The content is drawn from various sources and blended to center on each unit's topic (e.g., Michigan's Native populations, the fur trade, the auto industry) rather than organized according to the separate disciplines (e.g., Michigan history, geography, economics). The following topics are typically addressed in K–6 social studies programs:

Kindergarten: Self, home, school, community. Discovering myself (Who am I? How am I alike and different from others?), school (my classroom, benefits of school), working together, living at home, community helpers, children in other lands, rules, and celebrating holidays

Grade One: Families. Family membership, recreation, work, cooperation, traditions, families in other cultures, how my family is alike and different from others, family responsibilities, the family at work, our school and other schools, and national holidays

Grade Two: Neighborhoods. Workers and services in the neighborhood; food, shelter, and clothing; transportation; communication; living in different neighborhoods; my role within the neighborhood; neighborhoods and communities in other cultures; farm and city life; and protecting our environment

Grade Three: Communities. Communities past and present, different kinds of communities, changes in communities, community government and services, communities in other countries, cities, careers, urban problems, business and industry, and pioneers and American Indians

Grade Four: Geographic regions. World regions, people of the world, climatic regions, physical regions, population, food. Also, state studies: our state government, state history, people of our state, state laws, state workers, communities past and present. [Note: K–6 or K–8 social studies series typically cover geographic regions in their fourth-grade texts. However, local districts often omit purchase or minimize use of these texts and instead mandate that fourth grade be devoted to study of the state, using state-specific textbooks.]

Grade Five: U.S. history and geography. The first Americans, exploration and discovery, Colonial life, revolution and independence, westward movement, war between the states, immigrants, the Roaring 20s, lifestyles in the United States, values of the American people, and the United States as world power. Sometimes U.S. history is only covered up to the Civil War in fifth grade, with later history taught in middle school. Also, some fifth-grade texts include units on U.S. regions, Canada, and Mexico.

Grade Six: World cultures/hemispheres. Political and economic systems, land and resources, people and their beliefs, comparative cultures. Western hemisphere: early cultures of South America, the major contemporary South American countries, Central American countries, Canada, Mexico, historical beginnings of the western world. Eastern hemisphere: Ancient Greece and Rome, Middle Ages, Renaissance, Middle East, Europe, Africa, India, and China.

The expanding communities framework can accommodate most emerging topics (environmentalism, multicultural education, etc.), and it can be taught with very different mixtures of the five perspectives described by Martorella (1994). It also can be taught with different degrees of emphasis on across-subjects integration, causal explanation, life applications, and associated skills and dispositions.

Hanna (1963) rationalized the expanding communities approach as being (1) logical, in starting with the family and then moving outward toward progressively wider human communities; and (2) convenient, in allowing for a holistic, coordinated approach to the study of people living in societies. He recommended that students study the ways in which people in each community carry out basic activities associated with cultural universals, such as providing for their physical needs, transporting goods and people, communicating with one another, and governing their societies.

Children would begin with small, familiar communities and then study the same issues in larger, less familiar communities. If implemented as Hanna envisioned, the expanding communities curriculum would produce systematic social studies instruction structured around powerful ideas. However, elementary social studies texts that supposedly implement the model have been criticized as ill-structured collections of factual expositions and skills exercises that follow the letter but not the spirit of Hanna's recommendations.

They also have been criticized for being dull and boring; being too traditional and middle-class oriented in their treatment of families and communities; being sequenced according to adult rather than child logic (for example, a state is just as abstract a concept as a nation, so there is no reason why children must study the state before studying the nation); fragmenting the curriculum so that students do not get enough opportunity to see relationships that exist across communities; and failing to integrate skills instruction with instruction in content (Akenson, 1989; Frazee & Ayers, 2003).

Some critics claim that primary-grade children are interested in stories about heroes, the exotic, and the "long ago and far away," so primary curricula should concentrate on these topics rather than on familiar aspects of the family, neighborhood, and community (Egan, 1988; Ravitch, 1987). Others want students to develop a global rather than a more narrowly American purview. They note that television now brings non-Western lands and cultures into the home early, so that if one waits until the sixth grade to begin teaching world geography and cultures with an emphasis on human commonalities, it may be too late to overcome ethnocentrism that has already developed (Merryfield & Wilson, 2005). The increasing interdependence of the world's peoples and the speed at which the world is changing make a strong case for the importance of global education. UNICEF has acknowledged these phenomena and supported projects designed to provide guidelines that teachers around the world can draw upon as they develop global awareness instruction in their classrooms. This instruction provides you with opportunities to take advantage of whatever geographical and cultural diversity is represented among your students and their families (Selby et al., 2000).

Recent efforts to interpret the expanding communities approach more broadly have led to shifts in content coverage (e.g., from a focus on me and my community to my community and other communities in the nation and world) in some of the newer curriculum documents around the country. For example, California's *History—Social Science Framework* (California State Department of Education, 1997) labels the first-grade curriculum "A Child's Place in Time and Space." Yet the expanding communities approach remains fairly entrenched. It is familiar to teachers and so far has proven adaptable enough to incorporate new content and respond to criticisms without changing its basic structure.

Dissatisfaction with the Textbook Series

Whether or not the expanding communities sequence is identified as the culprit, there is widespread dissatisfaction with the curriculum content and instructional materials associated with this framework. Most of this criticism is focused on the primary grades. Surveys of teaching practices indicate that social studies is taught irregularly in Grades K–3, and critiques of instructional materials indicate that its content is not driven by coherent social education goals (Haas & Laughlin, 2001; Howard, 2003; VanFossen, 2005). There is broad agreement that (1) the content base of K–3 social studies is thin and redundant, and (2) most of this content, at least as it is presented in the textbooks, is trite, uninteresting, and either already known by students or likely to be learned by them through everyday experience (and thus not worth teaching in school).

A major reason for these problems is that the textbook series fail to articulate K–3 social studies as a coherent subject designed to develop connected sets of fundamental understandings about the social world and to move students toward clearly identified social education goals. As a result, most elementary teachers view (and teach) social studies as a collection of disconnected content and skill clusters, rather than as a coherent, goal-oriented curriculum composed of connected networks of knowledge, skills, values, and dispositions to action.

Reforms Suggested by Others

These concerns have led to calls for more substantive and coherently organized content for elementary social studies. Most of the reforms suggested by others are variations on three basic types. We will review these briefly before outlining the direction that we advocate pursuing.

Cultural Literacy/Core Knowledge

E. D. Hirsch, Jr. (1987) proposed cultural literacy as the basis for curriculum development. He produced a list of over 5,000 items of knowledge that he believed should be acquired in elementary school as a way to equip students with a common base of prior knowledge to inform their social and civic decision making. We agree with Hirsch that shared common culture is needed, but we view his list of ostensibly important knowledge as dubiously extensive and fragmented. Furthermore, because it is a long list of specifics (e.g., Alexander's horse was named Bucephalus), it leads to teaching that emphasizes breadth of coverage of disconnected details over depth of development of connected knowledge structured around powerful ideas.

Subsequently, educators inspired by Hirsch's book have used it as a basis for developing the CORE curriculum, which encompasses science, social studies, and the arts. The social studies strands are built around chronologically organized historical studies, with accompanying geographical and cultural studies. Thus, first-graders study ancient Egypt and the early American civilizations (Mayas, Incas, Aztecs). Second-graders study ancient India, China, and Greece, along with American history up to the Civil War. Third-graders study ancient Rome and Byzantium, various Native American tribal groups, and the thirteen English colonies prior to the American Revolution.

As a content base for social studies in the primary grades, the CORE curriculum is a considerable improvement over Hirsch's unorganized list of assorted knowledge items. However, it focuses on the distant past. We believe that an approach that begins with what is familiar to the students in their immediate environments and then moves to the past, to other cultures, and to consideration of the future has more to offer than ancient history as a basis for introducing students to the social world. It constitutes a better rounded and more powerful social education and equips students with many more concepts and principles that they can use to understand and explain their social experiences, thus providing them with bases for appreciating the value of social studies and developing related perceptions of self-efficacy.

History/Literature Focus

A second approach to reform is advocated by proponents of the academic disciplines that underlie social studies. These critics favor abandoning social studies as a subject designed to pursue citizen education goals using integrated content. Instead, they would offer separate courses in the academic disciplines, simplified as needed but designed to pursue the goals of history and the social sciences rather than the goals of citizenship education. This was the approach taken by "structures of the disciplines" advocates who developed the "new social studies" programs in the 1960s and 1970s. These programs never caught on in the schools for a variety of reasons, including the perceptions that they were not effective for addressing broad citizenship education goals and that they focused young children on relatively narrow and specialized disciplinary concerns prematurely, before they had acquired a basic social education.

More recently, Kieran Egan (1988), Diane Ravitch (1987), and others have advocated a variation of this approach that calls for replacing the early social studies curriculum with a heavy focus on history and related children's literature (not only historical fiction but also myths and folk tales). We believe that although K–3 children can and should learn certain aspects of history, they need a balanced and integrated social education curriculum that includes sufficient attention to powerful ideas drawn not only from history but also from the various social sciences. Consequently, we do not believe that their social education needs are well served by replacing most social science content with history content.

Similarly, we acknowledge that certain forms of children's literature (e.g., historical fiction, stories of life in other cultures) are useful social education tools, but we do not see much social education value in replacing reality-based social studies with myth and folklore. Stories about Paul Bunyan or Pecos Bill might be interesting to children, and the story of George Washington and the cherry tree might be a convenient fiction to use when teaching them about honesty, but:

1. These are fictions, not historical accounts of actual events.
2. At a time when children are struggling to distinguish what is true and continuing from what is false or fleeting, an emphasis on myth and lore is likely to interfere with their efforts to construct a reality-based model of the world.
3. As students discover that they have been taught myth, lore, and other fictions, they may begin to question the credibility of teachers or of social studies as a school subject.
4. Most of the content of myth and lore and the reasons for their development in the first place reflect the thematic preoccupations and entertainment needs of pre-modern agrarian societies, not those of contemporary Americans.

Whatever value the study of myth and folklore may have will be realized primarily within the language arts curriculum. In our view, allocating significant social studies time to myth and folklore, and for that matter to most forms of children's literature, amounts to an extension of the language arts curriculum at the expense of attempts to develop a coherent social studies curriculum focused on citizen education goals. Furthermore, proponents of this approach have made no attempts to test it empirically, and exemplary elementary teachers whom we have interviewed do not favor it. Finally, our own and others' analyses of curriculum guidelines (California's History and Social Science Framework) and textbooks that are based on the approach have identified some important problems with it (Alleman & Brophy, 1994b).

Issues Analysis

A third approach to reform has been suggested by social studies educators who believe that debating social and civic issues is the most direct way to develop dispositions toward critical thinking and reflective decision making in our citizens (Engle & Ochoa, 1988; Evans & Saxe, 1996). Most proposals for issues-centered social studies have focused on the secondary grades, but some have suggested that primary-grade social studies should de-emphasize providing students with information and instead engage them in inquiry and debate about social policy issues. We agree that reflective discussion of social issues and related decision-making opportunities should be included in teaching social studies at all grade levels. However, we also believe that a heavy concentration on inquiry and debate about social policy issues is premature for primary-grade students whose prior knowledge and experience relating to the issues often are quite limited.

The Approach That We Recommend:
Overview

We agree that reforms are needed in at least the K–3 portion of the elementary social studies curriculum because much of the content taught in those grades is trite, redundant, and unlikely to help students accomplish significant social education goals. However, the problem lies not with the topics addressed within the expanding communities framework but with the way that these topics have been taught. Many of these topics—families, communities, food, clothing, shelter, government, occupations, transportation, and communication, among others—provide a sound basis for developing fundamental understandings about the human condition. They tend to be *cultural universals*—basic human needs and social experiences found in all societies, past and present. If these topics are taught with appropriate focus on powerful ideas, students will develop a basic set of connected understandings of how the social system works; how and why it got to be that way over time; how and why it varies across locations and cultures; and what all of this might mean for personal, social, and civic decision making.

Two key points anchor our position as summarized in the previous paragraph: (1) shifting from the expanding communities sequence to *basic understandings about the human condition* as the major rationale for selecting content for elementary social studies, and (2) structuring this content around *powerful ideas* developed with emphasis on their connections and applications. We elaborate on these points in the following sections.

Shifting Emphasis from the Expanding Communities Sequence to Developing Basic Understandings about the Human Condition

Since its introduction, the expanding communities sequence has been subjected to a variety of criticisms, but it has remained popular for 75 years and proven adaptable to the times. It cannot be dismissed easily and perhaps should remain in place. However, we agree with its critics that there is nothing inherently necessary about the scope and sequence of topics typically included within the expanding communities sequence.

Piaget's cautions against getting too far away from children's experience base to the point of trying to teach abstractions that will yield "merely verbal" learning are well taken. However, his ideas about what children are capable of learning at particular ages were too pessimistic. More recent research indicates that children can learn a great many things earlier and more thoroughly if guided by systematic instruction than they would learn on their own. Also, they can use schemas built up through prior knowledge and experience as templates for understanding information about how people in other times and places have responded to parallel situations. In short, children's ability to understand social content does not hinge on its distance in time or space from the here and now but on the degree to which it focuses on people operating from motives and engaging in goal-oriented actions that match (or at least are analogous to) motives and goals that are familiar from their own life experiences.

Thus, there is no need to confine the primary grades to the here and now before moving backward in time (and outward in physical space and scope of community) in subsequent grades. Children can understand historical episodes described in narrative form with emphasis on the motives and actions of key individuals, and they can understand aspects of customs, culture, economics, and politics that focus on universal human experiences or adaptation problems that are familiar to them and for which they have developed schemas or routines. This is one reason why we have developed a revision of the traditional rationale—one that emphasizes structuring content around human activities relating to cultural universals rather than around the expanding communities sequence. Our approach can be implemented within that sequence, but it does not need to be.

Human Activities Related to Cultural Universals as Core Content

A second reason is that the term *expanding communities curriculum* is misleading. It is true that the elementary social studies curriculum is usually organized within the expanding communities *sequence,* but the categories in this sequence refer primarily to the levels of analysis at which content is addressed, not to the content itself. That is, although there is some material on families in first grade, on neighborhoods in second grade, and on communities in third grade, the *topics* of most lessons are the human social activities that are carried on within families, neighborhoods, and communities. These activities tend to be structured around cultural universals—basic needs and social experiences found in all societies, past and present (food, clothing, shelter, communication, transportation, government, etc.). *In short, the traditional elementary social studies curriculum is mostly about fundamental social aspects of the human condition related to satisfaction of culturally universal needs and wants, not about "expanding communities."*

Revised Rationale for This Core Content

In our view, teaching students about how their own and other societies have addressed the human purposes associated with cultural universals provides *a sound basis for developing fundamental understandings about the human condition,* for several reasons. First, activities relating to cultural universals account for a considerable proportion of everyday living and are the focus of much of human social organization and communal activity. Until they understand the motivations and causal explanations that underlie these activities, children do not understand much of what is happening around them all the time.

Second, children from all social backgrounds begin accumulating direct personal experiences with most cultural universals right from birth, and they can draw on these experiences as they construct understandings of social education concepts and principles. Compared to curricula organized around the academic disciplines or around forms of cultural capital closely linked to socioeconomic status, content structured around human activities relating to cultural universals is easier to connect to all children's prior knowledge and to develop in ways that stay close to their experience.

Third, because such content is inherently about humans taking action to meet their basic needs and wants, it lends itself well to presentation within narrative formats. Bruner (1990), Egan (1988), and others have noted that implicit understanding of the narrative structure is acquired early, and this structure is commonly used by children to encode and retain information. Narrative formats are well suited to conveying information about human actions related to cultural universals (including developments over time in technology and culture).

Fourth, narratives focused on humans engaged in goal-oriented behavior provide frequent opportunities to introduce basic disciplinary concepts and principles, to explore causal relationships, and to make explicit some of the human intentions and economic or political processes that children usually do not recognize or appreciate. Stories about how key inventions made qualitative changes in people's lives or about what is involved in producing basic products and bringing them to our stores can incorporate process explanations (of how things are done) and cause–effect linkages (explaining why things are done the way they are and why they change in response to inventions).

In summary, structuring the curriculum around human activities relating to cultural universals helps keep its content close to the students' life experiences and thus meaningful to them, and representing the content within narrative structures makes it easier for them to follow and remember. It also "unveils the mysteries" that the social world presents (from the children's perspective), helping them to view the cultural practices under study as rational means of meeting needs and pursuing wants.

This approach also offers two important bonuses. First, precisely because it focuses on people taking actions to meet basic needs and pursue common wants, students are likely to view the content as relevant and to appreciate follow-up activities as authentic (because they will have applications to life outside of school). Thus, it offers motivational as well as cognitive benefits. Second, the approach makes it easy to attend to diversity in natural and productive ways. When lessons deal with life in the past or in other cultures, they focus on commonalities (people pursuing familiar needs and wants), so they highlight similarities rather than differences. This helps students to see the time, place, and situation through the eyes of the people under study and thus to see their decisions and actions as understandable given the knowledge and resources available to them. Such promotion of empathy helps to counteract the tendencies toward presentism and chauvinism that are common in young children's thinking about the past and about other cultures (Brophy & Alleman, 2005; Davis, Yeager, & Foster, 2001).

Focus on Powerful Ideas

Along with focusing the content on basic understandings about the human condition, our approach to elementary social studies emphasizes the importance of structuring this content around powerful ideas developed with emphasis on their connections and applications. The importance of the latter principle has been recognized at least since Dewey (1902, 1938), who emphasized using powerful ideas to connect subject matter to children's prior knowledge in ways that make their learning experiences transformative. Transformative learning does not merely add to our fund of knowledge but enables us to see some aspect of the world in a new way, such that we find new meaning in it and value the experience (Girod & Wong, 2002). When students explore in depth the concept of biological adaptation, for example, they begin to notice aspects of the appearance and behavior of animals that they did not notice before and to hypothesize about relationships between these observed traits and the ways that animals have adapted to their environments (Pugh, 2002).

Others who have addressed the classical curricular question of what is most worth teaching have reached similar conclusions. Whether they refer to powerful ideas, key ideas, generative ideas, or simply big ideas (Smith & Girod, 2003), they converge on the conclusion that certain aspects of school subjects have unusually rich potential for application to life outside of school—most notably, powerful ideas developed with focus on their connections and applications.

Powerful ideas have several distinctive characteristics. First, they are fundamental to the subject area in general and the major instructional goals in particular. In the context of elementary social studies, we consider ideas to be powerful (or big, key, generative, or transformative) to the extent that they help students develop connected understandings of how significant aspects of the social system work; how and why they got to be that way over time; how and why they vary across locations and cultures; and what all of this might mean for personal, social, and civic decision making.

Powerful ideas tend to cluster in the midrange between broad topics such as transportation and particular items of information such as the fact that the fuel used in airplanes is not the same as the fuel used in cars. These ideas tend to be concepts, generalizations, principles, or causal explanations. Examples within transportation include the categories of land, sea, and air transportation; historical progression from human-powered to animal-powered to engine-powered transportation; the importance of transporting goods and raw materials, not just people; the role of transportation in fostering economic and cultural exchange; and the development of infrastructure to support a given form of transportation once it gets established (e.g., roads, service stations, traffic control mechanisms).

Powerful ideas are embedded within networks of knowledge and connected to other powerful ideas. Teaching about an object, tool, or action principle, for example, ordinarily would include attention to propositional knowledge (knowledge about what it is, why and how it was developed, etc.), procedural knowledge (how to use it), and conditional knowledge (when and why to use it).

Some aspects of a topic are inherently more generative or transformative than others. Powerful teaching about Iowa, for example, would call attention to its salient historical and geographic features, especially those that help explain its current population makeup and economic emphases. In contrast, there is little or no application potential in teaching about the state's flag, song, bird, and so on.

We developed our appreciation of the power of big ideas through our research on the activities included or suggested in the teachers' editions of social studies textbook series. We found many good activities but also many others that were mostly busywork: word searches, cutting and pasting, coloring, connecting dots, memorizing state capitals and state symbols, and so on. In analyzing what made the good activities good and the bad ones bad, we noted that the former consistently were focused around significant goals and big ideas, but the latter were not. Furthermore, we came to realize that a focus on goals and big ideas is important not only to help ensure that students perceive the content as interesting, relevant, and worth learning but also to help ensure that the activities based on this content are authentic and engaging.

A goal-oriented curriculum designed to teach important ideas for understanding and application will provide a basis for authentic activities that call for students to think critically and creatively in the process of conducting inquiry, solving problems, or making decisions. In contrast, a parade-of-facts curriculum restricts one's options to reading, recitation, and seatwork activities—mostly low-level ones calling for retrieval of definitions or facts (matching, filling in blanks) or isolated practice of part-skills. You cannot improve parade-of-facts curricula simply by replacing their worksheets with better activities; you must first replace the knowledge component, or at least supplement it in ways that emphasize big ideas that can provide a content base capable of supporting better activities (If you doubt this, try designing worthwhile activities based on information about the states' flags, songs, birds, etc.). Big ideas lend themselves to authentic applications, of which many will be generative and even transformative; trivial facts do not.

Summary

Social studies is a pandisciplinary subject that focuses on the social aspects of the human condition. It is informed primarily by history, geography, and the social sciences, but it also draws content from the humanities, physical sciences, local connections, current events, and other sources. In addition to academic learning goals, social studies bears special responsibility for citizen education—promoting civic competence by helping young people develop the ability to make informed and reasoned decisions for the public good as citizens of a culturally diverse, democratic society in an interdependent world.

Most social studies educators share this commitment, but they differ in their views about what should be the primary purposes, goals, and content of the social studies curriculum. Most proposed models involve some combination of transmission of the cultural heritage, social science, reflective inquiry, informed social criticism, and personal development. Traditionally, the elementary social studies curriculum has featured transmission of a celebratory version of the cultural heritage, couched within the expanding communities sequence. This curriculum has been heavily criticized, particularly in the primary grades where the content in the textbooks is thin and trite.

Many critics have blamed the expanding communities sequence for this, but closer analysis indicates that the problem lies neither with that sequence nor with the unit and lesson topics typically couched within it but instead with textbook treatments of these topics that feature parades of trivial facts and low-level activities instead of goal-oriented development of powerful ideas applied authentically.

The approach taken throughout this book reflects our revision of the traditional rationale for elementary social studies. Our revision emphasizes two key changes: (1) shifting from the expanding communities sequence to basic understandings about the human condition as the major rationale for selecting content, and (2) structuring this content around powerful ideas developed with emphasis on their connections and applications. Many fundamental understandings about the human condition concern human activities related to cultural universals, as these activities have developed over time and across locations and cultures. Powerful ideas tend to be concepts, generalizations, principles, or causal explanations that equip students with capacities for generative or transformative thinking about the topic in potential application situations that occur in or out of school. Powerful (or big, key, etc.) ideas can be appreciated by students as worth learning and can provide a content base for designing authentic applications. This is not true of content that can be described accurately as mile-wide but inch-deep, parade-of-facts, or trivial pursuit.

Reflective Questions

1. Given your priorities concerning social studies purposes and goals, what are the implications for your teaching?
2. Imagine that the local school board is recommending that the teaching of social studies be temporarily suspended. How will you respond? Why?

3. Imagine that an interviewer asks you to compare the priorities of your former K–6 social studies teachers (based on what you recall from instruction) to your own priorities. How would you respond?

4. As you reflect on your social studies vision and what the authors had to say in this chapter, what is currently missing in your approach? What do you plan on doing about it?

Your Turn:
What Is Social Studies?

For most people, trying to put together a large jigsaw puzzle without any idea of what the finished product should look like would be a pretty frustrating experience. For many children, social studies lessons are like puzzle pieces that are examined individually but never connected to a big picture. These children experience years of content and learning opportunities without ever understanding, appreciating, or applying social studies. They rarely can articulate why social studies is important and how it impacts their lives.

We suggest that you prepare a written statement describing what social studies means to you and how you will explain this to your students. Make sure that the statement reflects your social studies purposes and goals and their implications for your teaching. As you develop your plan, take into account the following elements drawn from this chapter.

Social studies is an interdisciplinary subject.

Social studies bears a special responsibility for citizenship education.

Social studies tends to be couched within the expanding communities model, but its real focus should be on teaching fundamental but powerful ideas about the human condition.

There are many approaches to teaching social studies, including the following: (1) as citizenship transmission; (2) as a social science with emphasis on disciplinary knowledge and data-gathering skills; (3) as reflective inquiry with emphasis on analyzing values and making decisions about social and civic issues; (4) as informed social criticism with emphasis on opportunities for examination, critique, and revision of past traditions, existing social practices, and methods of problem solving; and (5) as personal development with emphasis on a positive self-concept and a strong sense of personal efficacy.

One teacher whom we have observed does a remarkable job of helping students see what social studies is all about, using maps, charts, cultural artifacts, real-life problems, historical documents, and so on, and explaining how students will come to make sense out of these as a part of life's story. As a result of analyzing this information and values connected to it, they will be prepared to make informed decisions about geographic, social, historical, civic, and other issues that impact their lives now and in the future.

Another teacher connects content examples with student projects from the previous grade. She then spends time reflecting on the content covered, insights acquired, and so on, and begins showing how those prior experiences are connected to this year's social studies curriculum. At the end of the year, the students are interviewed by the upcoming teacher about what they have learned, and the teacher helps them begin to form links with the social studies subject matter that will be addressed next year.

After you have carefully planned your approach on paper, collect visuals to illustrate your key points. Share your plan with a peer and elicit feedback. Remember, if we want our students to be excited about social studies, we need to let them in on what it is and why it is important, using more than just words. Knowing what that picture on the puzzle box will look like—at least in broad terms—will go a long way toward creating a desire to participate in "making meaning" from it.

CHAPTER 2

HOW CAN I BUILD A LEARNING COMMUNITY IN MY CLASSROOM?

Kristina Utley, First-Year Teacher

Setting up an effective learning community is the basis for creating a successful classroom that promotes powerful learning and allows students to feel secure. This chapter explains step by step how to create an effective learning community, how to incorporate social studies learning into it, and how to include collaboration while motivating students to learn.

Thinking about how you are going to set up a learning community can be overwhelming. Not only do you have to think about what your classroom will look like but also about different ways in which you are going to engage students into all subjects, set up different routines, and encourage students to work collaboratively as well as independently. This chapter allowed me to visualize how I could set up my classroom so that on the first day of school, I knew how it would look and how I would carry out different routines throughout the year. I also combined real-life application of social studies into my learning community, allowing students to have a say in how their classroom works. This was an effective way to bring in social studies learning, and it gave the students a feeling of ownership of their classroom.

I have also implemented the idea of allowing the students to set up goals as a group as well as individually. These goals give the students an idea of what is expected of them and establish accountability for their work. When I facilitate this goal-oriented learning, I find a very positive outcome in what the students can produce.

This chapter emphasizes that your learning community is ongoing. Continuous modifications will need to be made throughout the year. It is OK to make mistakes. As teachers, we are ongoing learners, and what works well for one class may not work for another. It helps to get feedback from your students. This is an authentic way to realize how your learning community is working and what you may need to adjust to make it even more effective.

As you begin reading this chapter, I encourage you to read slowly and try to picture how your classroom can work with the different ideas mentioned. As a beginning teacher, I found this chapter extremely beneficial. You can use this chapter to customize a learning community that works for you and meets the specific needs of your students.

A Scenario

The week before schools starts, Mrs. Paul's students receive her letter, personally prepared, signed, and mailed. This letter is important to them because it comes from their new teacher. It fills them with anticipation, hopes, and dreams. They are eager to join her in Room 104 to begin collectively building a learning community. Her letter has given them a preview of the formal curriculum—the content to be experienced and the overarching goals to be achieved, the planned field trips and visits by resource people, and so on. It also has communicated high expectations for all learners. Most importantly, it has addressed the "hidden" curriculum— Mrs. Paul's expectations concerning the overall classroom climate and students' orientations toward learning, their teacher, and one another. Celebrating differences, fairness, rights and responsibilities, caring, and sharing, it offers a vision that her new students will find compelling and curious. They think Room 104 sounds special, but they wonder, "Will we really play a role in making all of that happen?"

Anxiety, optimism, and uncertainty are written on the students' faces as they come to Room 104 on the first day of school. Unlike previous years, this day greets students with a welcome doormat, soft music, a partially decorated room that includes a special bulletin board depicting the personal history of the teacher, and other trappings that reflect the communal voice that is about to be introduced and allowed to grow.

Introductions and organizational matters are soon followed by reference to the learning community promised in the letter. Mrs. Paul begins with a description, accompanied by visuals, of her ideal learning community. She is quick to say that this is her "sketch," her "vision," and that she wants to hear about the children's. A lengthy conversation ensues. References are made to real communities, to gardens, and to other natural places where there are plans for building something special with common goals, hopes, and dreams, and where diversity is appreciated. The teacher's storyline is inspiring, authentic, and presented with direction and purpose, yet it contains room for allowances that children would view as important and engaging.

Mrs. Paul goes on to explain herself as the teacher who receives a paycheck for assuming the role of head educator who orchestrates learning opportunities for all students. She makes no apologies for being the designated leader in charge, but she likens her role to that of the President of the United States, who needs lots of help to be an effective leader of our country. She explains that a teacher needs cooperation and assistance from everyone in the class in order to promote democratic life in the classroom.

The president has a cabinet, and Mrs. Paul plans to have one too. Health, education, welfare, and social are among the communal functions that she draws upon for organization, attachment, and action. Initially, she assigns a chair and appoints members to each area. Over the next two or three weeks, the committees will engage in dialogue about their roles, rights, responsibilities, how they will function, and how they will monitor their performance. Individual committee meetings coupled with large-group discussions are the secret to effective planning and well-executed efforts. Individual committee role and function descriptions, student rights and responsibilities, expectations, and so on are developed and posted around the room to ensure effective communication and encourage life applications.

During the course of Mrs. Paul's storyline about learning community and cabinet member efforts from the past year, she shares that the welfare committee wanted to support students with special needs. Consequently, they decided to offer lunch money on an emergency basis for kids who had no lunch—either because they forgot to bring one or lacked the resources to purchase one. This group felt that these kids should "work off" their loans, so the welfare committee found school building tasks that the kids could get paid to do, in order to reimburse the committee. This committee held fund-raisers (i.e., used-book sales, popcorn and bake sales) to generate resources. Last year's welfare committee also created a supply trunk with hats, shoelaces, mittens, and other clothing, collected during a donation drive for the purpose of applying "good citizen" actions toward peers. [Note: We believe that elementary teachers should be willing to address socioeconomic and other family circumstance differences that impact their students, rather than pretend that they do not exist. However, it is important to acknowledge such differences matter-of-factly and respond to them within the spirit of learning community norms. Talk and act in terms of coping (and helping others to cope) with special needs, not labeling or pitying those who have them.]

Launching a Learning Community

You may want to begin your school year as Mrs. Paul does by putting forth a vision of your classroom as a learning community, using past class events, work samples, and personal stories to engender early interest and inject meaning and context. Each new class, however, would be encouraged to generate its own ideas. You would plan carefully to ensure that every child has classroom (departmental) responsibilities that are within his/her capacity, match committee goals, and fit the community vision. You also would set aside periodic committee and total-class reflection time to ensure that learning community efforts are contributing to social understanding and personal and civic efficacy.

Instead of using the president's office and cabinet as your metaphor, you could use a family, a sports team, a neighborhood, or the governor of an island or state with a supportive cabinet to build context and structure into your learning community. The main idea is to let your students get a sense of what it means to satisfy needs and wants and to participate in a community where rights and responsibilities are exercised in ways that allow community members to feel in control of their destinies. There is probably no better way to build a sense of personal efficacy—a contributing factor to student achievement.

The classroom community provides a forum for living informal social studies in a safe, orderly, and enjoyable environment. It serves as a natural way for connecting cognitive, socioemotional, and moral development. It also facilitates Dorsett's (1993) concept of a good curriculum as one that respects and balances the need to educate "three people" in each individual: the worker (in this case, a student whose work is to attend school), the citizen, and the private person. All of these dimensions can be experienced firsthand in a laboratory-like setting in your classroom community.

The story of Mrs. Paul launching her community is intended to position your thinking about a powerful teaching and learning opportunity that considers knowing, understanding, appreciating, and applying a "hands-on" approach to democratic life in your classroom (a microcosm of society). If you decide to give your community a name, be sure it does not distract from the values and expectations you want your microcosm to represent.

Your learning community and the strategic moves you make as you develop it pave the way for building an environment for addressing social studies and its foundational academic disciplines. For example, every child in the community has a place in space (geography), a cultural background (anthropology), a set of experiences across time (history), needs and wants (economics), roles, norms, and expectations (sociology), the need to be guided or governed (political science), and a developing personal identity (psychology). Through structured discourse, students will begin to realize that social studies is dynamic and is an integral part of their lives across the school day—even without leaving the classroom.

The remainder of this chapter expands on the notion of developing a sense of community, presents a series of steps for creating it, describes a unit on childhood (adolescence for upper grades), and explains how it can provide a natural segue into substantive social studies content yet deepen the students' understanding and appreciation of their community and its members. Then it addresses strategies for motivating students to learn within the learning community context.

Productive Communication and Interaction Patterns

Research on powerful social studies teaching underscores the importance of establishing a productive context for learning by encouraging the class to function as a learning community. This involves articulating and following through on expectations relating to both teacher–student and student–student interaction patterns. A learning community atmosphere is an open and supportive one in which students are encouraged to speak their minds without fear of ridicule of their ideas, criticism for mentioning taboo topics, or voicing forbidden opinions. Students appreciate that the purpose of reflective discussion of the meanings and implications of content is to work collaboratively to deepen understandings. Consequently, they are expected to listen carefully and respond thoughtfully to one another's ideas, and to work together to solve problems collaboratively.

Both in advancing their own ideas and in responding critically to others, they are expected to build a case based on relevant evidence and arguments, and to avoid inappropriate behavior. They are challenged to come to grips with controversial issues, to participate assertively but respectfully in group discussions, and to work productively with partners or groups of peers in cooperative learning activities. They are expected to assume individual and group responsibilities for managing instructional materials and tasks, and to develop an ethic of caring for the personal, social, and academic needs of every child and adult who is part of the classroom.

Four Steps for Creating a Learning Community

The first step is formulating overall classroom goals specific to a social education learning community. These goals will cut across the spectrum of cognitive, socioemotional, and moral development. For example, a cognitive goal might be for students to acquire knowledge, understanding, and appreciation for cultural diversity, and apply what they learn from their social studies units to life in the classroom. A socioemotional goal might be to develop the ability to question opinions in responsible ways, and a moral goal might be to treat one another with respect.

In Step 2, you focus on the physical environment: creating and maintaining a classroom climate that features shared responsibility, celebrates diversity, and provides the support needed for the realization of intended learning outcomes. Use of physical space, accessibility of instructional materials, and availability of visual supports (such as charts, schedules, and the daily agenda and calendar of events) all contribute to the setting. So do visual materials that promote learning of unit content or provide pictorial support for academic, socioemotional, and moral responsibility. Plants, music, rugs, special chairs, identifiable spaces for reading or writing, manipulative materials, maps, globes, and computer data all build a sense of engagement and connectedness to the classroom milieu.

Step 3 in building the learning community includes the establishment of rules, norms, roles, and procedures. These range from communicating with parents to beginning the school day, managing individual and group work, resolving peer conflicts, and promoting appropriate behavior in the classroom as well as on the playground, in the lunchroom, and on the school bus.

Step 4 involves returning to your initial metaphor or picture and, as a class, creating a vision for how all of this will function. As part of the dialogue, pose questions such as "What should our classroom look like to us?" "What should it look like to a bypasser?" "What should it sound like?" "Feel like?" Responses can be captured in words, pictures, and photographs to be displayed as reminders of goals and as self-monitoring aids for achieving them.

Your style as a teacher, your prior experiences, and your unique teaching situation and students will all contribute to how you begin "growing" your learning community. The four steps are elaborated during daily dialogues that focus on the learning community as it is evolving. Questions that might be a part of these conversations include: What is going well? What needs to be modified? Why? How do we need to change a procedure? Does the physical setting need modification?

Do we need more or fewer students on a given committee? Are the tasks clearly defined? Does everyone understand his/her role?

Lots of attention needs to be given to the maintenance of learning community ideas and expectations. Be careful about moving too quickly. After creating an overall vision and plan with the class, work on one facet of the community at a time, such as rules or guiding principles. Then move on, but continuously loop back to previous steps, procedures, and practices. Think of your learning community as an ongoing growth process that has existing expectations but is always moving to new heights of understanding and positive actions.

A Childhood Unit as Your Content Vehicle

A unit on childhood can provide a natural segue into substantive social studies content that draws heavily from the social science disciplines in pandisciplinary ways, aligns with several of the NCSS (1994) content strands, and deepens the students' understanding and appreciation of their community. A childhood unit fits well as an introduction to the year because it personalizes learning for both the teacher and the students in multiple ways; it can be adapted to a range of grade levels (for upper grades, shifting the focus to adolescence); it provides an array of learning opportunities for students to experience, value, and apply; it introduces students to geographic, historical, economic, cultural, and and other aspects of their lives that will be revisited throughout the year and lead to more sophisticated understanding; it affords opportunities to make the familiar strange and the strange familiar; and it appeals to students because the content includes them at the center.

Such a unit is also a perfect place to focus on the idea that all people share some common experiences as they progress through and beyond childhood, yet everyone is unique and the differences are to be respected. A part of building your classroom community should include conversations about diversity and respect. The content of the unit can deepen children's thinking about these matters in natural ways.

Early in the unit, you could provide a lesson on the elements of childhood or adolescence, underscoring the idea that children everywhere experience many similar physical, behavioral, and intellectual changes in their early years. Creating a classroom bulletin board depicting these changes with photos of student members of the community will stimulate interest in the topic and visually underscore the big ideas. Of course, your students will love to see photos of their teacher's childhood! Students will be learning a lot about each other, and through your planned lessons, constructing understandings of networks of ideas associated with childhood as a cultural universal.

While children all over the world are alike in many ways, each is unique (e.g., fingerprints, voice, cells of the body, face, the ways s/he thinks, feelings about things, talents, etc.). Lessons addressing inheritance, culture, environment, and other factors that contribute to specialness or uniqueness provide good opportunities for conversations about appreciating diversity and avoiding prejudice—topics that need to be revisited regularly in authentic ways instead of only on designated holidays or when there is reference to the term in a sidebar in a textbook.

There is a host of children's literature sources that you might consider as you develop and implement lessons about children around the world. *To Be a Kid* (Ajmera & Ivanko, 1999); *Wake Up, World!, A Day in the Life of Children Around the World* (Hollyer, 1989); and *Children Just Like Me* (Kindersley & Kindersley, 1995) are great examples illustrating how children's lives everywhere are alike in many ways yet different in other ways due to culture, geographic conditions, economic resources, personal choices, and so on. Authentic children's literature laced with interactive narrative, electronic pen pals, or resource people in the community can be used to deepen children's thinking about culture, especially as these resources connect to their own lives. Attention to chauvinism will occur naturally as you engage in conversations about cultural borrowing, prejudice, specialness, and so on.

Birthdays and rites of passage are other useful topics. Children all around the world have birthdays, although they may have very different celebration customs from ours and there are places in the world where individual birth dates go unnoticed and instead people have communal birthdays when everyone becomes one year older. Also, people all over the world celebrate major happenings in their lives. Creating lessons that focus on these ideas builds empathy and appreciation and goes a long way in ridding the classroom community of prejudice.

Designing lessons that focus on children and work can add both a historical and a cultural perspective. For example, in pioneer times, children in America worked to help support their families; later, some worked as apprentices; and still later, some worked in factories. Today, however, there are laws against this and children go to school, which is considered their work, until they reach at least age 16. Most go on to complete high school. Children also go to school as their work in many other parts of the world, but there are places where, due to limited resources, children work at least part-time in factories or fields. Exposure to these ideas will broaden your students' thinking and foster empathy and appreciation for children around the world in new ways. Subsequent lessons might address early schools and schools today, focusing on changes over time and how economic resources are a major factor everywhere in determining the amount and quality of schooling available to children.

A series of lessons on toys and entertainment might also be included, again using historical, economic, and cultural threads to build meaningfulness. Main ideas might include: Children and their families long ago often combined work and entertainment (e.g., husking bees, cabin raisings); families made most things themselves, including toys; toys and entertainment have become big businesses in our country, but in places where resources are limited, children's games and entertainment are still much like those enjoyed by American children long ago. These lessons would provide an ideal place for building empathy with people of the past. For example, as you share your family story about toys and entertainment, perhaps beginning with your great-grandparents and using an interactive timeline accompanied by drawings, photos, or props, you can talk about changes that have occurred—including many during your lifetime—and the trade-offs associated with them. You can explain how technology and new resources trigger change, bringing both progress and new challenges. After the change, we still have most of the things we had in the past, but the older things are used or played with less frequently. They are sometimes collected by a few people, and the best specimens are treasured and put on display for us to observe in museums. A related idea is that availability, as well as values and personal preferences, influences one's choices of material resources and products.

Other thematic strands that might be woven throughout your childhood unit include children as consumers (they play a role in making choices regarding goods and services that families purchase) and children making a difference. Citizenship can come to life in your classroom community if you take on a project to help a local family who has a need due to insufficient resources, a crisis, etc. A lesson on childhood talents and interests could provide a beginning look at careers and how they sometimes evolve.

Table 2.1 shows the alignment between the NCSS social studies strands and our own unit on childhood (Alleman & Brophy, 2003b). We encourage you to consider such alignment in planning your unit as well. We find the NCSS (1994) standards statement to be a useful tool in thinking about the content in multiple ways that in turn lead to comprehensive unit plans.

We also suggest that you create home assignments that match the goals of the lessons and link the main ideas developed in the classroom to out-of-school settings. These assignments will allow applications of the content that feed back into your development of classroom community, especially if you, the teacher, also complete them. Examples might include, "Interview a grandparent, neighbor, or friend about toys and entertainment when s/he was a child as compared to today," or "Talk with a family member about one new feature you would like to add to your next birthday celebration, given what you have learned about birthdays in other cultures. Ask family members about how they celebrated their birthdays as children."

As you share your responses and talk about how you experienced the big ideas in out-of-school settings, you and the students will learn about one another and your families. This creates intimacy within the classroom community and fosters appreciation of diversity. An added bonus is that what you learn about each home situation creates opportunities for personalizing school content in the future by relating it to the jobs, hobbies, cultural backgrounds, and so on of your students and their families.

In summary, the classroom learning community is a place for helping students practice democratic life, in addition to addressing the academic subjects. Social studies content developed around the topic of childhood offers an opportunity to bridge the formal and informal, to enrich and deepen personal connections within the community, and at the same time, to develop networks of connected ideas associated with history, geography, and the social sciences (with the child at the center).

TABLE 2.1

Lessons from the Childhood Unit, *Social Studies Excursions, Volume 3*

10 National Strands (NCSS)

10 National Strands (NCSS)	1. Elements of Childhood	2. Specialness	3. A Day in the Lives around the World	4. Birthdays	5. Rites of Passage	6. Children and Work	7. Early Schools	8. Today's Schools	9. Toys & Entertainment	10. Children as Consumers	11. Adults Provide for Needs	12. Childhood Talents and Needs	13. Children Can Make a Difference
I. **Culture**—the study of culture and cultural diversity	●	■	■	■	■	■		■					
II. **Time, Continuity & Change**—the study of human beings in and over time	●	●	●			●	■	●	●	●		●	
III. **People, Places & Environments**—the study of people, places, and environments	●	●	■	■	■	●		●	●	●	●		●
IV. **Individual Development & Identity**—the study of individual development and identity	■	■	●		■	●		●				■	■
V. **Individuals, Groups & Institutions**—the study of interactions among individuals, groups, and institutions	●			●	●	■	■	■		●	●		●
VI. **Power, Authority and Governance**—the study of how people create and change structures of power, authority, and governance						●		●	■	■			
VII. **Production, Distribution and Consumption**—the study of how people organize for the production, distribution and consumption of goods and services					●	■		■	●	●	●		●
VIII. **Science, Technology and Society**—the study of relationships among science, technology, and society				●		●					●	●	
IX. **Global Connections**—the study of global connections and interdependence		●	■			■		●		●	●		●
X. **Civic Ideals & Practices**—the study of the ideals, principles, and practices of citizenship in a democratic republic											■	●	■

■ = primary focus
● = supporting focus

Cooperative Learning in a Community Setting

Once the students begin to feel comfortable with one another and interact in ways that reflect learning community norms, they are ready to work collaboratively. Cooperative learning formats are often used in social studies because they fit so well with the overarching goals of the subject, for at least three reasons (Winitzky, 1991). First, social studies teachers tend to use group work more than other teachers, and research on cooperative learning provides practical suggestions for making these activities more effective. Second, important goals of social education, such as cross-ethnic acceptance and interaction and the integration of handicapped students, are highly congruent with behavioral outcomes associated with cooperative task structures. Finally, the values underlying democratic classroom climate and cooperative learning also align well with the values promulgated by social studies educators.

A large body of research evidence indicates that cooperative learning techniques can affect achievement in positive ways (Good & Brophy, 2003), although it is important to know which techniques to use and how to implement them. Slavin (1995) emphasized that cooperative learning approaches that facilitate achievement feature two key characteristics: The activities have clear group goals, and individual members of each group are held personally accountable for their contributions. This implies the need to assess students on their cooperative efforts and learning outcomes.

Effects on outcomes other than achievement are even more impressive. Well-implemented cooperative learning arrangements promote friendship choices and prosocial patterns of interaction among students who differ in achievement, gender, race, and ethnicity. They also promote the acceptance of mainstreamed handicapped students and frequently have positive effects on self-esteem, academic self-confidence, and liking for classmates. Students who are taught how to interact in a collaborative environment tend to spend more time on tasks (asking questions, giving feedback, checking answers) and to go beyond just giving answers by providing explanations designed to make sure the listener understands the concept or process.

Task Structures

Cooperative learning methods differ according to the task structures that are in effect. The term *task structures* refers to the nature of the task (its goal, the kinds of responses that it requires, etc.) and the working conditions that accompany it. Task structures may be individual, cooperative, or competitive. In *individual* task structures, students work alone; in *cooperative* task structures, they collaborate on learning or on producing some group product; and in *competitive* task structures, they compete, either as individuals or as teams, in various contests, debates, or games. Competitive task structures usually are not compatible with learning community principles, but both individual and cooperative task structures should be observed frequently in social studies classes.

Members of student teams or groups may cooperate in working toward either group goals or individual goals. When pursuing *group goals,* the members work together to produce a single product that results from the pooled resources and shared labor of the group. For example, the group might prepare a report, video, skit, or slide display about childhood long ago for presentation to the class. When working cooperatively to reach *individual goals,* group members assist one another by discussing how to respond to questions or assignments, checking work, or providing feedback or tutorial assistance. Individual students are responsible for their own assignments but are allowed to consult with one another as they work.

Cooperative task structures also differ according to whether or not there is task specialization. *Task specialization* is in effect when a larger task is divided into several subtasks that are assigned to different group members. In preparing a report on childhood in another country, for example, task specialization would be in effect if one group member were assigned to do the introduction, another to write about the country's geography and climate, another about its natural resources and economy, and so on. Group goals and task specialization are common features of cooperative learning methods that are popular in social studies.

In a robust learning community, whole-class instruction often will be complemented by small-group learning activities as well as individual opportunities for personalizing and applying the major understandings and skills. For example, in a lesson on birthdays, the teacher might share information and pictures describing various ways children celebrate this special day around the world. This could be followed by a cooperative group activity with students listing and discussing all the new practices that they learned about in the lesson. Finally, students could independently write a journal entry describing what they would like to do on their next birthday, incorporating a practice from another culture that they learned about during the lesson.

Cooperative Learning Techniques

Several cooperative learning techniques are especially suited to social studies. Among them are Jigsaw (Aronson, Blaney, Stephan, Sikes, & Snapp, 1978); Learning Together (Johnson, Johnson, & Holubec, 1998); Group Investigation (Sharan & Sharan, 1992); Jigsaw II, an adaptation of the original Jigsaw (Slavin, 1986); and Complex Instruction (Cohen, Lotan, Scarloss, & Arellano, 1999). Cooperative learning is a natural feature of a classroom where a democratic community context is in place. Students cannot merely be placed together and told to cooperate; they need to be taught how to work collaboratively, engage in productive dialogues, and provide constructive feedback and help. Having a learning community plan in place prior to the implementation of cooperative learning techniques provides a good foundation for successful results.

In original *Jigsaw,* students work in home groups in which they teach one another material that they have learned in their respective expert groups. For example, a class of twenty students might be divided into four home groups consisting of five students each, with one member of each home group being designated as Number One, Number Two, Number Three, Number Four, or Number Five. To set the stage for Jigsaw, the teacher divides a chunk of curricular material into five subsections (also numbered one through five). Each subsection is comprehensible in its own right but forms only part of the total content to be learned. Students first work in expert groups, leaving their home groups to join students from other home groups who share the same number, to learn the corresponding subsection of content. Members of expert groups are expected to work together to learn the information thoroughly enough to be able to teach it to the other members of their home groups. Once this learning has occurred, the expert groups dissolve and the members go back to their home groups and take turns teaching what they have learned to their home group peers. We recommend that specified amounts of time be established for completing both the expert group and the home group activities so that students are clear about their responsibilities and stay on task. The teacher can circulate during group times to monitor progress and intervene if necessary.

Jigsaw II is used when a chunk of textual reading needs to be completed in a short period of time to provide context or a data base for further inquiry. All of the students begin by reading a common narrative, then each member of a given team is assigned a separate topic on which to become an expert. Students from separate teams who have been assigned to the same topic meet in expert groups to dialogue, after which they return to their teams and teach what they have learned to their teammates. Teachers find Jigsaw II especially successful in diverse classes that subsume a wide range of reading abilities, although care must be taken to ensure heterogeneity within each group.

Learning Together features diversity within groups among students who differ in achievement level, gender, race, or ethnicity. Groups are expected to turn in a collaborative product and are praised for working well together as well as for good task performance. Traditionally, Learning Together has four features: positive interdependence, face-to-face interaction among all students, individual accountability for mastering assigned material, and instruction in appropriate interpersonal and small-group skills.

Group Investigation works very well when a social studies unit has several natural subtopics. For example, a unit focusing on a particular region might offer a range of subtopics such as environmental concerns, economic priorities, climatic conditions, and so on. Students are formed into interest groups to work together using an array of instructional materials and applying cooperative inquiry, group discussion, cooperative planning, and cooperative projects. Each member of the group chooses an individual task and carries out the appropriate activities to contribute to a group report.

If students have not had previous experience with Group Investigation, the teacher can guide the whole class through one of the subtopics, first paying particular attention to the big ideas to be developed. For example, the class could use maps, the globe, and textual information to determine the climatic conditions of the region and how they impact where people live, the kinds of work they do, how the conditions influence leisure activities, and so on. Then it would be appropriate to assign groups to examine each of the other subtopics in an effort to acquire a comprehensive picture of a region and the factors that contribute to decision making associated with it. The debriefing whole-class discussions following each of the group's reports with an eye toward the big ideas is essential if this method is to enhance meaning.

Having discussed establishing a learning community and incorporating cooperative learning methods, we now address the broad topic of student motivation. As the leader of your learning community, you want to stimulate your students' motivation to learn—their tendency to find lessons and learning activities meaningful and worthwhile and to try to get the intended learning benefits from them.

Motivating Students to Learn

Students' motivation is rooted in their subjective experiences (thoughts, feelings), especially those connected to their willingness to engage in lessons and learning activities and their reasons for doing so. Brophy (2004) reviewed existing theory and research on this topic, with emphasis on identifying strategies for motivating students to learn. He depicted motivation in the classroom as expectancy x value reasoning, within the social context of a learning community.

The expectancy x value model of motivation holds that people's willingness to expend effort on an activity depends on how much (1) they expect to perform successfully if they apply themselves (and thus get whatever rewards successful performance brings), and (2) they value those rewards or the opportunity to engage in the activity itself. Effort investment is not likely if either the expectancy factor or the value factor is missing entirely. People do not willingly engage in activities that they do not enjoy and that do not lead to valued outcomes, even if they know that they can perform successfully. Nor do they willingly invest in even highly valued activities if they believe that they cannot succeed no matter how hard they try. Students will be motivated to learn to the extent that they view classroom activities and home assignments as meaningful and worthwhile and believe that they can succeed at them if they invest reasonable effort.

In addition to these subjective thoughts and feelings, students' motivation is affected by interactions with their teachers and classmates. Some classroom climates are supportive of motivation to learn, but others interfere with it. So, a comprehensive look at student motivation requires attention to three factors: individuals' internal thoughts about expectancy and about value, and their external experiences in the social context (learning community).

The Expectancy Side of Motivation

Students who approach learning activities with success expectations (a sense of efficacy or confidence) tend to focus their complete attention on the activity and bring all of their resources to bear in responding to its demands. Free of concerns about failure, they enjoy appropriate challenges, look forward to gaining new knowledge and skills, and persist in seeking to do so. If they become confused or realize that they have made mistakes, they will attempt to diagnose and address the problem, or if necessary, get help. Their goals and learning strategies focus on acquiring the knowledge and skills that the activity is intended to develop.

In contrast, students with efficacy problems experience learning activities very differently. Because they are not confident that they can succeed (or worse, are convinced that they cannot succeed), they will not be able to focus their full attention on the activity's demands. Instead, they will be distracted by anxiety, feelings of helplessness, expectations of failure, and worry about its consequences. Over time, they will come to prefer easy and routine tasks over more interesting and challenging ones (because they would rather be bored than embarrassed). They will begin to give up easily at the first sign of difficulty rather than persist in trying to overcome confusion and mistakes, and become more concerned about not looking stupid than about acquiring new knowledge and skills.

As a teacher, you will want to help your students to maintain their confidence as learners and to approach learning activities with productive goals and strategies. Doing so requires coordination of appropriate curriculum, instruction, and assessment.

Curriculum. An appropriate curriculum presents students with content and activities that lie within their *zone of proximal development,* which refers to the range of knowledge and skills that they are not yet ready to learn on their own but can learn with help from teachers (Tharp & Gallimore, 1988). Your curriculum should continually challenge students within their zones of proximal development yet make it possible for them to meet these challenges by providing sufficient instruction, guidance, and feedback. Students' prospects for successful learning depend not only on the difficulty of the activity itself but also on the degree to which you prepare them for it in advance and scaffold their learning efforts through guidance and feedback.

Instruction. Most students do not find social studies particularly difficult (compared to mathematics and science, for example). However, some may show expectancy-related problems, especially with demanding assignments. They may be daunted at the prospect of planning and carrying out a complicated project in order to accomplish what seems like a distant goal, but they will respond positively if you explain and model coping skills such as breaking the project into stages that enable them to identify and pursue a series of proximal goals that eventually lead to the ultimate goal. In the process, teach them to look backward as well as forward so that they will appreciate the progress they are making as they complete each step. Also, help them to view learning activities as opportunities to increase their knowledge and skills, not as tests of their existing capacities. Explain that knowledge and skills are not fixed but are developed through engagement in learning activities, that you are prepared to help them to become successful learners, and that they can expect to do so if they apply themselves consistently.

Assessment. Think of assessment as a way to keep track of the progress of the class as a whole and alert you to the need for adjustments in your instructional plans, not as just a way to provide a basis for assigning grades. Ordinarily, daily participation in lessons and work on assignments, especially work on significant projects, should be used at least as much as tests for assessing progress and grading students. In talking about assessment with your students, emphasize its role in providing informative feedback about their learning, and portray yourself as allied with them in preparing for the tests, not as allied with the tests in pressuring them. Follow through by using the assessment information to provide informative feedback on progress made toward major instructional goals. Include "safety nets" for students who are struggling (e.g., opportunities to take an alternative test following a period of review and relearning, or to earn extra credit by producing some product to indicate that they have overcome the deficiencies identified in the test performance).

Low achievers and students who fear failure often perform considerably below their potential on tests because they become anxious when they are aware of being evaluated. You can minimize test anxiety problems using the following strategies:

1. Rather than "springing" a test on students, let them know the date of the test, its general scope and nature, and how they can best prepare for it.
2. Be friendly and encouraging when administering the test; avoid making the testing situation any more threatening than it needs to be.
3. Avoid time pressures.
4. Stress the feedback functions rather than the evaluation or grading functions of tests when discussing them.
5. Portray tests as opportunities to assess progress rather than as measures of ability.
6. Give pretests to accustom students to "failure" and provide base rates for comparison when you administer posttests later.
7. Teach your students stress management skills and effective test-taking skills and attitudes.
8. Help your students understand that the best way to prepare for tests is to concentrate on learning what they need to know, without spending much time worrying about what will be on the test or how they will cope with anxiety in the test situation. See Chapter 12 for more on assessment.

The Value Side of Motivation

Whereas the expectancy aspects of motivation focus on performance (Can I complete this activity successfully? What will happen if I fail?), the value aspects focus on the reasons for engaging in the activity in the first place (Why should I care about this activity? What benefits will I get from engaging in it?) Students commonly report serious deficiencies in the value aspects of their social studies motivation. Even though social studies is about people and therefore should be highly interesting, students consistently rate it as their least favorite among the major school subjects. Heavy emphasis on memorization and regurgitation of miscellaneous facts is usually given as the reason.

Traditionally, teachers have been advised to address value questions either by offering incentives for good performance (extrinsic motivation) or by emphasizing content and activities that students find enjoyable (intrinsic motivation). Unfortunately, these approaches have only limited value if you want to teach social studies for understanding, appreciation, and life application.

Extrinsic approach. Rewards are popular because teachers enjoy giving them and students enjoy receiving them. However, they are often used more as behavior management tools than as motivational tools. Rewards are likely to have positive effects on motivation to learn only under certain circumstances. First, it is important to deliver rewards in ways that provide students with informative feedback and call attention to significant achievements. You want students to think about applying themselves to their studies as worth doing because it leads to increases in knowledge and skills, not just because it can lead to extrinsic rewards.

Also, rewards can act as motivators only for those students who believe that they have a chance to get them. Too often, access to rewards (or to the most desirable rewards) is effectively limited to high achievers. Learning of an opportunity to earn a reward by getting a high grade will be motivating to these students but demotivating to students who know that they have little chance to earn such a grade. Thus, you will need to individualize success criteria so that all students have equal (or at least reasonable) access to the rewards. An alternative that avoids these complications is to limit yourself to rewards given to the class as a whole ("I know that you all put in a lot of work on your projects, and I am very pleased with them. As a token of my appreciation for your efforts . . ."). Such celebrations of everyone's efforts and progress also are more in keeping with the spirit of a learning community.

Teacher praise and encouragement also are potential sources of extrinsic motivation for students, but again, it is important to deliver them effectively. Students are likely to be motivated by sincere praise delivered privately or through notes written on returned assignments, but they may not appreciate being singled out publicly, especially for things that are not really significant achievements (such as sitting up straight and paying attention). Effective praise and encouragement are delivered privately; focused on expressing appreciation and providing informative feedback rather than making judgments; and focused on the effort and care that the student put into the work, on the gains in knowledge or skills that the achievement represents, or on the achievement's more noteworthy features. Praise statements should not include attributions of successful performance to high intelligence or aptitude ("Wow—you're really good at this!") because students who become accustomed to interpreting successes as evidence of high aptitude will also begin to interpret any difficulties they experience as evidence that they lack aptitude or have reached the limits of their abilities.

Another commonly recommended extrinsic motivator is competition. It is true that the opportunity to compete, whether for prizes or merely for the satisfaction of winning, can add excitement to classroom activities. However, most motivational researchers oppose the use of competition or place heavy qualifications on its applicability. Participating in classroom activities already involves risking public failure, and a great deal of competition is already built into the grading system. Also, competition is even more salient and distracting than rewards for most students, so they are likely to pay more attention to who is winning or losing than to what they are supposed to be learning. Finally, a root problem with competition is that it creates losers as well as winners (and usually many more losers than winners). Losers of individual competitions, especially if they lose consistently, may suffer losses in confidence, self-esteem, and enjoyment of school. Members of losing teams may devalue one another and scapegoat those whom they hold responsible for the team's loss.

For these reasons, we would discourage you from emphasizing competition as a motivational strategy. If you do use competition, minimize its risks by making sure that all students have an equal chance to win, that winning is determined primarily by degree of effort (and perhaps a degree of luck) rather than by level of ability, that attention is focused more on the learning than the competition, and that reactions to the outcome emphasize the positive (winners are congratulated but losers are not criticized or ridiculed; the accomplishments of the class as a whole, not just the winners, are acknowledged).

Extrinsic rewards may reinforce effort and persistence, but they do little to help students come to value the content and skills they are learning. In fact, if their use is mishandled, it can erode whatever intrinsic motivation the students may have for learning the content or skills. If you offer and deliver rewards in ways that imply that the only reason that students engage in learning activities is to get rewards for doing so, it is natural for them to infer that these activities have no value in their own right. And, if you use rewards in ways that foster competition among individuals or subgroups in your class, you undermine the collaborative norms that you should be emphasizing as part of maintaining a learning community. In conclusion, extrinsic rewards have been oversold to teachers. They can be helpful, or at least not harmful, if used appropriately, but they will not help you to encourage students to value curricular content and learning activities. Their effects tend to be short-term and not supportive of progress toward major long-term goals.

Intrinsic approach. The intrinsic motivation approach is similarly limited. Emphasizing content that students are already familiar with and interested in, along with activities that they enjoy, will please them but not expand their horizons or even necessarily increase their appreciation for curriculum-related knowledge and skills. As a teacher, your primary responsibilities are to see that your students acquire the knowledge and skills they are expected to acquire at the grade level, not to see that they enjoy themselves. It is desirable that students find school activities interesting and enjoyable whenever this is compatible with your major instructional goals, but accomplishing these goals is your first order of business.

One way to accommodate students' interests and preferences while at the same time pursuing your instructional goals is to allow them choices when possible. If you were going to ask your students to write a biography or make a presentation about a country, for example, you could allow individuals to choose the persons or countries they would report about (perhaps providing a menu of resources to select from, to make sure that their choices are appropriate to their ages and prior knowledge levels).

Another intrinsic motivation strategy is to engage students in activities that they find enjoyable. For example, most students enjoy collaborating in pairs or small groups, and these cooperative learning formats are well suited to many social studies goals. Students also tend to enjoy activities that provide them with opportunities to use a wide variety of skills (e.g., conducting and reporting research) rather than requiring boring repetition (e.g., filling in blanks on a worksheet), as well as activities that allow them to create a product that they can point to and identify with (e.g., a display or report).

These preferences were expressed in one of our studies that involved interviewing college students about learning activities they remembered from K–12 social studies (Alleman & Brophy, 1993–94). We coded the students' responses for what they said about the outcomes of the activities. Desirable outcomes were coded when they reported that an activity had produced interesting learning (e.g., enabled them to empathize with the people being studied and see things from their point of view). Negative outcomes were coded when the students disparaged the activities as pointless (e.g., learning about state birds) or as boring and repetitive (e.g., worksheets or assignments such as reading a chapter in a text and then answering questions about it).

The students frequently mentioned desirable outcomes, and never expressed negative ones, when describing thematic units (such as on pioneer life or a foreign country) that included a variety of information and activities, field trips, class discussion and debate activities, and pageant or role-enactment activities. They expressed less enthusiastic but still generally positive reactions to simulation activities, research projects, construction projects, and lecture/presentation activities. In contrast, they frequently expressed complaints about boring, repetitive seatwork that had to be done individually and silently.

Other intrinsic motivation approaches involve adapting school content or activities to students' interests. For example, Hidi and Baird (1988) found that students' interest in texts was enhanced when the main ideas in the texts were elaborated through insertions that featured one of the following motivation principles: *character identification* (information about people with whom the students could identify, such as inventors whose discoveries led to the knowledge under study), *novelty* (content that interested the students because it was new or unusual), *life theme* (connections to things that were important in their lives outside of school), and *activity level* (reference to intense activities or strong emotions).

People, fads, or events that are currently prominent in the news or the youth culture can be worked into everyday lessons as applications of the concepts being learned. For example, a teacher pointed out that the Ark of the Covenant described in an ancient history text was the same ark featured in the movie *Raiders of the Lost Ark*. Another teacher sparked interest in studying latitude and longitude by noting that the sunken remains of the *Titanic* can be located easily, even though they lie on the ocean floor hundreds of miles out to sea, because the discoverers fixed the location precisely using these coordinates.

Another way to incorporate student interest is to encourage students to ask questions and make comments about topics. This creates "teachable moments" that you can pursue by temporarily suspending a planned sequence of events in order to address issues raised by a student (which typically reflect interests shared by other students as well). It also is helpful to plan lessons and assignments that include divergent questions and opportunities for students to express opinions, make evaluations, or in other ways respond personally to the content.

You can stimulate students' curiosity or whet their anticipation by posing questions or doing "set-ups" that create a need to resolve some ambiguity or obtain more information about a topic. For example, prior to reading material about Russia, you might ask the students if they know how many time zones there are in Russia or how the United States acquired Alaska. It will be mind-boggling for most students to discover that one country encompasses eleven time zones or that the United States purchased Alaska from Russia. Calling attention to facts like these can make the difference between just another reading assignment and an interesting learning experience.

You also can use questions to put students into an information-processing or decision-making mode as they begin to engage in an activity. For example, you might create suspense by inviting students to consider competing ideas about the causes of the Civil War, or indicate that the content that they are about to study contains information that appears to contradict what they currently "know."

Surveys indicate that teachers' beliefs about effective motivation strategies tend to emphasize intrinsic approaches: cooperative learning, stimulating tasks, choices, role-play and simulations, projects, learning games, relating content to current events and students' lives outside of school, hands-on activities, and personalized content. Unfortunately, teachers' strategies typically focus on activities or involve adding interesting elements to content rather than helping students to develop appreciation for the content base itself. Many reported hands-on activities seem gratuitous—likely to generate interest but not lead to important learning. For example, Zahorik (1996) described a fifth-grade social studies unit on the 1950s that included singing Elvis Presley songs, impersonating Elvis, writing essays speculating on whether Elvis was still alive, and critiquing Elvis's movies. Hands-on activities will not produce important learning unless they include minds-on features that engage students in thinking about big ideas.

Motivating students to learn. Mitchell (1993) distinguished between catching students' interest and holding it. He found that motivational techniques such as presenting students with brainteasers or puzzles, allowing them to work on computers, or allowing them to work in groups were effective for catching initial interest but not for holding that interest in ways that led to accomplishment of significant learning goals. The latter outcomes were associated with meaningful content (students could appreciate its applications to life outside of school) and instructional methods that fostered involvement (students spent most of their time engaged in active learning and application activities, not just watching and listening). Other research reviewed by Brophy (2004) similarly concluded that sustained student motivation to learn curricular content and skills results from what Mitchell called "hold" factors. More specifically, the key to motivating students to learn is to structure the curriculum around big ideas and develop them with emphasis on their connections and applications to life outside of school.

Students do not need to enjoy school activities in order to be motivated to learn from them, but they do need to perceive these activities as meaningful and worthwhile. Therefore, you will need to make sure that your curriculum content and learning activities are in fact meaningful and worthwhile, and develop the content and scaffold your students' engagement in the activities in ways that enable them to see and appreciate their value.

In this regard, it is helpful to apply the notion of a zone of proximal development to motivation as well as learning. If the content domains and learning activities they encounter at school have been well selected, students can come to appreciate their value. However, exposure alone may not be enough. Just as it is important for you to scaffold the cognitive aspects of your students' engagement in learning activities, it is also important for you to scaffold the motivational aspects. Besides conveying big ideas and modeling strategies for applying them, *convey reasons why these ideas are worth learning, explain when and why they might be used, and model how it looks and feels when we use them* (e.g., by expressing appreciation of growth in your own knowledge, artistry, or craftsmanship). Besides coaching by cueing attention to key points at each step in a learning process, provide goal reminders and encourage students' appreciation for the learning domain and for their own development of knowledge and skills. Finally, besides providing feedback about correctness of responses and how to avoid mistakes, call students' attention to developments in their knowledge or skills, to signs of artistry in their work, or to unique "signature" elements that reflect their personal style of operating in the domain.

Induce appreciation for a topic or activity by explaining why students should value it. Better yet, arrange for them to experience this themselves by engaging them with a question or problem that requires the content for its solution. Much social studies content has value as grist for developing insights into the human condition or advances in personal identity and self-actualization. Stories about people in the past or in other cultures, for example, usually can be framed with reference to enduring dilemmas with which your students can identify. In addition, the stories can be rendered in ways that help students to appreciate how the experiences of people from another time or place compare and contrast with their own experiences in insight-producing ways.

These and other considerations involved in addressing the value issues involved in motivating students to learn will be elaborated in subsequent chapters. For now, bear in mind that even though most discussions of motivation emphasize praise and rewards or strategies for making learning fun, research findings point to structuring the content around big ideas developed with emphasis on their connections and applications as the key to motivating students to learn.

The Social Context's Effects on Motivation

The relationship between the social context and students' motivation is straightforward: Students will be more motivated to learn and better able to concentrate on doing so when the classroom climate is collaborative and supportive than when it is competitive and judgmental. This is one reason why we place so much emphasis on establishing a learning community in your classroom.

Embracing Cultural Diversity

Minority students and others whose family backgrounds place them at risk for school failure do especially well with teachers who share warm, personal interactions with them but also hold high expectations for their academic progress, require them to perform up to their capabilities, and see that they progress as far and as fast as they are able. These teachers break through social-class differences, cultural differences, language differences, and other potential barriers to communication in order to form close relationships with at-risk students, but they use these relationships to maximize the students' academic progress, not merely to provide friendship or sympathy to them (Baker, 1998; Delpit, 1992; Siddle-Walker, 1992; Tucker et al., 2002).

At-risk students also do especially well in classrooms that offer warm, inviting social environments. Therefore, help your students to value diversity, learn from one another, and appreciate different languages and traditions. Treat the cultures that they bring to school as assets that provide students with foundations of background knowledge to support their learning efforts and provide you with opportunities to enrich the curriculum for everyone. Think in terms of helping minority students to become fully bicultural rather than in terms of replacing one culture with another. If you are unfamiliar with a culture that is represented in your classroom, educate yourself by reading about it, talking with community leaders, visiting homes, and most importantly, talking with students to learn about their past history and future aspirations.

For example, Moll (1992) interviewed the families of students enrolled in a bilingual education class to identify resources available in the community that might be capitalized upon at the school, which was located in a primarily Spanish-speaking minority community. He identified the following *funds of knowledge* possessed by members of these households: ranching and farming (horsemanship, animal husbandry, soil and irrigation systems, crop planting, hunting, tracking, dressing game); mining (timbering, minerals, blasting, equipment operation and maintenance); economics (business, market values, appraising, renting and selling, loans, labor laws, building codes, consumer knowledge, accounting, sales); household management (budgets, child care, cooking, appliance repairs); material and scientific knowledge (construction, carpentry, roofing, masonry, painting, design and architecture); repairs (airplane, automobile, tractor, house maintenance); contemporary medicine (drugs, first-aid procedures, anatomy, midwifery); folk medicine (herbal knowledge, folk cures); and religion (catechism, baptisms, bible studies, moral knowledge and ethics).

Teachers can capitalize on these funds of knowledge whenever they connect with curriculum content, to personalize the curriculum for their students and occasionally to integrate parents intellectually into the life of the school. Opportunities for connecting the curriculum to the students' home backgrounds are often missed because instruction stays too close to what is in the textbooks. For example, usually at least some students in a class, and frequently a great many, have parents who are police officers, fire fighters, postal workers, and other service workers studied in "community helpers" lessons, but few teachers think to invite these parents to come to the classroom to talk about their jobs. Home–school connections are discussed in detail in Chapter 13.

Adapt your curricula to feature the cultures represented by your students. Modifications might include a somewhat different selection of content as well as treatment of many more topics as issues open to multiple perspectives rather than as bodies of factual information that admit to only a single interpretation. Expose students to literature or multimedia content sources that feature models who come from cultural groups represented in your classroom and portray these models not as stereotypes but as nuanced individuals with whom all students can identify. In addition, expose your students to actual, living models by arranging for classroom speakers, field trips, or current events discussions that will raise minority students' consciousness of roles and accomplishments to which they might aspire.

Knapp (1995) analyzed ways in which teachers working in ethnically heterogeneous classrooms responded to the cultural diversity of their students. The most effective ones explicitly accommodated the students' cultural heritages by communicating to them that their cultural backgrounds were not problems to be overcome but rather strengths to be acknowledged and drawn upon in schooling. For example, here is Knapp's description of a bilingual teacher of a combined first- and second-grade class composed of a mixed population of Hispanic, African-American, and white students:

> Mr. Callio holds high expectations for his students and demands strict accountability for the work assigned to them. He recognizes that his students do not arrive at school with all the skills he would like them to have and plans his instruction accordingly. At the same time, his approach builds in a respect for the strengths and backgrounds of the students in his class. For example, Mr. Callio's classroom is alive with pictures from different parts of the world, showing the different ethnic, racial, and cultural groups represented in his students. One display reads "Yo soy Latin y orgulloso" ("I am Latin and proud of it") in big letters surrounded by pictures of pyramids, indigenous Mesoamericans, and other Latino faces. Another reads "I am African American and proud" and displays pictures of African people, places, and artifacts. Mr. Callio argues that it is imperative to provide positive self-images and role models if a teacher expects students to be driven to succeed. Mr. Callio uses his Spanish extensively in the classroom—and not simply to help those students with limited English proficiency. Rather, he argues that Spanish is an important language to know and encourages his monolingual English speakers to try to learn it. One of the top students in the class, an African-American male, regularly tries to piece together Spanish sentences. (p. 39)

The Teacher's Role

The teacher's role pervades the process of building a learning community, implementing cooperative learning strategies, and motivating students to learn. It includes but is not limited to the following:

1. Creating a climate of mutual caring
2. Teaching specific cooperative learning skills and techniques
3. Showing sincere interest in each student's responses, ideas, experiences, and work products
4. Eliciting students' input on a regular basis
5. Giving reasons and thoughtful explanations regarding socioemotional, behavioral, and academic issues
6. Giving students the chance to examine and express the importance of what they do
7. Providing students with opportunities to participate actively in the evaluation of their academic work

8. Minimizing students' need for extrinsic rewards and their fear of embarrassment
9. Celebrating students' successes while also engaging with them in ongoing dialogue and reflection regarding their individual and class development
10. Planning a curriculum that consists of networks of connected content structured around big ideas, then developing this content with emphasis on its applications to life outside of school
11. Sharing your own background and experiences to model connections to the topics you teach

Many of these elements apply especially to powerful social studies teaching. In this role, the teacher has the added responsibilities of building appreciations related to the human condition and civic efficacy, connecting the unit content to life in the classroom and outside of school, and exposing students to learning resources that reflect multiple perspectives and connect to diverse ethnic and cultural backgrounds.

Conclusion

A collaborative learning community will be most effective when it is:

1. Goal-oriented
2. Pitched at the appropriate level of difficulty for the academic and socio-emotional levels of the students
3. Integrated into the total school day as a way of life in the classroom
4. Deliberate in shaping democratic activities and actions to ensure that they support progress toward overall social understanding and civic efficacy goals, as well as relating to the unit goals that are linked to the social science disciplines
5. Maintained and monitored on a regular basis
6. Successful in producing students who understand, appreciate, and are willing to apply social studies concepts, processes, and actions to democratic life outside the classroom

A productive learning community draws on all of the senses, is established on the premise of democracy, and shapes constructive human interactions. At the same time, it provides a natural framework for acquiring meaning in the social studies.

Summary

Establishing and maintaining your classroom as a collaborative learning community will provide an ideal context for both motivating students to learn and developing attitudes, beliefs, and dispositions to action that reflect the goals of preparing students for citizenship in a culturally diverse, democratic society. Whether or not it includes formal structures like those established by Mrs. Paul, your learning community should feature rules, routines, expectations, and social interaction patterns that foster respectful and egalitarian discourse and frequent collaboration in constructing understandings.

Approaches to teaching that can contribute to the development of the classroom community include modeling and explaining key attitudes, beliefs, and behaviors; beginning with a unit on childhood that provides many opportunities for students to learn about their classmates' personal characteristics and home backgrounds; frequent opportunities for students to work collaboratively in pairs or small groups; and emphasis on classroom management and student motivation strategies that emphasize collaboration over competition. Whole-class activities should feature assertive but respectful interaction in which the emphasis is on discussing opinions with reference to relevant arguments and evidence as a means toward negotiating common understandings.

A learning community provides a supportive atmosphere that enables students to focus on developing knowledge and skill without worrying about failure or embarrassment. Other keys to supporting students' motivation to learn include maintaining an appropriate level of challenge (students can succeed with reasonable effort) and focusing the curriculum on content that they can appreciate (value) as worth learning and applicable to their lives outside of school. With respect to both learning and motivation, teachers need to work in the zone of proximal development and provide their students with whatever structuring and scaffolding they may need in order to accomplish the intended goals.

Reflective Questions

1. The core democratic values are being emphasized in many state and local social studies curricula. What roles and functions do you think they can play within the context of building a learning community?
2. Learning communities are often referred to as the informal social studies curriculum. How would you explain this? Support your response with examples.
3. There is evidence in the literature that fostering a learning community is loosely coupled with student achievement. How would you explain this? Support your response with examples.
4. If your priorities are to develop students who have intrinsic motivation within a learning community, what will your classroom sound like? Look like? Feel like? Cite concrete examples.
5. Select a social studies project planned for future use in your learning community. Assess the degree to which it reflects the activity design principles of the expectancy x value model of motivation. If necessary, revise accordingly.

Your Turn:
Building a Learning Community in Your Classroom

Observe several classrooms and look for evidence that the students are functioning as a learning community. Attempt to interview each teacher afterwards. If you did not see much evidence of a learning community, seek explanations. Where learning communities were successfully implemented, talk with the teachers about their insights—and how they have actualized their visions.

If you have your own classroom, begin by asking someone to serve as an observer to determine what your classroom looks like, sounds like, and feels like to an outsider. The data can serve as a powerful informant and useful planning tool as you develop your community.

SAMPLE OBSERVATION SCHEDULE

How would you characterize the climate of the classroom?

Does the climate reflect mutual caring? (Evidence?)

Do you feel like you are "living" in a community? (Evidence?)

Is there a sense of shared values? (Evidence?)

Are specific cooperative-learning skills and techniques being developed? How?

Is there a sense of high expectations regarding positive behaviors and academic success? (Evidence?)

Does the teacher show sincerity and interest in each student's responses, ideas, experiences, and work products? (Evidence?)

Is student input elicited on a regular basis? (Examples?)

Are students provided with choices where appropriate? (Examples?)

Does the teacher help students view learning activities as opportunities to increase knowledge and skills? (Evidence?)

Does the teacher motivate using an intrinsic reward approach? (Examples?)

Does the teacher focus on big ideas as a way to motivate students? (Examples?)

Does the teacher foster appreciation for a topic or activity? (Evidence?)

Does the teacher give reasons and thoughtful explanations regarding socioemotional, behavioral, and academic issues? (Evidence?)

Do students get a chance to share and express the importance of what they do? (Evidence?)

Do students participate actively in the evaluation of their behavior? Of their academic work? (Evidence?)

Do they celebrate their successes while engaging in ongoing dialogue and reflection regarding individual and class development? How?

After reviewing this chapter and observing in at least one classroom, take a sheet of paper and fold it (vertically) in half. On one side list things that you can do as a teacher to build a learning community in your classroom, and on the other side list behaviors (such as distributing candy to reward good conduct) to avoid because they will detract from your learning community goals. Find a peer who would also be willing to participate in this exercise. After you have both compiled your lists, discuss them.

After this preliminary activity, review your list and add or delete if needed. Then find a quiet spot and, using the list as a starting point, spend at least an hour creating your vision for your classroom learning community (use drawings, pictures, etc. if you find this helpful). Then put your statement aside, but work on it for 30 minutes every day for a week. Finally, spend time developing a long-range plan for launching the learning community in your classroom. Remember, it is a yearlong process. Accumulated experiences will expand your understanding and build your confidence in implementing the learning community approach to democratic life in classrooms, yet you will begin anew each year as you meet a new class of students and journey through the process together.

Review the key points made in the chapter, noting especially those that were new to you. Remember that the maintenance component of your community is absolutely essential. Your efforts will be realized gradually. What you lose in instructional time during the first few weeks of school as you build your community will be returned tenfold by the end of the year.

After the key elements of the community are in place, an introductory unit focusing on childhood/adolescence can serve as a powerful springboard for learning a lot about your students, engaging them in very personal ways, and at the same time introducing them to the historical, geographic, economic, and cultural frames for their yearlong program. Select from the following topics to get started in planning your unit. You might consider working with a peer.

Elements of Childhood/Adolescence

Specialness

Children around the World

Birthdays

Rites of Passage

Children and Work

Schools—Past and Present

Children as Consumers

Adults Provide for Children's Needs

Childhood Talents and Interests

Children Make a Difference

Look for places where cooperative learning is appropriate. Keep a reflective journal as you teach the unit. See Alleman and Brophy (2003).

CHAPTER 3

WHAT DOES GOAL-ORIENTED INSTRUCTION ENTAIL?

Karen Berry, Second-Year Teacher

Curriculum planning can be a daunting task. There is a never-ending fine line between what we know will help our students learn and what is adopted by our school districts to meet local and state grade-level expectations. The key to success is carefully planned units that *motivate learning through appreciation and understanding as well as result in students making connections in their learning and applying it to life.*

As I create a learning plan for my fourth-grade social studies curriculum, I always begin with the text, but I never stop there! Just as this chapter explains, the social studies text usually provides disconnected facts and exercises that are read and completed with little thought. The text helps me know what is minimally expected, and then I am able to begin the quest to make a powerful unit. Using the guidelines in this chapter, I refine my instruction by selecting goals and big ideas that I know are important for students to make connections to their own lives and therefore see the importance of learning. I then carry this out by making lessons in the unit *meaningful, integrative, value-based, challenging, and active.*

For example, using the *goal-oriented planning guide* at the end of the chapter helped me shape a rather static unit on maps and globes into an active and memorable one. I was able to scaffold students through a set of carefully selected big ideas. These goals helped me create lessons that promoted higher-level thinking and activities that made connections to students' lives. For example, one lesson required students to sit within a mock city (masking tape for roads, chairs with index cards for houses and stores) and give directions to their "home" using the cardinal directions. I discovered that planning with big ideas and goals in mind resulted in a powerful lesson in which students understood the cardinal directions as applicable to their lives.

A curriculum is not an end in itself but a means, a tool for accomplishing educational goals. These goals are learner outcomes—the knowledge, skills, attitudes, values, and dispositions to action that one wishes to develop in students. Ideally, curriculum planning and implementation decisions will be driven by these goals so that each component—the basic content, the ways that this content is represented and explicated to students, the questions that will be asked, the types of teacher–student and student–student discourse that will occur, the activities and assignments, and the methods that will be used to assess progress and grade performance—will be included because it is believed to be needed as a means for moving students toward accomplishment of the major goals. The goals are the reason for the existence of the curriculum, and beliefs about what is needed to accomplish them should guide each step in curriculum planning and implementation.

Today's social studies textbook series feature broad but shallow coverage of a great range of topics and skills. Lacking coherence of flow or structure around key ideas developed in depth, they are experienced as parades of disconnected facts and isolated skills exercises. These problems have evolved as an unintended consequence of publishers' efforts to satisfy state and district curricular guidelines that feature long lists of topics and skills to be covered rather than succinct statements of major goals to be accomplished. If teachers use the textbooks and their accompanying ancillary materials and follow the manuals' lesson development instructions, the result will be a reading/recitation/seatwork curriculum geared toward memorizing disconnected knowledge and practicing isolated skills. Nevertheless, this is what many teachers do because most elementary teachers and many secondary teachers who are assigned to teach social studies courses have not had enough social studies preparation even to allow them to develop a coherent view of what social education is all about, let alone a rich base of social education knowledge and an associated repertoire of pedagogical techniques. Acting on the assumption that the series has been developed by experts far more knowledgeable about social education purposes and goals than they are, such teachers tend to concentrate on the procedural mechanics of implementation when planning lessons and activities, without giving much thought to their purposes or how they might fit into the larger social education program.

The first of these two italicized paragraphs summarizes the classical view of curriculum development as a goal-oriented process. The second paragraph summarizes findings of recent research on the status of social studies. The contrasts between the two paragraphs reflect major challenges that we see in contemporary social education.

An important reason for these challenges is that publishers of social studies textbooks and the teachers who depend on them have lost the forest for the trees—they have lost sight of the major, long-term goals that reflect the purposes of social education and should drive the development and enactment of social studies curricula. Textbook teachers' editions, pacing guides, lesson plans downloaded from the web, and other contemporary materials often emphasize knowledge and skill-oriented "goals" that are better described as objectives or behavioral indicators. They typically refer to disconnected facts or skill sets that, when taught in isolation, are not retained. Because of how they are taught—"grill and drill"—it does not even occur to students that they could be applied in other settings.

This approach lowers the level of intention and instruction. Recalling the names of the states and capitals or battles and generals, naming the longest river in the world, or listing the steps in how a bill becomes a law are facts of little importance unless used in consort with explanations associated with big ideas.

Consequently, we are calling for a return to the notion of developing curricula as means to accomplish major goals with an inclusion of knowledge/skill performance indicators where appropriate. To be most valuable for curriculum planning, these goals will need to be phrased in terms of intended student outcomes—capabilities and dispositions to be developed in students and used in their lives inside and outside of school, both now and in the future.

We will consider two connected sets of goals that we recommend as guides for planning curriculum and instruction in elementary social studies. The first set is generic to powerful teaching in any school subject; the second set is specific to social studies.

Generic Subject-Matter Goals:
Understanding, Appreciation, and Life Application

The *academic disciplines* are means of generating and systematizing knowledge. The *school subjects* that draw from them are means of preparing students for life in our society by equipping them with essential knowledge, skills, values, and dispositions. We want students not just to learn what we teach them in school but to access and use it in appropriate application situations. These goals will not be met if students merely memorize disconnected bits of information long enough to pass tests, then forget most of what they "learned."

Consequently, in planning curriculum and instruction in any school subject, it is important to emphasize goals of understanding, appreciation, and life application. *Understanding* means that students learn both the individual elements in a network of related content and the connections among them so that they can explain the content in their own words. True understanding goes beyond the ability to define concepts or supply facts. It involves making connections between new learning and prior knowledge, subsuming the new learning within larger networks of knowledge, and recognizing at least some of its potential applications. For example, in a unit on government and a lesson on voting, a goal might be to help students understand voting and how the process works in the United States.

Appreciation means that students value the learning because they recognize that there are good reasons for learning it. Along with potential practical applications, these reasons include the roles that the learning might play in enhancing the quality of the learners' lives. In the case of social studies, students might appreciate the value of their learning for helping them to understand how the world as we know it came to be and what is occurring in it now, as well as for helping them to make personal and civic decisions. They also might come to appreciate their own developing understandings—to take pride in seeing how what they have learned applies to their own lives, to appreciate their attainment of new insights, or to enjoy interpreting or predicting current events or enhancing their knowledge by reading or watching programs on social issues. In a unit on money and a lesson focusing on children donating money to help others, an appreciation goal might be to help students appreciate what it means to be a good citizen by learning about the what, why, and how of age-appropriate social actions that they can undertake in and out of school by actually donating time and money.

Life application goals are accomplished to the extent that students retain their learning in a form that makes it usable when needed in other contexts. Too often, the knowledge taught in social studies is not applicable in life outside of school, or if it is, its potential life applications are not made explicit. This is why we encourage you to include out-of-school learning opportunities as a part of your overall planning. Provide life-application assignments that encourage students to interact with their family and community members to enhance the meaningfulness of the big ideas/skills introduced and discussed in the classroom. For example, when teaching about exact and relative locations, design home assignments that call for students to discuss with family members how and when these big ideas apply to situations they encounter (e.g., in planning for the number of hours required for travel and the means of transportation, identifying the relative location of the destination is probably all that is needed, but if you needed to have a package delivered to a specific individual, the exact location would be necessary).

Research on Teaching for Understanding

Throughout the rest of the book, we will use the term *teaching for understanding* as shorthand for "teaching for understanding, appreciation, and life application of subject-matter knowledge." Recently, there has been a confluence of theorizing, research, and publication of guidelines by professional organizations, all focusing on what is involved in teaching for understanding. Analyses of these efforts have identified a set of principles that are common to most if not all of them (Bransford, Brown, & Cocking, 1999). These common elements, which might be considered components in a model of good subject-matter teaching, include the following:

1. The curriculum is designed to equip students with knowledge, skills, values, and dispositions that they will find useful both inside and outside of school.
2. Instructional goals emphasize developing student expertise within an application context, emphasizing conceptual understanding of knowledge and self-regulated application of skills.
3. The curriculum balances breadth with depth by addressing limited content but developing this content sufficiently to foster conceptual understanding.
4. The content is organized around a limited set of powerful ideas (basic understandings and principles).
5. The teacher's role is not just to present information but also to scaffold and respond to students' learning efforts.
6. The students' role is not just to absorb or copy input but also to actively make sense and construct meaning.

7. Students' prior knowledge about the topic is elicited and used as a starting place for instruction, which builds on accurate prior knowledge but also stimulates conceptual change if necessary.
8. Activities and assignments feature tasks that call for decision making, problem solving, or critical thinking, not just memory or reproduction.
9. Higher-order thinking skills are not taught as a separate skills curriculum. Instead, they are developed in the process of teaching subject-matter knowledge within application contexts that call for students to relate what they are learning to their lives outside of school.
10. The teacher creates a social environment in the classroom that could be described as a learning community, featuring discourse or dialogue designed to promote understanding.

These generic goals and key features involved in teaching school subjects for understanding are implied in what we say about good teaching in the rest of this book. In addition, we emphasize the goals of powerful social studies teaching as identified in a position statement published by the National Council for the Social Studies (1993).

Social Studies Goals:
Social Understanding and Civic Efficacy

Powerful social studies teaching helps students develop social understanding and civic efficacy. *Social understanding* is integrated knowledge of the social aspects of the human condition: how they have evolved over time, the variations that occur in different physical environments and cultural settings, and emerging trends that appear likely to shape the future. *Civic efficacy* is readiness and willingness to assume citizenship responsibilities. It is rooted in social studies knowledge and skills, along with related values (such as concern for the common good) and dispositions (such as an orientation toward confident participation in civic affairs).

The NCSS position statement goes on to identify five key features that must be in place if social studies teaching and learning is to be powerful enough to accomplish its social understanding and civic efficacy goals: Social studies teaching and learning is powerful when it is meaningful, integrative, value-based, challenging, and active. The implications of these key features are as follows.

Meaningful. The content selected for emphasis is worth learning because it promotes progress toward important social understanding and civic efficacy goals, and teaching methods help students to see how the content relates to those goals. As a result, students' learning efforts are motivated by appreciation and interest, not just by accountability and grading systems. Students acquire dispositions to care about what is happening in the world around them and to use the thinking frameworks and research skills of social science professionals to gather and interpret information. As a result, social learning becomes a lifelong interest and a basis for informed social action.

Instruction emphasizes depth of development of important ideas within appropriate breadth of topic coverage. Rather than cover too many topics superficially, the teacher covers limited topics and focuses this coverage around the most important content.

The significance of the content is emphasized in presenting it to students and developing it through activities. New topics are framed with reference to where they fit within the big picture, and students are alerted to their citizenship implications. Students are asked to relate new knowledge to prior knowledge, to think critically about it, and to use it to construct arguments or make informed decisions.

Teachers' questions promote understanding of important ideas and stimulate thinking about their potential implications. Teacher–student interactions emphasize thoughtful discussion of connected major themes, not rapid-fire recitation of miscellaneous bits of information.

Meaningful learning activities and assessment strategies focus students' attention on the most important ideas embedded in what they are learning. The teaching emphasizes authentic activities and assessment tasks—opportunities for students to engage in the sorts of applications of content that justify the inclusion of that content in the curriculum in the first place. For example, instead of labeling a map, students might plan a travel route and sketch landscapes that a traveler might see on the route. Instead of copying the Bill of Rights, students might discuss or write about its implications for particular court cases. Instead of filling in a blank to complete a statement of a principle, students might use the principle to make predictions about a case example or to guide their strategies in a simulation game.

The teacher is reflective in planning, implementing, and assessing instruction. Reflective teachers work within state and district guidelines, but they adapt and supplement those guidelines and their instructional materials in ways that support their students' social education needs. In particular, they select and represent content to students in ways that connect it with the students' interests and with local history, cultures, and issues.

Integrative. Powerful social studies teaching crosses disciplinary boundaries to address topics in ways that promote social understanding and civic efficacy. Its content is anchored by themes, generalizations, and concepts drawn from the social studies foundational disciplines. However, these are supplemented by ideas drawn from the arts, sciences, and humanities; from current events; and from local examples and students' experiences.

Powerful social studies teaching also is integrative across time and space, connecting with past experiences and looking ahead to the future. It helps students to appreciate how aspects of the social world function, not only in their local community and in the contemporary United States but also in the past and in other cultures.

Powerful social studies teaching also integrates knowledge, skills, beliefs, values, and dispositions to action. In particular, it teaches skills as tools for applying content in natural ways. The teaching includes effective use of technology when it can add important dimensions to learning. Students may acquire information through films, videotapes, CD-ROMs, and other electronic media, and they may use computers to compose, edit, and illustrate research reports. Live or computer-based simulations allow students to apply important ideas in authentic decision-making contexts.

Finally, powerful social studies teaching integrates across the curriculum. It provides opportunities for students to read and study text materials, appreciate art and literature, communicate orally and in writing, observe and take measurements, develop and display data, and in other ways conduct inquiry and synthesize findings using knowledge and skills taught in other school subjects. It is important, however, to see that these integrative activities support progress toward social understanding and civic efficacy goals.

Value-based. Powerful social studies teaching considers the ethical dimensions of topics, so it provides an arena for reflective development of concern for the common good and application of social values. Students are made aware of potential social policy implications and are taught to think critically and make value-based decisions about related social issues.

Such teaching encourages recognition of opposing points of view, respect for well-supported positions, sensitivity to cultural similarities and differences, and commitment to social responsibility and action. It recognizes the reality and persistence of tensions but promotes positive human relationships built on understanding and willingness to search for the common good.

Challenging. Students are expected to strive to accomplish the instructional goals through thoughtful participation in lessons and activities and careful work on assignments. The teacher encourages the class to function as a learning community, using reflective discussion to work collaboratively to deepen understandings of the meanings and implications of content.

The teacher stimulates and challenges students' thinking by exposing them to many information sources that include varying perspectives on topics and offer conflicting opinions on controversial issues. Students learn to listen carefully and respond thoughtfully, citing relevant evidence and arguments. They are challenged to come to grips with controversial issues, to participate assertively but respectfully in group discussions, and to work productively with peers in cooperative learning activities.

Active. Powerful social studies teaching and learning is rewarding, but it demands a great deal from both teachers and students. It demands thoughtful preparation and instruction by the teacher and sustained effort by the students to make sense of and apply what they are learning.

Rather than mechanically following instructions in a manual, the teacher adjusts goals and content to students' needs, uses a variety of instructional materials, plans field trips or visits by resource people, develops current or local examples to relate content to students' lives, plans questions to stimulate reflective discussion, plans activities featuring authentic applications, scaffolds students' work in ways that provide them with needed help but also encourage them to assume increasing responsibility for managing their own learning, structures the classroom as a communal learning environment, uses accountability and grading systems that are compatible with these instructional goals and methods, and monitors reflectively and adjusts as necessary. The teacher also adjusts plans to developing circumstances, such as "teachable moments" that arise when students ask questions, make comments, or offer challenges worth pursuing.

Students develop new understandings through a process of active construction. They process content by relating it to what they already know (or think they know) about the topic, striving to make sense of what they are learning. They develop a network of connections that link the new content to preexisting knowledge and beliefs anchored in their prior experience. Sometimes the learning involves conceptual change because the students discover that some of their beliefs are inaccurate and need to be modified. The construction of meaning required to develop important social understandings takes time and is facilitated by interactive discourse. Clear explanations and modeling from the teacher are important, but so are opportunities to answer questions, discuss or debate the meanings and implications of content, or use the content in activities that call for tackling problems or making decisions.

Teacher and student roles shift as learning progresses. Early in a unit, the teacher may need to provide considerable guidance by modeling, explaining, or supplying information that builds on students' existing knowledge. The teacher also may assume much of the responsibility for structuring and managing learning activities at this stage. As students develop expertise, however, they can begin to assume responsibility for regulating their own learning by asking questions and by working on increasingly complex applications with increasing degrees of autonomy.

The teaching emphasizes authentic activities that call for using content to accomplish life applications. Critical-thinking dispositions and abilities are developed through policy debates or assignments calling for critique of currently or historically important policies, not through artificial exercises in identifying logical or rhetorical flaws. Students engage in cooperative learning, construction of models or plans, dramatic recreations of historical events that shaped democratic values or civic policies, role-play and simulation activities (such as mock trials or simulated legislative activities), interviews of family members, and data collection from the Internet or the local community. Such activities help them to develop social understandings that they can explain in their own words and can apply in appropriate situations.

Planning Goal-Oriented Topical Units

Instructional planning should reflect the generic subject-matter goals of understanding, appreciation, and application as well as the more specific social education goals of social understanding and civic efficacy. *In addressing issues of content scope and sequence, we focus initially on the knowledge component of the curriculum rather than on its skills, values, or dispositional components.* We do not mean to suggest that the knowledge component is more important than the other components or that it should (or even can) be planned and taught separately from them. However, we believe that curriculum development will proceed most smoothly if it begins by asking what knowledge is fundamental to accomplishment of the instructional goals and how this knowledge might be developed in students. Given the goals of elementary social studies as discussed in Chapter 1, we would emphasize knowledge about how the social system works as it does, how it developed through time, how and why it varies across cultures, and what all of this might mean for personal, social, and civic decision making.

After addressing issues of content scope and sequence and framing your subject-matter goals of understanding, appreciation, and life application, we encourage you to revisit them with an eye on the skills or processes frequently referred to as procedural knowledge. Most skill sets (e.g., acquiring information, manipulating ideas, participating in groups, etc.), apply to several school subjects. Typically, the local curriculum or pacing guide indicates where the skill set should be introduced and taught. Subsequently, students should get opportunities to apply it in multiple places, often including social studies.

For example, data gathering, analyzing, and graphing might be introduced in mathematics lessons. These skills could be applied in social studies, however, if students were surveying community members regarding their preferred ways of communicating or their responses to natural disasters.

We advocate introducing new skills using familiar content and only later applying them to new content. If you attempt to introduce new content and new processes simultaneously, students tend to become confused.

The NCSS (1994) guidelines endorse the idea that social studies skills should be taught as an integral part of the program. This well-taken advice is often violated or ignored. The subsets of national and state standards referred to as performance indicators, benchmarks, and so on are typically skill-based and easily measurable. With the current pressures of standardized testing, teachers often never get beyond the knowledge and skill goals.

For example, recently we observed two different approaches to writing persuasive essays. In the first case, the teacher told the students that they were going to learn how to write such essays because they needed to be able to do so for the upcoming state test. After minimal modeling or formal instruction and lots of moans and groans, students were given time to practice. Even though they were given choices about what to write, they approached the assignment as a perfunctory task. In the second class, the teacher had taught the basics of persuasion and essay writing in literacy. As part of their unit on Canada, students were asked to write essays persuading their families that a trip to Canada would be a great choice for their next vacation. Before they launched into the writing, they reviewed the basics of a persuasive essay and brainstormed all of the possible ideas that might convince their families. The essays would be sent home, and family members would be invited to come to class, comment on the essays, and react to their persuasive arguments. This context of authenticity promoted interest. In fact, students were highly engaged and complained that the class period was too short.

The skills scope and sequence should be an integral piece that is mapped onto your goals of understanding, appreciation, and application. When skills are selected strategically and developed authentically, meaningfulness and long-term retention are by-products. Informed citizens, capable of decision making, will emerge.

Advantages of Topical Units

Instructional units featuring interdisciplinary treatment of topics provide the best basis for selecting and organizing content for elementary social studies. In comparison to disciplinary structures, topical units offer much more flexibility concerning the nature and sources of content. Guided by the social understanding and civic efficacy goals of social studies, the teacher can include any sources of content and skills that seem appropriate, drawing not only from the social studies foundational disciplines (history, geography, and the social sciences) but also from the arts, sciences, and humanities; from current events; and from the students' familial and cultural backgrounds. The point is to develop a basic network of useful knowledge about the topic, not to develop knowledge exclusively within a particular discipline. Often skill sets introduced in other content areas are useful in promoting meaningfulness.

The unit approach also offers flexibility with respect to teaching methods and learning activities. There is no exclusive reliance on direct instruction, inquiry, or any other single approach. There will be variation, both across units and across subtopics within units, in the proportion of time spent introducing new information, developing comprehension of key ideas through discourse, or engaging students in inquiry or application activities. The kinds of activities emphasized will vary with the content and learning outcomes to be developed. Thus, students might generate a report or product relating to one subtopic but engage in debate about another. Where subtopics lend themselves to it, activities would include hands-on projects, site visits, collection of data from the home or neighborhood, or other experiential learning.

We do not mean to imply that all topical units are effective. Such units will not have much value if they are developed around topics that do not have much potential as vehicles for accomplishing important social studies goals. Also, even if the topic is well chosen, it may not be developed in goal-oriented ways. The subtopics selected for emphasis might be trite details rather than powerful ideas, or the treatment might amount to a parade of disconnected facts that leaves students without a network of usable knowledge.

In fact, most of the problems with contemporary instructional materials can be traced to poor development of topics rather than to the choice of the topics themselves. Most of the unit topics are good ones because they are cultural universals that comprise the basic components of all social systems that have been developed in the past or exist currently in various human cultures. These topics strike us as truly fundamental to social understanding and thus as appropriate for introducing students to social studies. However, as we stated in Chapter 1, we see a need to shift from an emphasis on the expanding communities sequential scheme to an emphasis on teaching the fundamentals of the human condition when rationalizing the choice of these topics to teachers and in introducing them to students.

While the focus on cultural universals has typically been viewed as an early elementary approach, it can be applied to state and regional studies. For example, if your topic were Michigan, the historical dimension could illustrate how human activities relating to food, shelter, clothing, transportation, government, and so on have changed over time due to population growth, expanded knowledge base, technological advances, and so on. Shelters, for example, have evolved from caves and simple huts to sturdier and more permanent homes such as Native Americans' longhouses or pioneers' log cabins to modern weatherproofed homes that feature running, water, heat, lights, and so on. Technological advances have enabled us to meet our shelter needs and wants more effectively yet with less personal effort and time than in the past.

State or regional studies could expose students to geographical and cultural variations in food, shelter, clothing, transportation, and so on that can be understood with reference to climate, terrain, natural resources, cultural preferences, or other local conditions. Similarly, state or regional studies could include economic, contemporary, and life-application elements that establish authentic rationales for thinking deeply about the content and personalizing it. For many students, subject matter only seems relevant and worth learning when they can relate to it personally and see applications to their present or future lives outside of school.

In the next several chapters, we will consider how powerful units on these or other topics might be developed, beginning in Chapter 4 with principles for content selection and representation. If your school uses the expanding communities approach, we suggest that at the very least you connect each of the topics to your students' world and design home assignments that help them to apply the big ideas learned in the classroom to their lives outside of school.

Planning Tool

Good unit planning begins with specification of major goals and associated big ideas, then proceeds through the planning of content selection and representation, development of big ideas through discourse, application through authentic activities, and other elaborations addressed in subsequent chapters of this book. As a way to help you see the big picture of unit planning and how each of its components fits into it, we have provided a planning tool built around a running example of steps involved in planning a unit on government. The planning tool is presented in Appendix C. It is a resource that you can refer to after studying each of the following chapters, as a way to reconnect the content developed in each of those chapters to the big picture of unit planning.

Summary

Powerful social studies teaching is planned to accomplish major goals phrased as intended outcomes—the knowledge, skills, attitudes, values, and dispositions to action that we wish to develop in students. These goals should determine what content is selected for inclusion in the curriculum, how this content is represented to students, the kinds of discourse used to develop the big ideas, the activities and assignments used to develop and apply what is learned, and the methods used to assess progress. The teaching of all school subjects should reflect generic goals of teaching for understanding, appreciation, and life application. Within that, social studies instruction should be planned to accomplish the major social studies goals of social understanding and civic efficacy. Social studies teaching that is oriented toward those goals is powerful when it is meaningful, integrative, value-based, challenging, and active, as described in the NCSS (1993) vision statement.

We strongly recommend that instructional planning focus first on the unit level, rather than the more specific lesson or activity level, to ensure that the planning in general remains goal-oriented and that you as the teacher (and through you, your students) maintain awareness of how individual lessons and activities fit within the big picture. We also recommend that the content and skill components of the unit be integrated. This helps ensure that the knowledge content is applied and that the skill content is used for authentic purposes. This tends not to occur when the content and skill components are taught separately.

Planning of topical units focused around major social studies goals helps to ensure that the instruction is complete, balanced, and well suited to the needs and interests of elementary students. Content is pandisciplinary rather than confined to a single discipline, students develop a variety of skills as they process and apply the content, and multiple connections are made to their lives outside of school.

Reflective Questions

1. Why do you think goal-oriented planning is so challenging?
2. One of the ways teachers garner support for their ideas is by acquiring outside funding from mini-grants. What would you include in a proposal asking for funds to help you in designing a goal-oriented social studies unit (designate topic) focused on understanding, appreciation, and life application?
3. Suppose that this year you decide to revamp your social studies program by shoring up your goals. Where would you start? How would you proceed?
4. Imagine that your principal plans to observe your social studies class during the upcoming unit. You want him/her to see evidence of your teaching for understanding. What will this look like? Sound like? What about your teaching for appreciation? And your teaching for life application?

Your Turn:
Goal-Oriented Curriculum Planning

Begin by reviewing sample goals provided as a part of the planning tool. If the government unit maps onto your scope and sequence, expand the list of goals, making sure to emphasize understanding, appreciation, and application. If a unit on money better aligns with your curriculum, expand on the list of goals we have provided to get you started. If neither of these topics meets your needs, select a unit you will be teaching and generate a comprehensive set of goals. Make sure you embed specific knowledge and skill goals within networks structured around more general goals and big ideas to ensure powerful teaching.

Goal-Oriented Planning Guide

TITLE OF UNIT: MONEY

Sample Goal for Understanding	To help students understand that long, long ago there was no need for money.
Suggested Idea for Promoting the Goal	Retell the history of money. Use *The Story of Money* by B. Maestro, published by Houghton Mifflin in 1993 as a resource.
Sample Goal for Appreciation	To help students appreciate how money simplifies the exchanges of goods and services that make it possible for us to live highly specialized yet interdependent lives.
Suggested Idea for Promoting the Goal	Go through a typical school day with students and determine how money is involved in the experiences they have.
Sample Goal for Life Application	To help students apply what they learned about money in their social studies class to their lives outside of school.
Suggested Idea for Promoting the Goal	Talk to family members about the importance of money in their lives. Keep a log for a specified period of time to document the family's uses of money. Bring the log to school for sharing data with classmates during an upcoming lesson.

See Alleman, J., & Brophy, J. (2003). *Social studies excursions, K–3. Book three: Powerful units on childhood, money, and government.* Portsmouth, NH: Heinemann.

CHAPTER 4

WHAT DO SELECTING AND REPRESENTING CONTENT ENTAIL?

Kristy Tomford, Teacher Intern

One powerful point I took away from this chapter is that content needs to be taught as "networks of connected knowledge structured around powerful ideas." Teachers need to set goals and big ideas for the unit. Unrelated activities designed to meet the standards and benchmarks will lead to zero retention of the material. For example, family, a familiar topic to students, needs to be put into historical, geographical, and cultural perspectives. Classifying families into "big" and "small" groupings is not adequate, challenging, or particularly meaningful. Depth of understanding is wanting. Teachers must teach for meaning, not to simply cover the curriculum.

During the next few weeks, I will be teaching a mini-unit on Aztecs, Incas, and Mayas for sixth-graders. It will be important to cover the content with big ideas and goal-oriented and authentic activities. The students should understand the forces that hold a society together or pull it apart, not just memorize facts about the Mayan, Aztec, or Incan civilizations. They also should build knowledge about the history and culture of the civilizations, geographical relationships, economic systems, and government. The content must be discussed in terms of anthropological and sociological concepts, cause-and-effect relationships, and comparing and contrasting each civilization with modern-day Mexico. Teaching about the threads of social studies in relation to these civilizations will be much more significant to the children than teaching that "the Mayan civilization started in 500 B.C." and asking the students to reproduce it on a test. Co-constructing a web about the civilizations and relating the content to modern-day Mexico will be relevant to the students. A beginning web could look like this:

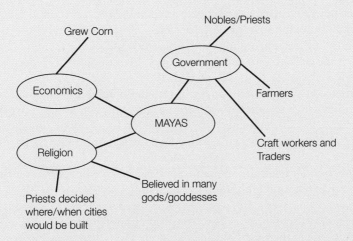

Students need to be involved in deep thinking about "why" and "how" these civilizations thrived in Mesoamerica. Discussing "why" and "how" will help students remember the big ideas of the unit.

Overall, I learned it is important to focus on big ideas developed in depth, not on breadth of content. Students must be taught content that is meaningful and applicable to their own lives. I imagine that someday my students will want to visit the Mayan ruins, for example, because of what they have learned and have become curious about seeing for themselves. Unrelated activities used simply to meet the curriculum requirements will not help the students appreciate the significance of the information or retain it. Big ideas and goals must be identified for a unit and then taught as a "network of connected knowledge structured around powerful ideas." Students need to be educated for life, not merely for standards and benchmarks!

Teachers do not have time to teach everything worth learning in social studies. Only so many topics can be included in the curriculum, and not all of these can be developed in sufficient depth to promote deep understanding of the topic, appreciation of its significance, and exploration of its applications to life outside of school. This tension between breadth of coverage and depth of topic development is an enduring dilemma that teachers must try to manage as best they can; it is not a problem that they can solve in any permanent or completely satisfactory manner. Still, teachers can develop compromise solutions that reflect the purposes and goals of their social studies instruction.

Recent research indicates that most social studies curriculum and instruction has drifted into an overemphasis on breadth at the expense of depth. Critics of textbooks routinely complain that they offer seemingly endless parades of disconnected facts, not coherent networks of connected content structured around powerful ideas. Reports of social studies teaching and learning observed in classrooms suggest a similar picture. Although there are exceptions, most of these descriptions portray teachers as hurriedly attempting to cover too much content and students as attempting to memorize as much as they can. Students spend too much time reading, reciting, filling out worksheets, and taking memory tests but not enough time engaging in sustained discourse about powerful ideas or applying these ideas in authentic activities (Goodlad, 1984; Shaver, 1991; Stodolsky, 1988).

Disconnected factual information is not very meaningful or memorable. Lacking contexts within which to situate their learning and richly connected networks of ideas to enhance its meaningfulness, students are forced to rely on rote memorization instead of more sophisticated learning and application strategies. They remember as much as they can until the test but then forget most of it afterwards. Furthermore, most of what they do remember is inert knowledge that they are not able to use in relevant application situations.

Scholars who have studied this problem are in general agreement about what needs to be done to enable students to construct meaningful knowledge that they can access and use in their lives outside of school. First, there needs to be a retreat from breadth of coverage in order to allow time to develop the most important content in greater depth. Second, this important content needs to be taught as networks of connected knowledge structured around powerful ideas. Instruction should focus on these important ideas and explain the connections among them as well as the ideas themselves. When this approach is used, students actually remember more facts as well, because they are tied to something that makes sense.

Goal-Oriented Development of Powerful Ideas

It ought to be easy to focus social studies instruction on important topics and develop these topics with emphasis on powerful ideas. Teachers would only need to pose the following questions and then follow through accordingly:

1. What topics are most useful as bases for advancing my students' social understanding and civic efficacy?
2. What are the most important understandings about the topics that my students will need to develop, and how do these connect to one another and to related skills, values, and dispositions?

If major social education goals were used in this way to guide curriculum development and instructional planning, they would yield coherent social studies programs. However, major social understanding and civic efficacy goals tend to get lost as operational plans are developed for implementing state and district curriculum guidelines. Planning gets driven by content and skill-coverage lists rather than major goals. Content standards, benchmarks, performance indicators, and even pacing guides are rarely written as goals and often appear disjointed. As a result, the content of many lessons and even entire units becomes disconnected and trite, often lacking in life-application potential and thus having little social education value. For example, Naylor and Diem (1987, p. 51) cited the following hierarchy of curriculum goals as typical for social studies:

District-wide goal (taken from the NCSS guidelines): to prepare young people to become humane, rational, participating citizens in a world that is becoming increasingly interdependent

Program-area goal for social studies, K–12: to enable students to recognize and appreciate that people living in different cultures are likely to share some common values but also to hold other different values that are rooted in experience and legitimate in terms of their own culture

Grade-level goal for social studies, Grade 1: to understand and appreciate that the roles and values of family members may differ according to the structure of the family, its circumstances, and its cultural setting

Unit-level goal for social studies, Grade 1: to understand that families differ in size and composition

Notice that the last (unit-level) goal is phrased in purely descriptive, knowledge-level language and that it is trite for a unit goal even at the first-grade level. It makes no reference to the anthropological and sociological concepts (cultures, roles) or to the values and dispositions (multicultural appreciation, citizen participation) referred to in the higher-level goals. Unless the teacher has a coherent view of the nature and purposes of social education and thus is aware of how this topic fits within the big picture, the result is likely to be a unit that is long on isolated practice of facts or skills but short on integration and application of social learning. Students will learn a few obvious generalities about families, such as that they differ in size and composition, that they grow and change, and that their members work and play together. However, they will not learn much about variations in family roles across time and culture, the reasons for these variations, or the lifestyle trade-offs that they offer. There will be little to advance the students' knowledge of the human condition, to help them put the familiar into broader perspective, or even to stimulate their thinking about family as a concept.

Several consequences follow from limiting the unit-level goal to developing the understanding that families differ in size and composition. The "composition" part at least has potential: If developed properly, it could lead to informative and thought-provoking lessons on family composition and roles as they have evolved through time and as they exist today in different societies. To have much social education value, however, such lessons would have to emphasize not merely that such differences exist but why. For example, the students might learn that a major social effect of industrialization is a reduction of the extended family's role as a functional economic unit and that this precipitates a shift to the nuclear family as the typical household unit. Instead of living and working together as a large extended family, small nuclear families live in separate households and spend much of their time with nonrelatives. Their members may pursue more varied occupational and lifestyle options than exist in nonindustrialized societies, but they usually must do so without the continuing involvement and support of a large extended family. Teaching such conceptually based content about families (in age-appropriate language) will help students to place the familiar into broader perspective. In this case, it will help them to appreciate the trade-offs involved in various economic systems and associated lifestyles, and perhaps to function more effectively as family members within our society.

The "size" part of the unit-level goal statement appears to lack social education value. First-graders are already well aware that families differ in size, so what is the point of making this a major goal of the unit? Even worse, what is the point of following up such instruction with exercises requiring students to classify families as either "big" or "small"? Textbook publishers have discovered that a focus on family size provides an entry point for inserting certain generic skills exercises into the social studies curriculum. Thus, students are asked to count the members in depicted families or to compare and contrast big and small families. Other such exercises call for students to infer by indicating whether depicted families are "working" or "playing" or by inspecting drawings of families depicted before and after an addition has occurred and circling the family member who represents the addition.

Similarly, units on shelter usually convey the fact that people live in a great variety of homes but say very little about the reasons why they live in these different kinds of homes and nothing at all about advances in construction materials and techniques, weatherproofing, insulation, or temperature control that have made possible the features of modern housing that most children in the United States take for granted. Units on government mention a few titles (president, governor, mayor), places (Washington, state capitols), and symbols (flag, ballot box) but say little about the functions and services performed by various levels of government. Thus, students learn that the positions of mayor, governor, and president exist but not what these people or their governments do. In later grades, students are exposed to reams of geographical and historical facts without enough concentration on major themes and generalizations, cause-and-effect relationships, linkage to local examples and current events, or other instructional framing that might help them appreciate the significance of the information and consider how it might apply to their lives outside of school.

To bring social studies curriculum and instruction into better alignment with the major goals of social understanding and civic efficacy, we need to honor these goals not just in theory but also in practice. In particular, we need to use them as the functional bases for curriculum planning. An in-depth look at what this might mean is given in the following example.

A UNIT ON SHELTER

Social studies teaching in the primary grades usually emphasizes universal human characteristics, needs, and experiences (food, clothing, shelter, transportation, communication, occupations, social rules, government, and laws) addressed within the contexts of family, neighborhood, and community. We believe that an important social education goal for each of these topics is to build initial understandings that will enable students to grasp the basics of how that aspect of the social world functions, not only in the local community and in the contemporary United States generally but also in the past and in other cultures today. The idea is to expand the students' limited purviews on the human condition and especially to help them put the familiar into historical, geographical, and cultural perspective. This will increase their understanding and appreciation of social phenomena that most of them have so far taken for granted without much awareness or appreciation.

Thus, rather than just teaching that shelter is a basic human need and that different forms of shelter exist, the instruction would help students to understand the reasons for these different forms of shelter. Students would learn that people's shelter needs are determined in large part by local climate and geographical features, and that most housing is constructed using materials adapted from natural resources that are plentiful in the local area. They would learn that certain forms of housing reflect cultural, economic, or geographic conditions (tipis and tents as easily movable shelters used by nomadic societies, stilt houses as adaptation to periodic flooding, high-rises as adaptation to land scarcity in urban areas). They would learn that inventions, discoveries, and improvements in construction knowledge and materials have enabled many modern people to live in housing that offers better durability, weatherproofing, insulation, and temperature control, with fewer requirements for maintenance and labor (e.g., cutting wood for a fireplace or shoveling coal for a furnace) than anything that was available to even the richest of their ancestors.

They also would learn that modern industries and transportation make it possible to construct almost any kind of shelter almost anywhere on earth, so that it is now possible for those who can afford it to live comfortably in very hot or very cold climates. These and related ideas would be taught with appeal to the students' sense of imagination and wonder. There also would be emphasis on values and dispositions (e.g., consciousness-raising through age-suitable activities relating to the energy efficiency of homes or the plight of the homeless). Development and application activities might include such things as a tour of the neighborhood (in which different types of housing would be identified and discussed) or an assignment calling for students to take home an energy-efficiency inventory to fill out and discuss with their parents. Students would begin to see function and significance in elements of their physical and social environment that they were not aware of before, as well as to appreciate their current and future opportunities to make decisions about and exercise some control over aspects of their lives related to their shelter needs. The following unit on shelter illustrates our ideas about teaching and how we apply the principles of goal setting and content selection and representation.

The goals of this unit on shelter as a cultural universal are as follows:

1. To build on students' already-attained understanding that shelter is a basic need by helping them to understand and appreciate key features of contemporary homes and how the forms and functions of homes evolved over time, through space, and across cultures

2. To help students to appreciate the potential implications of this learning for decision making regarding personal housing needs and preferences

Basic social knowledge is about people—what they do and why they do it. It is not about the disciplines or about shelter, except in this context. In teaching about aspects of human social life, we will include a historical dimension (how it evolved over time) and a cultural dimension (how it varies across cultures). In addressing shelter, the historical dimension will emphasize the role of technology and inventions. People have to meet their basic shelter needs. Early on, they were at the mercy of their environments, but as technology developed, they became more able to control or even shape these environments. Today, we have selected and controlled environments suited to our chosen lifestyles, not just "shelter."

The cultural, and to some extent, the economic dimensions of shelter are connected to the distinctions between needs and wants. As architectural styles and technology developed, people could begin to exercise choice in meeting their shelter needs and wants. This led to a diversity of styles within and across cultures, and to the development of features such as landscaping, decorating, and so on.

Content selection and development will also reflect other "meta" ideas: human progress over time, making the familiar strange by placing it in historical and cultural context, choices open to students and the trade-offs embodied in these choices, human applications of knowledge and technology to achieve control over the environment (but with trade-offs here too), and the social reality of homelessness.

The first lesson plan is provided in its entirety, and topics, general comments, goals, main ideas, and assessments are included for the others. For complete lesson plans, see Alleman and Brophy (2001).

LESSON 1: Functions of Shelter

Resources
- Pictures, books, electronic sources, and computer in an interest center focusing on shelter
- Strips of paper with questions related to shelter posted throughout the classroom
- Bulletin board depicting the functions of shelter
- Photos (exterior and interior) of the teacher's home, illustrating its functions
- A Look at Our Home: Home Assignment Sheet

Children's Literature
Kalman, B. (1994). *Homes around the world*. New York: Crabtree.
Morris, A. (1992). *Houses and homes*. New York: Lothrop, Lee & Shephard.

General Comments
To launch the unit, collect the instructional resources and display visual prompts to generate interest in the topic. Post questions (written on wide strips of paper) around the room and on the bulletin board. For example: What is shelter? Why do we need shelter? Why do people choose different kinds of homes? What types of homes do we have in our community? How do climate and physical features influence the types of homes we have? Why do people sometimes have portable shelters? What are some of the decisions people have to make when choosing a home? Why are there so many different kinds of shelters?

General Purposes or Goals
To help students (1) become aware of the possible questions to be answered about shelter; (2) understand why people need shelter (it provides protection against

the elements, provides a place to keep one's possessions, and is a home base for daily life activities); (3) acquire an appreciation for the diversity that exists in the nature and functions of shelter.

Main Ideas to Develop
- Shelter is a basic need.
- Throughout history, people have needed shelter for protection from the elements (sun in hot weather, cold in cold weather, precipitation, wind, etc.), places to keep their possessions, and places in which to carry out their daily activities.
- Other factors that people take into account in deciding the kind of home to build or buy include economic resources, cultural considerations, personal preferences, and the availability of building materials.

Introduction—Lesson
Pose questions regarding the meaning of *shelter* and its functions. Sample questions might include: What is shelter? Why do people need shelter? Why are there so many different kinds of shelters? How do climate and physical features influence the types of shelters people have? What types of shelters do we have in our community?

After a preliminary discussion of these questions and an explanation about answering these and other questions as the unit unfolds, show the class a bulletin board that you have begun that focuses on the functions of shelter.

Use your home as an example to illustrate the functions of shelter. Show photos of the exterior and interior of your home as you share "your story."

Protection
People need places to live that provide protection from cold, heat, storms, insects, animals, and so on. Even in warm climates, people need protection from the elements. People can choose from a variety of shelter types for protection. In our community, there are houses, apartments, duplexes, and manufactured homes. [A manufactured home is a house built in two sections, each on its own foundation that sits on a trailer to be hauled to a person's property. It is then put together. These homes can be quite luxurious, with island kitchens, fireplaces, master bedroom suites, and so on. These manufactured homes have replaced the simple trailer homes of the past.] Can you think of others? [Show a photo of your shelter and explain why you chose it. Describe the building materials that were used and why. If available, show samples.]

Places to Keep Belongings

The interior of the home is a place to store food, clothes, books, prized possessions, beds, furniture, and so on. [Through photos, take an imaginary walking tour of your home, showing your various belongings and explaining why they need to be kept inside.]

Home Base

The interior of the home is also a place for carrying out your daily activities, such as sleeping, eating, doing school work, watching television, spending time with family, and so on. [Continue the imaginary walking tour of your home, pointing out its uses as a home base.]

[Optional: If time permits, organize a walking tour of the immediate neighborhood, pointing out the different kinds of homes—contrasting in many ways yet all made of building materials suited to the physical features and climate. As you walk, underscore that each of these homes provides protection, a place for one's belongings, and a home base for daily activities. If possible, arrange to tour a home in the neighborhood and illustrate its functions. Explain its similarities to your home.]

Share the book entitled *Homes around the World* (Kalman, 1994) with the students (it contains numerous illustrations depicting the functions of homes). Explain that homes vary in size, shape, and type of building materials used, depending on physical features, climatic conditions, available resources, and people's personal choices. However, they all serve the same basic functions.

Activity

At the conclusion of the storylike presentation regarding the functional uses of shelter, ask the students to share in pairs the most interesting ideas they learned. Then, elicit ideas from the pairs and write them on the board. Ask students to indicate other questions that they would like to have answered about the functions (or other aspects) of shelter. Post the questions. Encourage students to peruse the books and electronic resources available in the shelter center in the classroom.

OR

Using a set of pictures and an activity sheet entitled "The Functions of Shelter," have students place the listed functions into categories and explain their reasoning.

Summarize Key Points

• Shelter serves several functions that are universal across time, culture, and place.
• Shelters are made of a variety of building materials, depending on natural and human factors.
• There are many kinds of shelters, such as apartments, duplexes, manufactured homes, houses, and so on, even in our community; however, they all provide protection, a place to store belongings, and a base for daily activities.

Assessment

Have the students brainstorm at their tables the things that they have learned about the functions of shelter. Then, as a class, complete a chart focusing on these functions. Encourage the students to give and explain examples. Then have students individually respond to the following open-ended statements (with assistance from upper-grade mentors or posted word cards reflecting the big ideas, if necessary).

People need shelters because _____.

My teacher's home protects her from _____.

My teacher's home provides a place for _____.

Day-to-day living activities at my teacher's house include _____,

_____, _____, and _____.

    *[If time permits, have students draw pictures to illustrate their responses.]

Home Assignment
Encourage the students to share with their families what they learned about the functions of shelter in their neighborhood and around the world, and about their teacher's home (using the open-ended statements as the springboard for the conversation). Also, encourage students to discuss with their families their shelter choices (i.e., why they live where they do) and the functions that their home fulfills for them.

Name _____

LESSON 1: Home Assignment: A Look at Our Home

With a parent or older brother or sister, look around your home. List examples of how your home functions. For example, the roof, walls, windows, doors, and so on keep out the rain. The roof provides shade from the sun. The door locks keep unwanted people from entering, etc. Attach pictures if available.

Parts of Our Home That Provide Protection	*Parts of Our Home That Provide Places to Keep Belongings*	*Parts of Our Home That Provide a Base for Daily Activities*

LESSON 2: Shelter Types in Our Community

General Purposes or Goals
To (1) stimulate curiosity, build interest, and get students into the habit of actively observing the range of shelter types that exist locally; and (2) develop knowledge, understanding, appreciation, and life application regarding shelter considerations and the factors that contribute to people's decisions about shelter.

Main Ideas to Develop
- There is a range of shelter types in our local community.
- Natural factors that contribute to the type of shelters that can be built in an area include climatic conditions, building materials found locally in large quantities, and physical features (terrain including hills, mountains, valleys, and plains; and bodies of water such as lakes and rivers).
- Factors contributing to family decisions about the type of shelter they will select include location in the community, cost, cultural influences, personal preferences, and so on.

Assessment

Tell the students to imagine they are local real estate agents familiarizing a newcomer to the types of homes available. Give each individual student a stack of cards depicting shelter types and ask him/her to identify those that illustrate homes found in the local area. When students have completed the task, conduct a class discussion focusing on their responses and their reasoning. If time permits, have students select one card depicting a shelter type not found in the local area and explain in writing where it would most likely be found and why.

LESSON 3: Shelter Types around the World

General Purposes or Goals

To (1) stimulate curiosity as well as build appreciation for the diversity of shelter types in the world, understood as inventive adaptations to time and place; (2) recognize and explain the types of shelters that would and would not be appropriate in the local environment; and (3) explain how people adapt to their local environment when making choices associated with shelter.

Main Ideas to Develop
- Geographic features, culture, economic resources, and personal preferences are among the factors that figure into people's choices about the type of shelter they will have.
- People all over the world adapt to their environment, and as a result, there are many types of shelters. Until recently, housing construction reflected the availability of local materials. This pattern still exists in some places, but in other places modern transportation has allowed choices to be expanded.

Assessment

Have students complete a series of open-ended statements. [Consider inviting upper-grade mentors to assist with the student writing. Make sure you model what you expect by completing your own form.]

- The shelter type I would like to learn more about is _____ because

  _____.

- The things I already know about this shelter type are _____ and

  _____.

- The questions I have are _____ and

  _____.

- The things this shelter type has in common with my home are _____

  and _____.

LESSON 4: Progress in Shelter Construction

General Purposes and Goals

To (1) help students understand and appreciate the types of homes that have been created over time, the changes they have undergone, and the reasons for these changes; (2) engender a positive attitude about history; (3) stimulate students' curiosity regarding shelter types, styles, and building materials; and (4) engender a sense of wonder regarding the range of shelters as home bases for family activities.

Main Ideas to Develop

- Until recently, housing construction reflected the availability of local materials. This pattern still exists in some places, but in other places modern transportation has allowed choices to be expanded.
- New construction techniques and technological improvements get invented and refined over time. Now, besides meeting our needs for protection from the elements, modern homes cater to our wants for a comfortable living space, hot and cold running water, electric lighting, comfortable beds and furniture, and so on.

Assessment

Give students individual blank timelines and ask them to show through drawings and words how shelter has progressed over time. If time permits, ask them to write a paragraph explaining which time period they would have most liked to live in because of the type of shelter they would have lived in and why.

LESSON 5: Progress in Shelter Construction (Continued)

General Purposes or Goals

To develop (1) an understanding and appreciation of progress in shelter construction; (2) some understanding about the steps in building a house and a range of people who are involved in the project; and (3) a "macro" understanding and appreciation for some of the features we currently label as modern conveniences, especially the control of light, heat, and water.

Main Ideas to Develop

- In the past, most housing construction was dependent on the availability of local materials. While this pattern still exists to some extent, modern transportation has allowed choices to be expanded.
- New construction techniques and technological improvements have been invented and refined over time. Now, besides meeting needs to protect people

from the elements, modern houses cater to our wants by providing a comfortable range of temperatures, hot and cold running water, electrical lighting, and so on.

• Today's homes are planned to take advantage of advances in new designs, technologies, materials, and so on. Many workers are involved to ensure that the plans are realized.

Assessment

Using word cards naming the steps in building a house, have each student sequence them. Then have the student select the one step and job that s/he might like to do as an adult. Write a short paragraph explaining the choice. Illustrate if time permits.

1. Purchase the land

2. Draw up blueprints

3. Be the building contractor

4. Dig a hole

5. Install footings and connections for sewer and water

6. Pour cement

7. Be a block layer and build outer walls

8. Be a carpenter and build floors

9. Be a carpenter and erect inner structure and roof

10. Shingle the roof

11. Install windows

12. Build chimney

13. Be a plumber and put in pipes

14. Install insulation

15. Be an electrician and add wiring

16. Install drywall

17. Add doors and cupboards

18. Paint interior and exterior

19. Install light fixtures

20. Lay carpets

 ## LESSON 6: Careers Associated with Shelter

General Purposes or Goals

To develop (1) knowledge, understanding, and appreciation regarding career opportunities that exist within the home industry; (2) understanding and appreciation for how technology can change the way work is done and how people can change the way homes look; and (3) a sense of efficacy among students—any one of them might invent a machine, a process, or a design that will benefit all of us in the future.

Main Ideas to Develop
- The home industry provides a range of opportunities for individuals to be creative and pursue careers.
- Today, it takes a variety of workers to perform specific steps in building a house or apartment.
- Many changes have occurred in the home-building industry over the past 200 years.

Assessment
Have each student complete the open-ended statements. Illustrations are optional.

The one career I would like to have in the home building industry is _____.

I think I would like that job because _____

_____

_____.

The one question I still have about it is _____

_____

_____.

LESSON 7: Costs Associated with Your Shelter

General Purposes or Goals
To develop (1) an understanding of and appreciation for the need to pay for a shelter/ home and for modern conveniences such as purified water, energy/electricity, and fuel delivered to our homes; and (2) an understanding of basic principles and options involved in buying or renting a shelter.

Main Ideas to Develop
- You can buy a house without putting down the full purchase price, although you can lose it if you do not continue to make your payments.
- Some people choose to live in an apartment temporarily while they save enough money for a down payment. Others choose apartments as permanent residences for other reasons such as convenience, fewer maintenance responsibilities, and so on.
- Banks (and sometimes private individuals) lend people the money to buy a house. The people have to pay back the amount of the loan plus interest. That is how banks make money.
- People have to pay to live in apartments. The rent money is kept by the owner of the building. Renting is a profit-making business.

- Whether you live in a house or an apartment, you pay utility companies for heat (fuel), water, and light (electricity).
- You pay money to the government (taxes) to maintain roads, provide police protection and fire protection, and operate schools. (If you are buying your home, you pay taxes directly to the government. If you are renting, some of the money you pay to the apartment building owner goes to the government for these services.)
- A large part of the family income goes for buying or renting and maintaining the property.

Assessment

Have students write paragraphs focusing on costs associated with buying and renting. [Option: Students could draw and label their responses.]

Why does buying a house take so much money? Write a short paragraph answering this question.

_____

_____

_____

_____

_____

Why does renting an apartment take so much money? Write a short paragraph answering this question.

_____

_____

_____

_____

 ## LESSON 8: Choice Making

General Purposes or Goals

To (1) enhance students' understanding regarding the forms of shelter that are available; (2) develop an appreciation for the opportunities that people may have to exercise choice in meeting their shelter needs/wants; (3) enhance students' understanding and appreciation regarding major choices that need to be made early in the decision-making process—namely, location and whether to rent or buy.

Main Ideas to Develop

- One of the choices people have to make is location—where they will live.
- Other choices concern such issues as the size of the residence, cost, length of expected stay, special features, and so on.
- Another choice is whether to rent or buy.

Assessment

Have each student complete the questioning exercise focusing on choice-making. [Optional: Invite upper-grade members or adult volunteers to serve as recorders.]

If, in the future, our family needs to move, we should ask several questions before we make a final decision about where we will live. Questions we need to ask—and be able to answer—include:

1. Why are we moving?

2. Do we have a house to sell? (If we do, we probably can't buy another until we sell the one we own now.)

3. Do we need to be near our parents' work?

4. Does our family have its own means of transportation?

5. Do we need to be near the schools? Interstate? Airport? Other? Why?

6. How long does our family expect to stay in this place?

7. How much does our family want to spend?

8. What are special features of the new shelter that we need? Want?

[Optional: If time permits, have students role-play their responses to questions associated with family choice-making.]

LESSON 9: Portable Shelters

General Purposes or Goals

To develop an understanding and appreciation (1) that portable shelters are intended and designed for portability; and (2) that some people depend solely on portable shelters because they are nomadic, while others use them for short periods of time to satisfy their short term needs (e.g., hunting, recreation).

Main Ideas to Develop

- Portable shelters are built out of a variety of materials, take many forms, and are used for a variety of reasons.
- Especially in the past, portable shelters have been used by nomadic societies.
- Today, portable shelters range from being primarily recreational in our area to being a necessity in a few places.

Assessment

Have each student complete an individual journal entry.

I learned that portable shelters _____

_____

_____

_____

_____

_____

_____

_____.

The most interesting portable shelter type to me is _____

because _____

_____

_____

_____

_____.

Questions I have about the most interesting portable shelter include:

_____

_____

_____

_____.

Our family would like to use a portable shelter on our next vacation.

_____ Yes _____ No

Reasons For   **Reasons Against**

1. _____   _____

2. _____   _____

3. _____   _____

4. _____   _____

LESSON 10: Design Your Ideal Future Home

General Purposes or Goals

To (1) draw on acquired knowledge and appreciation regarding shelter in order to "design" an ideal home; and (2) develop an appreciation regarding the range of considerations that need to be addressed when deciding on the ideal home. [Students are to project ahead as adults and be realistic. They should not plan for things that cost millions of dollars unless they also have a plan for making large amounts of money.]

[Note: This lesson will probably be most successful if older students could work as mentors in one-on-one situations.]

Main Ideas to Develop

- Location, climatic conditions, availability of materials, cost, and family size and composition are among the factors to consider when attempting to identify and "design" the ideal home.
- Individual tastes and preferences enter into the decision-making process.

Assessment

After completing the home assignment, as a family create a journal entry entitled "A Day in Our Ideal Home." Imagine that a guest was coming to your house to look at it—what would s/he see as s/he walked up the sidewalk, drove into the driveway, looked out the back door, and so on? Or imagine that a guest was coming to your house to look at it—describe four things you would want your guest to see.

Another option might be to have the students talk into a tape recorder, explaining their ideal homes.

LESSON 11: Homelessness

General Purposes or Goals

To help students (1) understand that in extreme cases people are unable to pay for shelter and may become homeless; and (2) acquire a sensitivity for homeless people and a desire to practice citizenship as it relates to assisting others in need. [*We recommend that you use children's literature to facilitate discussion about homelessness. Suggested resources include *Fly Away Home* (Bunting, 1991) and *Uncle Willie and the Soup Kitchen* (DiSalvo-Ryan (1991).]

Main Ideas to Develop

- Sometimes people cannot pay for shelter and utilities due to unemployment or underemployment, and some become homeless. Often these circumstances are due to illness, fire, flooding, loss of jobs, accumulation of bills, and so on.
- People who are homeless can secure help from community organizations (e.g., the United Way, Rescue Mission, Salvation Army, religious organizations).
- As members of the community, we can contribute to organizations that assist people in need by donating time, food, money, clothing, and so on.

Assessment

Have students respond to three open-ended statements:

1. Reasons people might become homeless might include _____,

   _____ and

   _____.

2. Our community helps homeless people by _____

   _____

   _____

   _____.

3. I can help homeless people by _____

_____

_____

_____.

 LESSON 12: Review

General Purposes or Goals
To (1) draw on prior knowledge, understanding, appreciation, and applications conducted in school and at home that collectively will enhance meaningfulness and continued curiosity in learning about shelter; and (2) revisit and reflect on the big ideas developed about shelter.

Main Ideas Developed throughout the Unit
Review mains ideas from Lessons 1–11.

Individual Assessment Activity: If True, Illustrate!
Read each of the statements to the class. [Each student will have his/her own copy.] Place a T by each statement that is correct. After you have marked all of the T statements, draw pictures to explain why you believe they are correct. [Model the directions by doing one as a class.]

T 1. Not all types of shelter exist in our community. (Draw one that does not.)

T 2. In the early days, housing construction reflected the availability of local materials.

F 3. Only some people need shelter.

F 4. All of the shelters in our community look the same.

T 5. Climate and culture influence the types of shelters people have.

F 6. People who own houses do not have to pay for water, heat, electricity, and so on.

T 7. There are many kinds of portable shelters.

T 8. A large part of the family income goes for paying for shelter and maintaining it.

Summary

Once you have clarified your major social studies goals for the year as a whole and for the unit you are planning, the next step is to determine what content relating to the unit's topic to develop and how to represent it to your students.

The content should be clustered around powerful ideas that students can apply to their lives outside of school and be developed in ways that connect to the students' prior knowledge and home experiences. Development of these big ideas should include their connections to one another and to related skills, values, and dispositions. These connections should not get lost in the process of moving from broader goals to more specific plans for units and lessons.

To illustrate what is involved in developing unit plans around goals and big ideas, we drew from our own twelve-lesson unit on shelter (Alleman & Brophy, 2001), showing (1) some of the introductory material that summarizes ideas relating to shelter that we view as powerful; (2) the first lesson in its entirety; and (3) the goals, main ideas, and assessment activities for the rest of the lessons. The unit is designed to deepen students' awareness and appreciation of activities relating to shelter in the contemporary United States, help them to view these within a broad historical and multicultural context, and help them to acquire anticipations and self-efficacy perceptions concerning their own future decision making related to meeting their shelter needs.

Reflective Questions

1. Selecting and representing meaningful content for social studies units requires thoughtful, goal-oriented planning. Assuming that you accept the importance of this work, at least in principle, how will you proceed?
2. Many school districts require grill-and-drill sessions in preparation for high-stakes testing at the expense of teaching substantive content in powerful ways. Suppose your conscience gets the best of you and you decide to challenge the principal regarding this practice. What will you do?
3. What arguments can you make for depth over breadth for both students and teachers? What do you view as the trade-offs? Challenges?
4. Teachers often feel disempowered and discouraged by the push for breadth, regurgitation, and mandated test preparation. How can you retain a positive attitude, maintain your integrity, and yet at some level accommodate the "system?" Or is that possible?

Your Turn:
Selecting and Representing Content

Identify the units you have taught—or plan to teach—this year. Examine them first by responding to the following questions:

1. What topics are most useful as bases for advancing my students' social understandings and civic efficacy?

_____

_____

_____

_____

2. What are the most important understandings that my students will need to develop, and how do these connect to one another and to related skills, values, and dispositions?

Key Topics	Major Understandings
1. _____	_____
2. _____	_____
3. _____	_____
4. _____	_____

Select a unit you have taught or plan to teach. Examine it carefully to determine whether it is reflective of the principles identified in this chapter for selecting and developing content. Where it is not, revise your plans accordingly. Share the results with a colleague. As you teach the unit—with the enhancements—be mindful of the changes. In your reflective log, document the results.

Principles	_Examples of Applications_
Principle 1 Use contemporary and familiar examples to help students understand how and why the social system functions as it does with respect to the cultural universal under study.	
Principle 2 Include a historical dimension illustrating how human responses to the cultural universal have evolved through time due to inventions and other cultural advances.	
Principle 3 Include a geographical/cultural dimension that exposes students to current variations in human responses to the cultural universal.	
Principle 4 Develop each topic with emphasis on its applications to students' current and future lives.	

FIGURE 4.1

Social Studies Strands

	Unit One	Unit Two	Unit Three	Unit Four
Culture				
Time, Continuity, Change				
People, Places, Environments				
Individual Development and Identity				
Interactions among Individuals, Groups, Institutions				
Power, Authority, Governance				
Production, Distribution, Consumption				
Science, Technology, Society				
Global Connections				
Civic Ideals and Practices				

Data from National Council for the Social Studies Task Force. (1994). *Curriculum standards for the social studies: Expectations of excellence* (Bulletin 89). Washington, DC: National Council for the Social Studies.

OR

In Chapters 5, 6, and 7, we provide principles for selecting content related to history, geography, anthropology (culture), psychology, sociology, economics, and political science that are traditionally taught at this level. Instead of skipping ahead, assess your units according to the curriculum strands published by the National Council for the Social Studies.

If one or more of these curricular strands have not been developed sufficiently, add appropriate content. (An option is to substitute your state's social studies standards.) Share your work with a colleague or with your school principal. This exercise also could serve as a valuable activity for members of the social studies curriculum committee.

CHAPTER 5

HOW CAN I TEACH HISTORY CONTENT MORE MEANINGFULLY?

Jennifer Klapper, Third-Year Teacher

In reading this chapter, I began to challenge myself as to how I teach historical content in my own fifth-grade classroom. Am I creating a learning environment where appropriate limits on the amount of content allow for students to focus on the powerful ideas and make important connections to their own lives? Employing strategies such as student-made timelines, sharing narratives, and using artifacts and visuals to enhance lessons, I find that I am on the right track. However, the chapter offers insights that I had not considered previously. For example, telling stories can have a powerful effect on a student's ability to connect details, but the student may overgeneralize the content. I need to be mindful of the possibilities and select narratives that are worth listening to *and thinking about,* with discussions that focus on the big ideas.

Providing students with different perspectives on history, using children's literature or narratives that represent people with whom students are able to relate, creating timelines, and effectively using artifacts—these are just some of the ideas this chapter addresses in depth. The chapter has provided an opportunity for me to revisit my lesson plans with a fresh approach. You too will discover that history is more meaningful for students when you "go beyond the text." Who knows? After reading Chapter 5, you might find that some of your methodology and philosophy in teaching this subject/discipline become "history"!

The K–12 school subjects draw much of their content from their respective foundational disciplines. For social studies, the primary foundational disciplines are history, geography, and the social sciences (anthropology, economics, political science, psychology, and sociology). Ongoing curricular disputes are often rooted in conflicting beliefs about what is the most appropriate relationship between the school subjects and their foundational disciplines. Consequently, before we address issues involved in representing the foundational disciplines of social studies, we will explain our position on this issue.

A Perspective on the Relationship between Elementary Social Studies and Its Foundational Disciplines

Curriculum theorists have noted that content for school subjects typically is drawn primarily from three sources: knowledge of enduring value (including but not limited to the academic disciplines), the learners (their age-related capacities and interests), and society (the learning outcomes that it deems most important to develop in its citizens). Many also include a fourth source: criticisms of contemporary society and ideas about how it might be improved (Kliebard, 2004). Most curricula in the K–12 school subjects can be understood in terms of their relative emphasis on these content sources. Conflict results when different groups push for curricula that represent contrasting content emphases.

One longstanding source of conflict in social studies, which continues through the present, pits those who want very close correspondence between K–12 courses and their respective foundational disciplines against those who want to draw social studies content from a broader range of sources and synthesize it as preparation for life in contemporary society. The former group wants single-subject courses (in history, geography, etc.) organized according to their respective disciplines and designed to socialize students to think accordingly (i.e., as historians or geographers). The latter group wants pan- or interdisciplinary courses (especially in the elementary grades), in which the emphasis is not on socializing students into the academic disciplines but on preparing them for life in general and citizenship in particular in contemporary society. Most approaches to elementary social studies, including ours, take the latter view.

Disciplinary practitioners have devoted their lives to their disciplines and value them highly, so they promote them enthusiastically if they get involved in efforts to specify social studies goals and standards. However, their zeal frequently leads to positions that are counterproductive in at least three ways. First, they tend to push for more curricular "airtime" than is reasonable. Some history advocates, for example, have seriously proposed replacing the entire social studies curriculum with history courses. Geography and social science content would be included only incidentally as it arose in the process of teaching history.

Second, advocates of the disciplines tend to produce curricular guidelines that are far too ambitious in their specifications of the nature and extent of content to be taught at each grade level. They tend to be professors accustomed to teaching college students and often are minimally knowledgeable about K–12 and especially elementary students, so their notions about appropriate content and activities often are unrealistic.

Third, and most fundamental, they typically fail to appreciate some important distinctions between disciplines and school subjects. Disciplines are communities organized to generate theory and research that will extend knowledge in their respective domains. As this occurs, the disciplines become subdivided and the work becomes more and more specialized. In contrast, school subjects are networks of knowledge, skills, values, and dispositions synthesized and organized to prepare young people for life in the present and future.

As Engle and Longstreet (1972) noted, most of the decisions we make in our daily lives are neither referred to nor guided by the disciplines. The disciplines concern themselves with intentionally isolated segments of existence, producing knowledge that is fragmented, abstract, and theoretical. Others have noted that disciplinary knowledge may be suitable for teaching to older students who are capable of appreciating its value, but elementary students need a topical approach that is better adapted to the realities of human situational learning and to what these students are able to comprehend and appreciate. Considering a topic in all of its aspects (rather than addressing only the aspects that fit within a particular discipline) and within the context of its implications for personal decision making should cause students to find social studies instruction relevant and meaningful (Barton & Levstik, 2003; Thornton, 2005).

Distinguishing between the school subjects and their foundational disciplines has implications not only for content but also for learning activities. Those who view the school subjects primarily as simplified versions of the disciplines tend to think of students as novices being socialized into disciplinary communities of discourse. Consequently, they call for activities that reflect the work that practitioners of the discipline engage in when they "do history," conduct economic inquiry, and so on. Many school activities that fit this disciplinary definition are not authentic with respect to life applications because they deal with specialized disciplinary topics or problems that are too esoteric for anyone but a disciplinary specialist to need to know or even care about. Such activities do not develop big ideas or basic skills that most people would count as preparation for life in contemporary society.

Relatedly, educators with a disciplinary focus tend to favor activities that call for students to use disciplinary tools and engage in disciplinary discourse genres in order to generate knowledge (e.g., by examining facsimiles of primary and secondary sources relating to a historical event, assessing the credibility of these sources, and drawing from them to construct defensible historical accounts). These disciplinary activities have been both oversold and misapplied in K–12 schooling. First, far too much importance has been claimed for them. In history, for example, limited exposure to historiography is useful to help students understand how historical accounts are constructed and appreciate the fact that history is primarily an interpretive discipline. However, history instruction is likely to be more meaningful to students and effective as preparation for life in general and citizenship in particular if it emphasizes opportunities for students to function as consumers rather than producers of historical knowledge (especially opportunities to discuss its connections to and potential implications concerning contemporary issues).

Historiographical activities have limited potential in this regard, and the potential they do have is often unfulfilled because they are misapplied (Barton, 2005). For example, one popular activity calls for students to examine varied accounts (from British soldiers, American rebels, newspaper articles, etc.) of the events at Lexington Green that are often identified as the beginning of the Revolutionary War (Yell, Scheurman, & Reynolds, 2004). It is usually organized as an inquiry designed to determine who fired the first shot (the British or the Americans?).

This activity is useful for learning about historiography because multiple accounts of the event have survived and there is no "right answer"—the most credible accounts disagree, so it is not possible to establish unequivocally who fired the first shot. This activity is authentic for disciplinary (history) purposes, but we do not view it as authentic social studies because it is not structured around big ideas with rich potential for life application. From a social studies perspective, who fired the first shot at Lexington Green is not very important. Escalating tensions were such that if hostilities had not broken out on April 19, 1775 at Lexington Green, they would have broken out someplace else shortly thereafter, and it would not have made any difference who fired the first shot. Consequently, we recommend that students studying the American Revolution spend little or no time on this activity but a lot of time learning about the issues that led to war between England and the colonies and how these affected the thinking of the framers of the Declaration of Independence and the Constitution, then discussing what all of this might mean for understanding American civic traditions and making decisions about contemporary constitutional issues.

In summary, we recommend a social studies curriculum that is rich in content drawn from the foundational disciplines but organized and represented with primary emphasis on preparation for life in general and citizenship in particular, not socialization into the separate disciplines. Furthermore, rather than cramming as much content into the curriculum as possible, we recommend limiting breadth in order to focus on developing powerful ideas in depth with emphasis on their connections and life applications. To better connect with students' prior knowledge and experiences, it is usually most effective to draw content from multiple disciplines and synthesize it with content drawn from the arts, the humanities, the physical sciences, current events, and other sources, organized within topical units. Disciplinary specialists might label much of this content as pre-, pan-, or protodisciplinary knowledge developed using relatively informal language rather than precise disciplinary terminology. However, such objections are beside the point if the content is valid and well suited to the needs and capacities of elementary students and goals of teaching social studies for life application (Gardner & Boix-Mansilla, 1994; Levstik, 1986).

That said, it remains true that the disciplines are key sources of enduring knowledge that is of value to the social studies curriculum. Consequently, it is important for teachers (including elementary teachers) to acquire a basic knowledge of the social studies foundational disciplines and to ensure that what they teach is consistent with these disciplines (as far as it goes).

History

The primary foundational disciplines for social studies are usually described as "history and the social sciences." This wording recognizes that history is different from the social sciences. History is an interpretive discipline concerned with particulars, not an empirical science concerned with developing theories meant to have broad applicability and explanatory power. Historians do seek to develop explanations, and they also follow rules for developing and interpreting evidence. However, their explanations focus on particular events in the past. Concerning the drafting of the U.S. Constitution, for example, historians seek to establish the chronology of key events and determine the motives and intentions of the framers so as to understand how the Constitution came to be written as it did. In the process, they draw on political science concepts and develop information that political scientists will find useful for their purposes, but they do not seek to develop and test political science generalizations (e.g., about relationships between mechanisms of government as described in constitutions and the ways that these tend to function in practice).

Unlike the sciences, the content of history is not organized into networks of knowledge structured around key concepts and generalizations. Historical information is mostly chronological and organized according to the place or people investigated (e.g., U.S. history or the history of the Seminole tribe) or according to the aspects of the human condition addressed (e.g., the history of medicine or warfare). The content in each of these "files" consists of an enormous collection of particulars, along with a few generalizations about trends over time or common patterns observed in parallel situations. Historical interpretations often conflict, if not on issues of what happened and in what order, then on issues of cause and effect (e.g., the possible causal roles of various factors that may have led to the Civil War and the roles that the war may have played in causing subsequent events). These features of the historical knowledge base make it very difficult to decide what history to teach in the schools.

Even though it is mostly a collection of particulars, history is often presented as a foundational and integrative subject that is or should be the core of the social studies curriculum. In this view, history provides a context for contemporary social education by grounding it in knowledge of the human condition as it has progressed over time, focusing in particular on development of the values and principles that guided the design of the nation's government and should guide political decision making today. We have provided a resource unit focusing on the American Revolution to illustrate a connected set of key ideas related to a specific time period (see Appendix A).

History in Elementary Social Studies

Even though it now is clear that elementary students can learn many aspects of history with understanding, extreme disagreements remain about how much history to teach in the elementary grades. A few social educators prefer to minimize the role of history and instead focus social studies on current events and issues, emphasizing critical discussion and reasoned decision making.

Most social educators, however, believe that history deserves an important place in the curriculum for several reasons, including its value as background knowledge that students can draw upon to develop contexts for understanding current events and issues.

At the other extreme from the "get rid of history" view are arguments calling for eliminating the social science content of elementary social studies and replacing it with content drawn primarily from history. As we noted in Chapter 1, we value history but also value the social science content needed to develop basic social understandings, especially content relating to cultural universals. Consequently, we reject the notion of eliminating this content from the curriculum in order to make more room for historical content.

The K–12 social studies curriculum typically includes three years of American history and at least one year of world history, and most other social studies courses include significant historical strands. In elementary school, the primary grades typically include the holiday curriculum and units on the history of the students' families and the local community, and on Native American and pioneer life; fourth-grade studies of the state or region usually include a lot of historical material; fifth grade includes at least a semester and usually a full year devoted to study of U.S. history; and sixth grade usually includes historical material in studies of the western hemisphere, the world, or ancient civilizations. Savage and Armstrong (2004) noted that the elementary grades commonly include historical activities such as the following:

Kindergarten features studies of the self in a social setting and may include activities intended to develop time and sequence concepts (sequencing daily routines, measuring calendar time in days and weeks and identifying changes in seasons, or charting personal growth and change), as well as more explicitly historical activities such as compiling a personal history booklet, reading stories about the past, and dress-up recreations such as those connected to the holiday curriculum.

Grade One focuses on family studies and often includes activities such as tracing changes over time in family size and composition, interviewing family members about the past, developing a family history (possibly including photos and artifacts, a timeline, and a family tree graphic), comparing family life at different points in history, reading stories of family life in the past, and handling and discussing historical artifacts such as old toys, photos, tools, or clothing.

Grade Two focuses on neighborhood studies and human activities related to meeting basic needs. Activities often include touring the neighborhood or visiting local historical sites to identify and discuss old buildings and learn about changes in the neighborhood, developing a history of the school or neighborhood, and studying changes over time in the neighborhood and in the technologies involved in meeting needs for food, clothing, and shelter.

Grade Three focuses on the community. This usually includes a significant historical strand involving learning about the Native Americans who inhabited the area before the arrival of Europeans, the origins of the Europeans who first settled the area and the reasons that they came there, the geographical and economic factors that became the basis for development of the community, and some of the community's more notable historical figures, buildings, and events. These activities might also include trips to local museums or historical sites, inspection and discussion of historical artifacts, or recreations of noteworthy events.

Grade Four focuses on state and regional studies. This includes an overview of the history of the state and region, featuring timelines showing key events and discussion of their causes and consequences. Activities might include historical inquiry or biography projects focused on significant people, places, or events in the state or region, developments in everyday life or in predominant economic activities, and projections concerning current and possible future trends.

Grade Five typically is devoted in whole or significant part to the history of the United States. This is the students' first exposure to sustained, chronological historical study, within units corresponding to the periods identified by historians (pre-Columbian native life, European exploration and settlement of the New World, the colonies, etc.). In addition to learning the basic chronology (timeline and salient facts), students should have opportunities to engage in historical thinking in the process of handling artifacts, conducting inquiry, learning about multiple perspectives on key events, and considering their causes and consequences.

Grade Six usually focuses on learning about people and cultures in different world regions. These geographical and cultural studies usually include a strong historical component and often include sustained study of ancient cultures.

Developments in Children's History Knowledge

Early research on children's history learning was heavily influenced by Jean Piaget's ideas about developmental stages, and it produced some initially discouraging results. In fact, for a time some social educators questioned the feasibility of teaching history to elementary students on the grounds that these students have not yet achieved the levels of cognitive development needed to learn history with understanding. However, subsequent debate and data collection led to the rejection of this argument. It is now generally accepted that elementary students can understand general chronological sequences (e.g., that land transportation developed from walking to horse-drawn carriages to engine-powered vehicles) even though they may be hazy about particular dates, and that they can understand age-appropriate representations of people and events from the past (especially narratives built around the goal-oriented activities of central characters with whom the students can identify) even though they might not be able to follow analytic treatments of abstract historical topics or themes (Barton, 1997; Barton & Levstik, 2004; Booth, 1993; Crabtree, 1989; Downey & Levstik, 1991; Thornton & Vukelich, 1988, Willig, 1990).

Barton and Levstik (1996) studied K–6 students' understanding of historical time by showing them pictures from various periods in American history, asking them to place the pictures in order and explain their reasoning. They found that even the youngest students could distinguish "long ago" from "close to now," explaining their judgments with reference to the relative modernity of the clothing, furniture, or objects shown in the pictures. Older students made increasingly differentiated temporal distinctions. Dates had little meaning for children before third grade; third- and fourth-graders understood their numerical basis; but only fifth- and sixth-graders typically connected particular dates with particular background knowledge.

Sansom (1987) noted that gradual advances occur in four key aspects of historical reasoning.

Causation. At first, children do not perceive any logic to historical causality—things happen without relationship to one another. The story "unfolds" but doesn't develop. Once children begin to realize that historical events have causes, they initially take a mechanistic view, thinking that events were the inevitable results of their preceding causal chains, that they had to happen the way that they did. Later, children begin to understand that events have multiple causes that act in combination, that things could have turned out differently, and that we cannot know all of the causes and give a comprehensive and final picture of the past.

Change and continuity. At first, children view changes as unrelated rather than as progressions in a causal chain. Then they believe that everything can be traced back to a first cause and that everything that happened in the past is an antecedent to the present. Eventually they begin to view historical change as gradual transformation, realizing that only some aspects of the situation change and that these changes may range from the trivial to the radical.

Motivation and intention of historical actors. Initially children do not empathize with people from the past. When exposed to accounts of what seems to be inexplicable behavior, they adopt a patronizing attitude, suggesting that the people acted as they did because they were stupid or not as developed as we are. Later they begin to understand that the people were acting rationally from their own perspectives. Initially they attribute vague or stereotyped motivation to these people ("his character," "their religion"). Later they attribute more specific motives, although still by projecting from a modern viewpoint. Finally, they begin to appreciate the need to reconstruct the probable perceptions and beliefs of historical actors, reasoning from whatever historical source materials may be available.

Evidence and historical method. At first, children equate evidence with factual information. They do not notice contradictory evidence or do not know how to make sense of it. Gradually, they come to understand that evidence must be interpreted, that different sources of evidence may conflict, and that historians need to follow disciplinary rules for evidence collection and use and then develop interpretations that are defensible but not final or definitive.

As a teacher, you can foster your students' development toward more advanced levels of history learning by emphasizing the more advanced levels during discussions of historical events. In teaching about the American Revolution, for example, you can explain that it was a major event that had multiple causes and multiple effects on government, including converting the colonies into a new nation, but few direct effects on everyday social and economic activities; note that the British might have won (and lead a speculative discussion about what might have happened subsequently); help students to empathize with the founders and appreciate that much of what they wrote into the Declaration of Independence and U.S. Constitution reflected their recent experiences with the British government (e.g., taxation without representation, forced quartering of troops in private homes); and help students recognize that accounts of the Revolution have been constructed by historians working from documents and artifacts that have survived from the time, and that different accounts conflict on some issues (e.g., the British have a different view of the nature of and justification for the Revolution than we do).

Hallden (1994) noted that history learning is complicated by the fact that students may process historical information using alternative frameworks that differ from the framework emphasized by a text author or teacher. Students tend to personify history by seeking explanations of historical events in the intentions, actions, and reactions of individuals. This hampers their efforts to follow lessons on general historical trends that are explained using structural rather than personal explanations.

Britt, Rouet, Georgi, and Perfetti (1994) asked students to read text selections, summarize them, and answer causal-temporal questions. Fourth-graders' summaries were disconnected lists of facts, fifth-graders' summaries were more coherent but focused on a substory rather than the main story, and sixth-graders' summaries were both coherent and focused on the main story. Students who gave more sophisticated summaries focused more on main events and learned more about the connections among them.

Barton (1992) described an emphasis on children's historical fiction in a case study of a fifth-grade unit on the American Revolution. He observed a heavy reliance on narrative structures, by both the teacher and the students, in representing knowledge about this historical period in speech and writing. The teacher and students used five overlapping structures to place their study of the Revolution into a narrative framework:

1. The unit as a whole was treated as a sequence of causally related events that together formed the "story" of the Revolution.
2. Each event was itself treated as a story with characters, problem, and resolution.
3. These stories emphasized the feelings and actions of these individuals.
4. Fictive conversations (e.g., between King George and his advisors) were spontaneously created in order to convey information.
5. Nations were endowed with human characteristics (e.g., motives, goals, plans, and other features common to central figures in stories).

In subsequent research, Barton (1996) noted that although narrative structures help students remember connected details related to the main storyline of a narrative, they also can lead to oversimplification of historical trends and events. The fourth- and fifth-graders he studied often collapsed lengthy and complicated historical processes into short time frames and simple narratives, such as crediting famous people for single-handedly bringing about monumental changes in a short period of time. For example, many spoke as if African-Americans began to be treated differently immediately after Martin Luther King, Jr. "gave a speech" and suddenly changed people's minds. Brophy and VanSledright (1997) found similar patterns in their interviews of fourth- and fifth-graders: Students described

European explorers as though they were a small band of associates in close contact with one another and thought that they returned to their home countries and personally led groups of settlers to the New World. They also conceived of English colonies in North America as though they were all small villages similar to Plymouth Plantation.

Much of the students' knowledge was represented in the form of storylike narratives that featured a setting, a plot focused on the motives and goals of one or more focal individuals or groups, and a resolution that carried implications for the futures of these people and others included in the story. The stories featured themes such as monarchs competing for power and glory through land claims and territorial wars, colonists uniting to proclaim and fight for their freedom from British rule, and pioneers struggling against adversity to establish new communities.

Less-sophisticated versions often were vague or inaccurate about the temporal and geographic specifics of the settings, and many of them featured stories personalized around hero figures. More-sophisticated versions were more specific and accurate about time and place, were formulated more as cause-and-effect explanations than as conventional stories, and described larger historical trends involving sizable populations or geographic areas rather than only recounting what happened to a particular individual or small group during the course of a particular event. There were few comments on the nature or quality of evidence, characterizations of the points of view of various stakeholder groups, references to alternative interpretations, or other indications of the kinds of historical reasoning brought to bear by disciplinary specialists.

The fifth-graders were able to overcome tendencies toward presentism and other biases in order to identify and empathize with some of the people they studied, especially if these people were portrayed as heroic figures or as victims of oppression. To the extent that they were encouraged and helped to do so, they also showed an ability to see both sides of an issue, such as the contrast between King George's views and the American rebels' views of the events that led to the American Revolution. However, they did not display advanced forms of historical empathy reflecting deep and contextualized knowledge of the people they studied. They did not, for example, evaluate historical figures' goals or strategies by taking into account the information available to the individuals at the time in question, or point to the individuals' prior philosophies or experiences that might have predisposed them toward particular views or courses of action.

The students expressed many inaccurate assumptions or misconceptions. Most of these were expressed prior to the instruction and were not repeated in the post-unit interviews, but some of them persisted, especially misconceptions related to the temporal or spatial relationships among the people and events being studied. The students clearly needed help in seeing how the historical content they were studying fit within the broader sweep of human history (contextualized with reference to timelines, landmark events and inventions, and social and political developments).

In the process of teaching history to fifth-graders, VanSledright (2002) found it necessary to address affective as well as cognitive barriers to children's construction of historical interpretations. Initially, his students showed strong preferences for simple storylines, free of ambiguities or complications. They wanted "the true history." Later, after exposure to multiple interpretations reflecting conflicting biases, they swung to the other extreme, thinking that there is no way to know what really happened, so one account is as good as the next. Still later, after learning about and applying basic principles of historiography, they began to understand that some accounts were more defensible than others because they were supported by more convincing evidence and arguments. Despite this developing understanding, however, their ultimate interpretations of historical events were strongly conditioned by their pre-existing knowledge and biases.

Research by Hynd and Guzzetti (1998) also suggests that teacher scaffolding of students' exposures to conflicting interpretations is needed to help them tolerate frustration and eventually achieve more sophisticated understandings. These authors found that students entered the study of Christopher Columbus with oversimplified heroic views of Columbus (he was adventurous, brave, and smart) that included some misconceptions (he was Spanish, landed on the North American continent, was the first to believe that the earth was round, and was regarded as a great man during his lifetime). They exposed the students to three different texts. The first was a traditional text that reinforced and elaborated the students' views of Columbus as unambiguously heroic. The second was a revisionist text that depicted Columbus as a greedy gold seeker who "discovered" only islands rather than continents and who cruelly mistreated the Native Americans he encountered. The third text offered a balanced view of Columbus's good and bad qualities, directly addressed and refuted common misconceptions about him, and concluded that if he had not sailed west and changed the world, someone else would have. The third text had the strongest impact on students, both in reducing their misconceptions and in inducing them to adopt a more nuanced rather than an unambiguously positive view of Columbus as a person. Most students apparently read the first text without noticing that some of its information contradicted their existing misconceptions, and many of them apparently rejected much of the content of the second text because they viewed it as biased.

Most of the research on children's thinking about history comes from studies of children in Grades 4 and above. However, our own interviews with K–3 students included questions about historical topics. They revealed that these younger students possessed bits and pieces of historical knowledge that they picked up from the holiday curriculum at school or (more typically) from children's literature or media. Furthermore, the knowledge they did have was very limited and often distorted by misconceptions. For example, when shown an illustration of a tipi, almost all of the students knew what it was, calling it a tipi or an Indian tent. However, none of the lower primary students and fewer than 10% of the upper primary students gave accurate explanations when asked why some native tribes lived in tipis (i.e., because they were nomadic plains tribes who followed the buffalo and had to have portable housing). A majority of these students had never heard of nomadic societies, so they did not even mention portability and instead generated such explanations as these tribes did not know how to make any other kind of home, tipis were constructed by people who lived alone or in only very small families and thus did not need a larger home, they were preferred by people who liked to do a lot of cooking and could do it inside a tipi because the smoke would go out the top, or these tribes had a lot of surplus buffalo skins and needed something to do with them (because Native Americans never wasted anything). The students' ideas about pioneer log cabins were more accurate but infused with presentism. Most of them disparaged these cabins as homemade and primitive, lacking modern heat, light, and running water. Some of them thought that the pioneers had no source of light in their cabins after sundown or that they had to tote water from a source a mile or more away. The latter students either did not know about wells or thought of them merely as holding containers for captured rainwater or water toted from a stream, not realizing that they tap underground water sources. When asked about life back in the cave days, many of the younger students provided responses clearly rooted in the Alley Oop or Flintstones cartoons (e.g., depicting people as traveling in vehicles with stone wheels).

Problems with History Texts and Teaching

Older generations typically complain that younger generations are ignorant of history, and periodic knowledge surveys appear to bear this out. However, analyses indicate that today's students know about as much history (although not the same history) as the students of previous generations did. Performance levels have remained constant over the last ninety years, and students do about as well on history tests as they do on tests in other subjects (Paxton, 2003).

On the other hand, both past and current surveys provide little cause for celebration. After several exposures to U.S. history, most students remain indifferent to and ill informed about it (Thornton, 2005; VanSledright, 2002). One reason for this is that history texts are especially prone to the problems summed up in the phrases "mile-wide but inch-deep," "parade-of-facts," and "trivial pursuit."

Commonly used fifth-grade U.S. history texts are difficult for students to understand because they lack coherence. Historical accounts should be built around causal chains indicating that events have causes and consequences. To learn history with understanding, students need to learn not only the elements in a chain but also how these elements are related—why certain actions caused some event and why that event led to subsequent events. In this regard, Beck and McKeown (1988) identified three major problems in fifth-grade history texts:

1. Lack of evidence that clear content goals were used to guide text writing (the text read as chronicles of miscellaneous facts rather than narratives built around connecting themes)
2. Unrealistic assumptions about students' prior knowledge (key elements needed to understand a sequence often were merely alluded to rather than explained sufficiently)
3. Inadequate explanations that failed to clarify connections between actions and events (in particular, causal relationships)

Follow-up studies confirmed that fifth-grade students' prior knowledge was much more limited and disconnected than the texts assumed, and that the students' attempts to learn from the texts seldom produced accurate reconstructions of the main storyline. To address these problems, McKeown and Beck (1990, 1994) revised textbook passages to make them more coherent and explicit. Students who read the revised versions recalled significantly more of their content, especially material concerning the sequential relationships of and explanations for the main events depicted. A second intervention involved providing students with background knowledge to make them better prepared for the material they would be reading. This intervention also improved comprehension, although not as strongly as making the texts more coherent did.

McKeown and Beck also developed interventions to improve students' engagement with the materials. One study involved rewriting texts to make them more interesting as well as more coherent. Another involved encouraging students to reflect on what they were reading by asking them to pause several times during the reading to talk about what came to mind. This think-aloud intervention was later extended to a small-group format. All of these interventions had positive effects, illustrating some of the things that textbook authors and teachers can do to improve the effectiveness of history instruction to elementary students.

We recognize that it is unrealistic to expect novice teachers to operate without texts and unnecessary to ask veteran teachers to do so (although some may prefer this option). However, it is important to view the textbook as just one among many resources to draw on in planning a history curriculum designed to accomplish social studies goals. To overcome some of the limitations of textbooks, you will need to examine them in light of your major social education goals in order to identify what content to ignore or downplay and what content to emphasize. You may need to augment the useful content if major ideas or themes are not well developed in the texts, as well as to identify pointless questions and activities to skip and to develop other questions and activities that will support progress toward major goals. If not only the texts but their related activities and assignments are focused on disconnected names, dates, and miscellaneous facts instead of big ideas and their implications, students will perceive history as boring and pointless.

Most school history texts are written in a bland style that features passive constructions and avoidance of controversial content. Especially when written for children, these texts ought to feature lively narratives that capture the drama that is inherent in much of the content. Joy Hakim's series, *The History of Us,* is a step in the right direction (Hakim, 1993).

The content emphasized in traditional history texts also leaves much to be desired. Political and military events and leaders are generally of less interest to elementary students than information about everyday life in the past and the influence of inventions; advances in freedom, equality, and social justice; and inspirational biographical material on the people most responsible for these advances. Finally, for students from immigrant families and minority groups, the heavily Eurocentric focus of traditional history does not offer them much to identify with and care about. They are likely to view such history as "someone else's facts," with little connection to their lives and concerns (Holt, 1990).

These problems suggest that although there are deficiencies in U.S. students' knowledge of history, the remedy does not lie in teaching them more history, if this means teaching history the way it has been taught traditionally. A more promising remedy is to focus history teaching around major goals and big ideas, teaching it for understanding, appreciation, and life application. We recommend establishing a network of basic understandings to provide a context for all history learning. Big ideas to emphasize in such a network include the following.

History is the study of the past. It includes the very recent past as well as ancient times, and the everyday lives of ordinary people in addition to the exploits of the famous and powerful. We study history to learn about developments through time in the human condition generally and in life at different places in the world; to learn about the origins and development of our country and its institutions and traditions; to understand the many ways in which today's world has been shaped by decisions and events of the past; to understand how these past events have influenced contemporary beliefs, attitudes, and life experiences, including our own and those of the groups with which we identify; to note parallels in comparable situations that developed at different times and places; and to consider the potential implications of all of this for personal, social, and civic decision making.

Historical accounts are developed through study of what has been preserved from the past. Usually this includes not only archaeological remains but also books, newspapers, maps, diaries, and other written material (and more recently, audiovisual material). These sources often disagree, especially when reporting on conflicts involving groups with competing interests. Usually there is at least some legitimacy to all the different points of view expressed. To construct defensible interpretations, historians need to sift through all of the relevant evidence (from people who were eyewitnesses on the scene vs. dependent on reports from others, and who were seemingly unbiased vs. committed to a particular group or point of view), then piece together a reconstruction that is consistent with the most credible evidence. This may include reference to situations in which the same events were perceived differently by different groups.

Historical study sometimes suggests "lessons" in the form of guidelines or cautions to keep in mind in coping with today's challenges. However, it is important to note the differences as well as the similarities between comparable situations. Also, developments that seem clear in hindsight may not have been very predictable at the time. To understand the thinking and behavior of people of the past, we need to adopt their purview—consider situations within the affordances and constraints of their time and place.

National Standards for History Teaching

Because of America's status as a nation of immigrants, teaching American values and political principles has received special emphasis in American schools, and the history curriculum has been considered a major vehicle for doing so. Rogers (1987) noted that decisions about what history should be studied are not fundamentally questions about history at all; they are questions about what things are important and therefore, which "histories" are most important to study. George Orwell observed that those who control the past also control the future. These characteristics have made history the most politicized of the school subjects so that controversies over the history curriculum often extend beyond the usual cast of players (state departments of education, academics, school administrators and teachers, textbook companies) to include presidential administrations, legislators, pundits, editorial writers, and issue-oriented lobbying groups.

In U.S. schools, history has been taught primarily as a way to socialize the young into American democratic traditions and prepare them to be citizens

(Bohan, 2005; Evans, 2004). Its focus has been on famous people and events, especially those connected with the origins of the nation and its subsequent geographic expansion and political and economic development. This celebratory view of American history continues to be emphasized by traditionalists, especially those such as Hirsch (1987) and Ravitch (1989), who fear that U.S. culture risks fragmentation if American children do not learn a body of shared information about the past to ground their civic thinking and decision making.

In recent decades, the traditional history curriculum has been criticized as too concerned with perpetuating the status quo. Social educators who emphasize a global purview and world interdependence want to see U.S. history embedded more clearly within world history and taught in ways less likely to induce chauvinistic attitudes in Americans. Those concerned with multicultural issues want to see a more inclusive selection of topics, treated in ways that represent more diverse points of view. Those concerned with gender issues would like to see more emphasis on social history and the lives of everyday people (especially women), and correspondingly less emphasis on political and military issues. Social critics would like to see more representation of the activities and views of workers relative to capitalists, oppressed or voiceless minorities relative to the establishment, and so on.

These tensions boiled over in the 1980s and early 1990s in a series of highly politicized movements to reform state history standards and eventually establish national history standards (Cornbleth & Waugh, 1999; Nash, Crabtree, & Dunn, 1997; Symcox, 2002). A great many issues were involved, but the conflicts essentially pitted "traditionalists, who favored a single grand narrative celebrating a shared and triumphant national past, against revisionists, who favored a more pluralistic rendering of our nation's history, with fewer heroes" (Symcox, 2002, p. 3).

Eventually, the federal government commissioned the National Center for History in the Schools (NCHS) to develop "voluntary" standards to guide K–12 curriculum and instruction in history. After several years of development and revision, which included soliciting and responding to feedback from a broad range of stakeholders, the NCHS published sets of standards that the developers believed to be representative of a broad consensus and thus noncontroversial. However, traditionalists denounced the standards as un-American—too reflective of political correctness and excessive multiculturalism while at the same time insufficiently celebratory of America's triumphs and heroes. This set off a lobbying effort that culminated in a U.S. Senate resolution condemning the standards.

As a result of this uproar, revised standards were published in 1996 (NCHS, 1996). The standards address both content and process. The *process standards* focus on five groups of historical thinking skills:

1. *Chronological thinking*—distinguishing between past, present, and future time; identifying the temporal structure of historical narratives or stories; establishing temporal order in the students' own historical narratives; measuring and calculating calendar time; interpreting data presented in timelines; creating timelines; and explaining change and continuity over time
2. *Historical comprehension*—reconstructing the literal meaning of a historical passage; identifying the central questions that the narrative addresses;

reading historical narratives imaginatively; developing historical perspectives; drawing on the data in historical maps; drawing on visual and mathematical data presented in graphics; and drawing on visual data presented in photographs, paintings, cartoons, and architectural drawings

3. *Historical analysis and interpretation*—formulating questions to focus inquiry or analysis; identifying the author or source of a historical document or narrative; comparing and contrasting differing sets of ideas, values, personalities, behaviors, and institutions; analyzing historical fiction; distinguishing between fact and fiction; comparing different stories about a historical figure, era, or event; analyzing illustrations in historical stories; considering multiple perspectives; explaining causes in analyzing historical actions; challenging arguments of historical inevitability; and hypothesizing influences of the past

4. *Historical research capabilities*—formulating historical questions; obtaining historical data; interrogating historical data; and marshalling needed knowledge of the time and place to construct a story, explanation, or historical narrative

5. *Historical issues-analysis and decision making*—identifying issues and problems in the past; comparing the interests and values of the various people involved; suggesting alternative choices for addressing the problem; evaluating alternative courses of action; preparing a position or course of action on an issue; and evaluating the consequences of a decision

The NCHS (1996) *content standards* are divided into three sections. There are separate U.S. history and world history standards for Grades 5–12, organized chronologically according to historical eras. For example, one of the eras identified for the U.S. history standards is The Revolution and the New Nation (1754–1820s). Standards associated with this era call for learning about (1) the causes of the American Revolution, the ideas and interests involved in forging the revolutionary movement, and the reasons for the American victory; (2) the impact of the American Revolution on politics, economy, and society; and (3) the institutions and practices of government created during the Revolution and how they were revised between 1787 and 1815 to create the foundation of the U.S. political system based on the U.S. Constitution and the Bill of Rights.

The content standards for Grades K–4 subsume both U.S. and world history. They are not organized chronologically within historical eras but instead are organized within eight historical themes identified for emphasis in the early grades:

1. Family life now, in the recent past, and in various places long ago
2. History of the local community and how communities in North America varied long ago
3. The people, events, problems, and ideas that created the history of the state
4. How democratic values came to be and how they have been exemplified by people, events, and symbols
5. The causes and nature of various movements of large groups of people into and within the United States, now and long ago
6. Regional folklore and cultural contributions that helped to form our national heritage

7. Selected attributes and historical developments of various societies in Africa, the Americas, Asia, and Europe
8. Major discoveries in science and technology, their social and economic effects, and the scientists and inventors responsible for them

The basic standards statement (NCHS, 1996) and related publications from NCHS elaborate on the standards and provide suggested activities to use in teaching to them. For a complete statement of the standards and information about related publications, see the NCHS website (www.ssnet.ucla.edu/nchs/standards/).

We believe that elementary teachers should familiarize themselves with these standards, especially if they form the basis for the history standards adopted by their state or school district. However, we also believe that the standards need to be adapted, rather than taken at face value, if they are used to inform instructional planning in the elementary grades. The standards are overly ambitious, reflecting unrealistic assumptions both about the curricular "airtime" that can be devoted to history and about the levels of prior knowledge and cognitive development that students at each grade level bring to historical study. In particular, some of the process standards dealing with historical analysis and interpretation and historical research capabilities, as well as much of what is implied in K–4 Content Standards 5, 6, and 7, ordinarily cannot be addressed seriously in Grades K–4. Nor can the content standards for subsequent grades be addressed at the level of detail and sophistication envisioned for Grades 5 and 6.

NCSS Standards Relating to History

The National Council for the Social Studies' (1994) curriculum standards include a thematic strand on Time, Continuity, and Change. In the early grades, it calls for experiences that allow students to demonstrate an understanding that different people may describe the same event or situation in diverse ways, citing reasons for the differences in views; demonstrate an ability to use correctly vocabulary associated with time such as past, present, future, and long ago; read and construct simple timelines; identify examples of change; recognize examples of cause-and-effect relationships; compare and contrast different stories or accounts about past events, people, places, or situations, identifying how they contribute to our understanding of the past; identify and use various sources for reconstructing the past, such as documents, letters, diaries, maps, textbooks, photos, and others; demonstrate an understanding that people in different times and places view the world differently; and use knowledge of facts and concepts drawn from history, along with elements of historical inquiry, to inform decision making about and action-taking on public issues.

The middle grades should include experiences that allow students to demonstrate an understanding that different scholars may describe the same event or situation in different ways but must provide reasons or evidence for their views; identify and use key concepts such as chronology, causality, change, conflict, and complexity to explain, analyze, and show connections among patterns of historical change and continuity; identify and describe selected historical periods and patterns of change within and across cultures, such as the rise of civilizations, the development of transportation systems, the growth and breakdown of colonial systems, and others; identify and use processes important to reconstructing and reinterpreting the past, such as using a variety of sources, providing, validating, and weighing evidence for claims, checking credibility of sources, and searching for causality; develop critical sensitivities such as empathy and skepticism regarding attitudes, values, and behaviors of people in different historical contexts; and use knowledge of facts and concepts drawn from history, along with methods of historical inquiry, to inform decision making about and action-taking on public issues.

As an example of the standards brought to life, the NCSS publication describes an activity in which small groups of primary-grade students are engaged in studying photographs taken in their own community in the past. To begin, each group receives a different photo and is instructed to study the photo and answer questions such as, "What is the most important thing you saw in the photo?" "Tell two things about the photo that surprised you," "Find two things in the photo that you might not see if it were taken today," and "Give the photo a title that accurately describes its contents." Next, the groups exchange photos and each group repeats the exercise with a different photo. Then, groups that examined the same photo join together and share their responses. These experiences help students to appreciate the fact that different observers will notice different details and take away different impressions from the same historical source. Follow-up activities include engaging the class in discussion of which photo was the oldest and having pairs of students collaborate to develop two illustrations of some aspect of the community (transportation, schools, stores, etc.), one showing it as it appears today and the other as it appeared long ago.

In another example, students study the experiences of immigrants by talking with family, friends, or neighbors about their own or their ancestors' immigrant experiences; gathering information about why the people left their homeland and what they thought about living in the United States; engaging in class discussion and developing lists of responses about each of these two topics; and conducting group interviews with recent immigrants whom the teacher recruits to come to the class for this purpose. Other examples included engaging students in learning about and then planning dramatic reenactments of interactions among key people involved in significant events in history, such as conversations among people participating in the American Revolution.

Other Guidelines for Teaching History

Most of what has been written about history standards has been rooted in concerns either about the discipline (make children into young historians) or the perceived needs of society (make them patriotic, focused on the common good, etc.). There should be more attention paid to the learners. We need to ask which history content and activities are most suitable for inclusion in the K–12 curriculum, and in the elementary grades in particular. The following sources provide some useful responses to these questions.

The Bradley Commission on History in Schools (1988) advocated teaching history in ways that develop important "habits of mind." These include understanding the significance of the past to our lives and to society as a whole; distinguishing between the important and the inconsequential; perceiving past events and issues as they were experienced by people at the time (developing historical empathy as opposed to present-mindedness); acquiring a comprehension of both diverse cultures and shared humanity; understanding cause-and-effect relationships in studying how things happen and how things change; recognizing not only the roles of human intentions but also of unpredictability and chance in affecting developments; appreciating the interpretive and often tentative nature of judgments about the past; resisting temptations to overemphasize "lessons" of history as cures for present ills; recognizing the importance of individuals who have made a difference in history and the significance of personal character for both good and ill; and reading widely and critically in order to recognize the difference between fact and conjecture and between evidence and assertion, and thereby to frame useful questions.

The Commission also suggested that historical study promotes personal growth because it can satisfy young people's longing for a sense of identity and of their time and place in the human story, that it furnishes a wide range of models and alternatives for political choice in a complicated world, and that it conveys a sense of civic responsibility through its graphic portrayals of virtue, courage, and wisdom—and their opposites. Others also have written eloquently about reasons for studying history and about how to teach it so that its potential may be realized.

John Dewey (1900/1956) suggested that history for elementary students be approached as an indirect form of sociology—a study of developments in the social aspects of the human condition. It would be taught with emphasis on its inspirational aspects—the heroic accomplishments of individuals and the inventions that helped people to solve problems and improve their life conditions. Instruction would draw on genuine historical content or historically based biography and fiction, however, not myths or fairy tales featuring fictional heroes solving fictional problems.

Hoge and Crump (1988) identified four purposes for teaching history in elementary school: (1) to make the past seem real; (2) to build insights into present circumstances and events; (3) to develop a love and respect for history learning, including an understanding of its limitations; and (4) to help students recognize their own relationship to history. These authors suggested four guidelines for teaching history for understanding. First, make history real to students by allowing them to manipulate artifacts or primary documents from the past. Struggling to read script in an old mill ledger or to operate an early corn sheller will help the students feel how hard people in earlier times labored intellectually and physically to survive. Second, transport students to the past through constructing, processing, and interacting within simulated environments (making hoe cakes on a hoe over an open fire, tracing origins of words, interviewing older people about home remedies). Third, question the text as a single authority and engage students in collecting information from other sources, discussing discrepancies, and writing their own accounts. Finally, make sure that students get the intended benefits from participating in "hands-on" activities by engaging them in reflective discussions about the activities and following up with assignments that require them to think and communicate about what they learned.

Knight (1993) emphasized developing historical empathy as a major goal of history instruction, arguing that the purpose of teaching history "is not directly to teach us lessons, nor to form laws which show the future. Rather, the past is to be studied on its own terms and 'from within': The intention is to try to recreate the understandings, the perspectives of people in the different societies which constitute the past. History, then, is a multicultural study. Like geography, its goal is to try to explain (often strange) others on their own terms, within their own cultures, set in their situations, and without the benefit of hindsight" (p. 84). He also indicated that elementary students are able to recognize that characters in the past had a perspective different from theirs; generate explanations that depend on taking another's perspective; predict outcomes of situations given another's perspective; and make evaluations of historical characters that involve handling evidence that can support more than one judgment.

Keep in mind these worthy purposes and goals of historical study as you plan and implement your history teaching. Help your students learn to approach historical episodes or periods not just as chronicles (lists of events in order of occurrence) but as narratives—stories worth learning and thinking about because they relate to important themes or issues.

Teaching History for Understanding, Appreciation, and Life Application

Theory and research on teaching history for understanding suggest several principles that are particularly relevant to elementary teachers. First, *focus instruction on the study of particular individuals and groups of people rather than on impersonal abstractions*; study these people with emphasis on developing understanding of and empathy for their contexts and points of view; and focus on general trends in the evolution of social systems rather than on particular dates or detailed chronologies (Knight, 1993; Levstik & Barton, 2005; Willig, 1990). Children in the primary grades are interested in and can understand accounts of life in the past that are focused on particular individuals or groups (cave dwellers, Native American tribes, the Pilgrims, life on a plantation or on the frontier in the 18th century). Fifth-graders are interested in and can understand an introduction to chronological study of U.S. history.

Represent historical material to students in the form of narratives that depict people with whom they can identify pursuing goals that they can understand. For example, primary-grade children could understand that the Pilgrims were persecuted for their religious beliefs and left England because they wanted to be free to practice their religion as they saw fit, but they could not follow an abstract analysis of the theological differences between the separatists and the Church of England. Similarly, fifth-graders could understand that the American colonists sold raw materials to England and purchased finished products manufactured in England, but they could not follow an abstract discussion of "the rise of mercantilism." Incorporating history teaching within strong narrative storylines is helpful for elementary students generally (relative to older students) but especially for students with attention deficits or other learning disabilities (Ferretti, MacArthur, & Okolo, 2001).

Virtually all sources of advice on teaching history emphasize *fostering empathy with the people being studied.* Just as there is a danger of chauvinism when we study contemporary cultures other than our own, there is a danger of presentism when we study people from the past with benefit of hindsight. Children are especially prone to presentism, often believing that people in the past were not as smart as we are today because they did not have all the social and technical inventions that ease our contemporary lives. You can foster their development of empathy by helping them to appreciate such things as bow-and-arrow hunting, horse-drawn carriages, or butter churns as ingenious inventions that represented significant advances for their times, not just as tools that seem primitive when compared with today's technology.

History educators also agree on the value of *exposing students to varied data sources and providing them with opportunities to conduct historical inquiry,* to synthesize and communicate their findings, and to learn from listening to or reading biography and historical fiction selections as well as conventional textbooks (Fertig, 2005; Harms & Lettow, 1994; Lamme, 1994; Levstik & Barton, 2005; Sunal & Haas, 1993). It is important, however, for you as the teacher to *guide your students in their use of these varied data sources.*

Elementary students lack a rich base of prior knowledge to inform their efforts at critical thinking and decision making, so they have difficulty knowing what to believe or how to assess conflicting accounts. They will need to learn that textbooks, and even eyewitness accounts or diaries, tend to emphasize aspects of events that support their authors' biases and interests. In studying the American Revolution, for example, it is helpful to expose students to information sources that will help them to realize that King George had a quite different view from that of the American rebels concerning how the events leading up the revolution should be interpreted and thus whether or not revolution was justified. Similarly, the students might come to see that the Boston Massacre would be viewed (and described later) quite differently by a British soldier seeking to avoid a confrontation than by an American rebel seeking to provoke one.

Many topics traditionally taught from a single perspective can be taught much more insightfully from a global and multicultural perspective. For example, traditional Columbus Day instruction typically was confined to a Eurocentric version of discovery of the New World in 1492, featuring a dramatized and largely inaccurate version of events occurring before and during Columbus's first voyage. A more accurate and informative version would depict the initial voyage as the beginning of an ongoing encounter between previously separated civilizations that eventually led to a great deal of cultural exchange and dramatically affected events not only in Europe and America but also in Africa (via the slave trade).

It is important that students see included in history (as represented in your curriculum) the racial, ethnic, and social class groups with which they identify. Several studies have shown that students take special interest in and assign special importance to people and events in history that accommodate such identification (Almarza, 2001; Epstein, 2001). For example, although mainstream European-American students talk about U.S. history primarily in terms of the establishment and growth of the nation and of its civic and political traditions, African-American students focus much more specifically on people and events related to African-American freedom and equality (Epstein, 2001). They also place relatively more trust in family members and relatively less in textbooks as sources of accurate historical information.

Rose (2000) took advantage of this by organizing her fourth-graders' study of Michigan history around the questions, "Why have people moved to Michigan and what was it like for them?" This provided many opportunities for students to gather information from their relatives and in the process, encounter evidence that conflicted with their own prior views or with what they were reading in their textbooks. For example, most of the students viewed racial discrimination as a southern problem that African-Americans could escape by moving to northern states (as many of their grandparents did in 1945–1965, coming to Michigan to take jobs in the auto industry). Consequently, they were surprised to find that their own or their African-American classmates' relatives frequently told of being unable to get served at certain restaurants and hotels, having trouble buying homes, or attending largely segregated schools in northern states. These stories produced a lot of curiosity, cognitive dissonance, and other motivation for students to conduct additional inquiry focused on understanding why these problems existed even in the North and what people and factors led to their gradual reduction.

Engaging students in learning about their own family histories is probably the most natural and motivating way to introduce them to both the content of history and the processes of historiography. Many methods of incorporating family history have been suggested, mostly involving having students interview family members about an assigned topic; develop (with their assistance) a report along with supporting documents, photos, or artifacts; and then bring these materials to school for sharing, discussion, and possible display. For example, Schwartz (2000) described assigning students to develop reports of noteworthy events in their families' histories, such as stories about when and how their parents met or the events of the day that the children were born. As another example, Hickey (1999) described a "different sides of the story" unit that uses family history to develop critical thinking skills. Students interview their family members to elicit their individual perspectives on a commonly experienced event (e.g., a tornado, election, or landmark event within the family). Then they compare the different perspectives and try to learn the "true facts." This leads to discussion of what ends up in press accounts, history books, and so on—the process of how history is made.

Using Children's Literature to Teach History

Most history learning is embedded within the context of storylines developed by the teacher, usually with the assistance of a textbook. However, it often is more useful to enrich these storylines using historical source material or historically based fiction written or adapted for children (biography or autobiography, fictionalized versions of historical events, diaries, newspaper articles, etc.). These sources usually are interesting to students and provide opportunities to expose them to multiple interpretations and to the views and experiences of women, children, minorities, and others whose voices are often excluded from textbook treatments of history (Causey & Armento, 2001). Well-chosen literature selections can serve at least three significant purposes that advance students' historical understanding: providing a sense of context by relating how some people thought about their worlds at the time, helping students learn to take the perspective of others, and exposing them to alternative interpretations of events. Although proponents of infusing literature into history teaching frequently advance these and other claims, it should be noted that the research base on the topic is quite limited and that many potential literature choices are distorted, chauvinistic, or otherwise unsuitable except as negative examples. However, appropriately selected literature used in support of relevant history-teaching goals can lead to positive affective and cognitive outcomes (VanSledright & Frankes, 1998).

History-based fiction can be helpful in "making history come alive" for elementary students. For example, the book *Sarah Morton's Day* (Waters, 1989) depicts a day in the life of an English child born in Holland in 1618 who came to Plymouth in 1623. Through engaging narrative and photographs (taken at the reconstructed Plymouth Plantation in Massachusetts), the book chronicles what might have been a typical day in Sarah's life. Much of it recounts the many chores that Sarah had to do during most of the time between dawn and dusk, but it also mentions lessons (in the home), social chat and games with a playmate, and excitement at the sighting of an incoming ship. In the process, the book communicates a great deal about what life was like in this colony, especially for children. It is based on an actual child and family and depicts events that are authentic given what is known about the time and place, although the depicted conversations are fictional. Most fifth-graders are quite taken with the story and especially with its details about the life of children in the colony, such as the notion that Sarah had to work on chores almost all day long and had to stand up while eating meals even though her parents were seated.

Comparisons of children's trade books with social studies textbooks indicate that the trade books have a great deal to offer as substitute or supplementary sources of curricular content. Historical trade books' emphasis on human motives, solving problems, and the consequences of actions compares favorably with the emphasis on facts, names, and dates in the textbooks, and the trade books' emphasis on ordinary people, the human aspects of famous people, and the effects of world or national events on the lives of common people compare favorably with the textbooks' emphasis on world leaders, famous people, and big events (Tomlinson, Tunnell, & Richgels, 1993).

Texts feature almost exclusively expository writing, but historical fiction features narrative writing; trade books feature longer and more complex sentences that nevertheless are easier to understand because they offer deeper elaboration of a smaller subset of topics and more cohesion across sentences and paragraphs than the texts do; the trade books are unrestricted by readability formulas, so they offer richer vocabularies, more varied styles, and more descriptive and elaborated language; in contrast to the use of past-tense verbs that lend a sense of distance and unreality to the events portrayed and make the people seem lifeless, trade books present the people and events as living and use present-tense verbs and dialogue that lend a sense of immediacy and reality; and trade books emphasize human stories well told that make for greater interestingness, reader involvement, and memorability (Richgels, Tomlinson, & Tunnel, 1993). However, you will need to exercise care in selecting historically based trade books meant for children because many of them offer romanticized rather than realistic portrayals of historical figures and events, feature chauvinistic or otherwise biased interpretations, or reflect other problems in content selection or representation that undermine their value as historical-content sources (Tunnell, 1993).

Children need help in keeping fictional sources in perspective so that they do not confuse the real with the fictional (like the student who named Johnny Tremain as a leader of the American Revolution) or overgeneralize from the specific (like the students who developed the notion that life for all children in all of the colonies was like Sarah Morton's life among the Puritans at Plymouth Plantation). These examples illustrate how the potential motivational and insight benefits that might be derived from using fictional sources must be balanced against their potential for inducing distorted learnings. Some distortions are inevitable, and most will be cleared up without great difficulty. Still, you should minimize such problems by screening historical-fiction sources for authenticity and by helping your students to understand the differences between fictional and historical representations (Levstik, 1989; VanSledright, 2002).

Using Timelines

Timelines are useful devices for helping students learn and remember landmark events in history. We recommend that at least one timeline be kept on permanent display in your classroom. You may be able to purchase commercially produced timelines suitable for use with your students, but if you teach in the primary grades, you might do better to develop your own timelines, preferably in collaboration with your students. We have seen the value of these "interactive" timelines while observing Barbara Knighton teach her first- and second-graders.

Barbara introduces her students to timelines by creating for them a timeline of her own life. She brings to class a collection of artifacts (trophies and keepsakes from childhood, graduation and wedding photos, etc.), sequenced by age. Then she displays each of these artifacts (and adds some simple drawings made quickly on the spot) during a lesson that highlights her life to date. Subsequently, she affixes these illustrations to a timeline that extends for several feet and is posted on a wall. As a follow-up, she assigns her students to develop their own personal timelines, working in collaboration with family members. At this point, they clearly understand that a timeline depicts significant events in the order in which they occurred.

Subsequently, when teaching the historical strands of her social studies units on cultural universals, Barbara develops additional timelines depicting key advances in each of these aspects of the human condition. Her timeline for the transportation unit, for example, depicts people walking and carrying or dragging things in the Long, Long Ago (cave days) section; people riding horses, carrying things in horse-drawn wagons, or using canoes or sailboats in the Long Ago (pioneer days) section; and trains, cars, trucks, and airplanes in the Modern Times section. Barbara's homemade timelines are not drawn to scale and do not usually include specific dates, but they are well suited to the content taught at the grade level. Furthermore, they are used as teaching and learning resources, not just displayed as decorations. Each artifact or drawing is used to illustrate a big idea emphasized in teaching about historical developments, and the completed timeline stands as a resource to which Barbara can refer in her subsequent teaching and her students can refer as they work on assignments.

Teaching with Artifacts and Historical Source Material

Today's teachers have access to a wonderful range of artifacts and documents that can enrich their students' history learning. Materials packets, CD-ROMs, and software collections of primary sources are available for purchase. Many historical societies, archival collections, and museums have digitalized their collections and made them available through the Internet, often with plans for documents-based lessons (Causey & Armento, 2001). In addition, the November/December 2003 issue of *Social Education* (Volume 67, No. 7) was devoted entirely to teaching history with primary sources. Its articles contain guidance on finding and evaluating such sources and planning lessons around them. The sources range from old objects found in the home to gravestones in local cemeteries to reproductions of our national documents accessed via the Internet.

Teaching ideas and even full-fledged lesson plans can be found on Internet sites devoted to history or social studies teaching and in the journals *Social Education* and *Social Studies and the Young Learner*. For example, Barton (2001) offered guidelines for scaffolding elementary students' analyses of historical photographs. Using as examples several photos of food stores, restaurants, and gas stations taken in the 1940s, Barton explained the value of posing questions about the pictures (In what year might they have been taken? At what time of day? What are the people doing?), eliciting responses and supportive reasoning, and then discussing the diverse opinions expressed to see if agreement might be reached. If the students have difficulty at first, the teacher can model some pertinent opinions and supportive observations, then cue students' observations by asking questions such as "What do you think stores were like then?" or "Do you think advertising was important then?"

As another example, Wyman (1998) described activities built around excerpts from diaries written by children and adolescents whose families were migrating west along the Oregon Trail in the middle of the 19th century. The excerpts communicate the sights, sounds, and feelings experienced by these young people as they traveled westward. Wyman suggested three ways in which they can be incorporated into useful learning activities: (1) identifying and discussing unexpected content; (2) identifying and discussing the implications of recurring events such as accidents, lost children, and contact with Indians; and (3) having students imagine that their families were traveling westward along the Oregon Trail and create their own imaginary diaries.

Sometimes a historical resource is not well suited to whole-class lessons but is useful as a focal point for activities in learning centers. Haas (2000) described such a use for *A Street through Time* (Millard, 1998), a richly illustrated children's book that offers "a 12,000-year walk through history." The book shows how a single place (a riverside street in Europe) changed through the centuries in response to innovations in culture and technology. Each illustration depicts the everyday activities of people of a variety of ages and occupations. Close study of each individual illustration reveals a great deal of information about life during the century it portrays, and comparisons across illustrations develop appreciation for changes over time. Haas explained how individuals, pairs, or small groups of students can study and discuss these illustrations, guided by questions calling for them to note the clothing, activities, or artifacts being used by different people for different purposes, the similarities and differences between consecutive illustrations, and so on.

Along with the sources cited previously, you may wish to consult the following sources for more ideas about teaching history to elementary students. First, you may wish to subscribe to or inspect issues of *Cobblestone: A History Magazine for Young People*. Designed for 8- to 14-year-old students, *Cobblestone* publishes 50-page issues devoted to a particular theme (person, event, period, or place) in American history. Each theme is addressed through nonfiction articles, historical fiction, poetry, and biography, and includes video and book bibliographies. The same company also produces *Appleseeds*, a social studies–based magazine for Grades 2–4; and *Footsteps*, a magazine celebrating the heritage and contributions of African-Americans. In each of these publications, the textual material is accompanied by good illustrations as well as puzzles, games, songs, cartoons, and other material related to the theme. You may want to adapt some of this material for use with your students in learning centers.

For information about historical trade books and other text supplements for use in teaching history to elementary students, see Brandhorst (1988), California State Department of Education (1991), James and Zarrillo (1989), Lawson and Barnes (1991), and Symcox (1991). Other recommended resources include the Levstik and Barton (2005) book on inquiry approaches to history teaching of elementary students, the McCall and Ristow (2003) book on teaching state history with a multicultural emphasis, and the Winston (1997) book on using family stories to address both social studies and literature goals with young students. For information about using computers and associated technology for teaching history, see Parham (1994), Schlene (1990), and Seiter (1988). Finally, for information about the History Teaching Alliance that offers training and resources for history teaching, see Beninati (1991).

Conclusion

Organizations and scholars concerned with history teaching have developed useful guidelines that can help you to teach history in ways that promote progress toward social understanding and civic efficacy goals. Along with more detailed and subject-specific advice, these sources emphasize the value of the following:

1. Replacing parades of facts with coherent networks of knowledge structured around powerful ideas
2. Studying people within the context of their time and place so as to develop empathy and avoid presentism or chauvinism
3. Focusing on causal explanations that will help students to understand not only what happened but why, and what this might mean for personal, social, or civic decision making

Summary

Much of the content of social studies is drawn from its foundational disciplines of history, geography, and the social sciences (anthropology, economics, political science, psychology, and sociology). However, this content is blended within holistic treatments of unit topics and taught with more emphasis on citizen education goals than on goals specific to the individual disciplines. Keep this distinction in mind as you learn about the pandisciplinary curriculum standards put forth by the National Council for the Social Studies, as contrasted with the discipline-specific standards put forth by advocates for history, geography, and the social sciences.

History is an interpretive discipline focused on particulars rather than a social science focused on developing and testing broadly applicable theories. Historians develop chronologies and explanations of events by assembling all potentially relevant evidence, assessing its sources (primary or secondary) and credibility (well informed, unbiased), and then constructing an account that best fits the most credible evidence. Even so, historians often disagree, especially when drawing conclusions about causes and effects.

Children in the elementary grades are not yet ready for detailed chronologies or abstract analyses, but they can understand basic historical sequences (such as the changes in farming or transportation brought about through inventions) and narrative accounts of events that focus on the goal-oriented actions of key figures. Most children show a pervasive presentism in their thinking about the past, so it is important to help them develop historical empathy: considering the decisions and actions of people in the past with reference to the knowledge and technologies available to them at their time and place, rather than viewing them only from hindsight.

Children's responsiveness to narrative formats acts as a double-edged sword in history teaching. Narrative formats make it easier to engage children's interest in history and help them to learn many aspects of it with understanding, but they prefer clean and simple storylines with clear-cut heroes and villains. Historical events are usually much more complicated than simple stories, and different stakeholder groups often have very different views about whether a particular event was desirable and whether key participants should be viewed positively or negatively. It is important to bring out these multiple perspectives as part of the larger effort to develop students' global and multicultural awareness.

The chronic tensions between those who want a celebratory and highly patriotic version of history and those who want a more balanced or even critical perspective have heated up recently in conflicts over national standards for history teaching. Relatively ignored amid these politicized conflicts has been the repeated finding that, whatever its political tint, history teaching has been relatively ineffective through the years because it has been overstuffed with too many names, dates, and other specifics, and because it has focused too much on political and military events at the expense of good coverage of family life and social history.

History learning in the elementary grades should begin early with students developing personal timelines and family histories that include narrative and supporting documents and artifacts. Later they can study and conduct inquiry into historical aspects of the local community. By the time they study state history in fourth grade and U.S. history in fifth grade, they should have acquired dispositions toward historical empathy and basic understandings about historiography as evidence-based interpretation that is open to multiple perspectives and does not always lead to unambiguous conclusions.

Reflective Questions

1. How would you respond to individuals who believe that the teaching of big ideas associated with history should relate to the development of students' life roles, including careers, family, citizen, and leisure? Provide examples to support your response.
2. Often classroom teachers introduce students to timelines by using the ones in their textbooks. What is your opinion of this?
3. Many educators believe that an approach that interrelates history with the social sciences is more appropriate than one that isolates it. What is your view and why?
4. What do you view as the historical priorities appropriate for your grade level and how might you teach them more meaningfully?
5. What do you view as the benefits of incorporating more big ideas associated with history into your current social studies curriculum?
6. Some educators believe that history is a multicultural study. Do you agree? Why? Why not? If you agree, what does this look like in your classroom?

Your Turn:
History in the Intermediate Grades

If the focus of social studies at your grade level is history, we suggest that you obtain and review the national history guidelines, guidelines available at the state level, and your district or school's curriculum guide at your grade level. Then carefully examine the textbook if one has been adopted. If you have developed your own units, you will want to revisit these materials, too. As you inspect all of these sources and reflect on what you have read in this chapter, use the grid shown in Figure 5.1 to plot specific examples that correspond to the principles for teaching history in your classroom. Once you have identified weak spots, spend time revising your program to be reflective of the principles. We think this exercise will bring you one step closer to presenting a social studies course in history that is meaningful and usable. Select one of the following options:

After planning a unit using the guiding principles for history teaching outlined in this chapter, share your plans with a "history buff." Elicit that person's reactions regarding the "love" of the subject you hope to impart—as well as the "meaningfulness" that you hope will result.

FIGURE 5.1

Specific Examples to Illustrate

	Unit 1	Unit 2	Unit 3	Unit 4
Develop and present networks of knowledge structured around powerful ideas				
Focus on the study of particular individuals and groups of people rather than on impersonal abstractions				
Expose students to varied data sources and provide them with opportunities to conduct historical inquiry, to synthesize and communicate their findings, to learn from biography, fiction, and texts, etc.				
Bring history to life for students				
Foster empathy with the people being studied				
Focus on causal explanations that help students understand what happened, why, and what it might mean for personal, social, or civic decision making				

OR

After teaching a unit using the guiding principles established in this chapter, interview students to determine their reactions regarding meaningfulness and enjoyment.

SAMPLE INTERVIEW QUESTIONS

Select questions that match your unit's goals and major historical understandings.

1. What were the big ideas you learned about the history of our (state/region/nation)?
2. Would you have liked to have been one of the early settlers to come to our area? Why or why not? What do you think life was like for them?
3. What groups of people do you think were the most influential in the development of our (state/region/nation)? Why?
4. If you could meet one historical figure who contributed to the development of our (state/region/nation), who would it be? Why? Describe how you would choose to spend a day with this person.
5. Have a range of data sources available that you used during the unit. Ask students to select those that were most inspiring, enjoyable, meaningful, and so on, and explain why.

6. If you could live during the early development of our region or today, which would you choose and why?
7. How do you think learning about the past can help you today? In the future? (These questions could be discussed in focus groups and tape-recorded for later analysis and reflection.)

Your Turn:
A Resource Unit for Fifth-Grade U.S. History:
The American Revolution (Appendix A)

The nature of the content and the students' lack of much background knowledge limit opportunities for experiential or independent inquiry, but the American Revolution provides a fruitful forum for structured discourse. Also, writing can be a natural outgrowth of the discussions, as well as a contributor to subsequent dialogues. Keeping this in mind, we recommend that you expand this resource unit into a teaching unit using discourse and writing as the key modalities. The writing pieces can serve as major entries for the student portfolio, a very appropriate authentic assessment measure given the nature of the goals, content, and strategies for developing meaningfulness. The net result should be powerful social studies teaching and learning.

Figure 5.2 is a "worksheet" to help guide your planning of structured discourse.

Select questions that focus on your goals and address the key understandings. Early in the discussion you will want to assess prior knowledge and determine apparent misconceptions. However, do not allow students to "wallow in ignorance" for too long. Textbook accounts, supplemental materials such as children's literature and information available on CD-ROMs, as well as audio and video commentary are among the content sources that can be used as vehicles for launching fruitful discussions with focus, boundaries, and interaction.

PORTFOLIO SUGGESTIONS FOR THE AMERICAN REVOLUTION UNIT

The potential portfolio contents for social studies are limitless, but those selected for emphasis should typify the powerful teaching and learning experiences that the students have had during the unit. Portfolio contents should be indicative of their continuous development. The portfolio should serve as a powerful stimulus for students to use as they articulate major understandings about the American Revolution and evaluate their own work.

We have included some sample writing entries that reflect Goal #1 identified on our "worksheet."

FIGURE 5.2

The American Revolution

Goal 1	Major Understanding	Content Source	Engaging Students in Reflective Discourse
To enhance children's understanding and appreciation of the circumstances that transpired between 1620 and 1776, setting the stage for the Declaration of Independence	During the 150 years between the founding of the first English colonies and the Declaration of Independence, ties with England gradually weakened.	Textbook account and/or story with pictures presented by the teacher, focusing on the conditions, issues, chain of events, and so on	Review the end-of-chapter material in Chapter 8. Incorporate each of the types of questions into this plan for structured discourse.

Possible Questions

What did you know about the time period from 1620 to 1776 prior to reading about it or hearing the "story" presented by the teacher?

What did you know about the English?

Do you remember hearing anything about England? Its people? Leadership? If so, explain.

What did the American Revolution make you think of when you heard of it for the first time?

If you were a colonist, how do you think you would feel about what was happening?

Who was right? Wrong? Why do you think so? Do you think there were circumstances beyond either group's control?

Do you think any single event or issue really broke things wide open between the two groups? Explain.

If you had lived during this time period, who would you like to have known? Would you have tried to influence that person's reactions regarding the conflict? If so, how? If not, why not?

How do you think the Declaration of Independence addressed the problem between the two groups? Was it necessary? Why or why not? How else might the differences between England and the colonists have been handled?

Goal 1	*Suggested Possible Portfolio Entries*
To enhance students' understanding and appreciation of the circumstances that transpired between 1620 and 1776, setting the stage for the Declaration of Independence	Pre-unit—What does the American Revolution mean to you?
	Post-unit—Repeat entry, drawing on what has been learned. What does the American Revolution mean to you?
	Imagine that you lived in England throughout the 150-year time period (between 1620 and 1776). Explain what life was like.
	OR
	Imagine that you lived in America during that same time period. Explain what life was like.
	OR
	Adopt the role of the King of England during this time period. Explain the situation from your perspective.
	OR
	Imagine you are a colonist. Write a letter to a relative in England explaining what your life in America was like in the mid-1700s.
	OR
	Imagine you are a journalist. Explain the trade-offs that occurred because the colonists were considered British subjects.
	(Encourage students to share their entries with their peers. If they wish to illustrate their writing, suggest they do it at home or when they have completed all of their assignments.)

Student-led conferences using the portfolios as springboards could serve as nice culmination activities for the learning. If structured properly, such conferences will provide powerful learning opportunities for students, especially with regard to key understandings about the American Revolution that they probably would not develop by studying disconnected facts to prepare for a conventional test.

CHAPTER 6

HOW CAN I TEACH GEOGRAPHY AND ANTHROPOLOGY CONTENT MORE MEANINGFULLY?

Mandy Ford, Teacher Intern, Sixth Grade

Social studies and especially geography and anthropology are content areas that I am passionate about as a learner and a teacher. This chapter gave me numerous ideas on how I can expand my instruction beyond rote memorization of disconnected facts to meaningful lessons focusing on the big picture or main ideas. I am currently planning a unit on Mexico, and this chapter encouraged me to look for patterns and focus on the big ideas. For example, Mexico is located in the lower latitudes, close to the equator; therefore, I would expect Mexico to have a relatively warm climate year round. Of course, other factors such as altitude come into play. I will encourage my students to make similar generalizations for the other themes of geography and the interfaces with culture. If my students are able to do this, they will be more likely to retain the information.

My students have told me that they think social studies is boring, which proves to me that the content is not being related to their lives. In this chapter, the authors discuss the importance of using the five themes of geography and culture to help students make connections to their world, resulting in increased enthusiasm and curiosity. Therefore, as I plan my social studies unit, this will be my challenge.

To help my students understand other regions as they relate to their lives, we will compare and contrast the characteristics of Mexico and other places we study. I will focus on how people in the world are alike because we have the same basic needs and also on how these needs often are satisfied differently due to geography, culture, personal preferences, availability of resources, and so on.

> Throughout my unit, I hope to change my students' perception of social studies. I want them to think of geography like geographers and anthropologists, asking the "how" and "why" questions. I will not stress rote memorization or disconnected facts and skills, but I will incorporate artifacts, pictures, slideshows, music, and art in my lessons to make the geography and anthropology of Mexico come alive.

Having addressed history teaching in Chapter 5, we shift attention in this chapter to teaching content drawn from geography and anthropology. We have grouped these two disciplines within Chapter 6 because they share an interest in culture, which is one of the most pervasive concepts in all of social studies. The remaining social sciences are addressed in Chapter 7.

Geography

Geography is the study of people, places, and environments from a spatial and ecological perspective. The *spatial aspect* refers to where different places in the world are located, both precisely (at a particular intersection of latitude and longitude, within a particular nation and region) and relative to one another (in terms of direction and distance), as well as the patterns of distribution of human activities occurring at different places (land use, settlement, industry, and other economic activities). The *ecological aspect* looks at characteristics of the physical environment, such as climate, landforms, and vegetation, which provide affordances and constraints for human habitation and in turn are affected by human activities (Geography Education Standards Project, 1994).

Geography is a broad field that is not easily classified. If viewed as a science, it can be seen as partly a *natural science* (the study and mapping of landforms, weather patterns, natural resources, etc.) and partly a *social science* (the study of the ways that people adapt to and change their physical environments). Viewed as a *field of study,* geography is not so much a subject as a point of view that draws on and integrates other subjects (Knight, 1993). Viewed as a *discipline,* it is whatever geographers do, which subsumes quite a range of activities and fields of knowledge (Demko, 1992; Marshall, 1991).

What geographers have in common is the *spatial point of view* that they bring to bear on the topics they study. However, as Knight (1993, p. 48) noted, "Geography is necessarily concerned with location, much as history is necessarily concerned with time, but geography is no more *about* location than history is about time." Libbee and Stoltman (1988) also compared historians and geographers. They noted that *historians* approach issues or events as developments in *time* and ask what happened, why it happened at that time, what preceded and perhaps caused it, what else was happening at the same time, and what the consequences were for the future. In contrast, *geographers* approach the issues or events as developments in *space* and focus on where the event happened, why it happened where it did, how things at that place and perhaps at other places helped to cause it, and what the consequences were for the place and for other places. Both historians and geographers seek to understand and explain why phenomena occur, not just to locate them on timelines or maps.

Geography in the Elementary Grades

Geography pervades the elementary social studies curriculum. Texts for each grade typically include a unit on map and globe studies, placed at the beginnings or ends of the books. These units focus on building basic knowledge and skills and are not integrated with the content of the other chapters. The characteristics of places influence local human activities relating to food, clothing, shelter, transportation, and most of the other cultural universals, so instruction on these topics in the primary grades should include significant geographic strands (e.g., looking at how and why different places in the world feature contrasting crops and food consumption patterns, types of homes constructed, and so on). Studies of communities, states, nations, and regions that occur in the middle grades are by nature studies of places, so units on these topics should include use of maps and globes as well as the study of ways in which the local geography provides affordances and constraints to human activities. Finally, historical studies should include geographical elements, routinely to note the locations at which significant events occurred and frequently to identify geographical factors that help explain why the events developed as they did (e.g., the major reason why slavery proliferated in the southern states was that cotton developed as a major crop in this region, and harvesting cotton was a labor-intensive industry that required a great many field hands; a major reason why the Americans won the Revolutionary War was that England had to ship soldiers across the Atlantic Ocean to fight on unfamiliar territory, whereas the Americans were locals operating on familiar territory with much more local support).

Developments in Geographic Knowledge

Research on children's geographic knowledge indicates that it accumulates gradually across the elementary years. Preschool and early elementary children tend to identify with their own country and to be aware of at least some other countries, although they usually do not possess much specific knowledge unless they have traveled abroad. Their beliefs combine accurate information with stereotypes and misconceptions. This is especially true of their ideas about Africa, which tend to emphasize images of jungles, wild animals, witch doctors, and people starving, living in huts, and living primitive lives generally (Palmer, 1994; Wiegand, 1993).

Primary children have difficulty understanding nested geographical relationships (e.g., local community within the state, within the region, within the nation, within the hemisphere). However, they can learn these relationships through exposure to map-based instruction, and there is some evidence that their understandings have improved in recent decades (Harwood & McShane, 1996).

Primary-grade children's knowledge about their own country is mostly vague and symbolic, and their knowledge about other countries is even vaguer and often riddled with stereotypes or misconceptions. American children typically develop positive attitudes toward their country, say that they are happy to live in it, and select positive adjectives as descriptive of it. These tendencies are less pronounced among minority group members and are not always observed among children from other countries (much depends on the country's history and the kinds of messages about it to which children are exposed).

These early positive attitudes toward the home country are not necessarily accompanied by negative attitudes toward other countries, but as children begin and progress through elementary school, however, many acquire at least temporary negative stereotypes of particular nations or world regions. As they learn more, they come to appreciate that there are both positives and negatives about any nation (Barrett, 2005).

Our own research (Brophy & Alleman, 2005) identified several generic characteristics of K–3 students' thinking that mediate their understandings of geographical information. First, the children tended to focus on individuals, families, and local settings. They rarely made reference to effects of events on the nation, let alone the world or the human condition at large. For example, when asked about how the invention of printing changed the world, most of them said that the people who made books no longer had to copy them by hand or that the people who read them found them easier to read, rather than saying that printing made it possible to make multiple copies of books much more quickly so that many more people would have access to them.

Second, although they were familiar with human actions relating to cultural universals that they could observe in their homes and neighborhoods, they usually knew little or nothing about how and why these practices vary across locations and cultures. Few children have much knowledge about the affordances and constraints that local geography provides even to people living in their region until they develop basic knowledge of the range of local geographies in the world and the trade-offs they embody.

Third, their thinking reflected a child's rather than an adult's purview. In talking about the location of their ideal home, for example, they seldom mentioned convenience to good schools or to the parents' job sites (instead, they emphasized convenience to parks and restaurants). When asked about why most settlements were located initially around rivers or bodies of water and later around rail lines, they talked about people wanting to go swimming or take a ride but not about transportation connecting the settlement to other communities and facilitating exchange of resources and products. When asked why the Chinese eat more chicken and rice but Americans eat more beef and bread, most talked about cultural differences in preferences (the Chinese like rice, but Americans like bread), not about geography-based differences in patterns of crop planting and animal raising.

In general, the children showed limited awareness of environmental affordances and constraints that help explain contrasting cultural and economic practices, as well as little awareness of the land-to-hand progressions involved in processing natural products or creating manufactured ones. When asked how developments in communication and transportation had "shrunk the world," most failed to grasp the metaphor and were unable to respond. Although their answers to geographic questions (when they were able to generate answers) reflected limited geographic exposure and a child's purview, most were valid as far as they went. However, some children did communicate clear misconceptions, such as the idea that rivers flow inland from the oceans or that highways are literally high (elevated above the surrounding land).

Some geographical misunderstandings are easily corrected because they are rooted in word ambiguities (the term *country* can refer either to a nation or to a rural area) or in overgeneralizations of associations or stereotypes (assuming that polar bears live in Antarctica, that penguins live at the North Pole, or that everyone who lives in or near a jungle pursues a hunter–gatherer lifestyle) (Scoffham, 1998, 2000). Other confusions may take longer to overcome because they require more complicated explanations (downflow of fresh water from higher elevations creates rivers that eventually reach sea level and flow into the salt water oceans) or because they involve abstractions that are difficult for children to remember (cities are located within states, which are located within the nation) or coordinate (map symbols, scale, directional coordinates).

Problems with Geography Texts and Teaching

Opportunities for developing geographical understandings are not exploited effectively in most elementary classrooms. Research on elementary geography textbooks and teaching typically reveals an emphasis on miscellaneous and often trivial facts rather than on understanding and using powerful geographical knowledge. Textbooks typically stress the physical aspects of geography over its human aspects and feature parades of facts presented without sufficient attention to connections, explanations, or critical thinking (Beck, McKeown, & Gromoll, 1989; Brophy, 1992; Haas, 1991). Similarly, studies involving interviewing teachers and observing in classrooms indicate that teachers' planning, instruction, and assignments relating to geography focus on map work and factual details (capital cities, major exports) without much emphasis on understanding why places are where they are and have the characteristics that they do (Farrell & Cirrincione, 1989; Muessig, 1987; Stoltman, 1991; Thornton & Wenger, 1990; Winston, 1986).

A major reason for this is that teachers usually possess only limited knowledge of geographical information and of geography as a discipline, which is not surprising given their limited and somewhat distorted exposure to the subject as students. Along with confusion about the nature of geography and about what aspects of it to teach, other problems include instruction in incorrect or out-of-date facts or concepts (such as an oversimplified environmental determinism as an explanation for human behavior in a particular place), a need to balance an emphasis on regions with a global perspective stressing our interdependent world, and tendencies toward ethnocentrism or stereotyping in treatments of other cultures.

Geography was strongly represented in early 20th-century curricula, but it gradually faded because much of it seemed pointless (memorizing of capitals, imports and exports, etc.) and because social educators developed interest in content drawn from the social sciences. However, it has been making a comeback lately in response to poor performance by American students on national assessments, concerns about developing a shared cultural literacy, and increasing recognition that Americans need to become better informed about the rest of the world in order to understand global economic and political issues (Gregg & Leinhardt, 1994;

Haas, 2001). Geographical content is well worth emphasizing for these and other reasons (e.g., developing empathy, minimizing chauvinism, helping students to understand and appreciate the reasons for variation in economies and cultures). However, this potential will not be realized unless geography instruction shifts from confronting students with endless parades of facts to teaching them to think about the world the way geographers do.

The Five Fundamental Themes

Professional associations have cooperated to help teachers understand geography as a discipline and to suggest powerful ideas to emphasize in teaching it. The first major step was publication of the *Guidelines for Geographic Education: Elementary and Secondary Schools* (Joint Committee on Geographic Education, 1984). These guidelines provide a clear content and skills framework for K–12 geography that is structured around the five fundamental themes outlined in this section (Petersen, Natoli, & Boehm, 1994). They include a scope and sequence for Grades K–6 that outlines concepts and learning outcomes for each grade level.

The sponsoring organizations later created the Geographic Education National Implementation Project (GENIP) to advance the spirit of the guidelines by developing teaching materials, reviewing teacher certification standards, sponsoring workshops for teachers, and advising groups who prepare diagnostic and competency tests in geography. GENIP's work has included publication of a key document for elementary teachers: *K–6 Geography: Themes, Key Ideas, and Learning Outcomes* (GENIP, 1987) and a book on how teachers can connect their theme-based geography teaching to the social understanding and civic efficacy goals of social studies (Stoltman, 1990).

The efforts of GENIP have been assisted by the National Geographic Society, which established its Geography Education Program to develop statewide alliances for geographic education in each state. These alliances are partnerships between teachers and university geographers. They circulate materials and sponsor summer workshops and other geographic education programs for teachers. You can contact your state's geographic alliance for information and resources to help you with your geography teaching. The National Geographic Society also has produced a map of the United States that demonstrates the five fundamental themes (GENIP/NGS, 1986) and circulated a teacher's handbook based on the themes (Ludwig et al., 1991).

Finally, Boehm and Petersen (1994) developed an elaboration of the five fundamental themes based on experience in using them with teachers. They noted that the themes provide a convenient and adaptable format for organizing geographical content and avoiding the practice of teaching geography through rote memorization. The five themes are as follows.

Location: Position on the earth's surface. Absolute and relative location are two ways of describing the positions of people and places. Location is the most basic of the fundamental themes. Every geographic feature has a unique location or global address, both in absolute terms and in reference to other locations.

Absolute location: We can identify locations as precise points on the earth's surface using reference grid systems, such as the system of latitude and longitude.

Maps of smaller segments of the earth (such as cities or states) often use alpha-numeric grids. Different types of maps show locations of population centers, climate zones, political entities, or topographic features. Projections are needed to transfer information from a spherical earth to a two-dimensional map. This process often leads to distortions in distance (size), direction, or shape. The grids used in location systems allow us to measure distances and find directions between places.

Relative location: Relative location is a way of expressing a location in relation to another site (Peoria is 125 miles southwest of Chicago, Australia is in the southern hemisphere, etc.). Both absolute and relative locations have geographical explanations (e.g., why places are located where they are or why they have certain economic or social characteristics). Over time, certain aspects of relative location may change even though absolute location does not (e.g., as transportation routes in North America shifted from inland waterways to railroads to highways, cities at various locations saw shifts in their relative importance in the transportation system and in the nature of their links to other cities).

Place: Physical and human characteristics. Location tells us where, and place tells us what is there (in particular, what makes the place special). All places have distinctive characteristics that give them meaning and character and distinguish them from other places.

Physical characteristics: These include the place's landforms (mountains, plains, natural harbors, etc.) and the processes that shape them, its climate (reasons for it and implications for human and animal life), its soils, its vegetation and animal life, and the nature and distribution of its fresh water sources. These physical characteristics are studied with emphasis on how they affect one another and support or challenge human occupation of the place.

Human characteristics: These include the racial and ethnic characteristics of the people who live in the place; their settlement patterns and population factors; and their religions, languages, economic activities, and other cultural characteristics. Also included are the perceived characteristics of places, which may vary across individuals or time periods (Central America might be viewed as a place of political turmoil, an attractive vacation site, or an interesting blend of Hispanic and Indian cultures).

Human-environmental relations (relationships within places). All environments offer geographical advantages and disadvantages as habitats for humans. For example, high population densities tend to accumulate on flood plains, and low densities in deserts. Yet, some flood plains are periodically subjected to severe damage, and some desert areas, such as those around Tel Aviv or Phoenix, have been modified to support large population concentrations. People continually modify or adapt to natural settings in ways that reveal their cultural values, economic and political circumstances, and technological abilities. Centuries ago, the Pueblo tribes developed agricultural villages that still endure in the desert southwest. Later, Hispanic and Anglo settlers established mines and mineral industries, cattle ranches, and farms in these deserts, relying on manipulation of water resources. Today, contemporary Americans look to the desert Southwest for resort and retirement developments, military training and research, and high technology industries.

Geography focuses on understanding how such human–environment relationships develop and what their consequences are for people and the environment. Subthemes include the role of technology in modifying environments (with attention to pollution and other costs as well as to benefits), environmental hazards (earthquakes, floods, etc., as well as human-induced disasters), the availability of land and natural resources and the limits this places on human possibilities, the purposes pursued and methods used by people to adapt to environments, and the ethical values and cultural attitudes that affect their behavior.

Movement: Humans interacting on the earth (relationships between places). Places and regions are connected by movement. Over time, humans have increased their levels of interaction through communication, travel, and foreign exchange. Technology has shrunk space and distance. People travel out of curiosity, and they migrate because of economic or social need, environmental change, or other reasons. Movement can also be traced in physical forces—traveling weather patterns, ocean and wind currents, flowing water, or plate tectonics.

Several subthemes surround the reasons for movement and the forms that it takes: transportation modes, everyday travel, historical developments, economic reasons for movements, and mass movements of physical systems. Other subthemes surround global interdependence: the movement of goods, services, and ideas across national and regional borders; and the development of trade and common markets. Still other subthemes surround models of human interaction: the reasons why people move (e.g., from rural areas to cities) and issues relating to the size and spacing of urban areas and the relationships between cities and their surrounding regions.

Regions: How they form and change. The basic unit of geographic study is the region, an area that displays unity in terms of selected criteria (types of agriculture, climate, land forms, vegetation, political boundaries, soils, religions, languages, cultures, or economic characteristics). Regions may be larger than a continent or smaller than your neighborhood. They may have well-defined boundaries, such as a state or city, or indistinct boundaries, such as the Great Plains or the Kalahari Desert.

Subthemes include uniform regions, functional regions, and cultural diversity. Uniform regions are defined by a common cultural or physical characteristic (the wheat belt, Latin America, the Bible Belt). Functional regions are organized around a focal point (the San Francisco Bay area, a local school district). Understanding regions sharpens appreciation of the diversity that exists in human activities and cultures, and of the ways in which different groups of people interact with one another within regional contexts.

A resource unit on Mountain Regions is included as an appendix (see Appendix B). It serves as an example to illustrate the possibilities of combining the physical and social aspects of geography built around the big ideas from the field. This unit could serve as a springboard for your planning, giving balanced attention to the five themes.

The National Geography Standards

Along with the five fundamental themes, the guidelines for geographic education identified five basic geographical skills: (1) asking geographic questions (Where is it? Why is it there? What is important about its location and how does it relate to other locations?), (2) acquiring geographic information (from maps, data bases, etc.), (3) organizing geographic information (using maps, models, and graphs to display the information in addition to summarizing it in text), (4) analyzing geographic information (interpreting and drawing conclusions from geographic texts and displays), and (5) answering geographic questions (acquiring relevant information and using it to draw conclusions or make generalizations). Subsequently, the sponsoring organizations elaborated the five fundamental themes and the five basic skills to create a more comprehensive set of national geography standards (see Figure 6.1). There are eighteen such standards, clustered within six essential elements of geographic education.

NCSS Standards Relating to Geography

The National Council for the Social Studies' (1994) curriculum standards include a strand on People, Places, and Environments. In the early grades, it calls for experiences that allow students to construct and use mental maps of locales, regions, and the world that demonstrate understanding of relative location, direction, size, and shape; interpret, use, and distinguish various representations of the earth, such as maps, globes, and photographs; use appropriate resources, data sources, and geographic tools, such as atlases, data bases, grid systems, charts, graphs, and maps, to generate, manipulate, and interpret information; estimate distance and calculate scale; locate and distinguish among varying landforms and geographic features, such as mountains, plateaus, islands, and oceans; describe and speculate about physical system changes, such as seasons, climate and weather, and the water cycle; describe how people create places that reflect ideas, personality, culture, and wants and needs as they design homes, playgrounds, classrooms, and the like; examine the interaction of human beings and their physical environment, the use of land, building of cities, and ecosystem changes in selected locales and regions; explore ways that the earth's physical features have changed over time in the local region and beyond and how these changes may be connected to one another; observe and speculate about social and economic effects of environmental changes and crises resulting from phenomena such as floods, storms, and drought; and consider existing uses and propose and evaluate alternative uses of resources and land in home, school, community, the region, and beyond.

For the middle grades, additional activities related to this theme will allow students to elaborate mental maps; create various representations of the earth; use appropriate resources, data sources, and geographic tools, such as aerial photographs, satellite images, geographic information systems (GIS), map projections, and cartography, to generate, manipulate, and interpret information such as atlases, data bases, grid systems, charts, graphs, and maps; estimate distance,

---

FIGURE 6.1

National Geography Standards

The geographically informed person knows and understands:

The World in Spatial Terms

1. How to use maps and other geographic representations, tools, and technologies to acquire, process, and report information from a spatial perspective.

2. How to use mental maps to organize information of people, places, and environments on Earth's surface.

3. How to analyze the spatial organization of people, places, and environments on Earth's surface.

Places and Regions

4. The physical and human characteristics of place.

5. That people create regions to interpret Earth's complexity.

6. How culture and experience influence people's perceptions of places and regions.

Physical Systems

7. The physical processes that shape the patterns of Earth's surface.

8. The characteristics and spatial distribution of ecosystems on Earth's surface.

Human Systems

9. The characteristics, distribution, and migration of human populations on Earth's surface.

10. The characteristics, distribution, and complexity of Earth's cultural mosaics.

11. The patterns and networks of economic interdependence on Earth's surface.

12. The processes, patterns, and functions of human settlement.

13. How the forces of cooperation and conflict among people influence the division and control of Earth's surface.

Environment and Society

14. How human actions modify the physical environment.

15. How physical systems affect human systems.

16. The changes that occur in the meaning, use, distribution, and importance of resources.

The Uses of Geography

17. How to apply geography to interpret the past.

18. How to apply geography to interpret the present and plan for the future.

Data from The Geography Education Standards Project (1994). *Geography for life: National geography standards 1994.* Washington, DC: National Geographic Research & Exploration, pp. 34–35.

calculate scale, and distinguish other geographic relationships, such as population density and spatial distribution patterns; locate and describe varying landforms and geographic features, such as mountains, plateaus, islands, rain forests, deserts, and oceans, and explain their relationship within the ecosystem; identify geographic patterns associated with physical system changes, such as seasons, climate and weather, and the water cycle; describe how people create places that reflect cultural values and ideals as they build neighborhoods, parks, shopping centers, and the like; examine, interpret, and analyze physical and cultural patterns and their interactions, such as land use, settlement patterns, cultural transmission of customs and ideas, and ecosystem changes; describe ways that historical events have been influenced by, and have influenced, physical and human geographic factors in local, regional, national, and global settings; and propose, compare, and evaluate alternative uses of land and resources in communities, regions, nations, and the world.

A recommended activity that can be done even with kindergarten children is to represent a highway linking two towns (using a strip of paper extending along the classroom floor or just drawing it on the board) and engage students in questions about people's experiences as they drive (eliciting such responses as getting hungry or needing gas). This leads to discussion of businesses that might develop along the highway, and individuals or groups within the class might be appointed to take the roles of a restaurant owner, a gas station owner, and so on. Subsequent discussion would focus on where these businesses should be located, their specific nature (e.g., fast food or more upscale restaurants), where these business owners would like to live (near their businesses on the highway or in the towns), where schools or banks are likely to locate, and so on. This activity could be limited to discussion within a single lesson or extended to include construction projects, role-play, related writing assignments, and other elaborations that would continue for a week or more. The main point would be to develop students' understandings about the relationships between people's needs and wants and the locations of homes, businesses, and other features of the built environment that enable people to provide for their needs and wants. Other activities include having students develop bird's-eye views (i.e., maps) of their bedrooms or homes, the school, or the neighborhood and locating on the globe the place from which the ancestors (or in some cases, the immediate families) of the students emigrated to America.

Using the Five Themes in Your Teaching

The National Council for Geographic Education makes available at reasonable prices both basic geographical standards and guidelines statements and related publications on standards-based curriculum, instruction, and assessment. Up-to-date information about these publications can be found at the Council's website (www.ncge.org). Although we find the NCSS strand on People, Places, and Environments and the National Geography Standards' list of basic skills and list of eighteen national standards helpful, we believe that the five fundamental themes will provide the best guidance to teachers as they plan lessons and activities. These themes are very powerful ideas that anchor the geographic perspective on the human condition. They should be brought to bear, not only on explicitly geographic activities but also on activities relating to most of the social studies curriculum.

Consistent emphasis on these five themes helps to ensure that you teach all aspects of geography (not just details of location and place), and in ways that lead students through levels of abstraction from the simple to the complex. Note, however, that the themes are not meant to be used as unit topics and taught one after another. Instead, they are meant to be organizers of the content taught about unit topics, such as states, nations, or regions. Good teaching of most geographic topics requires consideration of several, if not all five, of the themes, with attention to their relationships.

In this regard, elementary social studies texts leave much to be desired. Texts for the primary grades tend to emphasize basic geographical concepts and skills, such as the globe, the earth's rotation, daily and seasonal cycles, the cardinal directions, understanding of maps as two-dimensional representations of bird's-eye views of sections of the earth, and experiences with different kinds of maps. Some of them are quite good at introducing and scaffolding students' learning of basic map and globe skills. However, these aspects of the program tend to be separate from the content dealing with cultural universals.

In the intermediate grades, units on places and cultures tend to include maps and descriptions of physical geography so that they do at least communicate basic information about where places are located and how they support and constrain human habitation. However, the texts usually do not draw on the five themes as much as they should to develop understanding of why places have the characteristics that they do and why humans have adapted to them in the ways that they have. It will be important for you as the teacher to help your students to focus on the most important facts about a place, to see the connections among them, and to begin to ask and acquire answers to the "why" questions that geographers ask about places.

Successful teaching of geographic concepts and principles begins with good planning and preparation. First, stock your classroom with a range of maps and at least one globe, for reference in locating places and movements between places that are featured in the curriculum (not only in social studies but also frequently in science, reading, or writing activities). Maps and globes vary in level of detail, beginning with simple, often schematic, versions that show and label only the continents and oceans and progressing to the most detailed versions that include information on national boundaries, major cities, rivers, mountains, latitude and longitude lines, and so on. Simple, uncluttered versions are ideal for the introductory map and globe lessons taught in the primary grades.

More generally, there usually is an optimal level of complexity to any maps and globes that will be used for particular purposes at particular grade levels. For example, to locate England in a lesson on colonial America or to locate Afghanistan in a current events lesson, a somewhat simplified map or globe that uses color coding to differentiate bordering nations would be preferable to a map or globe in which the color coding reflects elevations above sea level and national boundaries are hard to follow because they are indistinct lines crisscrossed by many other lines representing rivers, and so on.

Simplified maps have been constructed to emphasize many geographical features besides political boundaries, such as distribution patterns for annual rainfall, production of various crops or manufactured items, or languages and religions. These resources are preferable to more familiar political maps for teaching about many geographical topics. The major map companies produce very good sets of maps for use in social studies teaching. Also, the Internet is an increasingly rich source for such specialized resources.

Another aspect of preparation for good geography teaching is thoughtful previewing of the curriculum as a whole (not just social studies) to identify lessons that feature particular places and thus offer opportunities for infusing geographical understandings. This might include locating these places on a map or globe and emphasizing some of their salient geographic features, especially those most relevant to the topic of the lesson. For example, to build background knowledge for appreciating a story about an Inuit family living in a remote area of Alaska, you might present or elicit key information about the far northern location, the very cold climate, the need to depend on hunting and fishing for food, and so on. Also, familiarize yourself with the map and globe concepts and learning activities suggested for use at your grade level. Rather than wall these off from the rest of the curriculum by teaching them in isolated skills exercises, you might find places where at least some of them could be attached to lessons that would provide authentic opportunities for using the skills being developed.

Frequent reference to maps and globes in the context of the five fundamental themes of geography will help children construct a network of basic generalizations to anchor their understandings of the social world. They should understand, for example, that the climate becomes cooler and eventually colder as one moves away from the equator toward the poles or upward from sea level toward mountain tops; that shipping and fishing are important industries in coastal and island communities; that farming is a major activity in parts of the world that feature rich soil and mild climates; that extraction industries are emphasized in areas that are rich in coal, copper, oil, or other underground resources; that populations tend to be dense in greenbelts but sparse in deserts or polar areas; and so on. They also should develop a sense of ways that humans have overcome or compensated for geographical constraints by altering land forms (building canals, tunneling through mountains, constructing dams) or developing specialized technology (irrigation in dry areas) or knowledge-based industries (Swiss watch-making, Japanese electronics).

Early map work with children should include opportunities for them to construct maps, not just answer questions about or color in portions of supplied maps. Developing a schematic map of a small surface such as a table or desktop (on which a few items have been strategically placed) will help them to understand that maps offer a bird's-eye perspective from above and that symbols or geometric shapes are used to represent salient features. Subsequent construction of maps of their rooms at home, of the classroom or school, of the playground, and so on will help them to acquire other basic understandings, such as that maps are representations constructed with particular purposes in mind; that they are constructed to scale, so that the relative sizes of the included features and the distances between them correspond to those in the real world; and that map makers help readers to interpret the maps by including a compass rose (typically but not always indicating that the map is oriented with North at the top) and a legend that explains the meanings of symbols.

To build understandings and skills in using maps to orient oneself and note relevant directions and distances, you can use maps of the school or neighborhood. For variety, use maps of places that are popular with children, such as zoos, shopping malls, or amusement parks. Frequent reference to maps and globes in the process of teaching about places and events that come up in the curriculum will help students learn that maps provide representations of a broad range of geographic information and therefore are useful for addressing a broad range of geographic questions, not just for planning trips. Children can be helped to appreciate this by viewing and engaging in activities built around the maps used in television weather reports; plotting the origins and movements of their own families on maps; or by studying and discussing the implications of maps showing such things as where the population is increasing or decreasing, where certain key products are developed and exported or must be imported, and so on (Haas, 2001).

Also, as a way to build interest in geography and develop basic geographical knowledge and skills, teachers who use centers in their classrooms should include one or more geography centers. These centers might include book-, map-, and photo-based activities on world nations or regions, tourist destinations, and sites of recent natural disasters or other current events, as well as software-based activities such as the popular *Carmen Sandiego* series or simulated travel programs that allow students to plan trips (including the forms of transportation and routes taken) and learn about the places they will encounter along the way. For additional ideas about activities built around geographic themes, consult the most relevant journals (*Journal of Geography, Social Education, Social Studies and the Young Learner*) and websites, notably www.nationalgeographic.org.

Anthropology

Anthropology is the study of cultures. It usually is associated with studies of past or present societies (e.g., the Inca, the Masai), but it can be applied to studies of any group engaged in what amounts to a shared culture (e.g., rock groupies, college football fans, elementary teachers). Anthropologists seek to depict cultures as they are viewed by insiders, by learning about their perceptual categories and language genres and using these to describe their kinship relations or other societal structures, the nature of and reasons for any subgroups that exist within the larger group, the goals and meanings of the groups' activities and the social mores and skills involved in carrying them out, and so on. Their data collection and analysis procedures are designed to ensure (as much as possible) that anthropologists observe enough different situations and interview a sufficient range of informants to enable them to construct a reasonably complete and balanced depiction of the culture portrayed as insiders would portray it themselves, free of filtering through the anthropologists' own assumptions and beliefs.

When it addresses ancient cultures, anthropology overlaps with archaeology, and some anthropologists view archaeology as a subdiscipline. When it addresses contemporary societies, anthropology overlaps with cultural geography. The main difference is that anthropologists tend to look first to belief systems as explanations for a culture's social and economic activities, whereas geographers tend to look first to climate, landforms, and other aspects of the physical environment.

The social studies curriculum usually does not include formal courses in anthropology, and anthropological organizations have not established standards for K–12 education. Nevertheless, social studies includes a lot of anthropological content, especially in the middle grades when students study life in different geographic regions and in ancient cultures. Lessons usually focus on material culture (arts and crafts, household items, architectural styles, clothing, transportation, economic activities and the technologies involved in carrying them out), but they sometimes include coverage of religious or political beliefs and customs. Historical material is usually couched within a "development of western civilization" theme. Contemporary material is usually either selected to illustrate geographical affordances to and constraints on human activity or couched within a "human family" theme that emphasizes commonalities and cultural universals over differences and exotic practices.

Developments in children's knowledge and thinking about other countries and cultures were summarized in a previous section of this chapter. Most American children acquire early and retain a preference for their own country and culture but show mixed and evolving attitudes about other countries and cultures. They sometimes pick up negative attitudes from family members or the media, but what they learn in school and through personal travel experiences usually supports positive attitudes (Barrett, 2005). Unless they have visited a country or studied it systematically at school, children's impressions of another country tend to be limited to famous landmarks (e.g., the Eiffel Tower) and whatever they have gleaned about its culture (e.g., they may associate fish eating, chopsticks, pagodas, samurais, martial arts, and tofu with Japan).

Given children's implicit orientations toward chauvinism and toward noticing differences (especially the exotic or bizarre) more than similarities, it is important for teachers to represent other cultures in ways that reflect the goals of anthropologists and social studies educators. In particular, it is important to help students see each culture through the eyes of its own people rather than through outsiders' stereotypes, to emphasize cultural universals and similarities in purposes and motives more than differences, and to show that what at first may seem exotic or bizarre upon closer inspection usually can be seen as sensible adaptation to the time and place or as parallel to certain features of our own culture.

NCSS Standards Relating to Anthropology

The National Council for the Social Studies' (1994) curriculum standards call for experiences that provide for the study of culture and cultural diversity. In the early grades, this means experiences that allow students to explore and describe similarities and differences in the ways groups, societies, and cultures address similar human needs and concerns; give examples of how experiences may be interpreted differently by people from diverse cultural perspectives and frames of reference; describe ways in which language, stories, folktales, music, and artistic creations serve as expressions of culture and influence behavior of people living in a particular culture; compare ways in which people from different cultures think about and deal with their physical environment and social conditions; and give examples and describe the importance of cultural unity and diversity within and across groups. Culture-related activities in the middle grades should call for students to compare similarities and differences in the ways groups, societies, and cultures meet human needs and concerns; explain how information and experiences may be interpreted by people from diverse cultural perspectives and frames of reference; explain and give examples of how language, literature, the arts, architecture, other artifacts, traditions, beliefs, values, and behaviors contribute to the development and transmission of culture; explain why individuals and groups respond differently to their physical and social environments and/or changes to them on the basis of shared assumptions, values, and beliefs; and articulate the implications of cultural diversity, as well as cohesion, within and across groups.

Guidelines for Teaching Anthropology

The geography teaching guidelines that deal with human adaptation and cultural development also apply to the teaching of anthropological content. More specifically, when studying past or present societies and cultures, it is helpful to organize content around cultural universals and related dimensions that facilitate comparison and contrast. For example, Hanna, Sabaroff, Davies, and Farrar (1966) presented detailed suggestions about ways to organize such studies around nine basic human activities:

1. Protecting and conserving life and resources
2. Producing, exchanging, and consuming goods and services
3. Transporting goods and people
4. Communicating facts, ideas, and feelings
5. Providing education
6. Providing recreation
7. Organizing and governing
8. Expressing aesthetic and spiritual impulses
9. Creating new tools, technology, and institutions

Similarly, Fraenkel (1980) suggested that systematic study and comparison of past or present societies can be organized around the following questions:

1. Who were the people being studied?
2. When did they live?
3. Where did they live?
4. What did they leave behind that tell us something about them?
5. What kinds of work did they do and where did they do it?
6. What did they produce or create?
7. What did they do for recreation?
8. What family patterns did they develop?
9. How did they educate their young?
10. How did they govern and control their society?
11. What customs and beliefs did they hold?
12. What events, individuals, or ideas are they especially known for, and how did these affect their lives?
13. What problems did they have?
14. How did they try to deal with these problems?

Certain key ideas appear repeatedly in sources of advice on how to teach elementary students about societies and cultures. One is the importance of focusing on *cultural universals* because these are fundamental categories of the human condition that children can understand based on their own prior experiences. A second is the value of *comparison and contrast* across well-chosen examples that illustrate and promote understanding of the variation to be found on key dimensions. A third is the importance of *explaining cultural adaptations within the context of their time and place* to help students empathize with the people involved and begin to see things from their point of view (as opposed to focusing on the exotic in ways that make the people seem stupid or crazy).

For example, we recommend studying Native Americans within historical and geographical context, focusing on a few well-selected tribes in sufficient depth to allow students to develop some appreciation of the similarities and differences in their cultures. We might include an Eastern Woodlands tribe, a Plains tribe, a Southwestern Pueblo tribe, a Pacific Northwest tribe, and (if not already included) a tribe that lived (or better yet, still does live) in your local area. Key ideas to develop might include the following:

1. Native Americans are believed to have crossed from Asia on a land bridge now beneath the Bering Strait, then gradually spread through North and South America.

2. Different tribes developed quite a diversity of cultures, although many of them shared common elements centered around knowledge about living off the land and beliefs featuring respect for natural elements and resources. Seasons of the year and local plants and animals often figured prominently in cultural customs and beliefs.

3. Depending in part on local geography, climate, and resources, different tribes used different forms of shelter (longhouses, tepees, pueblo apartments), clothing (animal skins, woven cloth), food (meat from hunting and trapping, vegetables from farming, seafood from fishing), and transportation (dugouts, canoes, travois pulled by dogs and later by horses). Some tribes were nomadic, moving with the seasons to follow the animals that they hunted, but most tribes lived continuously in the same place and emphasized farming supplemented with hunting and fishing.

4. In contrast to what happened in most of Africa and Asia, discovery of the New World by Europeans led not just to colonization or establishment of trade relations, but also to heavy immigration and ultimate repopulation. The land was attractive to Europeans because of its many natural resources and familiar climate and geography. Also, the Native Americans were vulnerable to encroachment because their tribes were mostly small and spread thinly. From a European point of view, vast amounts of desirable land were there for the taking, unowned by anyone in particular. At first, some Native Americans welcomed these newcomers and enjoyed friendly social and economic interactions with them. Resentments began to accumulate as immigrants kept coming and pushing the frontiers of settlement forward, but there was little that the local tribes could do against armies equipped with firearms. Some became assimilated into European settlements or lived on small, locally negotiated reservations, but the major tribes were continually pushed back beyond the frontiers. Eventually, decimated by war, disease, and starvation, they were forcibly relocated to reservations established by the U.S. government.

5. Today, many Native Americans still live on these reservations and retain their tribal customs, but many others have moved into ordinary communities and become assimilated into mainstream American culture. (Elaborate

with examples, especially of the activities and accomplishments of Native Americans residing locally; conduct inquiry into some of the social and policy issues relating to local tribes).

This treatment of Native Americans would draw on the five fundamental themes of geography, a well as on the principles for developing historical content presented in the previous chapter. It also would develop knowledge of where Native Americans came from, what happened to them over the last 500 years, and where and how they live today. In the process, it would attack stereotypes (e.g., that all Indians lived in tipis and hunted with bows and arrows) and help students to see the diversity and appreciate the contributions of various tribes and individuals.

In addition to or instead of using these guidelines to study a single culture in considerable detail, you might want to compare selected cultures on a more limited set of dimensions. The NCSS (1994) standards document suggests two ways for doing this. In the first, students would compare and contrast family needs and wants for people who live in sharply contrasting climates or physical environments. Activities related to this idea would help students develop appreciation of the influences of natural environments on cultural developments.

The second approach would involve developing and charting information about how people meet their needs for food, clothing, and shelter in the home community and in cities located in nations from which your students' families or ancestors migrated (e.g., Juarez, Hanoi, Lagos, Frankfurt). This might be the core of a unit that also would include map and globe activities, videos or other audio-visual input, Internet activities, or classroom visits by parents or others who could show and tell about the other nations' cultural artifacts and practices.

Older students might conduct inquiry into questions such as "Why did the people who lived in what is now southern Arizona (or some other purposefully selected location) at different points in history develop the economic and cultural activities they developed?" Scaffolded research and discussion relating to this question could help students begin to appreciate that technological, economic, and cultural developments within the region and even the world at large can lead to new uses for and even physical reshaping of particular locations. In this case, the same local environment has been used primarily for subsistence farming by the Pueblo tribes; for mining and ranching by European-Americans in the more recent past; and for retirement communities, tourism activities, and military and technological purposes today.

Anthropologists often speak of using examples of cultural diversity to "make the familiar strange" and "make the strange familiar." This involves helping students to appreciate that not only are many things done very differently elsewhere than they are here but in some cases, our way is unusual (e.g., our nonmetric weights and measures and our relatively large cars and houses). People in some countries use chopsticks instead of forks, wear white instead of black at funerals, or bow rather than shake hands. Most such differences are merely means for accomplishing the same ends (bringing small pieces of solid food to the mouth, expressing grief and sympathy at a funeral, performing a greeting ritual as a prelude to social interaction). Many are not arbitrary but explainable with reference to resources and economic or cultural practices.

Whenever you teach about culture, it is important to convey an "insider's perspective" by helping students to view cultural practices as their practitioners do, as well as to convey a large and balanced picture of the culture rather than overemphasize the exotic. As Merryfield (2004) put it, "If Japanese students made quilts, ate Southern fried chicken and Boston baked beans, and sang 'Old MacDonald Had a Farm,' would they have acquired information that leads to understanding of Americans today?" (p. 270).

Anthropologists typically emphasize the importance of authentic representations of other cultures and toward that end recommend liberal use of photos, videos, and cultural artifacts (or at least, authentic facsimiles). We recommend that you develop artifact kits to support your instruction about particular cultures. Many such kits can be purchased from supply houses catering to teachers. You also can collect useful materials on your own (e.g., during visits to Native American reservations or foreign countries). Besides using the collected materials during instruction, you can feature them within centers where your students can go to learn more about the culture. Good children's literature (both fiction and nonfiction) also is available for use as a resource in teaching about cultures. Field (2003), for example, identifies more than twenty such sources for use in a unit on Mexico and provides guidelines for selecting additional sources and using them in learning activities.

Summary

Geography is the study of people, places, and environments from a spatial and ecological perspective. Much of the knowledge that geographers have accumulated can be organized within the five themes of absolute and relative location (position on the earth's surface), the physical and human characteristics of places, human–environmental relationships within places, movement between places, and the formation and development of regions. Good geographic instruction builds understandings developed around these themes, rather than confronting students with parades of geographical facts (place names, import/export data, etc.).

Children enter school not only without much geographic knowledge but without much geographic awareness. They have not yet come to appreciate how landforms, climate, and natural resources affect human population patterns and economic activities. They also harbor implicit leanings toward chauvinism, tending to prefer the familiar to the strange and to prefer their own country (or other people or entities with whom they identify) over others. Consequently, it is important to teach geography in ways that develop not only cognitive understandings but also dispositions toward empathy and multicultural respect.

The textbook series offer generally good lessons and activities relating to map and globe skills but in isolation from the rest of the curriculum. We recommend integrating them and in particular, routinely pointing out places on the map or globe as they arise in teaching (in any subject, not just social studies), and informing or reminding students about any features of these locations that might be relevant to the big ideas of the day's lesson. Use geographic illustrations that are well suited both to your students (level of complexity) and to your instructional goals (illustrating clearly those aspects of the place that you want to emphasize).

Because geographers attend not only to the physical characteristics but also the human characteristics of places, they are interested in cultures. Anthropologists, however, focus more specifically on cultures. They seek to depict cultures as they are viewed by insiders, which is an important part of developing empathy and avoiding chauvinism. Anthropologists also emphasize "making the strange familiar" and "making the familiar strange," which facilitates crosscultural comparisons and helps us to transcend our own ethnocentrism by learning to understand our familiar cultural practices within larger global and historical contexts. Emphasizing commonalities or variations on common themes (such as human actions relating to cultural universals) when teaching about cultures also fosters empathy and other desired multicultural dispositions, whereas overemphasizing the bizarre or exotic can foster chauvinism.

Reflective Questions

1. How would you respond to individuals who believe that the teaching of big ideas associated with geography and anthropology should relate to the development of students' life roles, including careers, family, citizen, and leisure? Provide examples to support your response.
2. Often classroom teachers begin the school year with a map and globe unit. What is your opinion of this and why?
3. What do you view as the geographic and anthropological priorities appropriate for your grade level?
4. What do you view as the benefits of incorporating more big ideas associated with geography and anthropology into your current social studies curriculum?
5. Many social studies educators are convinced that American students need to become better informed about the rest of the world in order to understand global, economic, and political issues. If you agree, how might you address this matter in your classroom?

Your Turn:
Geography

If the focus of social studies teaching at your grade level is geography, we suggest that you secure a copy of the Guidelines for Geographic Education. Then contact your state's geographic alliance for information and resources to help you. Review the school's curriculum guide at your grade level and carefully examine the textbook, if one has been adopted. If you have developed your own units, you will want to revisit those materials as well.

As you inspect all of these sources, use the following grid to plot the key ideas that correspond to the Five Fundamental Themes (see Figure 6.2). Once you have identified the weak spots, spend time developing the key ideas for each. This activity will bring you one step closer to geographic teaching in depth instead of breadth.

FIGURE 6.2

Key Ideas That Connect to the Five Fundamental Themes of Geography

UNIT

Five Fundamental Themes   *Related to the Five Themes*

Location: Position on the Earth's surface

   • Absolute location

   • Relative location

Place

   • Physical characteristics

   • Human characteristics

Human–environmental relations

Movement: Humans interacting on the Earth (relationships between places)

Regions: How they form and change

After teaching a unit using the five themes, interview your students using questions that focus on the themes. Study their responses to determine the degree to which they have acquired the big ideas.

SAMPLE INTERVIEW SCHEDULE QUESTIONS

Select questions that match your goals and major geographic understandings for the unit.

1. Using a range of map types such as physical, political, and climatic, describe the Southwest of the United States.
2. Using a road map, plan a trip to Santa Fe, Phoenix, etc.
3. Using a range of map types, explain what is special about Salt Lake, Tucson, White Sands, Reno, etc.
4. What specifically have you learned about the people who live in the Southwest? What are some of the groups we have studied about and what is special

about each? Explain the settlement patterns of various groups. What are some of their traditions, customs, beliefs, and values? What types of economic activities would you expect to find in the Southwest? Why?

5. Would you expect high or low population densities in the Southwest? Why? Describe how specific parts of the Southwest have been modified to support large concentrations of population.

6. Explain why certain parts of the Southwest are attractive for retirement developments.

7. How has technology influenced life in the Southwest?

8. Why are certain parts of the Southwest growing so rapidly?

9. How would you characterize the Southwest as a region? Compare it to the region in which you live. How are they the same? Different? Which would you prefer to live in as an adult? Why?

Your Turn:
A Resource Unit on Mountain Regions

There are numerous ways to examine and enhance the mountain region resource unit. We suggest that you develop your plans with an eye toward the integrative aspects because the content naturally lends itself to more than one subject for the development of "meaningfulness." Remember, content, skills, and activities included in the name of integration should be educationally significant, desirable, and authentic. Such content, skills, and activities should be selected because they foster rather than disrupt or nullify the accomplishment of major social studies goals.

We have provided a framework and an example for you to use as you expand your unit (see Figure 6.3).

After you have completed the framework, review it carefully using the guiding questions for successful integration.

- Does the integrated activity clearly match the social education goal?
- Would an "outsider" clearly recognize the activity as social studies?
- Does the activity allow students to meaningfully develop or authentically apply important social studies content?
- Does it involve authentic application of skills or knowledge from other disciplines?
- Will students understand its social education purpose?

Your Turn:
Enriching Your Units with Social Science Content

Revisit your social studies curriculum for the year, paying particular attention to those social science disciplines that are underdeveloped. Select one that would naturally fit and add a new layer of meaning to the content. Read the section in the chapter, paying particular attention to the NCSS suggestions.

FIGURE 6.3

Mountain Regions: Sample Page from Unit Overview Chart

Goal 1	Key Ideas	Specific Activities to Match the Goal	Other Subjects Included	Materials Needed
Help students to understand the nature of mountains, the physical environments that they create, and the advantages and limitations that these environments pose for human activities	Mountains are not just hills but are very high elevations of land. They were formed by movements of the earth's surface plates or by volcanic activity erupting from below the surface. Often, people make a living in these regions through occupations that require specialized skills more than abundant raw materials. Mountain features and their cloistered effects often stimulate creativity.	Have students locate the nearest mountain range, first on a physical map, then on a topographical one. Using the scientific method, have the students speculate about how the range was formed. Examine together the line of inquiry. Have students gather data to establish evidence. Then have them gather information about the human activities found in this range. Beware of "make-and–take," cutesy-type volcano experiments that are not authentic and detract from the social studies understanding.	Science	Topographical maps, pictures of mountains, reference books, video of mountain region—acquire from the tour bureau or travel agency and adapt them to the unit goal. Have students observe the characteristics of mountains. As they observe, have them imagine the advantages and limitations these environments pose for human activities.
		Have students investigate the type of specialized skills that people in the mountain region nearest them possess. If possible, have an artist, writer, or musician whose work has been inspired by the mountains visit the class.	Art, music, literature	Books, paintings, music scores of individuals inspired by the nearby mountain region.

Example

- Unit Topic: Urban Communities
- Added Social Science Discipline: Anthropology

- Added Big Ideas:
  - Communities benefit from the influence of people who have come from different countries and who have different experiences.
  - Communities celebrate holidays. Holidays can be celebrated in many different ways.
  - The cultures represented in a community determine in some ways the use of its resources.
  - In some communities, people speak the language of the country they came from.
  - Cultural borrowing occurs when people share their beliefs, traditions, and customs with others.

To help you plan at the next level of specificity, we encourage you to revisit the section of the chapter that focuses on the select discipline. List key features that naturally fit with your unit topics.

Features	*My Plan of Action*
Constructing understandings about why people do what they do (goals and motives of a lot of people)	When teaching about the Native Americans, for example, I will explain that they made decisions about what sort of shelters to build based on the climate, available resources, their need for mobility, etc.
Connecting new content to students' prior knowledge, misconceptions, etc.	When beginning a new unit, I will do some form of assessment (e.g., TWL, pose "I wonders," interview students in groups)
	I will also spend time acknowledging students' exposure to fanciful stories and fictional worlds—and explain the differences between factual and fictional.
Providing for the study of culture and diversity	
Representing other cultures in ways that reflect goals of the anthropologists and social studies educators	
Organizing content associated with past and present societies around cultural universals (human activities)	
Addressing issues of diversity, including race, ethnicity, gender, and social and economic differences	
Addressing production, distribution, and consumption of goods and services	
Providing opportunities for students to engage in decision making	

CHAPTER 7

HOW CAN I TEACH THE OTHER SOCIAL SCIENCE CONTENT MORE MEANINGFULLY?

Laura DeGrendel, Third-Year Teacher

This chapter provides teachers with substantive content knowledge and useful teaching strategies. As teachers, we often sift through textbooks only to find superficial information that is inadequate for our classroom situations. While the social sciences can seem daunting to a new or preservice teacher, the authors offer a solid base for explaining issues associated with psychology, sociology, economics, civics, and government. This chapter provides many suggestions for putting the information to practical use. Personally, I will be able to take several of these ideas and carry them out in my own classroom. For example, when I design my unit on money, I will revisit the economics section and use the main ideas as the heart of my planning, making sure that I select appropriate instructional activities. I also will check out the possibilities that Mini Society has to offer. When designing my unit on our state government, the section focusing on political science will serve as a valuable source for decisions about what subject matter to include.

Finally, the authors' statement about teacher attitudes and beliefs really struck a chord with me. In fact, it has caused me to step back and ask, "How am I projecting myself and my beliefs to students? Am I authentic? Am I exposing children to real-life situations and allowing them to form their own opinions?" This chapter also opened my eyes to the crucial role social studies plays in developing contributing members of society.

The social studies curriculum in the primary grades typically consists of pandisciplinary units on human actions related to cultural universals, organized within the expanding communities sequence and emphasizing content drawn from history and geography. Beginning in the middle grades and continuing throughout high school, it shifts to courses in history and the social sciences. Usually, courses in civics/political science, economics, and sociology are included, and sometimes courses in anthropology/archaeology and psychology.

Especially at the upper-secondary level, the social science courses tend to be survey courses in their respective disciplines, more akin to college courses than to the pandisciplinary social studies courses taught in elementary school. They organize and represent content within the disciplines' major subdivisions and concepts, and typically focus on introducing students to the types of questions that each social science asks, the research tools and discourse genres employed to study these questions, and the major sets of findings developed to date. Depending on the district's guidelines and the philosophies of local schools and teachers, these secondary courses may or may not be planned to emphasize social studies goals of citizenship preparation in addition to narrower disciplinary goals.

Such survey courses in the social sciences are too abstract and too dependent on advanced levels of prior knowledge and information-processing skills to be feasible for the elementary grades. However, Grades K–6 usually include considerable content drawn from the social sciences (e.g., material on rules, laws, and government from civics/political science; and on needs, wants, and opportunity costs from economics). This content is introduced where it emerges naturally within the pandisciplinary social studies curriculum, and it is developed relatively informally. That is, even where it appears within its own units, instruction in this content is confined to developing a cluster of concepts and principles without attempting to provide a general introduction to political science or economics.

Consequently, there is no need for elementary teachers to be prepared to teach social science courses like those taught in high school. However, you should acquire sufficient familiarity with all of the social sciences to enable you to represent them faithfully when teaching aspects of their content. If you have not had basic courses in some of these disciplines, we recommend that you study introductory textbooks in each of them, continuing until you have a clear idea about how practitioners of the discipline think about and carry out their work. This will help ensure that the social science content you teach is both accurate and true to the spirit of the discipline that produced it.

In the rest of this chapter, we will consider psychology, sociology, economics, and civics/government content typically taught in the elementary grades. We will address the nature of this content, students' likely prior knowledge and misconceptions relating to it, and standards and other guidelines for teaching. Finally, we will argue the value of subsuming this and other social studies content within a global and multicultural perspective, and suggest strategies for doing so.

Psychology

Psychology is not formally taught in the K–12 curriculum except for a single (usually elective) course in high school. However, this social science is relevant to elementary social studies in at least four respects.

First, studies of developments in children's social knowledge and thinking indicate that children tend to think as psychologists before they begin learning to think as anthropologists, sociologists, economists, or political scientists (Brophy & Alleman, 2005; Carey, 1985). Until they start school, and sometimes for a year or two thereafter, their purviews are mostly restricted to their personal experiences within their families and neighborhoods. They get a lot of exposure to fanciful stories and fictional worlds (e.g., Harry Potter's) but not to factual information about life in the past or in other cultures. Furthermore, even what they know about their own society is focused on the goal-oriented activities of everyday living, which they make sense of by inferring people's intentions and motives.

When asked to explain macro-level social phenomena, children tend to respond with narratives that personalize the events around the goals and motives of a few people, without reference to macro-level cultural, social, economic, or political trends or principles. They are likely to say that the New World was discovered because Columbus wanted to find gold; African-Americans attained full civil rights because Martin Luther King, Jr. gave a speech; the government consists of the president and a lot of helpers; banks give families money to use to buy houses because the nice people who work there want to be helpful; certain native tribes built tipis because they had a lot of unused animal skins that they did not want to waste or because they could cook in them and the smoke from the fire would escape through the open top; Americans eat more bread, but the Chinese eat more rice because we like bread better and have butter knives but they like rice better and have chopsticks; and so on.

Second, because of its focus on human actions related to meeting culturally universal needs and wants, elementary social studies is essentially an introduction to the human condition, with attention to its development over time and variation across cultures. Furthermore, much of it is rendered in narrative formats that structure the content around people's goals and motives. Thus, its content matches up well with children's tendency to think in micro-level psychological terms rather than macro-level social science terms when constructing understandings of why people do what they do. This matching offers initial advantages to teachers because it makes it easier for them to connect new content to students' prior knowledge and develop it in ways that sustain interest and understanding. It also presents challenges, however, because instructional goals usually include not only adding new elements to students' existing knowledge structures but also constructing new ones and restructuring old ones. At least initially, students may be confused by, and may even resist, teachers' attempts to expand their purviews. For example, children's familiarity with narrative structures often leads to preferences for unambiguous storylines culminating in clear conclusions and moral implications, so they may be frustrated with aspects of history that are open to multiple interpretations and unlikely to be resolved through consensus on a single "real story" (Barton & Levstik, 2004).

Third, much of the content traditionally taught in kindergarten and first grade involves learning about the self and developing personal identity (both basic topics in psychology).

Fourth, we and many other social studies educators emphasize the importance of teaching content not only for understanding but also for appreciation and life application. This implies helping students see connections between the content and their personal identities and agendas, as well as developing the content using examples and activities that support students' self-efficacy perceptions with respect to their ability to apply what they are learning in their personal, social, and civic decision making and behavior. Thus, if you have not already done so, you should acquire familiarity with basic principles of child development, motivation, and other relevant aspects of psychology.

NCSS Standards Relating to Psychology

The National Council for the Social Studies' (1994) curriculum standards include a thematic strand on Individual Development and Identity. In the early grades, it calls for experiences that allow students to describe personal changes over time, such as those related to physical development and personal interests; describe personal connections to place—especially place as associated with immediate surroundings; describe the unique features of one's nuclear and extended families; show how learning and physical development affect behavior; identify and describe ways family, groups, and community influence the individual's daily life and personal choices; explore factors that contribute to one's personal identity, such as interests, capabilities, and perceptions; analyze a particular event to identify reasons individuals might respond to it in different ways; and work independently and cooperatively to accomplish goals. The middle grades should include experiences that allow students to relate personal changes to social, cultural, and historical contexts; describe personal connections to place—as associated with community, nation, and world; describe the ways family, gender, ethnicity, nationality, and institutional affiliations contribute to personal identity; relate such factors as physical endowment and capabilities, learning, motivation, personality, perception, and behavior to individual development; identify and describe ways regional, ethnic, and national cultures influence individuals' daily lives; identify and describe the influence of perception, attitudes, values, and beliefs on personal identity; identify and interpret examples of stereotyping, conformity, and altruism; and work independently and cooperatively to accomplish goals.

Guidelines for Teaching Psychology

Much teaching of psychology in the early grades focuses on developing concepts and attitudes relating to self and personal identity. Children's ideas about themselves tend to focus on their physical characteristics (e.g., size, hair color) and behavior (e.g., skills, hobbies, interests), not their personal, social, or moral traits. To the extent that they draw comparisons, it is with siblings or frequent playmates. They do not yet have much knowledge about the range of individual differences that exists among age peers in their own community, let alone the world at large.

The majority of most children's opportunities to think about themselves within larger contexts (our society, the world, the human condition through time and across locations) occur at school.

Supporting students' personal development is part of the informal curriculum that is embedded in the socializing that teachers do in the process of explaining rules and behavioral expectations and molding their classes into learning communities. These interactions with students provide many opportunities not just to teach rules but also to develop positive social self-concepts—to encourage students to think of themselves as prosocial individuals who are caring and helpful toward others and good citizens of the classroom community and society generally. In some school districts, the curriculum features a guidance strand that includes units on moral education and character development.

Within the academic curriculum, most teaching about self and personal identity occurs in social studies classes, especially in the early primary grades. Lessons and activities focusing on physical characteristics are common (e.g., measuring heights and weights; outlining body parts or even entire bodies; or filling out questionnaires on physical characteristics such as eye color, then constructing and discussing a table or graph). "Student of the Week" displays and "Show and Tell" activities provide additional opportunities for students to collect information about themselves and discuss it with classmates. Commonly taught lessons focus on topics such as growth and change with development, birthdays and rites of passage, ways in which individual children are special or even unique, children's talents and interests and their potential implications for occupational choices, and ways that children can make a difference in the lives of other people (for examples, see Alleman & Brophy, 2003b).

The particular activities that teachers use to help students develop their concepts of self and personal identity are not as important as the attitudes and beliefs that teachers project in the process. The goal here is to help children articulate tacit knowledge and acquire new information about themselves and others within an overall positive context of acceptance (or where relevant, celebration). Two teaching strategies are especially important. First, be matter-of-fact, descriptive, and explanatory (but not emotional or judgmental) when talking about individual characteristics over which children have little or no control (size, appearance, physical coordination, socioeconomic status, etc.). Where relevant, talk about trade-offs (e.g., smaller size is an advantage for certain sports and physical activities). In any case, avoid talking about individuals' characteristics in ways that are likely to make them feel handicapped or cause them to become objects of pity from classmates. The idea is to socialize students to expect and value diversity as the norm, and thus to respond with matter-of-fact acceptance to unusual personal characteristics and behavior (except for antisocial behavior).

Second, when teaching or talking to individuals about knowledge or skills, portray these as developed through commitment to learning activities, not as limited by genetic endowment or other factors beyond the students' control. Students who consistently receive these two kinds of messages from their teachers are likely to feel good about both themselves and their classmates and to think in terms of reaching short-term goals as steps toward longer-term goals, rather than worrying about embarrassing themselves or feeling the need to put down others.

Children's literature is an especially rich source for teaching about individual development and identity. As Krey (1998) notes, good children's literature provides students with an insider's perspective that includes the emotions of human events, as well as with opportunities to identify with characters or emotions that connect to their own personal experiences. Krey's book includes annotated recommendations of children's books useful for teaching about all ten of the curriculum strands in the NCSS standards. For the standard dealing with individual development and identity, these selections include a book that celebrates human diversity in the context of making observations about physical differences; a portrayal of an eight-year-old, northern, urban African-American girl's visit to the rural North Carolina farm on which she was born; a book in which a girl tells the story of how she was adopted; and a book in which a wheelchair-mobile boy with muscular dystrophy talks about how his life changed after he acquired a service dog trained to respond to his commands.

Sociology

Sociology is the study of social life, social change, and the social causes and consequences of human behavior. Sociologists investigate the structure of social groups, organizations, and society as a whole, and how people interact within those contexts. In particular, they look at contrasting social statuses and the roles and expectations associated with them (e.g., gender, social class, race, and ethnicity; minority-group membership; childhood, adolescence, and adulthood; power and positions of leadership; business ownership, management, and labor; social, political, and religious organizations; crime, poverty, and other social problems; the media and mass communications). These areas of interest overlap considerably with those of anthropologists. However, anthropologists tend to study small groups or societies and focus on belief systems, whereas sociologists tend to study large and complex modern societies and focus on social status and role expectations.

Sociology is not formally taught in the K–12 curriculum except for a single course in high school, but the curriculum contains a lot of sociological content. History instruction frequently makes reference to advances in gender or racial equity, social movements, labor relations, and other sociological topics. Studies of the family, the neighborhood, and the community in the primary grades typically include content dealing with social statuses and roles, occupations, and social organizations, and material on these and other sociological topics is included in what is taught about development of the state and nation in Grades 4 and 5.

Children's Knowledge and Thinking about Sociology

Children enter school not only well aware of sex differences but usually somewhat knowledgeable and often strongly opinionated about gender roles and expectations. They identify with their own sex and want to learn about and display behaviors associated with it and avoid behaviors associated with the opposite sex. Most of their gender-related thinking is focused on salient aspects of the culture of childhood: preferences for toys, games, books, hobbies, and so on that are associated with their own sex. However, they also have some knowledge of gender typing in adult roles and occupations, including awareness of associated status differences (Durkin, 2005).

Children also enter school with some awareness of social and economic differences, at least at the level of recognizing extremes of wealth and poverty. Primary-grade children usually cannot explain these differences or else offer explanations confined to differences in personal characteristics such as intelligence or ability (i.e., wealthier people have jobs that require more education, effort, or talent). By the middle grades, their explanations also begin to incorporate sociological factors such as political power, prejudice and exploitation, or limited opportunity structures and life chances. Even as they develop awareness of constraints on occupational choice, they remain optimistic about their own occupational chances.

Children's ideas about social inequalities are influenced by their social backgrounds. Compared to working-class children, middle-class children are more aware that the income differences between people from different socioeconomic classes are sizeable rather than minor, offer more complete explanations for these differences, and are likely to view them as fair or deserved (Emler & Dickinson, 2005).

Young children also begin school well aware of racial and ethnic differences in skin color and other physical characteristics, but this does not seem to affect their social behavior (e.g., playmate preferences, patterns of interaction with children of different races). As they continue to develop, the degree to which they attach importance to racial and ethnic differences and associate them with beliefs that lead to prejudice and discrimination varies with the socialization influences to which they are exposed (Hirschfeld, 2005; Lo Coco, Inguglia, & Pace, 2005). Sometimes, what children learn from their families or peers competes with teachers' efforts to celebrate diversity.

NCSS Standards Relating to Sociology

Sociological topics are emphasized in the thematic strand on Individuals, Groups, and Institutions in the National Council for the Social Studies' (1994) curriculum standards. In the early grades, it calls for experiences that allow students to identify roles as learned behavior patterns in group situations, such as student, family member, peer play group member, or club member; give examples of and explain group and institutional influences, such as religious beliefs, laws, and peer pressure, on people, events, and elements of culture; identify examples of institutions and describe the interactions of people with institutions; identify and describe examples of tensions between and among individuals, groups, or institutions, and how belonging to more than one group can cause internal conflicts; identify and describe examples of tension between an individual's beliefs and government policies and laws; give examples of the role of institutions in furthering both continuity and change; and show how groups and institutions work to meet individual needs and promote the common good, and identify examples of where they fail to do so. Activities related to this theme in the middle grades will allow students to demonstrate an understanding of concepts such as role, status, and social class in describing the interactions of individuals and social groups; analyze group and institutional influences on people, events, and elements of culture; describe the various forms institutions take and the interactions of people with institutions; identify and analyze examples of tensions between expressions of individuality and group or institutional efforts to promote social conformity; identify and describe examples of tensions between belief systems and government policies and laws; describe the role of institutions in furthering both continuity and change; and apply knowledge of how groups and institutions work to meet individual needs and promote the common good.

Teaching Sociological Content

The NCSS performance expectations relating to this curriculum strand strike us as overly ambitious, especially those dealing with institutions and other macro-level aspects of society. However, even young children have experience with some social organizations and structures (family, school, community, church, organizations dealing with youth sports and recreation activities). Discussions of their involvements with these groups and institutions can help them begin to appreciate concepts such as role and the tensions that exist between individuals, groups, and institutions (e.g., time demands and conflicting schedules can create role conflicts for children trying to simultaneously keep up with their school work, play on both soccer and hockey teams in youth sports leagues, take piano lessons and keep up with practice expectations, and complete the chores expected of them at home).

Children also can understand and profit from discussion of certain aspects of macro-level social phenomena that come up in history or current events (discrimination and equity issues as they relate to women and minorities; conflict over laws or political policies between groups representing different economic or value positions). Learning basic information about conflicts over issues such as minimum-wage laws or environmentally sensitive mining or forestry operations can help students to appreciate the fact that different people have conflicting vested interests in these issues and tend to join organizations that lobby in support of their interests. Classroom debates about such issues can be valuable learning experiences, especially if they are scaffolded to ensure that all students become well informed about both sides of the issue.

The NCSS (1994) standards publication identifies several recommended activities relating to individuals, groups, and institutions. In one, second-graders working in small groups brainstorm issues of concern within their community, identify organizations in the community that address that concern, and then develop ideas about how they can become personally involved with these efforts. In another, the teacher introduces her third-graders to the concept of role through studies of an ant farm and bee hive, then has them apply the concept through analyzing the roles (and related behavioral expectations) played out by themselves and others in situations they experience in and out of school.

To teach about tensions between individuals and social or governmental institutions, a fourth-grade teacher used biographical readings and research to acquaint students with civil rights and social acceptance groundbreakers such as Martin Luther King, Jr., Jackie Robinson, Amelia Earhart, and Cesar Chavez, calling attention to the obstacles they had to overcome and the approaches they used in doing so. Recommended activities for the middle grades included learning about and then creating political cartoons to represent group or institutional conflict and researching historically noteworthy groups involved in such conflict (e.g., the labor movement, the Ku Klux Klan).

We believe that instruction about social and political organizations and institutions should occur within a context of emphasis on values basic to preserving a healthy democratic society. One is that although it is understandable and appropriate for different groups to pursue the agendas of most importance to them, conflicts need to be bounded by concern for the common good and protection of everyone's rights. A related principle is that, where possible, leaders should develop negotiated solutions that are acceptable to as many stakeholders as possible, rather than thinking in terms of battles in which winners will impose their will on losers. Finally, it is worth helping students to recognize that although voluntary group membership usually brings many benefits to participants, it also can create conflicts when the leadership or the majority of group members favor a policy that conflicts with one's interests or values. In these cases, one must decide whether to "go along to get along" or to opt out of that activity or even from a group. Most children experience these conflicts periodically, outside if not inside school (as when their friendship group is contemplating doing something immoral, illegal, or dangerous).

Economics

If you have never taken a course in economics, you may think that the subject is simply about money—personal savings and bank accounts, budgeting, and making decisions about purchases. However, economists define their discipline much more broadly, as study of the production, distribution, and consumption of goods and services. It addresses decision making about obtaining and using all kinds of resources, not just money but others such as time, energy, or raw materials. Also, the scope extends from the micro level of personal economics to the macro level of national budgets, gross national products, and international markets and banking systems.

Elementary students are not ready for most aspects of macroeconomics, but they can and should learn microeconomics and most of the basic concepts and principles of the field. Many of these (needs and wants, scarcity, supply and demand, opportunity cost) lend themselves to experiential learning through activities calling for students to make decisions about how to spend their time or money. Economics lessons teach important skills involved in making good decisions. They also dispose students toward becoming well informed about relevant issues and considering the likely consequences of their choices before committing themselves to action.

In the elementary grades, instruction rarely focuses directly on economics except for a few lessons on personal economics and very basic economic concepts. However, economic themes and content pervade the curriculum even in the early years. Developments in the technologies used to exploit natural resources and produce goods and services are the focus of much of history instruction, and economic goals and motives are emphasized as reasons for many if not most major historical events (e.g., the development and expansion of trade, voyages of discovery, colonization, wars of acquisition). Similarly, studies of communities, states, nations, or geographical regions typically include a strand focused on natural resources, industries, occupations, and the goods and services produced by the people who live there.

Children's Knowledge and Thinking about Economics

Research on developments in children's economic understanding has shown that young children tend to believe in a benevolent world in which people get whatever money they need from banks simply by asking for it and shopkeepers sell items for the same price at which they were bought (Berti & Bombi, 1988; Byrnes, 1996; Furnham, 1996). Yet they also recognize that entrepreneurs do not have to be honest to be profitable (Siegler & Thompson, 1998). Even when economic understandings are valid, they often are limited: Children may know that money is printed by the government but not realize that the amounts of money in circulation are carefully regulated; they may know that banks are places to keep money safely but not know anything about other banking operations; or they may think that the value of an item depends only on the resources that go into producing it. In addition, certain misconceptions are common: The price of an item depends on its size; property is owned by those who use it; or the value of money depends on its color, picture, size, or serial number (Schug & Hartoonian, 1996).

Berti (2002) identified the following trajectories in children's knowledge about economics. Preschoolers typically show no understanding of economic institutions, and they do not understand the value of money or how it is used in buying and selling. If offered coins, they may prefer larger, more familiar, or more attractive coins to more valuable ones. They are aware that their parents make money by working, but they also think that money is available on request from banks and obtained as change from shopkeepers. In the early primary years (ages 6–8), they develop initial comprehension of the value and function of money and begin to represent banks as places where people deposit their money to protect it from thieves (rather than as sources of money).

Older children (ages 8–10) mention several sources of money that owners can use to pay their employees, such as earning it through their own job, getting it from banks, getting it from the government, or even getting it from the employees themselves (who must pay in order to be hired). Knowledge about shop profits and banking operations (deposits, loans, interest, and their relationships) usually is not acquired until at least ages 9 or 10, although it can be taught earlier (Berti & Monaci, 1998). Until then, children do not realize that employees are paid with money acquired from the sale of goods or services produced by their work and that retail prices must be higher than wholesale prices to enable shopkeepers to make a living. Most children do not know about bank interest, and even if they do, they usually do not understand how banks make a profit through the difference between deposit interest and loan interest.

Studies of children as consumers indicate that they are often brand conscious but seldom price conscious when asked to represent shopping or purchases (John, 1999; McNeal, 1992), even though probing may reveal that they know the approximate costs of the items (Pliner, Freedman, Abramovitch, & Darke, 1996). As they progress through the early grades, they gradually become more knowledgeable about the value of money and more sophisticated about managing it planfully. These developments emerge sooner among children who are high achievers in mathematics or who have had direct economic experiences (receiving an allowance, saving for a purchase, having their own bank account) (Abramovitch, Freedman, & Pliner, 1991; Sonuga-Barke & Webley, 1993).

Our own research (Brophy & Alleman, 2005) replicated many of these findings and generated some new ones. We found that K–3 students often were vague about the difference between renting or buying housing or described the difference in terms of planning to live in the home for a short vs. a long time rather than in terms of acquiring ownership of the home. Despite some intuitive understanding of the limitations of bartering systems, they could not explain that money systems were invented because purchasing with money is easier and more convenient than trading. They were vague about where money comes from (i.e., that it is made by the government). Many described banks simply as places where people put extra money for safekeeping (each person's money is kept in a separate box) or as places to go to get money (simply by asking for it). Some mentioned using banks to pay bills or cash checks, but none said anything about checking accounts, loans, or other financial services. Most knew that checks are used to get or transmit money, but only a minority knew that the money specified on checks that people write is debited from their bank accounts. Similarly, most children knew about when and where credit cards would be used, but only a minority understood that using them generates bills and eventually reduces one's bank account.

When asked about acquiring the money needed to start a business or purchase a home, students talked about building it up through savings or getting it as a gift or personal loan from a friend or relative but not about securing a loan from a bank. When asked about prices (why things cost what they do), they talked about the presumed inherent value of the object, the need to pay the person who made the object, or the seller's decision to set and insist on a given price but did not mention supply and demand or the idea that something is worth whatever the market will pay.

These and other responses to our interviews led us to include the following as main ideas in an instructional unit on money developed for primary-grade students (Alleman & Brophy, 2003b):

- Money is a medium of exchange, needed in all but the simplest and most isolated societies.
- Several denominations of coins and currency are needed to make it convenient for people to compile exact amounts or make change.
- Before the idea of a medium of exchange was invented, people had to rely on trading (barter).
- Money eliminates several problems associated with trading and makes economic exchanges much easier.
- Early forms of money (such as wampum or precious stones) were less convenient to store and use than more modern coins and paper money.
- U.S. coins and bills include a representation of a past president or another significant American on one side and an American symbol on the other side; words and numbers indicating the value of the coin or bill; and other material such as slogans, information about the depicted person, and information about when and where the money was manufactured.

- Money is made in factories (mints) run by the federal government.
- Banks not only provide safekeeping for money but also pay interest on accounts and provide loans, checking accounts, credit card accounting, and other financial services.
- Budgets are plans for managing finances (and in particular, keeping spending within one's means).
- Writing checks and using credit cards allow people to transfer money without having to exchange bills and coins, but they need to keep track of these transactions because the money is deducted from their accounts at their banks.
- When people want to start a business or buy a home and do not have all of the money needed to do so, they can get a loan from a bank (they will have to pay back the loan plus interest, but they are willing to do so because this allows them to start the business or purchase the home now, without having to wait until they accumulate the full amount).
- The value of an item ultimately comes down to what potential purchasers are willing to pay for it.
- Most people earn most of their money by working at jobs.
- Ordinarily a country's money is good only in that country, but it can be exchanged for an equivalent amount of another country's money, which then can be spent in that country.

Key Economic Concepts for the Elementary Grades

The Center for Economic Education at the University of Nebraska–Omaha suggested the following as economic concepts appropriate for introducing at each of the elementary grades (and subsequently reviewing).

Kindergarten

- Scarcity: the condition of not being able to have all the goods and services that we want
- Choice: what someone must make when faced with two or more alternative uses for a resource
- Goods: objects that can be held or touched that can satisfy people's wants
- Services: activities that can satisfy people's wants

First Grade

- Opportunity cost: the next best alternative that must be given up when a choice is made
- Resources: all natural, human, and human-made aids to the production of goods and services

  Natural resources: "gifts of nature" that are present without human intervention

  Human resources: the quantity and quality of human effort directed toward producing goods and services (also called labor)

  Capital resources: goods made by people and used to produce other goods and services

- Barter: the direct trading of goods and services between people without the use of money.

Second Grade

- Interdependence: dependence on others for goods and services; occurs as a result of specialization
- Money: a medium of exchange, a good that can be used to buy other goods and services
- Production/producers: people who use resources to make goods and services, also called workers
- Consumers: people whose wants are satisfied by using goods and services
- Specialization: the situation in which people produce a narrower range of goods and services than they consume

Third Grade

- Division of labor: the process whereby workers perform only a single task or very few steps of a major production task, as when working on an assembly line
- Productivity: the ratio of output (goods and services) produced per unit of input (productive resources) over a period of time
- Markets: any setting where buyers and sellers exchange goods, services, resources, and currencies
- Price: the value of a good or service stated in money terms
- Public goods: goods and services that are provided by the government, often too expensive or impractical to be obtained by individuals

Fourth Grade

- Economic systems: the way a society organizes the production, consumption, and distribution of goods and services
- Market economy: an economic system where most goods and services are exchanged through private transactions by private households and businesses, with prices determined by buyers and sellers making the exchanges in private markets
- Circular flow: a model of an economic system showing the interactions between households and business firms as they exchange goods, services, and resources in markets
- Trade/exchange: trading goods and services with people for other goods and services or for money. When people exchange voluntarily, they expect to be better off as a result.

Fifth Grade

- Factors of production: resources used by businesses to produce goods and services
- Investment in capital resources: business purchases of new plants and equipment
- Investment in human services: activities that increase the skills and knowledge of workers

- Trade-offs: giving up one thing to get some of another
- Demand: a schedule of how much consumers are willing and able to buy at all possible prices during some time period
- Supply: a schedule of how much producers are willing and able to produce and sell at all possible prices during some time period
- Equilibrium price: the market clearing price at which the quantity demanded by buyers equals the quantity supplied by sellers

Sixth Grade

- Competition: techniques used by businesses to gain more customers and earn higher profits
- Costs of production: all resources used in producing goods and services for which owners receive payment
- Profit: the difference between the total revenue and total cost of a business; entrepreneurial income
- Entrepreneurship: the human resource that assumes the risk of organizing other productive resources to produce goods and services
- Incentives: factors that motivate and influence the behavior of households and businesses. Prices, profits, and losses act as incentives for participants to take action in a market economy.
- Taxes: required payments of money made to governments by households and business firms

  Income taxes: taxes paid by households and business firms on the income they receive

  Property taxes: taxes paid by households and businesses on land and buildings

  Sales taxes: taxes paid on the goods and services people buy

- Unemployment: the situation in which people are willing and able to work at current wages but do not have jobs
- Shortages: the situation resulting when the quantity demanded exceeds the quantity supplied of a good, service, or resource
- Surpluses: the situation resulting when the quantity supplied exceeds the quantity demanded of a good, service, or resource, usually because the price is for some reason above the equilibrium price in the market.

Elaboration of these concepts and links to resources for teaching them can be found at the Center's website (http://www.ecedweb.unomaha.edu).

National Standards for Economics Teaching

Different groups interested in economics have different interests and thus different priorities concerning what ought to be taught in the schools. Academic economists would emphasize the basic concepts, principles, and data collection and analysis methods used in the discipline. Business groups would emphasize savings, investments, and knowledge and values related to the free-market economy. Consumer advocates would emphasize critical thinking about advertising and good decision making about spending, credit, and other aspects of personal economics. These and other stakeholders have yet to agree on a single set of standards, let alone a complete economics curriculum.

The National Council on Economic Education (NCEE), an organization of economists and educators interested in economics education, developed a set of voluntary national standards for teaching economics as a discipline. Some of these standards deal with macro economics and are better suited to instruction in high school (e.g., monetary and fiscal policy, unemployment and inflation, the role of government in regulating the national economy), but others are appropriate for teaching to elementary students (e.g., scarcity, the role of incentives, specialization and trade, entrepreneurship and profit). Elaboration of these standards, including definitions, related concepts, standards and benchmarks, and links to classroom-tested lessons can be accessed at NCEE's website (www.ncee.net). The NCEE also sells curriculum guides and lesson plans targeted for the primary, intermediate, or upper grades, as well as a guide to teaching economics using children's literature. The lesson plans available through NCEE's site have been field-tested by teachers at the target grade levels and revised over the years. Other web-based sources of economics lessons for the elementary grades include the Indiana Council for Economic Education site (www.econed-in.org/) and the economic education site at James Madison University (http://cob.jmu.edu/econed).

Economics standards also appear in the National Council for the Social Studies' (1994) curriculum standards. One of the ten thematic strands calls for experiences that provide for the study of how people organize for the Production, Distribution, and Consumption of goods and services. In the early grades, such experiences allow students to give examples that show how scarcity and choice govern our economic decisions; distinguish between needs and wants; identify examples of private and public goods and services; give examples of the various institutions that make up economic systems, such as families, workers, banks, labor unions, government agencies, small businesses, and large corporations; describe how we depend upon workers with specialized jobs and the ways in which they contribute to the production and exchange of goods and services; describe the influence of incentives, values, traditions, and habits on economic decisions; explain and demonstrate the role of money in everyday life; describe the relationship of price to supply and demand; use economic concepts such as supply, demand, and price to help explain events in the community and nation; and apply knowledge of economic concepts in developing a response to a current local economic issue, such as how to reduce the flow of trash into a rapidly filling landfill. In the middle grades, activities relating to this strand allow students to give and explain examples of ways that economic systems structure choices about how goods and services are to be produced and distributed; describe the role that supply and demand, prices, incentives, and profits play in determining what is produced and distributed in a competitive market system; explain the difference between private and public goods and services; describe a range of examples of the various institutions that make up economic systems, such as households, business firms, banks, government agencies, labor unions, and corporations; describe the role of specialization and exchange in the economic process; explain and illustrate how values and beliefs influence different economic systems; differentiate among various forms of exchange and money; compare basic economic systems according to who determines what is produced, distributed, and consumed; use economic concepts to help explain historical and current developments and issues in local, national, or global contexts; and use economic reasoning to compare different proposals for dealing with a contemporary social issue such as unemployment, acid rain, or high-quality education.

Teaching about Economics

The NCSS (1994) standards document includes some interesting activities relating to production, distribution, and consumption. In one, a primary class is divided into two teams to make gingerbread cookies. One team works as an assembly line, with each person having a unique role; and the other works as individuals, with each creating his or her own version. Afterwards, the students discuss and write about the trade-offs embedded in the two methods (e.g., assembly lines facilitate speed and quality control, but doing the entire job as an individual affords more independence and opportunities for creativity).

To teach about trade and economic interdependence, a class is divided into seven groups, each representing a country about to build a new structure to house its government. The groups are each given a bag of supplies, but when they open them they discover that one group has only some glue and a pair of scissors, another has only crayons and paper, another only sticks, and so on. The groups discover that they can accomplish their construction task by trading surplus materials for the materials they lack, although it will be important to consider supply and demand in deciding what constitutes a fair deal.

In another example, an ongoing current event (debate about whether a local property should be developed as a park or as a strip mall and condos) was used to teach middle-grade students about opportunity cost at the community level. The class was divided into a park group and a developer group, each assigned to research the pros and cons of both sides and develop an argument designed to persuade the town council to adopt its plan. To enhance the authenticity of the activity, a group of school administrators, teachers, and other adults was assembled to simulate the town council in listening to the presentations and then making a decision (taking care to compliment both sides on the strengths of their presentations).

Economics educators often recommend using children's literature as a vehicle for teaching economics concepts and principles (VanFossen, 2003). Besides offering motivational benefits, stories provide contexts within which to embed authentic examples of economic decision making. Kehler (1998) recommended twenty children's literature selections suitable to this purpose, keyed to the voluntary national content standards in economics.

The most powerful and lasting economics lessons, however, are likely to be those that involve experiential learning in which students are engaged in economic activities or decision making followed by debriefing discussions focusing on key concepts and principles (Laney, 2001; Laney & Schug, 1998). For example, primary-grade children may find it difficult and confusing to learn the concept of opportunity cost (defined as the next-best alternative that one gives up when making a decision) if it is taught as an abstract concept in isolation from other, related content. However, the same children relatively easily not only come to understand but to appreciate the relevance and importance of the opportunity cost concept when engaged in a series of activities that call for them to make decisions about allocating their time or money. During debriefing discussions of these experiences, the teacher leads them to see that economic decisions involve trade-offs—that when you allocate some of your time or money to one purpose, you simultaneously forego the opportunity to use it for a different purpose (ordinarily, the next-best alternative). Appreciation of the opportunity cost concept will help them learn to approach economic decisions by considering not only the benefits but the costs of resource allocations (e.g., they can use part of their savings to buy a video today, but this will delay their opportunity to buy the bicycle they have been saving for).

Economics Programs for the Elementary Grades

Most elementary school teachers do not have much formal economic knowledge (McKinney, McKinney, Larkins, Gilmore, & Ford, 1990), which makes it difficult for them to develop activities around sound content. It also leaves them susceptible to reliance on corporately produced materials that include questionable financial advice (Stanger, 1997). So, make sure that you acquire enough economic knowledge to create meaningful economic learning activities for your students.

Some economics educators advocate the use of technology as an instructional tool to facilitate students' construction of meanings and economic relationships. Highlighting an activity comparing population patterns with locations of corporate polluters, Lucey and Grant (2005) encouraged the use of the NTeQ instructional model (iNtegrating TEchnology for inQuiry) (Morrison, Lowther, & Demuelle, 1999) to foster students' collection and analysis of economic information and associated relationships. Such technology functions as more than glamorous tutors for students by encouraging collaborative discourse that fosters both working understandings of technology and discovery of economic principles.

A well-established and successful program for teaching economics in Grades 3–6 is Mini-Society, an experiential learning program that teaches students basic economic concepts and principles along with related information about government, careers, consumer issues, and values (Kourilsky, 1983). The program is intended to be implemented three times a week for ten weeks, so it would require 25–50% of the time allocated to social studies in most elementary classrooms. It involves creating a Mini-Society in the classroom based on market mechanisms. The society includes a name, a flag, a currency system, civil servants (e.g., paymasters who are paid to distribute money to individuals), and mechanisms for introducing money into circulation (by allowing "citizens" to earn money by meeting criteria of good citizenship or accomplishment). Students then can use the Mini-Society money to purchase items from classmates in exchange for the special money, but the main focus switches to encouraging students to begin businesses that offer goods or services in exchange for Mini-Society money. In addition to consumption, incentives for developing businesses that will enable the students to acquire money include the need to pay various taxes and fees levied to pay civic servants for their work, pay the teacher for needed supplies and consultant advice, and pay the principal rent for use of space.

Once several businesses begin and a thriving market economy develops, students have experiences (business successes and failures, conflict between partners, indecision about how much to charge for one's product or service, etc.) that provide grist for debriefing discussions, which are the main mechanism for highlighting and formalizing the concepts and principles taught in the program. Experiences followed by debriefing discussions are used to develop topics such as goods and services, supply and demand, advertising, keeping financial records, opportunity cost, cost-benefit analysis, shortages and the rationing function of price, and the function of banks. If the implementation incorporates the option of establishing a formal government, there also will be debriefings on concepts such as democracy vs. dictatorship, the branches of government and their functions, and legal contracts and their implications.

Mini-Society requires considerable commitment of time, space, and teacher preparation (guided by a detailed manual that includes many duplicate masters). The program offers a great deal of excitement and enjoyment to students and provides them with a variety of experiences that can become valuable grist for learning economic concepts and principles. The degree to which their understanding is developed, however, will be determined heavily by the degree to which the teacher recognizes and exploits teachable moments and consistently leads the students through good debriefing discussions.

Laney (1997, 2001) provided a step-by-step example of good debriefing discussion. Students are confronted with a scarcity situation at school, then asked to describe it in detail in their own words and role-play it. Next, the students identify the central problem, and the teacher helps them to recognize that the existence of scarce resources is a relevant decision-making issue. Next, the teacher teaches or reviews the concepts needed for dealing with the problem. Students supply their own invented definition and label for the concept of scarcity, such as not-enough or too-few-for-so-many, and the teacher provides the conventional label and definition (scarcity occurs whenever people's wants exceed the available resources, which they usually do). Finally, the teacher guides the students in relating this new information to the current problem and to their own knowledge base and past experience. The students address the problem by brainstorming possible allocation strategies, discussing and role-playing positive and negative consequences of each strategy, selecting the one that appears best, implementing it, and living with the consequences.

Kourilsky (1992) also developed Kinder-Economy, an experience-based economics curriculum for Grades K–2. It also calls for students to experience situations that focus on real-world economic decision making and living with the consequences, but it does not involve creating a society, starting businesses, and the other more complicated aspects of Mini-Society. Students are asked to choose between two alternatives (e.g., which playground activity to participate in or which supplies to use in creating an art project), then are guided in using cost-benefit analysis to determine whether they made a good decision given their choice of alternatives.

Two other economic programs worth noting are Small-Size Economics and Children in the Marketplace. These are less ambitious, more conventional programs than Mini-Society but are designed to teach many of the same concepts. Small-Size Economics (Skeel, 1988) includes twenty lessons, ten for kindergarten or first grade (addressed within the contexts of self, family, or school) and ten for second or third grade (addressed within the contexts of neighborhood or community). Children in the Marketplace (National Council on Economic Education, 2005) is a series of eight lessons designed to teach basic economics principles to third- and fourth-graders. Each lesson is designed to provide opportunities for students to first hear about economics concepts and principles, then apply and experience them, then review them, and finally, generalize their applications to concrete situations.

Financial Literacy

Financial literacy is an emerging economic topic garnering increasing educational interest. The Jump$tart Coalition offers a set of personal finance standards to be met by Grades 4, 8, and 12 (http://www.jumpstartcoalition.com). However, the methods through which teachers implement these standards have strong bearing on their students' abilities to master financial skills. Activities that allow students to discover the meanings of financial choices and their associated consequences are especially desirable as financial literacy learning opportunities.

Civics and Government

Besides teaching content and skills, American schools traditionally have been expected to socialize each new generation, and the children of immigrants in particular, in American values and political traditions. These socialization goals are addressed not only through course content but also through school rules, learning communities established within classrooms, patriotic pageants and holiday celebrations, mock votes and other election-related activities, student governments, current-events discussions, and special units or events related to topics such as conflict resolution, law education, or celebrating diversity.

Within the academic curriculum, social studies bears special citizen education responsibilities. Along with knowledge and skills, this includes developing civic values (e.g., democracy, justice, equality before the law) and dispositions to action (e.g., voting and other forms of political participation). Social studies was conceived as a pandisciplinary curricular strand, rather than merely a placeholder for courses in separate disciplines, primarily as a way to ensure that citizen education goals received sufficient attention.

Educating students for citizenship is challenging because it requires addressing some enduring dilemmas, most notably the challenge of socializing students to adopt American political values while simultaneously respecting cultural diversity, and the challenge of fostering dispositions toward active political participation without foisting your own partisan political views on your captive audience of students. Unfortunately, most textbooks and many teachers shy away from these challenges, seeking to avoid controversy. Consequently, scholars who study civic education in the schools frequently lament that there is not enough of it and that what there is overemphasizes transmission of academic knowledge and traditional values at the expense of opportunities for students to discuss and debate social or civic policy issues, work on service learning projects, or get other opportunities for active political participation or experiential learning. They emphasize that partisanship can be avoided by focusing civic education around the core democratic values rooted in our Declaration of Independence, U.S. Constitution, and political traditions and by engaging students in civic service or improvement projects that people of all political persuasions can support.

A federal law that took effect in 2005 requires teachers to teach about the U.S. Constitution, and many states require instruction relating to core democratic values. The latter guidelines usually feature the following twelve values: life, liberty, the pursuit of happiness, justice, the common good, equality, truth, diversity, popular sovereignty, patriotism, the rule of law, and individual rights. These core values can be defined at varying levels of sophistication for students at different grade levels. For example, *justice* can be defined for younger children as taking turns and being fair to others but explained to older children in terms of treating people fairly in the eyes of the law without favoring particular individuals or groups. Information about how the core democratic values can be defined and taught at different grade levels (including recommendations for correlated children's literature selections) can be found at the website of the Michigan Department of Education (http://www.michigan.gov.mde).

Some elementary teachers, especially primary teachers, also shy away from teaching about government because they believe that their students are not interested in or ready for instruction in the topic. It is true that most elementary students will not respond well to macro aspects of the topic or to some of the drier traditional content, such as a lesson on how a bill becomes a law. However, even young children are very interested in issues of fairness and justice (as can be seen when they learn about slavery or past restrictions on women's rights). We also have found them to be responsive to lessons on government that emphasize basic reasons for and functions of government (rather than abstract political science concepts or details of governmental procedures).

Children can understand that people need governments to provide essentials that are too big, complicated, or expensive for them to provide for themselves, such as keeping us safe (military, police, fire, hospitals) and enabling us to function in the modern world (schools, roads, traffic regulation). They also are interested to learn other basic ideas about government: Governments collect taxes to pay for their activities; there is not always consensus on what government should be doing, which is why we have political parties and elections; and our country vests power in the people and elects its leaders, but other countries are ruled by monarchs who inherit the throne or by despots who forcibly seize power and maintain it through repression.

Children's Knowledge and Thinking about Government

More is known about children's thinking about government than about other major social studies topics. Early studies indicated that young children tend to depict a benevolent world in which political leaders are wise, caring, and attentive to the needs of everyone. American children's early political thinking is focused on the president, whom they depict as making laws and running the country by doing everything from managing the military and world affairs to providing individual assistance to people who telephone or visit the White House. They usually know little or nothing about Congress, the Supreme Court, federal departments and bureaucracies, or parallel governmental structures at the state and local level. Instead, they think of government as the actions of the president (and to a much lesser extent, the governor or the mayor), assisted by "helpers" who come to bring up issues or problems, get decisions, and then carry out orders.

Because they think of government as benevolent and put their trust in it, children have difficulty conceiving or approving of pressure groups, parties, conflict, and so on. They are somewhat aware that big corporations influence government, but they usually do not think that rich people have any more influence than average people. They idealize elections, believing that candidates should not say unkind things about one another, that the loser should join in support of the winner, and that the winner should be gracious and forgiving.

Although they occasionally refer to something quite specific (e.g., helping a person get a job), children's depictions of the president's actions are usually vague and generic. Initially, they talk about the president signing papers, making speeches, or running meetings, and later they add functions such as making laws, running the country, or solving problems. Although their thinking about governmental leaders focuses on the president much more than the governor or mayor, their thinking about governmental functions is much more local (they talk about providing roads, schools, police and emergency services, and so on). They sometimes confuse the public and private sectors, as in thinking that all utility companies and television stations are part of the government or in not realizing that mail carriers and most teachers do work for the government (Hess & Torney, 1967; Moore, Lare, & Wagner, 1985).

More recent studies have replicated and extended these findings. They again indicate that children's thinking about government focuses on leaders and face-to-face commanding rather than hierarchies of offices and levels of government. Children generally emphasize either or both of two main ideas: government as a source of authority and power over people's actions; and government as a benevolent resource that protects us, solves problems, and helps people in need. Most children are not very clear about who does what, but they share a general perception that the nation, state, and/or local community are run by competent people who take actions as needed to protect the health, safety, and general welfare of the citizens. A few display naïveté in describing the extent of governmental benevolence or the motivations behind it (e.g., keep the streets clean to protect birds from choking), and a few others display resentment against governmental exercise of authority (e.g., enforcing eviction notices), but most speak matter-of-factly when describing the nature and functions of government.

About half of primary students know that the president is elected. Others assume that the vice president moves up or that the new president is appointed by the previous president or some committee of knowledgeable leaders, based on display of competency (making good decisions, giving good speeches) and virtue (works hard, keeps promises). They do not assume that the office is hereditary. Thus, even young children who do not yet know much about our form of government already have learned that our country is neither a monarchy nor a totalitarian state, and have been conditioned to view it as a meritocracy. If asked to draw comparisons with kings and queens, children often depict monarchs as basking in the trappings of inherited luxury, while depicting presidents as working long hours for the good of the country during their limited time in office.

Most children convey a positive view of laws, depicting them as needed and helpful. However, their rationales tend to be limited to keeping us safe (traffic laws) or ensuring a well-ordered society and preventing chaos (laws against crimes). They rarely speak of laws as securing people's rights or making sure that they are treated fairly. They often are unsure about whether or how new laws might be introduced or older laws might be changed. When they are aware of particular laws, these tend to be laws regulating the behavior of individuals rather than commerce, corporations, or governmental processes, especially laws of special interest to children (focusing on bicycle safety, seatbelts, smoking, alcohol, drugs, or weapons).

Children are more aware of judges today than in the past because of the popularity of courtroom settings, both fictional and realistic, on television. They generally depict courtrooms in which the judge (rather than a jury) is the arbiter who decides which side wins the case and what subsequent actions will be taken. They depict judges as presiding over their courtrooms by banging their gavels, lecturing defendants about their behavior or questioning them about their motives, or questioning witnesses to clarify what they saw. If they mention other courtroom actors (e.g., juries, attorneys), they usually depict them as judges' advisors or helpers rather than as people with their own unique roles to play in deciding cases.

Children usually do not think or know much about where the money to pay for government comes from. If asked, the younger ones are likely to say that the government (and more specifically, the president or governor) gets money from banks or prints whatever money is needed. Later they begin to understand that money to pay for government comes from the people but are vague about how the process works. They may not know or use the term *taxes*. Those who do may understand *taxes* as bills to be paid but may confuse them with utility bills or house or car payments. Even those who do understand that taxes are paid specifically to governments to fund governmental activities are usually only aware of sales taxes, not income or property taxes.

Most young students do not realize that their own school is provided by the local government and that their teachers are paid using tax money. Many assume that the school is owned by the principal or some combination of people who work in the building, and that teachers are paid by the principal (using personal funds or money gotten from a bank) or their parents (via money paid for books and supplies) (Berti, 2005; Brophy & Alleman, 2005).

Finally, it is noteworthy that less than one-fourth of the students whom we interviewed said that they would like to be president when they grew up, and many of these were more focused on the perquisites attached to the office than on opportunities to use its power for the good of the country. Despite the tendency of most of these students to attribute near-omnipotent power to the presidency, they also associated the office with long hours, daunting responsibilities, and "political stuff." We need to do a better job of helping students to appreciate the many services and functions that governments perform and socializing them to aspire to public-service careers.

National Standards for Teaching about Civics and Government

The curriculum standards of the National Council for the Social Studies (1994) include two thematic strands relating to civics and government, one focusing on knowledge and the other on values and dispositions. The first strand calls for experiences that provide for the study of how people create and change structures of Power, Authority, and Governance. In the early grades, such experiences allow students to examine the rights and responsibilities of the individual in relation to his or her social group, such as family, peer group, and school class; explain the purpose of government; give examples of how government does or does not provide for needs and wants of people, establish order and security, and manage conflict; recognize how groups and organizations encourage unity and deal with diversity to maintain order and security; distinguish among local, state, and national government and identify representative leaders at these levels, such as mayor, governor, and president; identify and describe factors that contribute to cooperation and cause disputes within and among groups and nations; explore the role of technology in communications, transportation, information-processing, weapons development, or other areas as it contributes to or helps resolve conflicts; and recognize and give examples of the tensions between the wants and needs of individuals and groups, and concepts such as fairness, equity, and justice. In the middle grades, experiences related to this strand allow students to examine persistent issues involving the rights, roles, and status of the individual in relation to the general welfare; describe the purpose of government and how its powers are acquired, used, and justified; analyze and explain ideas and governmental mechanisms to meet needs and wants of citizens, regulate territory, manage conflict, and establish order and security; describe the ways nations and organizations respond to forces of unity and diversity affecting order and security; identify and describe the basic features of the political system in the United States, and identify representative leaders from various levels and branches of the government; explain conditions, actions, and motivations that contribute to conflict and cooperation within and among nations; describe and analyze the role of technology in communications, transportation, information-processing, weapons development, or other areas as it contributes to or helps resolve conflicts; explain and apply concepts such as power, role, status, justice, and influence to the examination of persistent issues and social problems; and give examples and explain how governments attempt to achieve their stated ideals at home and abroad.

The second strand addresses Civic Ideals and Practices. It calls for experiences that provide for the study of the ideals, principles, and practices of citizenship in a democratic republic. In the early grades, such experiences allow students to identify key ideals of the United States' democratic republican form of government, such as individual human dignity, liberty, justice, equality, and the rule of law, and discuss their application in specific situations; identify examples of rights and responsibilities of citizens; locate, access, organize, and apply information about an issue of public concern from multiple points of view; identify and practice selected forms of civic discussion and participation consistent with the ideals of citizens in a democratic republic; explain actions citizens can take to influence public-policy decisions; recognize that a variety of formal and informal actors influence and shape public policy; examine the influence of public opinion on personal decision making and government policy on public issues; explain how public policies and citizen behaviors may or may not reflect the stated ideals of a democratic republican form of government; describe how public policies are used to address issues of public concern; and recognize and interpret how the "common good" can be strengthened through various forms of citizen action. In the middle grades, activities that develop desired civic ideals and practices allow students to examine the origins and continuing influence of key ideals of the democratic republican form of government, such as individual human dignity, liberty, justice, equality, and the rule of law; identify and interpret sources and examples of the rights and responsibilities of citizens; locate, access, analyze, organize, and apply information about selected public issues—recognizing and explaining multiple points of view; practice forms of civic discussion and participation consistent with the ideals of citizens in a democratic republic; explain and analyze various forms of citizen action that influence public policy decisions; identify and explain the roles of formal and informal political actors in influencing and shaping public policy and decision making; analyze the influence of diverse forms of public opinion on the development of public policy and decision making; analyze the effectiveness of selected public policies and citizen behaviors in realizing the stated ideals of a democratic republican form of government; explain the relationship between policy statements and action plans used to address issues of public concern; and examine strategies designed to strengthen the "common good" that consider a range of options for citizen action.

The Center for Civic Education (1994) also released standards for teaching about civics and government. As shown in Table 7.1, they are organized around five key questions. Like the NCSS standards, these standards also address both knowledge/skills and values/dispositions, and are differentiated between the early and the middle grades.

Teaching about Civics and Government

To help students understand why governments are needed and what they do for their people, we recommend developing instruction around the basic idea that governments provide facilities and services that people need but are too big in scope, expense, and so on for individuals or families to provide for themselves. These include national defense and the armed forces; roads, airports, and transportation infrastructure; education from kindergarten through university levels; the criminal justice system; police protection and emergency services; parks and recreation facilities; the postal service; standards and regulations regarding product quality and safety; safety-net services for people with special needs; and so on. The tax money that is collected to pay for these services supports the common good.

An effective way to develop such appreciation is to prepare a photo essay illustrating events occurring in a typical day in the life of one of the students in the class and underscoring the role of government in facilitating these activities. For example, the photos might depict the child getting up in the morning wearing fire-resistant pajamas (per government regulations); washing using purified running water supplied by local government; changing into clothes inspected for quality

TABLE 7.1

National Standards for Civics and Government

Grades K–4	*Grades 5–8*
I. What is government and what should it do?	**I. What are civic life, politics, and government?**
Defining government	Defining civic life, politics, and government
Defining power and authority	Necessity and purposes of government
Necessity and purposes of government	Limited and unlimited governments
Functions of government	The rule of law
Purposes of rules and laws	Concepts of "constitution"
Evaluating rules and laws	Purposes and uses of constitutions
Limited and unlimited governments	Conditions under which constitutional government flourishes
Importance of limited government	Shared powers and parliamentary systems
	Confederal, federal, and unitary systems
II. What are the basic values and principles of American democracy?	**II. What are the foundations of the American political system?**
Fundamental values and principles	The American idea of constitutional government
Distinctive characteristics of American society	Distinctive characteristics of American society
American identity	The role of voluntarism in American life
Diversity in American society	American identity
Prevention and management of conflicts	The character of American political conflict
Promoting ideals	Fundamental values and principles
	Conflicts among values and principles in American political and social life
	Disparities between ideals and reality in American political and social life
III. How does the government established by the constitution embody the purposes, values, and principles of American democracy?	**III. How does the government established by the constitution embody the purposes, values, and principles of American democracy?**
The meaning and importance of the United States Constitution	Distributing, sharing, and limiting powers of the national government
Organization and major responsibilities of the national government	Sharing powers between the national and state governments
Organization and major responsibilities of state governments	Major responsibilities for domestic and foreign policy
Organization and major responsibilities of local governments	Financing government through taxation
Identifying members of government	State governments
	Organization and responsibilities of state and local governments
	Who represents you in legislative and executive branches of your local, state, and national governments
	The place of law in American society

Criteria for evaluating rules and laws

Judicial protection of the rights of individuals

The public agenda

Political communication

Political parties, campaigns, and elections

Associations and groups

Forming and carrying out public policy

IV. What is the relationship of the United States to other nations and to world affairs?

Nations

Interaction among nations

IV. What is the relationship of the United States to other nations and to world affairs?

Nation-states

Interaction among nation-states

United States' relations with other nation-states

International organizations

Impact of the American concept of democracy and individual rights on the world

Political, demographic, and environmental developments

V. What are the roles of the citizen in American democracy?

The meaning of citizenship

Becoming a citizen

Rights of individuals

Responsibilities of individuals

Depositions that enhance citizen effectiveness and promote the healthy functioning of American democracy

Forms of participation

Political leadership and public service

Selecting leaders

V. What are the roles of the citizen in American democracy?

The meaning of citizenship

Becoming a citizen

Personal rights

Political rights

Economic rights

Scope and limits of rights

Personal responsibilities

Civic responsibilities

Dispositions that enhance citizen effectiveness and promote the healthy functioning of American constitutional democracy

Participation in civic and political life and the attainment of individual and public goals

The difference between political and social participation

Forms of political participation

Political leadership and careers in public service

Knowledge and participation

Source: Adapted from Center for Civic Education (1994). *National standards for civics and government: Organizing questions and content summary.* The complete standards statement is available at the Center's website (www.civiced.org).

and safety; eating a breakfast consisting of foods inspected for quality and safety; boarding a safety-inspected, government-provided bus driven by a licensed driver; traveling to school on government-maintained roads patrolled by the local police force; attending school in a government-owned building; participating in learning activities using government-supplied materials assisted by government-supplied teachers; and so on.

Initial ideas about alternative forms of government can be developed by contrasting our system of representative democracy (leaders are elected to limited terms and must act within constitutional guidelines) with systems in which leaders ascend to power through other means (inheritance, military power), hold office indefinitely, and exercise totalitarian power. Contrasts can be brought home through discussion or simulation of what it is like to live in countries where there are no elections or at least no secret ballots, access to desired housing and jobs requires continued government approval, and people who resist government policies are subject to arrest.

Some of the details of how our system works are best addressed around election times via study of some of the issues and the reasons why different stakeholders would prefer one candidate or policy over another. Also, using examples easily understood by children, instruction can help students learn that debates about laws or policies often focus on means–ends relationships and tradeoffs rather than ultimate purposes (e.g., people who agree with the ultimate purpose of a proposed law or policy might nevertheless oppose it because they do not believe that it will accomplish the purpose or that whatever good it accomplishes will not be worth the costs in higher taxes, new restrictions on individual freedoms, etc.).

Lesson plans and children's literature resources on the presidency are plentiful but often focus on the trivial and stop well short of genuine civic education. This produces outcomes like the one reported by Haas (2004): A middle-school student who had completed a report on President Reagan recalled three facts: Reagan was called "the Gipper," he had a sense of humor, and he loved jellybeans. Children can and should learn much more substantive information about the presidency and about the major policies and initiatives of any individual presidents they study. For ideas about teaching about the presidency and presidential elections, see the Haas (2004) article, McGuire's (1997) book, or websites established for introducing students to government and the electoral process (Bensguide.gpo.gov/3–5/election/index. html; www. kidsvotingusa.org).

The Kids Voting website is especially useful during election years. It offers a program for students that provides information about registering to vote, the role of political parties in elections, and how to organize information to make voting decisions (through reading newspapers, analyzing political advertisements, and following debates about campaign issues). It concludes with a mock election held on the same day as the general election. Evaluation of the program indicated that it energizes students' interest in elections and increases their communication with parents about politics, their use of political media such as newspapers in the home, and their general knowledge about elections, with especially noteworthy effects on students from lower socioeconomic status families (McDevitt & Chaffee, 2000).

Key to successful civic and political education is thoughtful discussion of civic issues within an open classroom climate. Instruction in civic content increases students' civic knowledge but by itself usually has negligible effects on student attitudes related to eventual civic and political participation. However, both sets of outcomes are likely when students report frequently discussing issues, hearing and exploring alternative views, and feeling comfortable expressing their own opinions because the teacher maintains a classroom atmosphere that supports this kind of thoughtful discourse (Torney-Purta, Hahn, & Amadeo, 2001).

Teachers can convey basic information about taxes and address likely confusion about taxes and utility bills by sharing and leading discussions about their own personal documents. Most of the students will be familiar with sales taxes at some level, but showing the amounts added to the purchase price as listed on store receipts will help bring home the fact that sales taxes are attached to most purchases and provide a sense of the relative amounts involved. Similarly, sharing property assessments and local tax bills will help students understand how local governments raise money for schools and community services. Support of the federal (and if relevant, the state) government through income taxes can be made concrete by showing paycheck statements indicating that employers keep track of the taxes that their employees owe and deduct this money from gross pay to send to the government.

Once the students have developed some basic knowledge about common forms of taxation, where tax money is sent, and what is done with it, teachers can share utility bills and lead discussion of what is being purchased from utility companies, how it is used, and how the companies keep track of what customers owe them. Class discussion would be followed up with home assignments calling for students to interact with their parents in locating and observing the meters that measure water, gas, and electricity usage, as well as inspecting and discussing tax bills, utility bills, store receipts, and related documents.

Instruction about the civic aspects of government might begin with emphasis that students are members of a classroom community as well as a larger community that incorporates their homes and businesses. As members of the classroom learning community, they are expected to follow rules designed to help people get along, keep things fair, protect individual and school property, and keep people safe. The larger community has laws for similar reasons. Political office holders make sure that life in the community allows people to carry out their daily activities in a safe and orderly environment. Students might be introduced to local leaders through guest speakers who visit the classroom, field trips to government offices, or studying photos and listening to taped interviews.

The students might learn that the community leaders have three basic jobs: make plans and laws, solve problems, and make the community a pleasant place to live. Legislators make the laws that need to be followed by everyone. Some laws protect people's rights, some protect property (e.g., zoning ordinances), some protect health (e.g., pollution ordinances), and some promote safety (e.g., speed limits).

Laws help guide our lives and remind us of our responsibilities toward other people. They are enforced by police and judges who are part of local government, but they are intended to make the community a better place, not merely to limit individuals' behavior. To make this concrete, students might discuss why particular laws exist (e.g., considering what would happen if people drove at any speed they wanted and ignored stop signs). Once students have developed a basic understanding of and appreciation for local government, they are ready for lessons on state and national government, on voting and other aspects of responsible citizenship, and on comparisons of different forms of government.

Finally, the learning might include encouragement of and opportunities for practicing good citizenship. Some of these might involve government (e.g., writing to appropriate government leaders to suggest new laws or express a position on a current issue). Others might involve service learning (e.g., participation in anti-litter, recycling, or other volunteer activities), rationalized with the explanation that governments cannot be expected to do everything and that good citizens contribute to the common good as individuals. For a unit on government that incorporates these and other basic ideas, see Alleman and Brophy (2003).

Embedding Social Science Content within Global and Multicultural Perspectives

At the beginning of Chapter 5, when introducing our set of three chapters on disciplinary content, we emphasized that social studies is a pandisciplinary school subject that bears special responsibility for socializing students to fulfill their roles as citizens in a democratic republic. Much of this involves learning about the history, geography, and so on of the United States and its people. However, as the National Council for the Social Studies (1994) put it, "The primary purpose of social studies is to help young people develop the ability to make informed and reasoned decisions for the public good as citizens of a culturally diverse, democratic society in an interdependent world" (p. vii).

An ongoing source of concern to many social educators is that the "culturally diverse" and "interdependent world" aspects of this statement often do not receive the attention they deserve. This has led to calls for more attention to diversity, as well as development of curricular models featuring global and multicultural education. For in-depth treatment of these instructional models and the curricula and learning activities associated with them, see Banks (2005) and Nieto (2004).

The approach that we recommend calls for infusing global and multicultural perspectives throughout your teaching rather than planning special units that address global or multicultural topics but otherwise walling them off from the rest of the curriculum. This pervasive global and multicultural perspective would be advisable for teachers in any country, but especially a country of immigrants such as ours.

The big ideas emphasized by the foundational disciplines of social studies point toward the same conclusion (e.g., analyzing events within the context of the time and place in which they occur, portraying a culture from an insider's perspective, fostering empathy while avoiding presentism and chauvinism). You can accomplish these basics most naturally by routinely embedding social studies content within a global purview (where relevant, addressing the causes and consequences of events with reference to the world at large, not just the United States, and helping students to notice and appreciate the significance of current events occurring all around the world), as well as analyzing them with attention to multiple perspectives, including the beliefs and traditions associated with those perspectives. Recent events in our increasingly connected and interdependent world underscore the need for global awareness and a multicultural perspective. Far too many Americans are ignorant about other people and places (not only where they are located but also their needs, interests, priorities, concerns, and cultures generally).

Another fundamental principle to emphasize is capitalizing on the diversity that exists within your own classroom by connecting with your students' families and using them as resources for creating authentic learning experiences relating to global and multicultural issues. Whatever you are teaching about in social studies at any given time, it is likely that at least some of your students' families are connected to the topic in some way. Capitalizing on these connections allows you to personalize what otherwise might be an abstract learning experience for many students and in the process, to promote appreciation for cultural diversity and encourage conversations about school-related topics between students and family members.

Summary

This chapter addresses elementary social studies applications of content drawn from psychology, sociology, economics, and civics/government (political science). Psychological content as such appears primarily in kindergarten and first grade, in lessons about oneself and one's social relationships. However, it is helpful to bear in mind that young children tend to take a psychological/narrative perspective on social studies content, rather than a social science/analytic perspective. Also, supporting the development of positive personal identities is part of the rationale for the mutual respect and celebration of diversity aspects of creating a learning community.

Sociology content is emphasized in studies of neighborhoods and communities, as well as in content dealing with social status and associated roles studied in lessons on history or cultures. Elementary teachers have many opportunities to sharpen students' awareness of their social involvements and the trade-offs associated with them. Children are very interested in issues surrounding fairness and justice, which makes them very interested in social studies content dealing with past or present inequities related to gender, race, ethnicity, or other status characteristics.

Economics addresses decision making about all kinds of resources, not just money. Elementary students can learn many of its most basic concepts experientially through activities calling for them to make decisions about how to spend their time or money. Although they often have personal experience in saving for and buying toys, most children do not know much and often harbor misconceptions about even basic economic aspects of society (business transactions and profits, banking operations, home financing, credit cards, the effect of supply and demand on prices). Economists have done a good job of identifying the most basic economic concepts and principles and developing experiential learning programs for use in the elementary grades.

Elementary social studies features considerable content relating to civics and government, although not teaching of political science as such. Basic appreciations about the need for rules to regulate social interactions are developed as part of establishing a classroom learning community. Subsequently, an emphasis on core democratic values should pervade all social studies teaching (not just lessons on civics and government). Focusing on these values and the knowledge content associated with them will help you to address potentially controversial content authentically while avoiding either an overly celebratory or an overly critical treatment of American political traditions. Given the divisiveness and polarization that has characterized the nation's political climate in recent years, we would emphasize two key goals in teaching about civics and government: (1) developing appreciation of why governments are needed and the kinds of resources and services they provide for people, and (2) emphasizing the importance of serving the common good and accomplishing as much as possible for as many as possible (rather than winning or losing battles) as basic orientations to politics.

Finally, the primary purposes and goals of social studies imply that discipline-based content ought to be embedded within global and multicultural perspectives. This includes analyzing events within the context of the time and place in which they occur, portraying cultures from insiders' perspectives, and fostering empathy while avoiding presentism and chauvinism. Students should learn to notice and appreciate the significance of events occurring all around the world (not just in the United States) and to analyze them with attention to multiple perspectives.

Reflective Questions

1. How does developing content in the social science disciplines link to the goal of preparing students for their life roles?
2. How can a novice teacher include the social sciences within units of instruction (that go beyond the textbook) without becoming overwhelmed?
3. If you were to expand your social studies program by addressing the social sciences described in this chapter, how would you prioritize them at your current or preferred grade level? Why?
4. Economics traditionally has been minimized in the elementary grades. Why? What do you propose can be done to overcome this mind-set?
5. Imagine you have been charged with embedding social science content within global and multicultural perspectives. What would this look like at your grade level?

Your Turn:
Applying Social Science Concepts within Your Learning Community

Our hope is that you have already accomplished a lot toward the development of your learning community—if you have your own classroom. (If you are at the stage of observing or interning, begin by putting your plans on paper.) You can help your students see the connections between life in your classroom (microcosm of society) and what goes on in other places by leveraging content associated with the disciplines and making it more explicit. Authentic representations will make the content more meaningful and memorable.

We encourage you to review this chapter and list the key concepts associated with each of the four disciplines. Then (1) prepare a matrix describing how each applies to your learning community; (2) add questions to be discussed in your class meetings that will stimulate conversation and critique associated with each; and (3) list possible unit infusions.

The matrix is intended as a planning tool. The general rule is that less is more; therefore, think about natural places for inclusion rather than attempting to infuse big ideas from each of the disciplines in every unit. Also, think about natural occasions for doing some foreshadowing, knowing that big ideas from a specific discipline will be emphasized in an upcoming unit.

NCSS STRANDS

IV. INDIVIDUAL DEVELOPMENT AND IDENTITY

Social Science Discipline	Learning Community	Optimum Places in My Unit Plans Where These Big Ideas Will Fit
[Psychology] Micro-level Psychological Terms	Use TWL as an introduction to units in order to figure out what students think they know based on the experiences they have had.	As I begin my unit on local government, I will ask my students what they think they know about government. I will record their responses on a large sheet of paper. I will use it as a daily reference as I plan and enact the lessons in an attempt to shift or enhance their thinking. I will address their misconceptions when appropriate.
Personal Identity	Promote conversations within the learning community that address the individual (e.g., What do you want to do? Why?). Move toward questions that guide students into acknowledging and respecting others—and making decisions accordingly.	
Self-efficacy	Promote conversations and learning community activities that foster "I can contribute," "I can make a difference for my class."	

V. INDIVIDUALS, GROUPS, INSTITUTIONS

Social Science Discipline	Learning Community	Optimum Places in My Unit Plans Where These Big Ideas Will Fit
[Sociology] Institutions Roles Expectations	Discuss the school as an institution and within the classroom, focusing on ideas that students have individual and group roles to play and expectations to meet. They have committee member responsibilities as well as individual subject-matter assignments. Similarly, out of school they participate in institutions such as church, scouts, gymnastics, etc. They have roles and expectations to meet. The challenge is to balance them with those they have within their classroom. Sometimes they seem to conflict.	As I assign committee members to certain tasks, we will discuss roles and expectations. We will create job charts and talk about how we will know when we have met our expectations as they relate to committee assignments and responsibilities.

VI. POWER, AUTHORITY, AND GOVERNANCE

Social Science Discipline	Learning Community	Optimum Places in My Unit Plans Where These Big Ideas Will Fit
[Political Science] Common good	I will introduce this core democratic value when we discuss our community service project.	During our unit on local government, I will prepare an interactive story-type lesson and explain that our core democratic values were created as part of the founding and establishment of our country. I will briefly introduce the Declaration of Independence and the Constitution. As the unit unfolds, we will look for places in our surroundings where the common good is being enacted.

VII. PRODUCTION, DISTRIBUTION, CONSUMPTION

Social Science Discipline	Learning Community	Optimum Places in My Unit Plans Where These Big Ideas Will Fit
[Economics] Opportunity cost	When we are making class decisions such as what to do/eat at our next class party, what to present at family night, or what community service project we would pursue, I will introduce opportunity cost—and explain that when you make choices, there are trade-offs. You always give up something.	This will fit nicely with our upcoming unit on money. We will address opportunity cost when we discuss personal budgeting. I will present several scenarios, then students will be asked to do some budgeting and explain their examples of opportunity cost.

HOW CAN I STRUCTURE CLASSROOM DISCOURSE TO HELP STUDENTS DEVELOP SOCIAL STUDIES UNDER-STANDING?

Anne Lehnert-Spalding, Teacher Intern

While it is not news, the idea that strategies need to match your goals cannot be overstated. Too often, as new teachers, we overuse our favorite strategy, or we get caught up in using one that has been popularized. I really like the idea of enhancing my instruction with more narratives. The segment on reflective discourse was very informative as well. Too often, we ask questions in classroom discussions that do not encourage students to think critically and in fact hinder them from being challenged and analyzing what they have learned. We need to develop questions that will make them look at the meaning in the content they learn. Another aspect I found very informative was the segment on teaching for thoughtfulness. I would be the first to admit that I need to spend more time planning and selecting strategies to make lessons more meaningful and challenging for the students.

    After reflecting on this chapter, I realized that I need to analyze my questions. I want to challenge my students, and classroom discussions are a good way to do that. I want them to think about their prior experiences and knowledge and connect them to the information they are learning. If they cannot connect anything from the lesson to their lives, they are not going to be able to internalize the new information, retain it, or make it memorable.

> I will also use the checklist at the end of the chapter. It is a valuable tool and guide to decision making and serves as a reminder of my responsibility as the teacher.

Until recently, most models of effective teaching emphasized the teacher as the dominant actor in the classroom: explaining content to students, checking their understanding, and then supervising their work on practice and application activities. The once widely disseminated model of Madeline Hunter (1984), for example, suggested that effective lessons contain the following elements:

1. Anticipatory set (prepare students to learn and to focus on key ideas)
2. Objective and purpose (tell students the purpose of the lesson)
3. Input (provide them with new information)
4. Modeling (demonstrate skills or procedures)
5. Checking for understanding (through questions or requests for performance)
6. Guided practice (under direct teacher supervision)
7. Independent practice (once students know what to do and how to do it)

Hunter's approach typifies what has become known as the *transmission view* of teaching and learning. The following assumptions are implied in this view (Good & Brophy, 2003):

1. Knowledge is treated as a fixed body of information transmitted from teacher or text to students.
2. Teachers and texts are viewed as authoritative sources of expert knowledge to which students defer.
3. Teachers are responsible for managing students' learning by providing information and leading the students through activities and assignments.
4. Teachers explain, check for understanding, and judge the correctness of students' responses.
5. Students memorize or replicate what has been explained or modeled.
6. Classroom discourse emphasizes drill and recitation in response to convergent questions, with a focus on eliciting correct answers.
7. Activities emphasize replication of models or applications that require following step-by-step procedures.
8. Students work mostly alone, practicing what has been transmitted to them in order to prepare themselves to compete for rewards by producing it on demand.

The transmission view embodies some important principles of good teaching, especially in its emphasis on the role of the teacher in stimulating students' motivation and readiness for learning, providing them with needed information and modeling, and structuring and monitoring their learning experiences. However, this view treats students as relatively passive receivers or copiers of knowledge. It does not convey images of students undergoing conceptual change as they construct new understandings, engaging in debate or carrying on sustained discussions rather than just responding to recitation questions, or collaborating in pairs or small groups as they work on cooperative learning activities.

In contrast, contemporary models of effective teaching and learning emphasize the role of the student as well as the role of the teacher. In Chapter 3, we noted that the following principles have emerged from research on teaching for understanding: The students' role is not just to absorb or copy input but also to actively make sense and construct meaning; activities and assignments feature tasks that call for problem solving or critical thinking, not just memory or reproduction; and the teacher creates a social environment in the classroom that could be described as a learning community, featuring discourse or dialogue designed to promote understanding. In Chapter 3 we also summarized the implications of the NCSS (1993) position statement that depicts social studies teaching and learning as powerful when it is meaningful, integrative, value-based, challenging, and active. All five of these key features, but especially the latter two, emphasize the need for active student engagement in knowledge construction, particularly through reflective teacher–student and student–student discourse.

Knowledge Construction

These contemporary models of effective teaching reflect the emergence of a *constructivist view* of learning. Constructivists believe that students learn by making connections between new information and existing networks of prior knowledge. They emphasize the importance of relating new content to knowledge that students already possess, as well as providing opportunities for students to process and apply the new learning. Before knowledge becomes truly generative—usable for interpreting new situations, reasoning, or solving problems—students must elaborate and question the new content, examine it in relation to more familiar content, and build new knowledge structures (Resnick & Klopfer, 1989). Otherwise, the knowledge may remain inert—recallable when cued by questions or test items like the ones used in practice exercises but not accessible when it might be useful in everyday living.

Active Construction of Meaning

The core idea of constructivism is that students develop new knowledge through a process of active construction. They do not merely passively receive or copy input from teachers or textbooks. Instead, they actively mediate it by trying to make sense of it and relate it to what they already know (or think they know) about the topic. Each student builds his or her own unique representation of what was communicated, and this may or may not include a complete and accurate reconstruction of what the teacher or textbook author intended to convey. Sometimes the learning is incomplete or distorted.

Even when the basic message is reconstructed as intended, different learners construct different sets of meanings and implications of "the same" set of ideas. For example, after reading about mountain climbers who overcame potential disasters to scale a peak successfully, one student might remember and think about the text primarily as a story about achievement motivation, another as a story about the value of teamwork, another as a story about how shared adventure seals the bonds of friendship, and yet another as an illustration of the challenges and specialized techniques involved in mountain climbing. The students all read the same story and their reconstructions all include the same basic story line, but they emphasize different meanings and potential implications.

Students routinely draw on their prior knowledge as they attempt to make sense of what they are learning. Accurate prior knowledge facilitates learning and provides a natural starting place for instruction, but inaccurate prior knowledge can distort learning. If new content gets connected to existing ideas that are over-simplified, distorted, or otherwise invalid, students may develop misconceptions instead of the target conceptions that the teacher is trying to teach. For example, students learning about U.S. history for the first time often overgeneralize what they learn about Jamestown so that they come to think of colonies as very small villages surrounded by wooden stockades. Most of these students later elaborate their concept of "colony" as they learn about events that occurred between 1607 and 1776. Some of them do not, however, so that they retain their original "Jamestown" image of a colony even when they begin studying the American Revolution. As a result, these students may emerge from fifth grade with an image of the American Revolution as a spat between King George and a few villages, rather than as a significant war between two large and populous nations.

Conceptual Change

Besides adding new elements to a child's existing cognitive structure, active construction of knowledge may involve changing that structure through processes of restructuring and conceptual change. Sometimes the needed restructuring is relatively minor and easily accomplished, but sometimes students need to undergo more radical restructuring that involves simultaneous changes in large networks of connected knowledge (Chinn & Brewer, 1993).

Merely exposing students to correct ideas will not necessarily stimulate needed restructuring because the students may activate long-standing and firmly believed misconceptions that cause them to ignore, distort, or miss the implications of aspects of the new learning that contradict these powerful misconceptions (Kendeau & van den Broek, 2005). It may be necessary first to help students to see the contradictions between what they currently believe and what you are trying to teach, and then to appreciate that the target ideas are more valid, powerful, or useful than their existing concepts. Drawing out students' ideas during whole-class lessons and engaging them in pair or small-group discussions are two ways to help students to recognize and correct their misconceptions.

Socially Constructed Knowledge

Some constructivist accounts of learning, especially those that have been influenced heavily by the developmental psychology of Jean Piaget, depict learning as primarily a solitary activity. They focus on the individual child who develops knowledge through exploration, discovery, and reflection on everyday life experiences. However, most constructivist accounts are variants of social constructivism. In addition to emphasizing that learning is a process of active construction of meaning, social constructivists emphasize that the process works best in social settings in which two or more individuals engage in sustained discourse about a topic. Participation in such discussions helps the participants to advance their learning in several ways. New input from others makes them aware of things that they did not know and leads to expansion of their cognitive structures. Exposure to ideas that contradict their beliefs may cause them to examine those beliefs and perhaps restructure them. The need to communicate their ideas to others forces them to articulate those ideas more clearly, which sharpens their conceptions and often leads to recognition of new connections. As a result, cognitive structures become better developed (both better differentiated and better organized).

Social constructivists' ideas have been influenced heavily by the writings of the Russian developmental psychologist Lev Vygotsky (1962, 1978). Vygotsky believed that children's thought and language begin as separate functions but become intimately connected during the preschool years as they learn to use language as a mechanism for thinking. Gradually, more and more of their learning is mediated through language, especially learning of cultural knowledge that is difficult if not impossible to develop through direct experience with the physical environment. Children initially acquire much of their cultural knowledge through overt speech (conversations with others, especially parents and teachers). Then they elaborate on this knowledge and connect it to other knowledge through inner speech (self-talk, or thinking mediated through language).

Social studies consists mostly of the kinds of cultural knowledge that Vygotsky viewed as socially constructed. He suggested that this learning proceeds most efficiently when children are consistently exposed to teaching in the zone of proximal development. The *zone of proximal development* refers to the range of knowledge and skills that students are not yet ready to learn on their own but could learn with help from teachers. Children already know things that are "below" the zone or can learn them easily on their own without help. They cannot yet learn things that are "above" the zone, even with help.

In some ways, ideas about teaching within the zone of proximal development resemble ideas about readiness for learning. However, readiness is passive in its implications. It suggests that teachers can do little but wait until children become ready to learn something (presumably due to maturation of needed cognitive structures) before trying to teach it to them. The notion of teaching within the zone of proximal development assumes that children's readiness for learning depends much more on their accumulated prior knowledge about the topic than on maturation of cognitive structures. A related notion is that advances in knowledge will be stimulated primarily through the social construction that occurs during sustained discourse, most rapidly with respect to topics currently in the student's zone of proximal development (Moll, 1990; Newman, Griffin, & Cole, 1989; Tharp & Gallimore, 1988).

Social constructivists emphasize teaching that features *sustained dialogue* or discussion in which participants pursue a topic in depth, exchanging views and negotiating meanings and implications as they explore the topic's ramifications.

Along with teacher-structured whole-class discussions, this includes cooperative learning that is constructed as students work in pairs or small groups.

Earlier in this chapter, we listed the key features of the transmission view of teaching and learning. Standing in contrast to the transmission view is the *social constructivist view*. Its key features are as follows (Good & Brophy, 2003):

1. Knowledge is treated as a body of developing interpretations co-constructed through discussion.
2. Authority for constructed knowledge is viewed as residing in the arguments and evidence cited in its support (by students as well as by texts or teachers, so that everyone has expertise to contribute).
3. Teachers and students share responsibility for initiating and guiding learning efforts.
4. Teachers act as discussion leaders who pose questions, seek clarifications, promote dialogue, and help the group recognize areas of consensus and of continuing disagreement.
5. Students strive to make sense of new input by relating it to their prior knowledge and by collaborating in dialogue with others to co-construct shared understandings.
6. Discourse emphasizes reflective discussion of networks of knowledge so that the focus is on eliciting students' thinking through questions that are divergent but designed to develop understanding of the powerful ideas that anchor each network.
7. Activities emphasize applications to authentic issues and problems that require higher-order thinking.
8. Students collaborate by acting as a learning community that constructs shared understandings through sustained dialogue.

The transmission view and the social constructivist view represent opposite extremes on important dimensions of teaching. In practice, most teaching lies somewhere in between these extremes, incorporating features of both views (with the particular mix depending on the situation). Table 8.1 presents the key features of these two views, with corresponding features arranged side by side. Study these comparisons to develop an appreciation of the contrasting forms of classroom discourse they create.

The Need to Build a Content Base

Teaching content-rich subjects (primarily science and social studies) is especially challenging in the early grades, as well as in multicultural classrooms or in settings where there is a wide range of achievement levels. In the first place, although students almost always have at least some experiential base to bring to bear, their prior knowledge about topics addressed in these subjects is often very limited. Furthermore, this limited knowledge base is mostly tacit (not organized or verbally articulated, and perhaps never even consciously considered), and it often includes many misconceptions. Consequently, primary-grade teachers and upper-grade teachers who have very diverse classrooms often are faced with the task of helping their students to develop

TABLE 8.1

Teaching and Learning as Transmission of Information versus as Social Construction of Knowledge

Transmission View	*Social Construction View*
Knowledge as fixed body of information transmitted from teacher or text to students	Knowledge as developing interpretations co-constructed through discussion
Texts, teacher as authoritative sources of expert knowledge to which students defer	Authority for constructed knowledge resides in the arguments and evidence cited in its support by students, as well as by texts or teacher; everyone has expertise to contribute
Teacher responsible for managing students' learning by providing information and leading students through activities and assignments	Teacher and students share responsibility for initiating and guiding learning efforts
Teacher explains, checks for understanding, and judges correctness of students' responses	Teacher acts as discussion leader who poses questions, seeks clarifications, promotes dialogue, and helps group recognize areas of consensus and of continuing disagreement
Students memorize or replicate what has been explained or modeled	Students strive to make sense of new input by relating it to their prior knowledge and by collaborating in dialogue with others to co-construct shared understandings
Discourse emphasizes drill and recitation in response to convergent questions; focus is on eliciting correct answers	Discourse emphasizes reflective discussion of networks of connected knowledge; questions are more divergent but designed to develop understanding of the powerful ideas that anchor these networks; focus is on eliciting students' thinking
Activities emphasize replication of models or applications that require following step-by-step algorithms	Activities emphasize applications to authentic issues and problems that require higher-order thinking
Students work mostly alone, practicing what has been transmitted to them in order to prepare themselves to compete for rewards by reproducing it on demand	Students collaborate by acting as a learning community that constructs shared understandings through sustained dialogue

and begin to integrate an initial knowledge base in the domain. This requires taking little or nothing for granted, teaching (in some respects) as if the students know nothing at all about the topic.

In these situations, teachers usually have to assume most of the burden of conveying new information to their students. You cannot rely on texts for this purpose because kindergarten and first-grade students cannot yet read informational texts fluently and many older students have not yet acquired a critical mass of reading fluency and study skills that would allow them to learn efficiently from reading. So, most of the content that you believe is important for your students to learn will have to be conveyed by yourself personally during lessons. You may use books, photos, physical artifacts, or other instructional resources in the process, but your students' initial exposure to new information will come mostly from listening to what you say during teacher-led classroom discourse.

You will need to work within certain constraints as you construct and manage this discourse. Your students' attention spans are limited, and they are not yet able to retain lengthy and complicated explanations, so extended lecturing is not a feasible teaching method. Also, these students do not yet possess a critical mass of cognitive development and domain-specific knowledge that would enable them to comprehend and use the disciplinary content structures and associated discourse genres that are used in teaching subjects at relatively abstract and advanced levels. For example, they have experiences with money and personal economic exchanges but know nothing of macroeconomics; they can comprehend basic ideas about rules, laws, and authority but not about comparative governmental structures or other advanced aspects of political science; and they can understand stories about everyday life and key events in the past but not abstract analyses of macro-level historical trends.

It is just as important for younger students as for older ones that you offer curricula featuring networks of knowledge structured around big ideas, but you cannot do this through lengthy presentations of content organized as systematic explication of concepts, principles, logical arguments, or other advanced disciplinary structures that young students are not yet prepared to understand and use. Instead, you need to stick to aspects of a domain that can be made meaningful to students because they can be connected to the students' existing knowledge, and especially to their prior experiences. In addition, it helps to convey this content using text structures and discourse genres with which the students already have some familiarity (and preferably, some fluency).

Narrative Structures as Teaching Tools

One particularly useful tool that meets these criteria is the narrative structure, because even the youngest students are already familiar with it through exposure to stories. Bruner (1990), Egan (1988, 1990), Downey and Levstik (1991), and others have noted that even very young children are familiar with and adept at using *narrative modes of thinking* for describing and remembering things that are important to them. That is, they formulate and remember in story form. The stories are built around one or a small group of central figures and include attention to their goals, strategies undertaken to accomplish those goals (often involving solving problems or overcoming obstacles in the process), and the outcomes of these actions for the central figures and others in the story. The narrative format provides a natural way to remember a great many of the details used to fill out the story, organized within the goal–strategy–outcome "story grammar."

This makes the narrative format a powerful vehicle for teachers to use in helping students bridge from the familiar to the less familiar. Children can understand information about long ago and far away when the information is represented as stories of people pursuing goals that the students can understand by doing things that the students have done themselves, can be shown, or can be helped to imagine. Just as children can understand fictional creatures (e.g., Hobbits) and worlds (e.g., Harry Potter's) conveyed through narrative formats, they can understand stories about life in the past or in other cultures so long as the depicted events lie within their own experiences or can be understood and imagined based on those experiences.

Many aspects of elementary social studies are amenable to representation within narrative structures, especially those that involve human actions that occur in steps, stages, or series of events unfolding over time. History is the most obvious example. Although it has its abstract and analytic aspects, much of history involves reconstructing stories of specific events (e.g., the American Revolution) or changes over time (e.g., in modes of transportation). Studies of children's historical learning indicate that much of what they retain about history is organized within narrative structures, usually compressions of larger trends into stories that focus around goal-oriented activities or conflicts involving a few key figures (Barton & Levstik, 2004; Brophy & VanSledright, 1997). They tend to think of the American Revolution, for example, as a fight between King George of England and George Washington and other Americans who resented his taxes and unfair treatment, not as a protracted and multifaceted conflict between a sovereign nation and a federation of colonies about to become a nation.

Elementary-grade children may be limited in their ability to understand the geopolitical aspects of the past, but they can understand wars as stories of attempts to gain control over land or other resources, voyages of discovery as attempts to satisfy curiosity and acquire riches, immigration as attempts to escape oppression or exploit economic opportunities, and so on. Most historical events and trends involved people engaged in goal-oriented behavior and thus can be conveyed using narrative formats.

Although it is less commonly recognized, narrative formats also are well suited to conveying information about many of the geographical and social science aspects of social studies, especially those involving human actions related to cultural universals. To teach about societies and cultures, whether past or present, teachers can construct narratives explaining how the people meet their basic needs for food, clothing, and shelter within the affordances and constraints of local climate and natural resources; how they communicate and travel locally and across longer distances; and how they act both individually (or as families) and collectively (through their governments) to meet needs and pursue agendas.

These stories will provide frequent opportunities to introduce basic concepts and principles of geography, economics, political science, sociology, and anthropology. Also, because they focus on humans engaged in goal-oriented behavior, they provide frequent opportunities to explore causal relationships and make explicit the human intentions and economic or political processes that underlie and explain human behavior but often go unrecognized and thus unappreciated by children. Stories about how key inventions made qualitative changes in people's lives, about why Americans eat relatively more wheat and beef but the Chinese eat relatively more rice and chicken, or about the land-to-hand processes and occupations involved in producing common foods and fabrics and bringing them to our stores all incorporate process explanations (of how and why things are done as they are and how products are developed) and cause–effect linkages (explaining why things are done the way they are and why they change in response to inventions).

This approach also offers two important bonuses. One is that, precisely because the stories focus on people taking actions to meet basic needs and pursue common wants, students are likely to view their content as interesting and relevant, and such a content base leads to follow-up activities and assignments that are authentic because they involve applications to life outside of school. Second, when the stories deal with life in the past or in other cultures, teachers can convey them in ways that help their students to see the time, place, and situation through the eyes of the people under study and thus to see their decisions and actions as understandable given the knowledge and resources available to them. This helps to counteract children's tendencies toward presentism when thinking about the past and chauvinism when thinking about other cultures.

Teaching for Thoughtfulness

Important social education goals such as helping students see the time, place, and situation through the eyes of people under study require engaging them in higher-order thinking and teaching for thoughtfulness. Newmann and his colleagues (Newmann, 1990; Onosko, 1990) described *teaching for thoughtfulness* as challenging students to interpret, analyze, or manipulate information in response to a question or problem that cannot be resolved through routine application of previously acquired knowledge. They identified six key indicators of thoughtfulness based on their studies in high school social studies classes. These indicators can serve as important guidelines for elementary teachers as well, provided that students are adequately prepared to engage in carefully structured discourse.

1. Classroom discourse focuses on sustained examination of a few topics rather than superficial coverage of many.
2. The discourse is characterized by substantive coherence and continuity.
3. Students are given sufficient time to think before being required to answer questions.
4. The teacher presses students to clarify or justify their assertions, rather than accepting and reinforcing them indiscriminately.
5. The teacher models the characteristics of a thoughtful person (showing interest in students' ideas and suggestions for solving problems, modeling problem-solving processes rather than just giving answers, acknowledging the difficulties involved in gaining clear understandings of problematic topics).
6. Students generate original and unconventional ideas in the course of the interaction.

Thoughtfulness scores based on these indicators distinguish classrooms that feature sustained and thoughtful teacher–student discourse about the content from two types of less desirable classrooms: (1) classrooms that feature lecture, recitation, and seatwork focused on low-level aspects of the content; and (2) classrooms that feature discussion and student participation but do not foster much thoughtfulness because the teachers skip from topic to topic too quickly or accept students' contributions uncritically.

Teachers whose classroom observation data yielded high thoughtfulness scores were more likely to mention critical thinking and problem solving as important goals that focused their lesson planning. In talking about the satisfactions of teaching, they tended to cite evidence of good student thinking about the content, whereas low-scoring teachers tended to talk only about student interest or positive response to lessons.

All teachers felt pressure to cover more content, but high-scoring teachers experienced this primarily as external pressure and tended to resist it by favoring depth over breadth. In contrast, low-scoring teachers experienced it primarily as internal pressure and thus emphasized breadth of content coverage over depth of topic development. All teachers mentioned that students are likely to resist higher-order thinking tasks, at least initially, but high-scoring teachers nevertheless emphasized these tasks in their classrooms. As a result, students described their classes as more difficult and challenging but also as more engaging and interesting.

Finally, thoughtfulness scores were unrelated to prior levels of student achievement, indicating that teachers can structure thoughtful discourse at all achievement levels. Taken together, these findings suggest that thoughtful, in-depth treatment that fosters higher-order thinking about social studies topics is feasible in most classrooms (not just those dominated by high achievers) and that teachers can overcome initial resistance and bring students to the point where they see higher-order thinking activities as more engaging and interesting than lower-order recitation and seatwork.

Fraenkel (1992) drew on case studies of high school social studies classes to identify factors associated with differences in effectiveness. He also found that the major factor determining the success of a class was the teacher, not student achievement levels. Less-effective teachers tended to present ideas ready-made rather than to ask students to develop ideas for themselves. They tended to talk to students rather than with them. Often they did not seem to have a clear sense of where they were heading. They tended to engage students in busywork and to stress memorization and regurgitation of facts rather than understanding of ideas. Many did not seem to like what they were doing, to like their students, or to be having much fun. Unsurprisingly, their students rarely were active learners and often were discipline problems.

In contrast, the more-effective teachers often engaged students in discussions. When they did lecture, they combined speech with use of the overhead or showing pictures, maps, or other visuals. Their questions tended to elicit discussion (not just recitation), and they often asked students to respond to one another's comments. Students often worked in pairs or small groups while the teacher circulated and interacted with them. They were often required to function as active learners by role-playing or giving presentations in class. The teachers made a point of engaging students in activities designed to help them understand and require them to use the ideas they were learning.

These teachers appeared to like what they were doing, like their students, and like their subject matter. They had high expectations for the students, emphasized depth rather than breadth of coverage, were able to explain things clearly using examples that related to the students' lives, had good wait times and were good listeners when students talked, demonstrated patience when students did not understand initially, varied their instructional approaches and types of activities, and displayed considerable command of their subject and ability to relate it to a variety of daily-life examples.

They also were highly attuned to their students. They encouraged students to take public risks by contributing their opinions to discussions and publicly discussing their mistakes. Yet they were quick to notice indicators of confusion or anxiety and to react by providing additional explanations, alternative assignments, or other scaffolding. They emphasized bringing to light students' thought processes for public examination and discussion. They maintained personal contacts with their students and arranged for frequent interaction among students through cooperative small-group activities.

Elementary Grades

While only limited research relevant to these methods has been done in elementary social studies, Thornton and Wenger (1990) reported observing lessons that exhibited many of the characteristics of thoughtfulness as described by Newmann and by Fraenkel, and Stodolsky (1988) reported that the quality of students' task engagement was higher during more cognitively complex activities than during lower-level activities. In addition, White (1993) described several case studies in which teachers set up contexts and arranged tasks to allow students to construct meaning interactively instead of relying on a low-level textbook/recitation approach.

Other chapters in the same collection of case studies (Brophy, 1993) provide examples of desirable forms of classroom discourse. Levstik (1993) presented the case of Ruby, whose approach to teaching history to at-risk first-graders featured a great deal of inquiry and discussion. Sosniak and Stodolsky (1993) presented the case of Carol Olsen, a teacher who used a conversational approach to teach inner-city fourth-graders about geography, history, and world cultures. In both of these cases, the students had limited prior knowledge and thus needed to be provided with bases of information from which to work, but the teachers nevertheless were able to emphasize social construction of knowledge rather than recitation as their primary discourse pattern.

Engaging Students in Reflective Discourse about Powerful Ideas

When preparing your lesson plans, develop sets of questions that will stimulate your students to reflect on what they are learning and engage in thoughtful discussion of its meanings and implications. Reflective discourse is most successful once students have acquired a common content base through teacher explanation, interactive narrative, independent reading, watching a video, and so on. You also may have occasion to use drill activities to reinforce learning that needs to be memorized, as well as recitation activities to check and correct understanding of the initial knowledge base. However, most of your questions should be asked not just to monitor comprehension but to stimulate students to think about the content, connect it to their prior knowledge, and begin to explore its applications.

Thus, *questioning* ordinarily should not take the form of rapidly paced drills or attempts to elicit "right answers" to miscellaneous factual questions. Instead, questions should be used as means for engaging students with the content they are learning. They should stimulate students to process that content actively and "make it their own" by rephrasing it in their own words and considering its meanings and implications. Furthermore, the questions should focus on the most important elements of the content and guide students' thinking in ways that move them systematically toward key understandings. The idea is to build an integrated network of knowledge structured around powerful ideas, not to stimulate rote memorization of miscellaneous information.

For each subtopic to be developed, *ask questions in sequences designed to help students construct connected understandings*. Use different kinds of question sequences to accommodate different instructional goals. To develop an unfamiliar topic, for example, you might begin with questions designed to stimulate interest in the topic or help students connect it to their prior experiences, then move to questions designed to elicit key ideas, then move to questions calling for reflection on or application of these ideas. Where students have more prior knowledge about a topic, you might wish to place them into an application mode immediately, such as by posing a problem, eliciting alternative solution suggestions and rationales, and then engaging the group in reflective discussion of these ideas.

Do not try to develop complete scripts for question sequences and proceed through them rigidly. This would not be possible because students' responses to teachers' questions are only partially predictable. Nor would it be wise, because teachers need to adapt their lesson plans to developing situations and take advantage of "teachable moments" that students create by asking questions or making comments that are worth pursuing. Nevertheless, an important part of goal-oriented planning is the planning of purposeful sequences of questions designed to help students construct key understandings. Such planned question sequences are much more likely to yield thoughtful classroom discourse than the inefficient patterns of questioning that occur when teachers have not thought through their goals in developing a particular subtopic.

Certain aspects of questioning technique can enhance the power of your questions for stimulating student thinking. First, *questions ordinarily should be addressed to the entire class or group* rather than to a single designated student. This will encourage all students, and not just the designated individual, to think about the question. Second, before calling on anyone to respond, *allow sufficient wait time to enable students to process and formulate responses to the question*. You may need to emphasize to students that you are more interested in thoughtfulness and quality than in speed of response so as to discourage overly eager students from blurting out answers, distracting their peers by saying "I know!" or pleading with you to call on them. Finally, it is a good idea to *distribute response opportunities widely rather than allow a few students to answer most of your questions*. Students learn more if they are actively involved in discussions than if they sit passively without participating, and distributing response opportunities helps keep all students attentive and accountable.

Even if a discussion begins in a question-and-answer format, it should evolve into an exchange of views in which students respond to one another as well as to you, and in which they respond to statements as well as to questions. To conduct effective discussions, you will need to have your goals clearly in mind, establish a focus based on the big ideas you are attempting to develop, set boundaries, and facilitate interaction but in other respects assume a less dominant and judgmental role than you assume in recitation activities.

If you are collecting ideas, record them (list them on the board or on an overhead projector), but do not evaluate them immediately. Once the discussion is established, continue to participate in it periodically in order to point out connections between ideas, identify similarities or contrasts, request clarification or elaboration, invite students to respond to one another, summarize progress achieved so far, or suggest and test for possible consensus as it develops. However, do not push the students toward some previously determined conclusion (this would make the activity a guided discovery lesson rather than a discussion).

The pace of discussions is slower than that of recitations, with longer periods of silence between bursts of speech. These silent periods provide participants with opportunities to consider what has been said and to formulate responses to it.

Dillon (1988, 1990) has shown that teachers' statements can be just as effective as their questions for producing lengthy and insightful responses during discussions. Questions even may impede discussions at times, especially if they are perceived as attempts to test students rather than to solicit their ideas. Instead of continuing to ask questions, you sometimes can sustain discussions nicely by simply remaining silent, by asking students to respond to what their peers have said, by probing for elaboration ("Tell us more about that" or "Perhaps you could give some examples"), by asking indirect questions ("I wonder what makes you think that" or "I was just thinking about whether that would make any difference"), by summarizing or restating what a student has said, or simply by making some declarative statement that adds to the discussion and indirectly invites further comment from students.

To encourage your students to participate optimally in discussions and get the most from them, you will need to socialize them to function as a learning community. Students will need to understand that the purpose of reflective discussion is to work collaboratively to deepen their understandings of the meanings and implications of content. They will be expected to listen carefully, respond thoughtfully, and participate assertively but respectfully in group discussions. Both in advancing their own ideas and in responding critically to their peers, they should build a case based on relevant evidence and arguments but avoid divisive or other inappropriate behavior.

In summary, recent theory and research suggest that, even in the early elementary grades when students are just beginning to acquire a content base, teachers' questions should be designed to emphasize sustained interactive discourse, not mere recitation. To the extent necessary, students should be taught to participate in such discourse in ways that support the development of the class as a collaborative learning community.

Summary

Traditional transmission models of teaching depicted teachers as actively explaining, modeling, and checking for understanding, with students mostly listening passively except when answering relatively closed questions. In contrast, social constructivist models of teaching emphasize development of key ideas through sustained discourse in which teachers ask more open-ended questions and students actively collaborate in constructing understandings by sharing and responding to ideas. Good social studies teaching will include both transmission and social constructivist elements, along with other elements that are not easily classified as one or the other.

To discuss a topic profitably, students need a common knowledge base from which to work. Elementary students (and especially primary students) often have only limited prior knowledge about topics addressed in the curriculum. Consequently, they often will need modeling or explanation from you or input from some other source to provide grounding for subsequent discussion. Your explanations should feature informal narrative (storytelling) rather than formal lecturing. Once the needed knowledge base is established, you should shift from an explainer to a discussion leader mode, asking sequences of questions designed to stimulate students to think about the meanings and applications of big ideas (and if appropriate, confront their misconceptions). The resulting discourse should feature sustained examination of a few key ideas, substantive coherence and continuity, sufficient wait time following questions, and other indicators of thoughtfulness. As much as possible, the teacher–student discourse in your classroom should feature the thoughtful exchange of ideas associated with the term *discussion* rather than the quizzing to elicit right answers associated with the term *recitation*.

Reflective Questions

1. Imagine an observer were in your classroom to determine how your students develop social studies understandings. Describe what will be occurring.
2. Imagine you are planning one of the early lessons in your next social studies unit. How will it look? Describe one of the final lessons. Compare the two.
3. Reflect on your last social studies unit. Describe how the phenomenon of conceptual change unfolded.
4. Describe how you will address the zone of proximal development in an upcoming social studies unit.
5. Reflect on a recent or current social studies unit. What does it take to seriously build a content base with your students? Make sure you consider your students with special needs.
6. How can the narrative format serve students from diverse backgrounds?
7. What aspects of your social studies curriculum are amenable to representation within narrative structures?
8. Think about an upcoming lesson built around discourse. What elements will you consider and why?

Your Turn:
Developing Content through Classroom Discourse

While you may not want to plan every lesson in your social studies curriculum to the level of specificity called for in the following activity, it will give you an opportunity to test your level of understanding of the content in this chapter. We encourage you to develop content using narrative and to apply our guidelines for using discourse. Questions need to be selected and scaffolded so as to elicit the desired social construction of knowledge among members of the class.

Unit topic: _____

Specific lesson topic: _____

Specific goal(s) for the lesson: _____

Major understandings to be developed: _____

Identify questions you will use to assess existing networks of prior knowledge.

_____

_____

Identify questions you will use to detect misconceptions. _____

_____

_____

Identify questions you will use to encourage students to connect prior knowledge with new information. _____

_____

Write the narrative structure for building a content base. (Imagine you are presenting new information to students based on their responses to previous questions. Write down your "story.") _____

_____

_____

_____

Identify specific questions you will use to stimulate students to think about the new content you have presented, connect it to prior knowledge, and begin to share its applications. _____

_____

Identify specific questions and/or summary comments you will use to bring closure to the lesson. _____

_____

_____

After you have carefully structured your lesson using classroom discourse as the major modality for developing content, prepare to tape-record it. Select several of the following criteria to guide assessment of your lesson. You can monitor your progress toward becoming an effective scaffolder of classroom discourse by continuing to tape your lessons and expanding the criteria for your reviews. This activity can also be effective for peer coaching and collaboration. Share the results with your principal. Listen for coherence, continuity, and wait time.

Students' work habits

- Do they give auditory evidence of working collaboratively to deepen their understandings of meanings and implications of the content?
- Do they clarify or justify their assertions?
- Do they generate original ideas?
- Do they show evidence of respect for each other's ideas?
- Do they make content their own by rephrasing it and considering its meanings and implications?

Teacher's behaviors

- Do I show interest in students' ideas?
- Do I model problem-solving processes?
- Do I acknowledge the difficulties involved in gaining clear understandings of problematic topics?
- Do I emphasize higher-order thinking?
- Do I distribute response opportunities widely?
- Do I combine lectures and discussions with illustrative materials and minds-on/hands-on learning activities?
- Do I encourage students to interact among themselves and respond to one another's comments?
- Do I demonstrate good listening skills?
- Do I encourage students to share their thinking in large- and small-group settings?
- Do I emphasize questions that move students systematically toward the key social education understandings?
- Is my pacing appropriate, giving students time to reflect, question, and formulate responses?
- Do I summarize and refocus when necessary?

CHAPTER 9

HOW CAN I DESIGN, IMPLEMENT, AND EVALUATE INSTRUCTIONAL ACTIVITIES?

Angela Barry, First-Year Teacher

It is the teacher's responsibility to create ideal social studies lessons and sets of activities. Teachers cannot rely on instructional materials that often require artificial exercises without authentic applications. For example, during my internship year I was required to implement a first-grade unit on communities. I was given a social studies textbook and instructional manual from which to teach. However, the activities in the manual involved many rote exercises, such as worksheets that asked students to color homes that were different and circle homes that were alike in a drawn depiction of a neighborhood. I knew that these activities were not authentic, so I planned a unit that was. The authors recognize these challenges that teachers face today and outline criteria for teachers to follow when developing their own authentic social studies units.

As I read this chapter, I began to write down criteria that make a social studies activity good. I plan to keep this list posted near my desk to remind me of the standards that I should strive for when developing my own authentic social studies activities. I also found myself reflecting on my past elementary and secondary social studies experiences. This caused me to add to my list of what makes a social studies activity good and possibly ideal.

For example, because of the strong emotional response that each movie elicited, I strongly remember watching *Roots* in the ninth grade and *Schindler's List* in tenth grade. As I watched these movies, I felt that I was being placed in the lives of the people of the past. The instructional activities that followed enhanced my understanding and engendered appreciations that I still retain. I also strongly remember learning about economics in the twelfth grade because it related directly to my life. I was taught how to invest in stocks and property, and I could actually use these skills to invest my own money. The activities associated with that memorable course matched its goals, and besides fulfilling all of the primary principles for activities, the activities also had strong motivational value.

Although I mostly remembered social studies content from my secondary education, this chapter showed me that powerful social studies learning can also occur at the elementary level. Elementary students also should experience social studies on an emotional level and be expected to apply the content to their lives outside of school. It is the teacher's responsibility to provide activities that enable them to do so.

Therefore, this chapter challenged me as a teacher. It reminded me that I am accountable for the level of learning that my students engage in. Even though the social studies textbooks and instructional manuals that I am given to work with may not be ideal, I can still create exceptional social studies activities using the resources in our natural environment. After all, "social studies is not what is in books but what is all around you."

In one of our studies (Alleman & Brophy, 1993–1994), we asked preservice teachers in senior-level social studies methods classes to reflect on their elementary-school social studies experiences. For each of three grade ranges (K–3, 4–6, and 7–8), we asked them to identify at least one activity that they remembered clearly and to explain what they learned from it. Here is what was written by a preservice teacher who apparently experienced a relatively barren K–8 social studies curriculum:

Powerful/Memorable Activity	*Explanation of What You Learned*
GRADES K–3	
(No memory)	(No statement of learning)
FOURTH GRADE	
We wrote letters to a specific state (Texas) and requested information about that state. When we got the information, we wrote reports and drew the flag, flower, and so on.	I learned how to write a formal letter, learned a great many facts about Texas, and learned from other students' posters and reports.
SEVENTH GRADE	
We used maps and grease pencils to learn geography, latitude, and longitude. For every chapter, we had to read and outline it.	I learned how to locate places by reading maps and using lines of latitude and longitude. I learned to outline.
EIGHTH GRADE	
We had to research a particular subject and write a report on it. My topic was the Holocaust.	I learned how to use the library and to find research materials, and I learned a great deal about the Holocaust.

The next preservice teacher's memories were typical in most respects, except that she reported a cultural unit rather than a First Thanksgiving activity at the K–3 level.

Powerful/Memorable Activity	*Explanation of What You Learned*
FIRST GRADE	
We did a unit on the Hopi Indians. I remember that we did a little program for the parents because I got to be the narrator and had the most lines. I thought this was because I was the best reader.	I don't remember anything about the play or what I read. All I remember is that the Hopi did not live in tepees like I thought all Indians did at that time.
GRADES 4–6	
I can faintly remember doing a report on a European country. Each person chose a country and researched it, then turned in a written report and presented an oral report to the class.	I studied Belgium. I learned what flax was and that it was one of Belgium's main resources.
SEVENTH GRADE	
By seventh grade I had a strong dislike for social studies and my teacher did not help one bit. All we did in his class was worksheets that were multiple choice.	(No statement of learning)
EIGHTH GRADE	
At one point we did a report on a president. I chose Andrew Jackson just because I liked the name. We had to research the president and then write a research report.	I found out that Jackson wasn't that great of a guy after all. I didn't find out about any of the other presidents, though, because no one shared with the class the information we gathered.

Our third example is from someone who reported unusually rich activities and learning outcomes:

Powerful/Memorable Activity	*Explanation of What You Learned*
THIRD GRADE	
We learned about economics by dividing into groups and "selling" supplies. Each group of sellers were also purchasers. Each buyer was given a different amount of money to simulate different income levels. Groups would set prices based on the competition. In the end, results were recorded and the class discovered how high and low prices and purchasing power had affected obtaining supplies.	Through this activity I learned how prices are set (competition), how high and low prices affect the supply of the seller and the demand of the buyer, and how income level affects what and how much a person can buy.

GRADES 4–6

Create a country. We were required (at year end) to integrate what we had learned about government, monetary systems, cultures, and geography to create our own country with currency, government, and so on. All had to be workable but could be unique.

This project taught me how interrelated and complex the components of society are. For example, geography determines climate and growing conditions. This in turn affects imports and exports, which then affect the economy.

EIGHTH GRADE

We viewed several movies on Nazi Germany and their treatment of Jews. Each movie was very graphic, portraying the true horrors. We then had to write about the impact we thought these atrocities had on history and the Jewish community.

I learned that history is not just past events' determiners and predictors of the future. I remember experiencing social studies emotionally and not just intellectually. This made learning history a completely different experience.

Before reading further, try this exercise yourself. What activities do you remember from elementary social studies? What do you think these activities were intended to teach you? What did you actually learn from them? What do your responses imply concerning your own ideas about good versus poor learning activities?

We will return to these examples and summarize the findings from our study at the end of this chapter. First, however, we will offer our principles and suggestions for selecting and implementing learning activities.

In previous chapters, we underscored the importance of using major social education purposes and goals to guide planning but also noted that such goal-oriented planning is not often evident in the content found in textbooks or in the recitation-dominant discourse patterns observed in classrooms. We suggested that the way to improvement lies in focusing content development more clearly around powerful ideas associated with social understanding and civic efficacy goals.

We continue with these themes in the present chapter. We use the term *activities* to refer to the full range of classroom tasks, activities, and assignments—anything that students are expected to do in order to learn, apply, practice, evaluate, or in any other way respond to curricular content. Activities may call for speech (answer questions; participate in discussion, debate, or role-play), writing (short answers, longer compositions, research reports), or goal-directed action (conduct inquiry, solve problems, construct models or displays). Activities may be done either in or out of the classroom (i.e., as homework); in whole-class, small-group, or individual settings; and under close and continuing teacher supervision or largely independently (on one's own or in collaboration with peers).

Our research has addressed fundamental questions about the nature and roles of learning activities: What are the intended functions of various types of activities? What is known about the mechanisms through which they perform these functions (if they do)? What is it about ideal activities that makes them so good? What faults limit the value of less-ideal activities? What principles might guide teachers' planning and implementation of activities?

Our work on activities began with a critique of two elementary social studies series (Brophy & Alleman, 1992). This work reaffirmed frequently voiced complaints about the activities components of these series, such as that too many of the activities were fill-in-the-blank worksheets or involved practicing skills independently of the content developed in a unit (instead of using the skills to apply that content in natural ways). Our analyses also pointed to several additional problems: Activities often were built around peripheral content rather than key ideas, were built around misrepresentations of content, were too cumbersome or time consuming to justify the trouble it would take to implement them, or ostensibly provided for integration across subjects but in reality did not promote progress toward significant goals in either subject. In subsequent work, we developed a framework for thinking about learning activities.

The Nature and Functions of Learning Activities

Our position on learning activities has been influenced by the ideas outlined in earlier chapters; the work of John Dewey, Hilda Taba, Ralph Tyler, and other major curriculum theorists; and the work of other authors who have been influenced by them. Zais (1976), for example, stated that the primary standard for the selection of learning activities should be how well the activities contribute to students' attainment of curricular goals. Other criteria for good activities were that they provide for the attainment of multiple goals, engage students in active forms of learning, help them to develop values and critical-thinking capacities, are built around important content, and are well matched to students' abilities and interests.

Fraenkel (1980) similarly suggested that good activities feature: justifiability (serve goal-related purposes); multiple focus (further progress toward multiple objectives such as knowledge, thinking, skills, and attitudes); open-endedness (encourage a variety of responses rather than just retrieval of answers to closed questions); potential for increasing self-confidence in ability to learn (encourage students to inquire, think for themselves, or solve problems); sequential structure (build on what came before and prepare for what will come later); transferability of acquired knowledge (enable students to apply what they have learned to new or different situations); and variety (suitable mixture of intake, organization, demonstration, and expression/creation activities).

Raths (1971) suggested that activities should provide opportunities for students to make informed choices about how to carry out tasks and to reflect on the consequences of their choices later; play active rather than passive roles as learners; engage in inquiry into key ideas, apply important intellectual processes, or address personal or social policy problems rather than just learn factual information; work with actual objects rather than just read about them or view pictures of them; examine or apply a previously learned idea in a new setting; examine topics or issues that citizens in our society do not normally examine; take intellectual risks; rewrite, rehearse, or polish initial efforts; share the planning or carrying out of an activity with peers; address their own expressed purposes; or assess their work using criteria drawn from relevant disciplines. He also suggested that an activity would be more worthwhile to the extent that it could be accomplished successfully by children operating at different levels of ability.

We have built on these lists and other writings on activities in four ways. We have (1) expanded them to include additional principles, (2) grouped the principles according to priority levels, (3) distinguished principles that apply to each individual activity from principles that apply only to groups of activities considered as sets, and (4) added principles describing how teachers might structure and scaffold activities for their students. Our theoretical position and set of principles are as follows.

Basic Assumptions about Ideal Curricula

Our position is rooted in certain assumptions about key features of ideal curricula. Most of these assumptions reflect basic principles that are commonly stated in curriculum texts but seldom reflected in the instructional materials used in today's schools.

Curriculum development should be driven by major long-term goals, not content coverage lists. Thus, activities should be included because they are viewed as means for helping students to acquire important dispositions and capabilities, not just to acquire cultural literacy construed in a narrow, "Trivial Pursuit" sense.

Content should be organized into networks structured around important ideas, and these ideas should be taught for understanding and for application to life outside of school. Teaching social studies for understanding and application requires concentrating on key concepts and generalizations that help students understand and appreciate how the social world works, how and why it has evolved as it has, how these understandings can be used to predict or control social outcomes, and what the implications may be for personal values or social policies. *Content provides the cognitive base for activities.* Coherent content structured around powerful ideas leads naturally to activities that call for students to think critically and creatively about what they are learning and use it in applications involving inquiry, invention, problem solving, or decision making. However, parade-of-facts content leads to low-level activities calling for retrieval of definitions or facts (matching, fill-in-the-blanks) or isolated practice of part-skills. There will not be many opportunities for authentic applications to life outside of school.

Activities are not self-justifying ends in themselves but instead are means for helping students to accomplish major curricular goals. They are designed to fulfill this function by providing structured opportunities for students to interact with content, preferably by processing it actively, developing personal ownership and appreciation of it, and applying it to their lives outside of school.

The knowledge and skills components of the curriculum should be integrated in ways that are consistent with the previous assumptions. Thus, the skills included in a unit should be the ones most naturally suited to important applications of the knowledge taught in that unit. Critical thinking skills and dispositions are developed most naturally through assignments calling for addressing value or policy issues that come up in the process of studying particular content. There is no need to manufacture artificial exercises to develop these skills. For example, instead of engaging students in artificial exercises in identifying logical or rhetorical flaws, you would engage them in policy debates or assignments calling for critique of currently or historically important policy arguments or decisions. To the extent necessary, you would model and provide instruction in the skills required for these tasks, but the skills would be developed through authentic applications rather than artificial exercises.

Different types of activities serve different functions, and these functions evolve as units develop. When introducing new content, you might emphasize activities designed to stimulate interest, establish an anticipatory learning set, or link the new learning to prior learning (such as by providing students with opportunities to compare/contrast or make predictions from the old to the new). When developing content, you might stress activities that allow students to extend and apply their learning. When concluding the unit, you might plan activities that help students to appreciate connections or provide opportunities to synthesize their learning.

In combination, the assumptions stated so far imply that *sets of activities* embedded within units should be assessed with reference to the degree to which they are cost effective as methods for accomplishing major goals and that *particular activities* should be assessed within this larger context. Given a unit's major goals, an activity under consideration for inclusion might be considered (1) essential; (2) directly relevant and useful, although not essential; (3) directly relevant but not as useful as another activity that serves the same functions more effectively; (4) tangentially relevant but not very useful because it does not promote progress toward major goals; or (5) irrelevant or inappropriate to the goals. For example, we have noted that we would emphasize the development of American political values and policies in teaching U.S. history to fifth-graders. With these primary goals, a unit on the American Revolution would emphasize the historical events and political philosophies that shaped the thinking of the writers of the Declaration of Independence and the Constitution. Certain activities might be considered essential for such a unit: activities calling for research, debate, or critical thinking and decision making about the issues that developed between England and the colonies and about the ideals, principles, and compromises that went into the construction of the Constitution. Other activities might be considered less essential but still relevant and perhaps useful: studying more about the thinking of key framers of the Constitution or about the various forms of oppression that different colonial groups had experienced. Still other activities might be rejected because of their focus on peripheral content: studying the lives of Paul Revere or other revolutionary figures who are not known primarily for their contributions to American political values and policies, or studying the details of each of the economic restrictions that England imposed on the colonies. Finally, certain activities would be irrelevant to the unit's goals: studying the details of particular Revolutionary War battles or constructing dioramas depicting these battles.

The key to the effectiveness of an activity is its cognitive engagement potential— the degree to which it gets students actively thinking about and applying content, preferably with conscious awareness of their goals and control of their strategies. If the desired learning experiences are to occur, student involvement must include cognitive engagement with important ideas, not just physical activities or time on task.

The success of an activity in producing thoughtful student engagement with important ideas depends not only on the activity itself but also on the teacher structuring and teacher–student discourse that occur before, during, and after the time period in which students respond to the activity's demands. Activities are likely to have maximum impact when the teacher (1) introduces them in ways that clarify their purposes and engage students in seeking to accomplish those purposes; (2) scaffolds, monitors, and provides appropriate feedback concerning students' work on the activity; and (3) leads the students through appropriate postactivity reflection on and sharing of the insights that have been developed.

Principles for Designing or Selecting Activities

Consistent with these assumptions, we suggest the following principles for designing or selecting activities. For more details, see Alleman and Brophy (1992) or Brophy and Alleman (1991, 1992).

Primary Principles That Apply to Each Individual Activity

This first set of principles identifies *necessary criteria that should be met by each individual activity considered for inclusion in a unit.* Failure to meet any of these criteria constitutes a fatal flaw that would disqualify the activity from further consideration.

Goal relevance. *Activities must be useful as means of accomplishing worthwhile curricular goals (phrased in terms of target capabilities or dispositions to be developed in students).* Activities may serve many goals, but each activity should have a primary goal that is an important one, worth stressing and spending time on. Activities that amount to mere busywork do not meet this criterion. Nor do games and pastimes, no matter how enjoyable, that lack a significant curricular purpose. Nor do activities that are limited to reinforcement of vocabulary or skills that are never used in authentic applications.

The content base for activities should have enduring value and life application potential, not just cultural literacy status as a term that students might encounter in general reading or social discourse. Even if a word, person, or event is currently a common term of reference, you should ask why this is so and whether there are good reasons for it to continue to be so indefinitely. If there are, the reference is probably useful as a way to remember some important principle. Thus, it might be worth including Franklin's quote about hanging separately if we do not hang together or Lincoln's quote about not fooling all of the people all of the time in a history curriculum, and perhaps even building activities around them (discussion of their meanings or debate of their validity or application). There would be much less justification, however, for including quotes such as "Don't shoot until you see the whites of their eyes," or "Shoot if you must this old gray head . . . ," let alone for making them the focus of activities.

There must be at least logical (preferably research-based) reasons for believing that an activity will be effective in accomplishing its primary goal. This seemingly obvious principle is violated with surprising frequency. For example, many supposedly motivational activities are not actually likely to develop motivation to learn the content. Consider introducing a unit on rules and laws by having students teach classmates some of their favorite games and by spending time playing those games. It is true that one can make connections between game rules and social rules or laws, but there are important differences between game rules and social rules. Using the former as an analogy to the latter may create misconceptions; time-consuming play is not needed to introduce the concept of social rules; and there is no reason to believe that playing games will motivate students to want to learn about social rules (if anything, it may cause them to resent this intrusion into their fun). Remember, an activity suggested in a teacher's manual will not necessarily fulfill the functions stated for it (if any). In fact, it may have no significant pedagogical value at all (it may have been selected via computer simply because it fits the theme or topic, with no concern for goals and major understandings).

Activities should be built around powerful ideas, not isolated facts or other peripheral content that lacks life-application potential. The geography components of current social studies curricula frequently fail to meet this criterion because they engage students in memorizing miscellaneous facts about a country instead of developing understanding and appreciation of how and why the country developed as it did and what some of its current trends and issues are.

Be sure that key ideas that provide the content bases for activities are represented accurately so that the activities do not induce or reinforce misconceptions. Activities often are based on vague or somewhat incorrect definitions (e.g., products are things that we use). Others feature misleading rather than prototypical examples (e.g., cultural studies activities that encourage students to develop chauvinistic stereotypes rather than well-informed understandings, such as singing slaves' spirituals or participating in "Indian powwows").

Appropriate level of difficulty. *Each activity must be pitched within the optimal range of difficulty (i.e., the students' zones of proximal development). It must be difficult enough to provide some challenge and extend learning but not so difficult as to leave many students confused or frustrated.* You can adjust difficulty levels either by adjusting the complexity of activities themselves or by adjusting the degree to which you structure and scaffold those activities for your students.

Structuring and scaffolding of an activity must be sufficient to enable students to accomplish its primary goal if they invest reasonable effort in attempting to do so. If they cannot engage in the activity with enough understanding to be able to perform its required tasks, or if these tasks are (in effect) performed for them by the teacher or by the structuring built into the materials, the activity's value will be nullified.

Ordinarily, activities should not combine difficult new processes with difficult new content. Difficult new processes should be introduced in the context of applying easy or familiar content. When the main purpose is to get students to apply new content, activities should employ easy or familiar formats and processes. Violations of this principle can cause students to become so concerned about the procedural requirements of unfamiliar activities (such as role-playing) that they fail to attend sufficiently to their content-related purposes (Blumenfeld, Mergendoller, and Swarthout, 1987).

Feasibility. *Each activity must be feasible for implementation within the prevailing constraints (space and equipment, time, types of students, etc.).* Some activities are difficult to implement because they require more noise or commotion than is feasible in most classrooms. Others are difficult to justify because they involve significant risk to students' emotional security or would be offensive to significant elements in the community.

Cost effectiveness. *The educational benefits expected to be derived from an activity must justify its anticipated costs (for both teacher and students) in time and trouble.* Some activities are not worth the time and trouble it would take to implement them. Often this is the case for activities suggested as ways to generate interest in a new topic or to culminate curriculum units. Other examples include time-consuming construction of murals or dioramas and overly ambitious pageant-like simulations and games.

Activities should not be burdened with needless complications that may distract students from their primary goals. Simple worksheet activities that should only require circling, underlining, or writing in answers often call for coloring, cutting and pasting, or other modes of response that take up time and distract students from content-related purposes. Many activities are complicated in counterproductive ways by converting them into games that place more emphasis on speed of response than on thoughtful understanding or that focus students' attention on winning a competition rather than on learning or applying content.

Secondary Principles That Apply to Each Individual Activity

The principles in this section refer to features of activities that are *desirable but not strictly necessary*. Each individual activity in a curriculum should embody all of the primary principles listed previously and as many of the following secondary principles as can be incorporated in ways that are consistent with the primary principles.

Multiple goals. *An activity that simultaneously accomplishes many goals is preferable to one that accomplishes fewer goals (so long as it is just as effective in accomplishing the primary goal).* In social studies, activities that allow for integration across subjects or inclusion of special topics (e.g., career education) or skills (e.g., debate) may be desirable. However, such integration should not interfere with accomplishment of the primary social education goal.

Most successful integrations occur, not as a result of deliberate attempts to inject integration into the curriculum, but as natural by-products of goal-oriented attempts to provide opportunities for authentic applications of big ideas. This process will identify numerous activities that incorporate various inquiry and thinking skills, as well as knowledge or skills associated with language arts or other school subjects. If this does not occur sufficiently, you might look for ways to adapt planned activities so as to incorporate more content from other areas or to shift from individual to cooperative formats. Be sure, however, that any such changes are consistent with the overall goals of your social education program and with the primary goal of each activity. See Chapter 11 for more about curricular integration.

Motivational value. *Other things being equal, activities that students enjoy (or at least find meaningful and worthwhile) are preferable to activities that students do not enjoy.* Typically, authentic, holistic, life-application activities not only are of greater pedagogical value but also are more enjoyable to students than information recognition or retrieval worksheets; isolated skills practice exercises; or boring, repetitive seatwork.

Like integration, motivation is an important but nevertheless secondary principle. Too often, curriculum developers or teachers treat it as primary by planning "fun" activities that lack goal relevance. No matter how much students may enjoy an activity, it has no curricular value unless it promotes progress toward some worthwhile goal.

Topic currency. *Activities that are constructed around currently or recently taught powerful ideas and that cohere as a set that builds toward major goals are preferable to "orphan" activities that are constructed around isolated content.* Inserted skills exercises or activities that are built around disconnected topics tend to disrupt the continuity and thrust of the students' progress through curriculum units. Furthermore, the isolated nature of these intrusions minimizes their value as learning experiences.

Whole-task completion. *Opportunities to complete whole tasks are preferable to isolated practice of part-skills, matching of words to definitions, or other work that does not cohere and result in closure as completion of a meaningful task.* This is another principle that will mostly take care of itself if activities are planned with emphasis on major goals and authentic life applications.

Higher-order thinking. *The best activities challenge students not just to locate and reproduce information but also to interpret, analyze, or manipulate information in response to a question or problem that cannot be resolved through routine application of previously learned knowledge.* This principle incorporates Newmann's ideas about thoughtfulness in academic activities. It implies that good activities will engage students in sustained and thoughtful discourse or writing about content in ways that cause them to think critically and creatively about it as they attempt to conduct inquiry, solve problems, make decisions, or engage in citizen action projects. The most desirable discourse activities involve discussion or debate rather than just recitation, and the most desirable writing assignments involve sustained writing rather than just filling in blanks.

Adaptability. *Activities that can be adapted to accommodate students' individual differences in interests or abilities are preferable to activities that cannot.* Other things being equal, activities that offer students some opportunity for choice in deciding what to do or autonomy in deciding how to do it are preferable to activities that lack these features. Similarly, activities that students of differing ability levels can address at differing levels of difficulty or sophistication are preferable to activities that require all students to use the same process in order to produce the same outcome.

Principles That Apply to Sets of Activities

The principles in the previous two sections apply to each activity considered individually. In contrast, the principles in this section apply to *sets* of activities developed as part of the plan for accomplishing the goals of a unit. Each principle might not apply to each separate activity in the set, but *the set as a whole should reflect these principles* (insofar as it is possible to do so while still meeting the primary goals).

Variety. *The set should contain a variety of activity formats and student response modes.* Within the range of activities suited to the unit's goals, variety is desirable as a way to accommodate individual differences in students' activity preferences. There might be both individual and cooperative activities, for example, as well as variety in communication modes (reading, writing, speaking, listening) and information-processing requirements and task forms (communicating understanding, responding critically, conducting inquiry, solving problems, making decisions).

Progressive levels of difficulty or complexity. *Activities should progressively increase in levels of challenge as student expertise develops.* As students become more accomplished in meeting the demands of various activity formats, they can take on more complex assignments, assume greater autonomy in deciding how to organize their responses, gather data from a broader range of sources, and so on.

Life applications. *Students should get to apply what they are learning to current events or other aspects of their lives outside of school (in ways that make sense given their levels of development).* Even if they do not involve taking action, such applications should at least include opportunities to develop understanding and appreciation of how the ideas currently studied in school apply to issues that call for personal and civic decision making. Much current instruction fails to include such applications, and when it does, many of the so-called applications are confined to decontextualized "academic" examples or cases that do not apply to students' lives outside of school. For example, students sometimes are asked to make predictions about a fictional country based on what they are told about its geographical features. If students are to develop appreciation for the value of geographical principles, however, they will need authentic opportunities to see how the principles can help them to understand actual past and current developments in our country and elsewhere in the world.

Full range of goals addressed. *As a set, the activities should reflect the full range of goals identified for the unit.* In particular, to the extent that values or citizen action goals are included along with knowledge and skill goals, the set should include activities designed to develop values or citizen action dispositions. Whenever a goal implies doing, activities should include actual doing, not just reading or talking about it.

Concrete experiences. *Where students lack sufficient experiential knowledge to support understanding, sets of activities should include opportunities for them to view demonstrations, inspect artifacts or photos, visit sites, or in other ways to experience concrete examples of the content.* Concrete experiences are especially important in connection with knowledge that children ordinarily do not get much opportunity to develop through their everyday experiences. To learn about conditions of life in past times or in different cultures, for example, children may need to handle artifacts, view photos or films, or read or listen to factually based children's literature in addition to reading textbooks. Resources of this kind are increasingly available on the Internet or in video and CD-ROM formats.

Connecting declarative knowledge with procedural knowledge. *Students should learn relevant processes and procedural knowledge, not just declarative or factual knowledge, to the extent that doing so is important as part of developing basic understanding of a topic.* In the case of facts or conditions that reflect the end results of series of understood processes, students should not only learn that a thing exists but also how it is produced and why. For example, sets of activities in government and civics units should go beyond teaching facts about government (capitals, names of officeholders) to include activities designed to develop understanding of governmental processes (what different levels of government do and how they do it) and citizen-participation dispositions and skills (voting, lobbying). Similarly, in learning about different forms of maps, graphs, and other data display formats, students should learn not just that the different forms exist but why they exist and how they can be used as tools to accomplish particular purposes.

"Natural" applications. *Activities that are "naturals" for developing understanding of a unit's content should be included in the set for the unit.* Retrieval charts and related comparison/contrast methods should be used whenever the content has focused on different examples of concepts (Native American tribes, geographic regions, governmental forms) or generalizations (e.g., population development tended to follow water transportation routes prior to the invention of motorized vehicles). Activities designed to develop understanding of sequences of causes, effects, and subsequent implications are "naturals" in teaching history. So are activities built around comparisons of historical events with contemporary events that appear to be following similar patterns.

Principles for Implementing Activities with Students

The principles discussed in previous sections refer to the features of activities themselves. The following principles identify ways that teachers might structure and scaffold the activities for their students.

Completeness. *A complete activity ordinarily would include the following stages:*

1. Introduction (the teacher communicates the goals of the activity and cues relevant prior knowledge and response strategies)
2. Initial scaffolding (the teacher explains and demonstrates procedures if necessary, then asks questions to make sure that students understand what to do before releasing them to work on their own)
3. Independent work (individuals, pairs, or small groups work mostly on their own but with teacher monitoring and intervention as needed)
4. Debriefing/reflection/assessment (teacher and students revisit the activity's primary goals and assess the degree to which they have been accomplished)

Effective activities require not just physical actions or time on task but also cognitive engagement with important ideas, which depends in part on the teacher structuring and teacher–student discourse that occur before, during, and after students' responses to the activity's demands. Even for an inductive or discovery learning activity, an optimal type and amount of teacher structuring and teacher–student discourse will be needed to maximize the activity's impact.

Introduction. *Students will need to understand the intended purposes of the activity and what these imply about how they should respond to it. These understandings are not self-evident, so you will need to develop them in the process of introducing the activity to the students. Good introductions to activities fulfill at least four purposes or functions:*

1. Motivating students' interest in or recognition of the value of the activity
2. Communicating its purposes and goals
3. Cueing relevant prior knowledge and response strategies
4. Establishing a learning set by helping students to understand what they will be doing, what they will have accomplished when they are finished, and how their accomplishments will be communicated or evaluated

Be sure to make the goals and purposes of activities clear when introducing them. Students should understand that activities call for goal-oriented cognitive and affective engagement with important ideas, not just completion of a series of steps to fulfill a requirement.

Also, cue any relevant prior knowledge. This might include comparison or contrast with previous activities, asking students to use their prior knowledge to make predictions about the upcoming activity, explaining where the activity fits in a sequence or bigger picture, or helping students to make connections between its content and their personal knowledge or experiences.

Initial scaffolding. *Before releasing students to work mostly on their own, provide whatever explicit explanation and modeling that students may need in order to understand what to do, how to do it, and why it is important.* To the extent that the activity calls for skills that need to be taught rather than merely cued, your introduction should include explicit explanation and modeling of strategic use of the skills for accomplishing the tasks that are embedded in the activity.

Independent work. *Once students have been released to work mostly on their own, monitor their efforts and provide any additional scaffolding or responsive elaboration on the instructions that may be needed to structure or simplify the task, clear up confusion or misconceptions, or help students to diagnose and develop repair strategies when they have made a mistake or used an inappropriate strategy.* These interventions should not involve doing tasks for students or simplifying the tasks to the point that they no longer engage students in the cognitive processes needed to accomplish the activity's goals. Instead, interventions should involve scaffolding within the students' zones of proximal development in ways that allow them not only to handle as much of the task as they can at the moment but also to progress toward fully independent and successful performance.

Students will need feedback about their performance—not only information about correctness of responses but also diagnosis of the reasons for errors and explanation of how their performance might be improved. To the extent possible, provide immediate feedback as you circulate to monitor performance while students are engaged in an activity, not just delayed feedback in the form of grades or comments provided at some future time.

Debriefing/reflection/assessment. *Bring activities to closure in ways that link them back to their intended goals and purposes.* Provide students with opportunities to assess their performance and to correct and learn from their mistakes. Ordinarily there should be a teacher-led *postactivity debriefing or reflection* that reemphasizes the activity's purposes and goals, reflects on how (and how well) they have been accomplished, and reminds students about where the activity fits within the big picture defined by the larger unit or curriculum strand.

For teachers, postactivity reflection also includes evaluating the effectiveness of the activity for enabling students to accomplish the goals. Depending on the relative success of the activity and the apparent reasons for it, you may need to take remedial actions now or adjust your plans for next year.

Optimal format. *Where alternatives are possible, implement an activity in whatever format will maximize the time that students spend in active and thoughtful cognitive engagement (and thus minimize the time that they spend being passive, confused, or engaged in busywork).* Many activities that involve communicating about or debating content, for example, are better done in pairs or small groups than as whole-class activities that offer active roles to just a few students and require the others only to listen.

Optimal use of instructional time. *If the independent work phase of an activity calls for forms of work that are time consuming but do not require close teacher monitoring, these aspects of the work can be done outside of the time allocated for social studies instruction.* Ordinarily, students should do activities such as reading and taking notes for a research assignment, editing initial drafts for grammar and spelling, or working on elaborate illustrations or constructions during general study periods or at home.

Extending the Curriculum through Out-of-School Learning Experiences

Learning opportunities in classrooms are necessarily limited and somewhat artificial compared to what is possible under more natural and unconstrained conditions. One way to compensate for this is to use the community as a living laboratory for social studies learning, and in the process, use the diversity of student backgrounds represented in the class as a resource for promoting social studies understandings. By "out-of-school learning experiences," we do not mean mere homework, which traditionally has focused on practice exercises designed to reinforce in-class teaching (Cooper, 1989). Instead, we refer to learning opportunities that expand and enrich the curriculum by causing students to think and collect information about how social studies concepts learned at school apply to family and community situations, then feed their findings back into subsequent class discussions (see Chapter 13).

College Students' Reports of Learning Activities Experienced in Elementary Social Studies

As an application and indirect test of the principles presented in this chapter, we asked preservice teachers to tell us about the social studies activities they remembered from their elementary years and to state what they believed they learned from engaging in those activities. It was important to ask what the students remembered learning because curriculum developers and teachers often cite salience in students' memories as justification for their activity selections ("Students may not remember the everyday stuff, but they all remember our reenactment of the First Thanksgiving"). Such justifications are questionable if the students remember the activities only because they were fun or if they report undesirable learning outcomes (e.g., stereotyped perceptions of Native Americans acquired through participation in First Thanksgiving reenactments).

We identified as "best" activities those that produced reports of noteworthy cognitive learning (a significant conclusion or insight) combined with desirable affective outcomes (interest or empathy). Thematic units, simulations, discussions/debates, and field trips most often emerged as "best" activities. Lectures/presentations were depicted positively by many students, mostly due to memorable media presentations or visits by resource people. Seatwork and construction projects were least likely to be named as "best" activities. Activities such as memorizing the state capitals, learning the states in alphabetical order, writing out definitions, answering questions about the text, coloring maps, doing ditto sheets, or memorizing the locations of states and nations often were criticized as boring or pointless.

Discussions and debates typically yielded positive reports (especially current events discussions, as opposed to discussions of events in the past). So did simulations, field trips, and activities that were embedded within thematic units that allowed for sustained study of a substantial topic (archeology, Native Americans, states, or nations). However, research reports on states or nations often produced little substantive learning. Apparently, these reports focused on activities such as looking up and listing the state's birds and flowers or the nation's exports and imports (without learning much about the reasons for these economic characteristics). Social studies goals would be better served if report assignments were structured with emphasis on learning the more important aspects of states or nations and the geographical, historical, and economic reasons why they have the characteristics that they do.

Many students reported constructing products. Often these were maps, photo montages, or other illustrations to accompany reports on states or nations, but many were time-consuming activities such as building a pyramid, making a papier-mâché globe, making flags, creating a puzzle of the United States, or building a bridge. The time involved in some of these construction activities raises cost-effectiveness concerns, especially because the learning outcomes associated with most of them were not impressive.

Low-level, repetitive seatwork was mentioned frequently and often disparaged as boring or counterproductive. Two other activities appeared infrequently but were singled out for pointed criticism when they were reported. The first was memorizing and reciting (the Gettysburg Address, the states in alphabetical order, etc.). Students who mentioned these activities usually did so contemptuously, pointing out that they no longer remembered much of what they had memorized. The other disparaged activity was taking turns reading aloud from the textbook. Rather than mere contempt, students reported this activity with resentment. In addition to sheer boredom, they mentioned the humiliation that it caused poor readers. Some of these students added that such activities made them "hate" social studies and/or the teacher.

NCSS Position on Powerful Teaching and Learning

The implications of the five key features of powerful social studies teaching and learning (meaningful, integrative, value-based, challenging, and active) described in Chapter 3 suggest the importance of combining content as described in Chapter 4 with activities that meet the criteria outlined in this chapter.

Meaningful learning activities and assessment strategies focus students' attention on the most important ideas embedded in what they are learning. The teaching emphasizes authentic activities and assessment tasks—opportunities for students to engage in the applications of content that justify the inclusion of that content in the curriculum in the first place. For example, instead of labeling a map, students might plan a travel route and sketch landscapes that a traveler might see on the route. Instead of copying the Bill of Rights, students might discuss or write about its implications for particular court cases. Instead of filling in a blank to complete a statement of a principle, students might use the principle to make predictions about a case example or to guide their strategies in a simulation game.

Meaningful. The teacher emphasizes authentic activities that call for using content for accomplishing life applications. Critical-thinking dispositions and abilities are developed through policy debates or assignments calling for critique of currently or historically important policies, not through artificial exercises in identifying logical or rhetorical flaws. Students engage in cooperative learning, construction of models or plans, dramatic recreations of historical events that shaped democratic values or civic policies, role-play and simulation activities (such as mock trials or simulated legislative activities), interviewing family members, and collecting data in the local community. Such activities help them to develop social understandings that they can explain in their own words and can apply in appropriate situations.

Integrative. Powerful social studies activities are integrative and cross disciplinary boundaries. For example, an activity that addresses multiple content goals might use one or more literacy genres. A group research project might draw from mathematics, literacy and even include a science-related activity.

Value-based. If the content goals focus on appreciation, activities might include ones that promote critical and analytical thinking, empathy, sensitivity to cultural likenesses and differences, and so on.

Challenging. Activities need to be intellectually challenging, not simple paper–pencil worksheets that require simple recall. Generally, more challenging activities will meet multiple goals. They typically involve higher-order thinking and require sustained and thoughtful discourse.

Active. Typically, "active" is associated with "hands-on" learning. This may or may not be appropriate depending on the content goals. For example, if students were studying shelter and the goal was to develop understanding and appreciation for the steps and challenges associated with construction, having students build gingerbread houses would not be appropriate. Visiting a construction site, observing the workers, and/or studying a series of photographs accompanied by an interactive discussion would be far more meaningful. "Minds-on" activities including prompts such as "think about," "listen for," and "observe" are examples of activities that are active yet do not include physical movement.

Summary

Instructional activities play a major function in elementary social studies. We encourage you to pay careful attention to the activities that are selected to ensure that they are all related to the goals, are at an appropriate level of difficulty, and are feasible and cost effective. Your activities should promote major social studies understandings. After all, what makes an activity worthwhile in the long run is not just that it is memorable but that it has led to important learning. There is a great deal of room for improvement here. It can be accomplished primarily by placing more emphasis on selecting learning activities with major social education goals in mind, emphasizing these goals when structuring and scaffolding the activities for students, and reemphasizing them in postactivity debriefing exercises.

Reflective Questions

1. How would you respond to a principal or teaching colleague who insists that all activities should be "hands-on" for meaningful learning to occur?
2. Imagine you have been asked to give a talk to building principals in your district. The topic is Instructional Activities. You have decided to use this chapter as the basis for your presentation. What unfamiliar but useful information would you include?
3. What previous misconceptions about instructional activities were dispelled as the result of reading this chapter? How will these inform your future practice?
4. How do you view the relationship between instructional activities and student achievement?

Your Turn:
Learning Activities

In order to assess your level of understanding regarding the principles for designing and selecting instructional activities contained in this chapter, we have provided an exercise focusing on a third-grade land-use unit. Study the goals of the unit carefully, then read each of the activities. Using the guiding principles, rate each activity as "good," "bad," or "conditional." Be prepared to give reasons for your decisions.

The content for this exercise was adapted from the third-grade Houghton Mifflin textbook, Unit 4, Chapters 9 and 10 (pp. 167A–215). The focus is the United States today. Chapter 9 addresses our current use of the land to meet our needs. Specifically, the chapter deals with agriculture, industry, and transportation. Chapter 10 focuses on some of the consequences of our use of natural resources, emphasizing the need for us to work together to solve environmental problems.

UNIT GOALS

- Develop an understanding and appreciation for how we use the land to meet our needs and wants. (The San Joaquin Valley is described to demonstrate how modern technology is used to produce huge amounts of food. Pittsburgh is used as the example of an industrial city because it occupied an important place in the industrial history of our country, its geographical location influenced its growth as an industrial giant, and its economic history reflects various periods in the economic development of our nation. Another theme woven into the chapter is the role of transportation, especially railroads, in carrying goods and people from coast to coast.)
- Develop an understanding and appreciation for the earth as our shared home, the importance of conserving our natural resources, and the consequences of our misuse of these resources.
- Develop understanding, appreciation, and life applications for solving environmental problems.

POSSIBLE ACTIVITY SELECTIONS

ACTIVITY	RATING	REASONS
1. Bring in five bunches of grapes and five empty tissue boxes without tops. Form five groups of students and have each group select one member to compete in a fruit-picking contest. Have students pretend that the bunches are fruit trees. The pickers are to neatly fill the boxes without damaging or bruising the fruit.		

2. Tell students that people have figured out how much each acre of farmland in the United States produces, on the average. The number is based on the total amounts of all types of farm products. Have students graph the following data on the overall increase in production, labeling the axes "Year" and "Amount": 1900, 146; 1925, 143; 1950, 213; and 1975, 440.

3. Have students work in small groups to investigate different types of farms, such as crop farms; flower farms; beef cattle, hog, and sheep farms; dairy farms; and poultry farms. Allow time for groups to present their findings in class, and encourage the use of visuals.

4. Arrange field trips to local farms of different types to give students firsthand knowledge of their operation.

5. Have each student make a chart of the produce grown in the San Joaquin Valley and indicate with a symbol which products could be harvested by machine and which by hand.

6. Assign groups of students to interview produce managers at local supermarkets. Have students find out where the store's fruits and vegetables are grown and how they were transported to the store. Ask each group to report its findings to the class.

7. Focus attention on the Benton painting on page 178, explaining that the year is 1930. Ask students what this steel mill would have smelled, sounded, looked, and felt like. Explain that steel workers form huge bars, sheets, and strips of steel from molten steel, which they must hammer, press, roll, and shape under very high heat.

8. Conduct a class discussion. Focus questions should include: "How might very fast freight trains be helpful to the farmers in the San Joaquin Valley?" "What do you think would happen to the transportation industry if someone invented a faster and cheaper way of moving goods?"

9. Work with a group. Make a model freight train out of shoeboxes. Draw on a shoebox to make it look like a certain type of train car. Load your train with freight. Decide where it is going and then tell the class.

10. Many tall-tale characters are heroes to certain industries. For example, Joe Magaree is a hero to the steelmakers, John Henry is a hero to railroaders, and Paul Bunyan is a hero to lumberjacks. Make up your own classroom tall-tale hero. Brainstorm the kinds of things your hero would do. Work in groups to write stories. Put all the stories together to make a classroom book. Vote on a title for your book. Choose someone to draw a cover.

11. Discuss wasteful practices with students, such as over-watering lawns, lengthy showers, and so on. Have students brainstorm others. Then have each student draw a picture of a wasteful practice that he or she might help eliminate.

12. Draw attention to the picture of Mt. McKinley on page 201. Tell students to pretend that this is not a protected national park and that they will determine its future. Divide the class into two groups. Have one group represent an environmental protec-tionist point of view and the other group represent ski resort developers. Provide time for students to prepare their arguments

and to present their debate. Explain to students that ideally we need to balance our use of resources and our protection of them. We cannot preserve all places as they are.

13. Create a large outline shape of a tree from used paper grocery bags. Attach it to the bulletin board and title it "Save This Tree." Then have students brainstorm a list of things they can do to save paper and trees. Have students write their ideas on pieces of paper bags, which they can color and cut into the shape of leaves to attach to the tree shape.

14. Have students work in small groups to create "Save Our Water" checklists. Their lists should include tightly turning off faucets, fixing drips and leaks, never letting water continue to run while brushing one's teeth, and using less water for showers and baths. Have the groups share lists and then compile a composite class list.

15. Have small groups compose letters to the Environmental Protection Agency, Waterside Mall, 401 M Street, S.W., Washington, DC 20406. Each group can request different information, such as a list of EPA agencies and their locations, information about what the EPA does, pamphlets about air pollution, brochures about how to start a recycling center, or information about a specific problem in the students' own community. Have students share the information they receive.

16. Conduct a class discussion. Focus it on the question, "How does farming in the San Joaquin Valley depend on natural resources?"

17. Have students draw a factory polluting the air, water, and soil. Suggest that students include billowing smoke stacks, a pipe dumping waste into a nearby river, and huge containers of waste in back of the factory. Then have the students make a second drawing of the same factory showing the pollution reduced through the use of filters, sealed containers, and so on.

18. Have students predict what would happen to a town in which no one stopped air, soil, or water pollution. Have each student write a paragraph describing the town after ten years of unchecked pollution.

19. Have students work in small groups. Use waste materials such as plastics, packaging, newspaper, and string to make a model of a national park.

20. Have the students participate in a class trial for some one who is accused of throwing trash in the park. Choose a judge, twelve jury members, witnesses, and the person who is accused of the crime. Have the witnesses tell the judge why they think the person is innocent or guilty. If the accused is guilty, the jury should decide what the punishment will be.

After completing the exercise, revisit those activities you have identified as good. Check your reasoning. Review the NCSS five elements of powerfulness. Which of them apply to the activities you designated as "good?"

CHAPTER 10

WHAT ARE SOME OTHER STRATEGIES FOR TEACHING SOCIAL STUDIES?

Susan Harvey, Teacher Intern

As I was reading this chapter, I could visualize the techniques and processes that went along with each approach. The questions asked in the opening paragraphs are thought provoking. They tend to make you ask yourself, "What are my big ideas? Why do I want to teach this particular lesson this way? Is it the best way for me to teach this concept?" Asking such questions helps us to formulate habits of good practice.

I will definitely use storytelling in my classroom; it's the greatest way for my students to begin visualizing concepts that they may never have experienced in their young lives. If I can make the stories "come alive" for my students, I have a better chance of "hooking" them to want to know more.

I would like to incorporate the arts into my classroom. In today's fast-paced, technologically savvy world, I believe the arts have been neglected. I would like to expose my students to all types of arts (relevant to the social studies we are learning), such as music, paintings, and literature. They can promote an atmosphere that is calming and thought provoking, yet exciting.

Children's literature will also be used. If it is fanciful, I will not use it to introduce new content during social studies; rather, I will select authentic sources. I want to avoid misconceptions. Curiosity will be piqued when we talk about far-off places that students never knew existed.

The teaching approaches that you use influence your students' attitudes about the content, their desire to learn about it, what they learn, their retention level, and its impact on their lives. Most principles and examples in the previous chapters featured teacher explanation, discussion, interactive narrative, and other common approaches to everyday lessons. In this chapter, we describe several other instructional strategies that we encourage you to consider as you plan your year. Pay especially close attention to those approaches that are least familiar to you, review the ones you have tried before with an eye toward new aspects to consider, and plan to incorporate at least one new strategy into each of your upcoming social studies units (one that fits the goals and enhances the development of the big ideas you have identified).

As you think about selecting approaches for specific units and questions, we encourage you to begin with your goals and big ideas. Ask yourself, "What do I want my students to know? Understand? Appreciate? Apply to their lives?" Next ask, "Which teaching approaches best fit my intentions?" Most often there will be more than one viable approach, and you should become familiar with a wide variety so that you can offer your students a range of possibilities with an eye toward balance. This is part of making teaching active, challenging, meaningful, integrative, and value based.

Some techniques require you to exercise almost continuous direct influence over how information flows to your students. Others place much more responsibility for managing the instructional flow on the learners, with you the teacher serving more as a guide. Most approaches represent mixed models, with the teacher and the lerners shifting responsibilities depending on the stage of the strategy.

As you plan your units and individual lessons, consider how children learn. For example, one way they learn is by direct experiences that incorporate the five senses: feeling, touching, tasting, smelling, and hearing. They also learn by acquiring knowledge through books, people, media, and so on. A third way is through the personal construction of knowledge that occurs when they engage in thought processes that connect new experiences with prior knowledge and organize them in some way that is meaningful for them. Chapter 13 features home–school connections that we view as powerful but underused venues for fostering memorable learning. Students can personalize in-school learning and organize it in ways that make sense to them by discussing it at home with family members.

Instructional strategies tend to feature three learning modalities through which learners receive, process, or respond to information (Ross, 1998). The most common involve expressing ideas audibly through sound (lecturettes, often referred to as direct instruction, storytelling, music, etc.); expressing ideas visually using paintings, photos/pictures, artifacts, co-constructed diagrams or graphic organizers, and so on; and expressing ideas kinesthetically through dramatic play, dance, and so on. Many strategies use a combination of these modalities.

While goals should be your first concern when determining which strategy to select, the nature of the content and learner profiles are other factors to consider. As you build your own repertoire of strategies, you will find that often more than one approach matches the goal and fits the content. Varying your approaches is usually a good thing because it helps maintain high interest in the subject area, but you need to think about students' familiarity with the selected strategy. For example, if you decide to use role-play in a lesson introducing new decision-making skills, make sure students have sufficient familiarity with role-play. If they do not, you might consider introducing role-play during literacy lessons, using a familiar story as the content. Then students will be positioned to apply the skills in social studies lessons. As a rule of thumb, avoid trying to teach both new skills and new content simultaneously.

Typically, you will start a new unit using strategies that call for direct experiences and knowledge acquisition, and end the unit with strategies that call for students to personally construct knowledge and have more influence over the instructional flow. There are instances, however, when your goals might lead you to reverse the order. For example, to build interest/foster curiosity in an upcoming unit on Canada, you might begin with an inquiry lesson. You might show a collection of artifacts (flag, coins, stamps, photos/pictures, maps, etc.), and pose the question, "What speculations can you make about Canada?" After a range of questions or hunches have been listed, you would shift to knowledge acquisition. You might show a video, take a virtual field trip to a part of Canada, or assign some selected reading. The key is to keep your eye on the goals and the big ideas to be developed.

As the unit unfolds, you might include storytelling, pen-pal communication activities, and a simulation. At some point, you might have students study the paintings of Cornelius Krieghoff, Robert Bateman, Emily Carr, and other prominent Canadian artists and discuss how the geography and history of Canada have influenced their work. At another point, you might have students debate the question, "Should (could) the province of Quebec survive as an independent entity?" The unit might conclude with a travel-brochure activity (with most of the busy-work, such as design, being done at home). The goal would be for the students to synthesize what they learned about Canada and share the information with an authentic audience—preferably local travel agents or families interested in traveling to Canada. The ultimate goal would be to educate the adults about Canada's unique features and convince them to put together a travel package and tour for interested community members. The students in the class could serve as assistant tour guides if distance is not an inhibitor and the trip is actually enacted.

It should be apparent from the range of strategies mentioned that the possibilities for a unit on Canada are endless. There are multiple resources to be tapped. The National Council for the Social Studies publication *Introducing Canada* (Joyce & Beach, 1997) is a gold mine of suggested approaches and available materials. It also provides content background for the teacher.

Bear in mind that you cannot depend on manuals supplied with the textbook series to determine which instructional approaches to use. You will need to assess suggested strategies to determine whether they offer sufficient educational value to merit inclusion in your unit. For judging strategies, consider the following questions:

- Does the strategy match the goal?
- Does it promote learning of the big ideas that I am attempting to develop?
- Do the students have the necessary skills to be successful with the strategy?
- What roles will I need to play to help students construct the big ideas?
- How will I balance the teacher and the student roles and functions based on the students' prior experiences, their familiarity with the content and skills, and the degree of dissonance they are experiencing?

- Across the unit, how will I accommodate the ways students learn: direct experience, acquired knowledge, and personally constructed knowledge?
- Across the unit, how will I vary the learning modalities to use those that fit the content most naturally?

In the rest of this chapter, we will describe strategies that are appropriate for elementary social studies and represent auditory, visual, and physical modalities and various ways that students learn.

Storytelling

Storytelling is a method of sharing our beliefs, traditions, and history with future generations. Rosen (1986) has suggested that the human brain is a narrative device that runs on stories. The knowledge that we store in our brain as part of our theory of the world is largely represented in the form of stories that are remembered far more easily than sequences of unrelated facts (Smith, 1988).

Stories and storytelling engage children and help them become personally interested in the past as well as the present. They help children realize how social studies is the study of people and their lives and not simply a parade of facts that they are expected to memorize for a test. Egan (1986) suggests that if teaching were regarded more as storytelling, the curriculum could become a collection of great stories of many cultures. This could make learning more engaging and likely to be remembered. Storytelling can be a powerful strategy when you select anecdotes that illustrate big ideas and general principles. Stories provide opportunities for children to make connections between their lives and those of people living in other times or places.

The stories can come from your own repertoire of personal experiences, from stories that have been passed down to you from previous generations, from children's literature, or from your own students. For example, if you were teaching about pioneer life, you might share stories that have been passed down through your ancestors about schools, curriculum and instruction, and approaches to discipline in the past. If you were teaching about the Depression, you might draw on what your grandparents have shared about their experiences with food and gasoline rationing or bartering among neighbors. Perhaps your family has letters, journals, or other artifacts to enhance the story about the stock market crash. If your class were studying social issues such as homelessness or hunger, you could draw on children's literature and retell stories such as *Fly Away Home* (Bunting, 1991) or *Uncle Willie and the Soup Kitchen* (DiSalvo-Ryan, 1991). These stories depict elementary school children in stressful situations, in ways that promote empathy and cognitive understandings.

Hamilton and Weiss (1990) describe several learning processes that are supported by storytelling. These include listening, speaking, sharing ideas with others and accepting their reactions, and marshaling ideas and stories to address a specific problem or topic. Of prime importance, however, is the shared experience among classmates and the bonding that ensues and transcends gender, social class, and culture.

As you develop your social studies units and search for ways of helping students make meaning and connect with the content both cognitively and affectively, consider the use of stories and storytelling. They offer familiar narrative contexts that support learning and can be very engaging. Make sure that the goal and big ideas do not get lost in details, and save enough time following the story for debriefing.

Visuals

The old adage that "a picture is worth a thousand words" expresses the power of visuals, but alignment with the unit's goals is essential. For introducing new content, you might select visuals such as pictures or photographs to stimulate interest, foster speculation and hypothesizing, establish an anticipatory learning set, or link the new learning to prior learning (such as by providing students with opportunities to compare and contrast or make predictions from the old to the new).

Other criteria for selecting visuals for new learning include selecting those that promote curiosity (e.g., a montage of photos that illustrates changes in communication over time); illustrate sequences or connections (e.g., photos that illustrate the land-to-hand relationship of wool to cloth and the idea that pioneer clothing was made out of local resources); broaden the meaning and cast the familiar within a global and multicultural perspective (e.g., photos that depict a range of shelter types and construction materials to underscore the idea that climate and culture, as well as availability of resources, influence the types of shelters that people build; photos to illustrate that children in various parts of the world dress more alike than differently).

Another criterion for selecting visuals is connection to your students or their families. For example, in a unit on family living, photos illustrating family life in Japan and Vietnam would be desirable if you had students who were native to those countries. They would help all of your other students to appreciate diversity and its contributing factors in new ways.

Visuals should be large enough for the whole class to see (if they are not, use multiple copies—one per table or group). They also should be up-to-date and timely; simple rather than complicated; likely to promote depth of understanding rather than emphasizing minutia or the exotic; gender and culturally sensitive; and free of stereotypes, misconceptions, and fanciful representations.

Do not think of visuals merely as appealing or entertaining. Rather, think of them as enhancing opportunities for students to thoughtfully process, integrate, and apply curriculum content that is structured in goal-oriented ways and accompanied by a great deal of teacher–student discourse.

Primary Historical Sources

Letters, diaries, documents, and sheet music are primary sources. They function as time machines by taking students back to faraway places and long-ago eras, making it easier for them to imagine the past and empathize about it. These first-hand examples are ideal for engaging the learners, stimulating higher-order thinking, and making the time or event more meaningful and memorable.

Your sources can be drawn from existing books that have compiled collections. They might include classic documents such as the Declaration of Independence or the U.S. Constitution; original newspaper articles acquired from the local newspaper's collection or online; or documents from government offices, individual businesses, or local museums. Residents in the community may also have deeds, journals, diaries, certificates, and other memorabilia to share. Perhaps least obvious, but extremely powerful, are materials you have in your possession such as your third-grade report card, your marriage certificate, your childhood diary, or a letter a family member wrote during military service.

The effectiveness of the primary source depends on its purpose, level of difficulty, and integration with other learning activities but most importantly on how its use is structured around big ideas with potential for life application. Questions to be answered when examining primary sources should be developed in advance as a guide for gathering information and interpreting and establishing meaning. Sample questions include: Who wrote the source? When and why do you suppose it was written? What values are expressed in it? How does this source align with other sources being used—or does it? Why do you suppose this source was preserved? A host of other questions could be generated—but as a general rule, less is more if you keep your eye on the goal and intended outcomes.

Artifacts

Artifacts are objects (such as tools or ornaments) that show human workmanship. They are products of civilization. They can be used as individual items to illustrate a point or show unique characteristics; they can be used in multiple numbers (such as a coin or stamp collection) to ground an inquiry lesson; or they can be used to display a range of objects and put together as an artifact kit to reflect characteristics of a group of people or items found in a certain type of environment. You can acquire commercially produced kits that focus on specific cultures, collect objects and create your own kits to focus on key ideas in your units, or ask your students to assemble kits representing major understandings being developed.

Artifacts add interest and meaning to content. If used as the heart of an inquiry lesson built around big ideas, they foster curiosity, sharpen observation skills, and stimulate speculation and higher-order thinking. Suppose you were studying money, and the general goals were to (1) pique students' interest in examining coins and bills up close and learning about them and how they are made; (2) develop an understanding and appreciation for the government's role in making money and controlling the amount that is in circulation; and (3) develop understanding and appreciation for the range of currencies that exist in the world, all of which are made very carefully and are exchangeable (Alleman & Brophy, 2003a). Showing a coin and bill collection could serve as a stimulus for unpacking some of the big ideas associated with the goals. In pairs or small table groups, students could examine the money, then as a class, make a list of observations and "I wonders."

Through interactive discussion, additional information provided by the teacher, exposure to informational texts, and perhaps some fact gathering on the Internet, the class could develop big ideas such as every country has its official unit of currency; governments are in charge of making money and regulating the amount in circulation; and currencies can be exchanged for equivalent value because of agreements among countries. Artifacts can be an excellent choice for addressing some goals and big ideas, if the artifacts are appropriately contextualized and used as but one piece of the learning sequence.

Computers

Computer technology has a place in the social studies curriculum, but there are issues associated with it, including philosophical matters, time constraints, and a lack of technology support (Buchanan, 2001). Technology is simply another tool and should not be used for its own sake. Its use must match the goals and enhance understanding of the big ideas under study.

Research has focused on the teaching of technologies and how software can affect student learning. Little has been written about the teacher's role in using technology to mediate students' learning, and in particular, learning of subject matter (Wallace, 2004).

Our own classroom observations as well as those described in social studies journals convince us that computers can be a valuable data-gathering source via the Internet. However, do not assume that if it is in cyberspace, it is credible. Cross-referencing is essential. A book by Berson, Cruz, Duplass, and Johnson (2004) entitled *Social Studies on the Internet* is a reputable source that provides an annotated collection of websites for use by social studies teachers.

Besides serving as a storehouse of information, the computer can serve as an electronic communication tool linking individual students and classrooms engaged in learning similar social studies information, a vehicle for inputting software for simulation games, or a way to take a virtual field trip via the Internet.

We remind you that the guidelines we offer for selecting instructional activities are equally appropriate for the use of technology: Does it match the goal? Is it at the appropriate level of difficulty? Is it feasible? Is it cost effective? For expanded explanations, we encourage you to revisit Chapter 9.

The Arts

The arts convey meaning and enlarge understanding. They can generate emotion by stimulating and expressing feelings. For example, a historian may craft language that puts the reader in touch with the time period; a painter can portray a character, a battlefield, or a landscape to enable the observer to acquire a sense of what it might have been like to be there; and a composer can create a mood that communicates the situation that inspired the composition. Artistic enhancements can promote meaningfulness by enabling students to participate in events vicariously and develop relationships with fictional or faraway people and places.

Visual Art

From ancient times to the present, people have expressed their thoughts and feelings through various art forms. Some of the most powerful influences on these creations have been the land and the people. Geographical features have always inspired painters, and native peoples, frontier people, trappers, and others have provided fresh material as well. Early painters tended to see the land and people through their own eyes or through the places where they were educated. This continues to be a pattern for some contemporary painters as well.

Art can be useful when engaged in the development of geographic understandings or learning about a specific historical period. We suggest you provide students with paintings—usually prints—that capture significant elements of place or time. Encourage students to discuss their observations using a set of guiding questions: What do you see? What does the painting suggest about the place or the historical period or event? Is it an accurate representation? Explain.

Music

Music is a powerful vehicle for extending communication about people and cultures across time and space. For example, through songs related to big ideas derived from a unit topic, students can experience feelings of loneliness, sadness, jubilance, struggle, and so on. If they are studying a particular culture, they can acquire a deepened appreciation for its customs and traditions through music and dance. For example, if Cuba or Argentina were being studied "up close," listening to folk music or watching video performances of the tango would evoke emotion and reveal cultural-borrowing phenomena in a very powerful way.

Music has potential for fostering respect for diversity in authentic ways. It can be used as a background to create atmosphere and interest in a topic, as a strategic part of a lesson to reveal a tone or feeling, or as a medium for communicating a point of view. Typically, students would not be asked to memorize lyrics or perform a dance, because in these instances the social studies understandings would be overshadowed by the "doing" of music and dance.

Children's Literature

Carefully selected children's literature has potential for deepening the cognitive and affective dimensions of content (Alleman & Brophy, 1994b). For example, in a unit focusing on family or a series of lessons about life during pioneer times, you might select *When I Was Young in the Mountains* (Rylant, 1982) for enriching students' understanding and appreciation for life in the past, or a chapter from *Little House on the Prairie* (Ingalls-Wilder, 1935) that describes the efforts and dangers involved in digging a well for the family. Both present powerful perspectives on family life long ago.

If you were teaching a unit on neighborhood or community, you might introduce the poem entitled *The General Store* (Field, 1991). Have the students listen to the poem, imagine what the store looks like, and determine if it is old or new. Questions to personalize the learning might include: "Would you rather shop with your family in a general store or a modern one? Why? What do the two types of stores have in common? Where could we go to find a general store? Why? Why are general stores disappearing? How is the modern store that your family shops in different?"

Literature often is inserted into social studies textbooks. In many instances, the selections run several pages and exceed space allotted for covering the content, causing many units to look more like language arts than social studies. Worse, the selections often focus on trivial and peripheral aspects of social studies.

Some even contradict intended goals or create stereotypes. For example, *The Little Red Hen* (Galdone, 1991) is a poor choice for a unit on friendship because it conflates personal friendship with prosocial and Golden Rule behavior. In the story, the Little Red Hen calls her friends to solicit their help in planting and harvesting a field of wheat. Her friends refuse to help her, so when it is time to eat the fruits of her labor, she refuses to share. The story features characters that are unhelpful and spiteful and carries an undertone suggesting that friendship is strictly conditional. These are not values we wish to instill in our social studies teaching.

Literature has potential for deepening cognitive and affective dimensions of the content, but it may introduce problems that you would prefer to avoid. Here are several questions you can use to guide your decision making: Does the literature source:

Match the social education goals for the lesson and unit?

Offer sufficient value as a source for social education activities to justify the social studies time allotted for it?

Seem to be of appropriate length given the social knowledge that needs to be included for adequate sense-making?

Enhance meaning and not trivialize the content?

Reflect authenticity and promote understanding of the content?

Enrich social studies understandings as well as promote language arts or other subject-matter content or skills?

Avoid misconceptions, unnecessarily shallow interpretations, or stereotypes in its depictions of people and events?

Creative Dramatics

One of the most basic premises underlying this book is that social studies instruction will have limited meaning for children unless it affords them opportunities to become actively involved in learning experiences that engage their heads and hearts and apply to their lives. Various forms of creative dramatics can add an engaging dimension to social studies lessons and promote empathy. Among the most valuable strategies of this type include dramatic play, role-play, simulation, and mock trials.

Dramatic Play

Unlike a drama which has a story, characters, props, and scenery and is intended to be acted out on stage, dramatic play has no script, no stage (in the usual sense), and no formal scenery; it simply has actors (your students) and an established place in the classroom for the learning experience. Often props are available as the students engage in the strategy. Students simply act out roles that allow the teacher to determine what they know, what misconceptions they might have, and what they wonder about. What children say and do as they act out the roles provides insights into the depth and quality of their learning and related feelings. Often, engaging students in dramatic play at the beginning of a unit stimulates their interest in the upcoming topic and allows you to do some foreshadowing during the class discussion that follows. Steps to follow for dramatic play include the following.

Arranging the environment. Establish a place in the classroom where dramatic play will occur. If, for example, you are about to embark on the study of clothing as a cultural universal, you might bring in a trunk of hats, shoes, play clothes, party clothes, work clothes, outfits from around the world that are worn for special celebrations, and so on. If you were about to launch a unit on immigration, you might have visas, passports, maps, globes, health records, luggage, an official-looking immigration officer uniform, currency from a range of countries, and so on.

Play. Part of a designated class period could be set aside for students to try on and talk about the clothes or manipulate the immigration props. Before you begin the play period, establish "ground rules" and share what you want the students to do and why. During the dramatic play period, look and listen as the students participate. On occasion, ask a question or engage individuals in conversation. One goal of dramatic play is to encourage students to have a vicarious experience that raises new questions that lead to further investigation.

Discussion. The debriefing that follows should examine what students felt, thought about, or were confused about as they engaged in the strategy. Typically, a list of questions (often cast as "I wonder . . .") sets the stage for upcoming lessons. Listing students' "I wonders" and noting misconceptions serve to inform future planning.

Research and future lessons. Depending on the age group and the topic under study, individuals, groups, or a combination of the teacher and groups will engage in research on questions and misconceptions that surfaced during the dramatic play. Typically, the results of the dramatic play comprise only a few of the big ideas for the unit.

Role-Play

In contrast to dramatic play, role-play tends to be more carefully organized and sequenced, and allows the students to grapple with a problem situation and resolve it. In role-playing, a few students enact a situation while the rest of the class act as observers. How a role-playing group resolves a problem—whether it be a decision about buying a bicycle (new or used, how to pay for it) or a decision about what to do if you witnessed a shoplifter while shopping in a toy store—becomes the focus for discussion and analysis after the enactment is completed. Role-playing situations are open-ended, and the role-players are asked to figure out how to resolve the situation.

The technique is often useful for helping students to develop a sense of social consciousness or to experience what it is like to "walk in another person's moccasins," and to view a problem from another person's perspective (Berman, 1990).

In *Role Playing in the Curriculum*, Shaftel & Shaftel (1982) recommend nine steps for role-play activities:

1. "Warming up" the group—setting the stage, identifying the problem to be resolved
2. Selecting the participants (for the early grades, it is usually a good idea to have the teacher as an active participant in the role-play)
3. Preparing the audience to participate as observers—establish with the observers what to look for, listen for, or think about
4. Setting the stage—during this time, the role-players should briefly plan what they are going to do. Since there is no script or predetermined answer, this should take only a few minutes. It merely involves the general line of action that is to occur. Steps 3 and 4 usually occur simultaneously. While the role-players are planning, the teacher prepares the audience.
5. Role-play enactment
6. Discussing the enactment
7. Further enactments—it is not necessary for every child to participant in an enactment. In fact, when this occurs, the strategy usually loses its effectiveness because students have to invent things to be different and the result is silliness.
8. Further discussion
9. Generalizing

The debriefing/discussions and overall attention to the goals and big ideas are the keys to role-play as an effective strategy. If used appropriately, it can enhance literacy skills and underscore the importance of thinking through decisions because they are usually multifaceted and do not have a single right answer.

Simulations

Simulations place students in situations that closely parallel those found in the real world. They simplify reality for the purpose of highlighting key ideas. The object is for each participant to make decisions and experience the consequences. The popularity of personal computers has enhanced the appeal of simulations. The California Gold Rush and Oregon Trail are two popular simulations for the middle grades that add a "real-world" dimension to instruction that many students find highly motivating.

If a class were studying conflict and the concept of territoriality, the "Road Game" could be a powerful learning opportunity. This simulation involves teams of participants competing to build roads through each other's land. It helps students recognize how conflicts develop as groups or nations pursue their own goals. Simulations, if properly selected, can go a long way toward "making meaning" that includes empathy.

After you have decided that a specific simulation is the best way to accomplish your goals and develop the big ideas to ensure maximum effectiveness, you should follow a basic sequence. It includes overview, training, activity, and debriefing. In the overview phase, you introduce your students to the simulation—what the goal is, what challenges the simulation presents, what you are trying to resolve, and so on. You assign the roles and lay out the rules.

During the training phase, you "walk through" the steps and confront potential problems. If the simulation requires groups, you work through both individual and group issues. Allow time for questions. Some teachers prefer to do a pretraining session with a select group of students who then serve as mentors during the class training session.

The simulation takes place during the activity phase. Your role as the teacher depends on the age level of the students, the complexity of the simulation, and the degree to which your students encounter difficulties. As the students gain confidence, your role shifts from clarifier and discusser to coach, and then finally to observer. Sometimes teachers interrupt the simulation to provide students with opportunities to reflect on their actions and the strategic moves they have been making.

At the conclusion of the simulation, you need to facilitate a debriefing discussion that addresses the conclusions or generalizations acquired, the strategies that were most effective, and what was learned about people's behavior under the conditions provided by the simulation.

Mock Trials

Enactments of trials include an element of competition that often stimulates high levels of student enthusiasm. Typically, they are used in upper elementary grades during the study of government, with specific attention to the legal system. They tend to take a lot of time, and the logistics often overshadow the development of big ideas. If a mock trial is the best approach for your goals, consider having students doing much of the work outside of class. The mock trial involves three stages.

Preparation. Introduce students to the purpose of a mock trial. Use fact sheets that explain information associated with both sides of the disputed issue. Next, identify the roles needed, assign them to individual members of the class, and provide these students with specific information about their responsibilities. Allocate time for students to engage in research in preparation for the trial.

Enactment. Savage and Armstrong (2004) provide a comprehensive explanation of how to set up mock trials, including the following sequence for the enactment:

- Opening of the court
- Opening statements by attorneys, with the prosecuting attorney going first and the defense attorney following
- Witnesses for the prosecution, with cross-examination by the defense attorney
- Witnesses for the defense, with cross-examination by the prosecuting attorney
- Closing arguments, with the defense going first
- Jury deliberations
- The verdict and adjournment

During each step, the clerk and judge make certain routine statements. You may want to give a basic script to the students playing the roles so the enactment more closely resembles a real court session.

Debriefing. During the debriefing, the big ideas are revisited and the general trial process is reexamined (to counteract students' tendency to focus only on the verdict).

Co-Constructing Learning Resources

This is a strategy in which the teacher and students work together to construct classroom resources, such as maps, charts, graphs, or lists of big ideas, as lessons unfold. This approach reduces dependence on commercially produced materials that often are narrow in scope, too "busy" (crammed with too much information), or likely to create misconceptions. Co-constructed materials have the handmade look of children's projects, and yet their logic and construction reveals the involvement of an adult (Alleman, Brophy, & Knighton, 2003).

Interactive timelines are examples of co-construction. Imagine yourself sharing a narrative with students about shelters in the cave days. Using a large sheet of paper and drawing a line horizontally for time, you could present big ideas, facts, humor, and appropriate drama as a way to establish a rich database. Artifacts, cut-out pictures, drawings, and teacher sketches (visuals preferred by many students) engender a sense for the way things were for a specific time period and pave the way for explaining how and why things changed.

Teaching about developments in transportation, for example, can be built around a timeline that begins with people traveling by foot and is structured around key inventions such as boats, wheeled vehicles, and engine-powered vehicles. Again, cut-out pictures, drawings, and teacher sketches can provide visual prompts as your presentation or an interactive narrative helps students realize that innovations such as dugout canoes for early water transportation were significant advances achieved through creative use of available resources. After constructing a rich knowledge base through the use of stories and interactive discussion, students can make their own timelines. They will still use the co-constructed one as a guide, as well as a visual prompt for the narratives that they may be asked to write in their journals.

Another example of co-construction involves *graphing*. Instead of trying to teach graphing skills using arbitrary information (data for use in that exercise only), you can co-create a graph that aligns with your social studies lesson, and guide the content and accuracy of the visual representation.

Sequence charts or *class-made books* are other examples. Suppose you were teaching the land-to-hand steps in the story of bread. As you initially teach the sequence, you can create the chart as a class, using the language of your students. During quiet reading time or independent work time, students will feel at ease in reading the co-constructed resource or drawing on the familiar words for their journal writing.

When teachers and students co-construct a resource in the classroom, it benefits both parties in several ways: Students feel energized and involved (as opposed to feeling passive or forced); they participate in the lesson and engage the content (since they are using what they have learned to create something new); and they render the content in their own words (making it easier for them to understand, remember, and work with later). The teacher relates to students as a member of the learning community (rather than only as an authority figure who stands alone and apart). Finally, both teacher and students have a visual display that they can use in the future (for reference, review, and example).

While co-construction might initially seem like a strategy for the early grades, we have observed its use in upper grades with tremendous success. It is engaging, and it particularly benefits students who have difficulty focusing or have challenges with language, spelling, and so on.

Field Trips

Field trips allow for direct experiential learning at sites within walking or short commuting distance from the school. Unfortunately, budgetary and liability concerns have reduced the frequency of field trips in recent years. However, the Internet has made it possible for students to take virtual field trips without leaving the school.

Many social studies units can be enriched through content-related field trips. For example, when studying the community and investigating the types of shelters available and the building materials that are used, one of the best ways to learn would be to walk around the neighborhood and observe firsthand single vs. multiple dwellings, houses, apartments, duplexes, condominiums, manufactured homes, and so on, and the resources uses to construct them.

The scope of the observations should be limited and focused. For example, when studying local shelters, it is not a good idea to meander from the goals and look at types of vehicles parked in the driveways, numbers of dogs and cats observed, or objects on the lawns. Similarly, if you are planning a trip to a local museum as part of your study of the lifestyles of Native Americans from your area, spending time in the geological section focusing on the rock collection would only be a distraction. Guidelines to follow for field trips include the following:

- Embed the learning opportunity within the context of the unit.
- Clearly establish the purpose or goal of the field trip.
- Make all the necessary preliminary arrangements and visit the site prior to taking your class.
- Prepare the class for the field trip. One way is to conduct a TWL activity: "What do we think we know about this? What do we want to find out?" Afterward, address "What did we learn?" Another approach is to have students predict what they will see on the field trip.
- As a class, prepare:

(A)	(B)	(C)
What will we see?	How it (they) will appear	What we observed

- Hold students accountable. You expect them to learn from the experience.

- Engage the students in appropriate follow-up activities. It is usually a good idea to have your students retrieve data on-site and record it for later discussion. With young children, provide volunteers with forms for keeping track of things and recording students' responses. Older students can do their own note taking individually or in groups. Back in the classroom, revisit the information to clear up any misconceptions and underscore big ideas. Typically, field-trip data are not adequately harvested. Follow-up activities should go beyond drawing pictures and writing thank-you notes.

Many potential field-trip sites would be nice to visit but are too costly or have other constraints such as schedules or numbers of observers allowed. Encourage families to visit them during out-of-school time (e.g., gathering specific data during the next trip to the supermarket or credit union, or eliciting adult volunteers to take their children to an evening meeting of the school board or township and encourage the children to report their "findings" to the whole class).

Case Method

A case study is an intense examination of an event, person, or thing. In social studies, it can be a way of helping students see the personal and human aspects of a culture or of a historical period, or the relationship of a historical document such as the Declaration of Independence or the U.S. Constitution to a contemporary issue. For example, fifth-graders typically study U.S. history. The Constitution and the Bill of Rights outline basic values that continue to serve as criteria for judging the adequacy of our laws and actions. Students could be presented with a case focusing on the right to privacy as related to such areas as the Internet, wiretapping, televised surveillance of public places, or searches of school lockers, with the goal being to understand the legal issues related to the case and how they apply to today, and to begin to realize that many legal issues involve a clash between two or more rights. Students can begin to get a glimpse of how the courts balance rights and responsibilities and reach a decision.

The local bar association could be an excellent source for securing a speaker to address the judicial power of the Supreme Court. For example, if your class were examining the rights of people accused of committing crimes, you might ask the resource person to explain the *Miranda vs. Arizona* case, which requires the police to inform the arrested person of his/her rights, including the right to remain silent; or the *Gideon vs. Wainright* case, which guarantees defendants subject to jail sentences the right to legal counsel. Generally speaking, the case approach is most powerful when it emphasizes contemporary issues. Linking classic cases to the here and now has potential for enhancing meaning and for helping students realize that court decisions are informed by policies, laws, and past practices. Guidelines to follow when using the case study approach include the following:

- Introduce the case.
- Identify the basic facts and explain the unfamiliar terms.
- Pose the key questions related to the case that link to the goals and big ideas.

- Allow time for students to study the case individually or discuss it in small groups.
- Conduct a whole-class discussion.
- Debrief to encourage your students to evaluate their reasoning by comparing their thinking to that of their peers as well as the judge who may have decided the case in a real court of law. Make sure the students adequately summarize and understand the relevant key ideas—for example, if the case were about privacy, the legal principles related to that right.

There are many commercial sources of cases prepared for classroom use. An example is a book entitled *Real-World Investigations for Middle and High School Social Studies* (Hoge, Foster, Nickell, & Field, 2004), which has a host of cases that can be adapted for use in the elementary grades. One is entitled "Mandatory School Uniforms," which fits nicely with a government unit. It provides a real-world exploration of power, authority, and governance.

Debate

Debate is a strategy used to highlight an issue by focusing attention on extreme viewpoints. The positions individuals take during the debate often reveal the depth of their understanding of the issues.

Debate is rarely used in elementary classrooms, apparently for lack of time. Social studies and literacy standards, however, call for students to learn to state a position and provide supportive evidence. These experiences pave the way for adult opportunities to actively engage in public debates related to civic action pursuits or politics.

Students can get very excited about subject matter that lends itself to taking a position and engaging in spirited discourse. For example, in fifth-grade U.S. history, as part of reviewing the contributions of past leaders, a question for debate might be, "Which leader had the greatest impact and why?" A fifth-grade class studying the Revolutionary period might be asked to debate the question: "Was the war justified? Why or why not? Provide evidence and cite examples to support your position." Another class studying individual rights and responsibilities might debate: "Should our school enforce a dress code that calls for uniforms? Provide evidence and cite reasons for your recommendation." If you had just completed a unit on Florida or the Southern states and were now launching a unit focusing on Illinois or the Midwestern states, you might ask students to decide which state or group of states would be the better location for beginning a designated type of business.

Preparing for a debate is an excellent way for students to sort through the issues and get clearer about what they think. Sometimes you might designate the position students must take in order to force them to grapple with both sides of the issue. Other times, especially if the class is divided in its position, you might allow students to stay with the view they initially favor. In either case, the task is to provide evidence, through research and concrete examples, that their position is more defensible.

Debates can be carried out in a group format, with each group responsible for gathering data to support its position. Group leaders should be designated to facilitate the preparation. Spokespersons for each side will present their arguments. A large group discussion should follow. Key points to keep in mind in scaffolding a debate include:

1. The question or debate issue should be stated clearly, specifically, and pointedly.
2. Each debate team should thoughtfully, and with adequate documentation, prepare its position.
3. Some class time should be allotted for exploring of the issue, gathering appropriate information, and preparing for the formal presentation, but students should work on their position outside of class as well.
4. Usually one class period is adequate for the debate. Time allotments for the speakers should be enforced.
5. Speakers should not be interrupted, but open discussion can follow immediately after all positions have been expressed.
6. Debating tactics should remain secondary to clear and forthright presentations of points of view and substantiation of claims. Examples to illustrate can add credibility to the position.

Inquiry

Inquiry teaching has been around for a long time. In fact, in John Dewey's classic book *How We Think* (1910), he outlined the basic steps of inquiry teaching that are still followed in principle. These include describing the key features of a problem or situation, suggesting possible explanations or solutions, gathering evidence that can be used to test the accuracy of the explanations or solutions, evaluating the solutions or explanations, and developing tentative conclusions.

Inquiry connotes "minds-on" learning—asking questions, exploring possibilities. It requires pulling ideas apart and putting them back together. It can be used at all grade levels; however, more guidance is needed in the early grades. While many experts characterize inquiry teaching as student centered, we believe that for it to be effective, it requires balance, with the teacher playing an active role throughout the process.

Let's imagine that you have designed a unit on shelter. Around the room you might display pictures, photos, building materials, and library books that reveal the range of shelter types around the world, the functions of shelters, careers associated with shelter, and so on. Provide time for students to peruse the range of resources and then conduct a class discussion focusing on "What do you wonder about shelters?" Students would be encouraged to make all sorts of speculations about shelters, including what types are found where, the materials that are used, how they are made, the functions they serve, the many careers associated with shelters, and so on. The speculations and questions should be recorded on a large piece of newsprint. They serve as the springboard for the unit and as a means of generating interest in the topic. Younger students and their teacher would then study the evidence throughout the subsequent lessons. Older students would be encouraged to gather information throughout the unit that would be used to test the accuracy of the original ideas. Explanations would be evaluated and conclusions drawn. Examples of some of the main points that would emerge through the inquiry/learning opportunity would include: shelter is a basic need; there are natural factors that affect the kinds of homes built in the local community as well as in other parts of the world; and there are a range of human factors that people take into account in deciding the kind of home to build, buy, or rent.

For an inquiry lesson focusing on a state, you could provide the students with a list of words frequently associated with it. For example, if your class were studying Michigan, an introductory list might include automotive industry, boating, skiing, mining, lumbering, Great Lakes, cherries, vineyards, and so on. The challenge for the students would be to first speculate as to what Michigan is like. After students' curiosities are sufficiently piqued, they should be asked to gather data to see how accurate their speculations were—and to see what they can unearth about Michigan that did not surface in the limited word list.

Another inquiry lesson might focus on the geography of a place. You could present students with a series of maps (i.e., physical features, rainfall, natural resources, etc.), one at a time. Each time, after studying the "new data," ask "Where would you place the capital and/or largest cities and why?" As more information is provided, students' ideas will be modified. Record their responses and revisit them during the unit. Part of class discussions should focus on student reasoning, clearing up misconceptions, and pointing out anomalies such as that the capital was relocated for political reasons.

While inquiry lessons are usually stimulating and curiosity is normally high, it is important for students to revisit their initial speculations and process their critical and analytical thinking as a part of the class discussion. Since inquiry is about extracting ideas and putting them back together again, it necessitates teacher involvement. At the onset of the lesson sequence, you need to set the stage and pose the important questions. During the data-gathering period, you might provide some information (or most of it in the early grades), monitor, and serve as a guide.

Even in the upper grades, your guidance is needed. For example, if you are asking students to work individually or in groups to address specific questions or hypotheses, it is usually a good idea to first "walk through" the process using one question or hypothesis with the whole class. Students' maturity levels and research skills will dictate the amount of the help you need to provide in gathering resources and synthesizing information. If the inquiry process extends over several days, posing questions to groups as they work and to the class as a whole will keep the focus on the goals and big ideas and enhance student accountability.

Summary

Because of the diversity of social studies content, the subject lends itself to a broad range of teaching strategies in addition to the ones discussed in Chapters 8 and 9. Presentation of content can be enriched through storytelling and the use of visuals, artifacts, information and illustrations accessed through the Internet, and the use of topic-relevant art, music, and literature. A particularly useful strategy in the elementary grades is teacher and student co-construction of learning resources such as timelines, maps, charts, graphs, or lists of big ideas. Other sources of enrichment include several forms of creative dramatics (dramatic play, role-play, simulations, and mock trials). Field trips and case studies provide opportunities for in-depth study of particular examples of concepts or principles emphasized in a unit. Debates provide an engaging way for students to learn and think about enduring issues, especially those that involve conflicts between basic rights or principles of justice. Inquiry activities call for students to conduct research on a problem or issue, then collate the obtained information and develop a well-argued conclusion or position. When used appropriately, these alternative strategies make social studies more powerful by enriching its content base or engaging students in synthesis, analysis, evaluation, or other higher-order thinking about the content.

Think carefully about your selection of teaching approaches to ensure it matches your goals, promotes understanding of the big ideas, is at the appropriate level of difficulty, does not call for the development of new content and skills simultaneously, and is cost effective in terms of time and trouble. Using a variety of approaches over time acknowledges diversity and establishes the groundwork for an interesting, engaging, and meaningful social studies program.

Reflective Questions

1. What strategies do you consider most challenging for students? Why? For teachers? Why?
2. Imagine you are encouraged by your school leader to consider incorporating all of the strategies described in this chapter over the course of the school year. How would you build them into your long-range plans?
3. Debate and role-play are examples of strategies that have been around for a long time, yet they do not typically occur in social studies. How would you explain this? Where might these approaches be used in your curriculum?
4. Co-constructing is a relatively recent strategy being used during social studies. What do you see as advantages? Disadvantages? How might you address them?
5. Storytelling, sometimes considered a disappearing art, is resurfacing as a powerful strategy for promoting memorable learning. What do you view as its inherent challenges? How will you overcome them in order to incorporate this powerful strategy into your repertoire?
6. Teachers often associate storytelling with the early grades. What modifications, if any, would you propose for fourth- through eighth-graders? What are content examples where storytelling could be particularly beneficial and why?
7. Although the use of inquiry has been around since the early 1900s, teachers and students' experiences have been varied. Describe an optimal inquiry lesson. Be sure you include the roles and responsibilities for both the students and the teacher. What makes the lesson exceptional?

Your Turn:
Strategies for Teaching Elementary Social Studies

Study an upcoming social studies unit carefully with an eye toward adding at least one new strategy that will potentially make the learning experience more memorable for your students. Ask yourself the following questions to ensure that you have made an intelligent choice:

- What strategy, if added, could enhance understanding of the selected set of big ideas?
- Does the strategy match the goals, and is it appropriate for the content I have selected?
- Do the students have the necessary skills to be successful with the strategy?
- What sorts of unique features does the selected strategy have—and have I adequately addressed them?
- Have I clearly thought through my role and function as the teacher? Students' roles and functions?
- Have I mentally mapped the steps/procedures that need to be followed?
- How can I describe what the strategy will look like to an outsider when in process in my classroom?
- What sorts of behaviors and understandings do I expect my students to acquire as the result of the selected strategy?

CHAPTER 11

WHAT IS THE ROLE OF CURRICULAR INTEGRATION?

JoAnne West, Michigan State University Honors College, Elementary Education Major

Instead of making a blanket statement that integration is always the best idea, the authors right away let the reader know that although integration can be effective, there are some very poor ways of integrating curriculum. They dissect the different types of desirable integration with good reasoning and examples. The specific books and lesson ideas for teachers were helpful too. The background information on research on literacy learning was particularly pertinent. As a future educator, I am more persuaded to engage in this approach to integration knowing that my students not only will learn more in their content areas (i.e., social studies, science, math, etc.) but also will improve their scores on standardized literacy tests. This example was great!

The authors' discussion of effective and ineffective integration activities also brought to mind some of the powerful social studies lessons I remember. For example, my fourth-grade teacher taught a unit on China in which we learned about the country and then assumed the role of Chinese students in dress, behavior, and lessons. We were taught in the style of a Chinese classroom but still worked on other core subjects, such as math, reading, and science. The unit was particularly effective in emphasizing major concepts and allowing us to apply our knowledge of China to our everyday lives. Powerful teaching does result in memorable learning.

Curriculum integration appears to be an obviously good idea. Articles and in-service speakers extol its potential for enhancing the meaningfulness of what is taught, for saving teachers' time by reducing the need to make so many preparations, for reducing the need to cover everything, and for making it possible to teach knowledge and skills simultaneously. For social studies and other subjects that suffered reduced time allocations as a result of the back-to-basics movement and high-stakes testing, integration is pictured as a way to restore needed content emphasis. In general, integration is seen as a viable response to problems of content balance and as a way to save time and make for more natural and holistic learning.

These seemingly compelling arguments have predisposed most educators to view integration in social studies as a desirable curriculum feature. Indeed, the implicit maxim is "the more integration, the better." A few years ago, we shared this view, and we still find it hard to resist the notion that integration is a good idea—in the abstract. However, we have become more cautious after examining the best-selling elementary social studies series, observing in classrooms, and talking to teachers about their integration practices. We have found some desirable forms of integration but also many undesirable ones.

Desirable Integration

The key to successful integration is that it results in enhanced understanding and appreciation of subject-matter content and processes in ways that promote progress toward social education goals. For example, adding content drawn from another subject can enrich the content of social studies (e.g., reading about and displaying the works of an artist can enhance the study of a historical period). Adding science content related to technology can enrich understanding of social issues. Using a powerful literary source can add interest and appeal to the study of the Revolutionary War and help develop students' understanding and appreciation of the origins of U.S. political values and policies.

Literary sources need to be chosen carefully, however, so as to develop topics in ways that promote progress toward major social education goals. For example, if the goal in the early grades is to enrich students' understanding and appreciation of family life in the past, *When I was Young in the Mountains* would be an appropriate selection to include. If the goal is to develop a perspective regarding pioneer life, a chapter or two from *Little House on the Prairie* might be more appropriate. The latter novel describes the efforts and dangers involved in digging a well. It is written from a child's point of view—very engaging to a youngster—and it presents a powerful glimpse of pioneer life that enriches the social studies curriculum.

Some forms of subject-matter integration are the result of necessity. For example, certain topics are primarily identified with one subject but require applications of another to be learned meaningfully. Map and globe studies are part of geography, and consumer education is part of economics, but both of these topics require mathematical knowledge and skills.

Recent research on literacy learning (Duke & Bennett-Armistead, 2003) suggests that acquiring skills in the use of informational texts results in both more informed citizens regarding content and higher scores on standardized literacy measures. Speaking and writing skills introduced and practiced during literacy and applied in social studies can enhance meaningfulness in both subjects. For example, students might be asked to interview business people about an urban renewal project as part of a social studies unit focusing on the city. Using the literacy skills in an authentic way results in acquisition of subject-matter knowledge, promotes a sense of efficacy, and makes learning more powerful.

Accountability Considerations

The focus of the instruction and the accountability pressures placed on students may be on the knowledge, the processes, or both. If students were asked to write to their political representatives about their legislative roles or policy positions, the assignment would be primarily a social studies activity, although it would include application of writing skills. In contrast, students might be asked to write about an imaginary visit to the White House as an exercise in descriptive writing. If the emphasis in structuring and grading this assignment were placed on the functions of the president, it would be mostly a social studies activity. However, if the emphasis were on technical aspects of composition and form, it would be mostly a language arts activity—and should not count against social studies instructional time. Of course, assessment and grading could be done using criteria drawn from both subjects.

As another example, students who were studying book-reporting skills in language arts and the American Revolution in social studies might be asked to write biographies on key Revolutionary figures. This assignment might promote progress toward important goals in both subjects, especially if the goals were made clear to the students and the reports were graded separately for compositional features and for historical content.

Examples of Appropriate Integrative Activities

For an activity to be considered part of the social studies curriculum, its primary focus should be on one of the social education goals established for the current social studies unit—a goal that would be pursued whether or not this particular activity were included. Other guiding principles that you can use to determine whether an integrative activity is appropriate for social studies include the following: The activity must represent social studies appropriately and not distort or trivialize its subject matter; the benefits to social education must justify the activity's costs in time and trouble; the activity must be geared to the appropriate level of difficulty; and it must be feasible for implementation within the constraints under which you must work.

Examples of appropriate integrative activities that we have found in social studies materials fall into three major categories:

1. Necessarily integrative activities that focus on topics that draw on content from more than one subject area

2. Authentic applications in which skills learned in one subject area are used to process or apply knowledge used in another
3. Enrichment activities that help personalize content, make it more concrete, enhance learner curiosity, or add an important affective perspective

Integrative Activities That Focus on Topics That Draw Content from More Than One Subject

Some topics inherently cut across subjects. For example, we have noted that map and globe studies are part of geography, but they also require applications of mathematical knowledge and skills. We encountered a map activity for the early grades that calls for students to go on a walking trip around the school campus, make sketches of its key features, and measure distances. After recording their measurements, they return to the classroom and make a map to scale. After completing the map, they are to revisit the route and make any necessary corrections. Finally, they are to add pictures to enhance the sketches and design a legend so that the map will make sense to visitors to the school and to new students who need to be oriented to the school site. Mathematics and geography combined make this a meaningful learning experience.

An elementary social studies unit that focuses on needs and wants includes teaching about an economic decision-making model. A key activity calls for applying this model to decide which bicycle is the best buy: a new model, last year's model, a used bicycle that can be purchased at a garage sale for a mere portion of the original price, or another used one that is in good condition but needs new tires. Prices are attached to each model. Students are then encouraged to use their economics and mathematics knowledge to decide what constitutes the best buy; discuss alternatives and consequences; and finally, individually and then as a group, decide which bicycle to purchase.

In an upper-grade unit in which a major goal is to develop understanding regarding the trade-offs that result from technological change, one activity calls for students to read a case study and discuss the pros and cons of introducing robotics into a factory setting. Both science and social studies issues are to be examined as a means of illustrating that change results in problems as well as fresh and efficient practices.

Integrative Activities in Which Skills Learned in One Subject Are Used to Process or Apply Knowledge Learned in Another

If planned carefully, the instruction and the accountability expectations may include both knowledge and processes. For example, in a unit addressing equity in America, assigning a report on a famous American who helped make U.S. society more equitable would be appropriate if the students had mastered report writing in language arts. However, bear in mind that activities ordinarily should not require students to cope with new processes and new knowledge simultaneously.

The following examples also focus on social studies content goals but integrate skills from other subjects. A history activity calls for students to write an essay explaining how the colonial plantation differed from today's large farms. With proper structuring and scaffolding by the teacher, this activity could be useful in extending understanding and promoting critical thinking about how the nature and economics of farming have changed over time in response to inventions. A creative writing activity calls for students to imagine that they were among the Native Americans forced to endure the Trail of Tears journey, and to write diaries describing their experiences, attitudes, and future expectations. This topic provides a good basis for creative writing. The assignment should deepen understanding of the events involved and help students to develop sympathetic and positive attitudes toward Native Americans.

Another activity, part of a unit on the Middle East, asks students to analyze newspaper and magazine articles to identify biases and to explain the points of view expressed and the factors that contribute to developing them. Here, communication skills addressed in language arts are applied to a real-life critical-thinking situation in ways that encourage students to begin to see the power in becoming thoughtful, astute readers.

Enrichment Activities That Help to Personalize Content, Make It More Concrete, Enhance Learner Curiosity, or Add an Important Affective Perspective

In an early elementary social studies unit on families, with a goal to develop understanding and appreciation for peoples' needs and wants, literature is used to enhance children's ideas. The teacher is directed to read a story to the students about a person wanting something (Cinderella, King Midas), then pose questions such as "Were these people wise to want the things they did?" "What were the things these people really needed?" The teacher is to continue the lesson by explaining that certain things people need and want cannot be purchased with money. Students are then to imagine what some of these resources might be (e.g., love, caring, kindness, and friends). This activity provides a nice departure from the often-sterile conception of needs and wants, and it appropriately adds an affective dimension that speaks to the ideas that valuable things cannot always be purchased and that there are ways, besides "things," to make people happy.

Activities that integrate music, literature, or art with social studies, when connected to social education goals, help to personalize the time and place being studied. For example, in a unit on France, students are asked to study Monet reprints, describe how he viewed France, and then, using geography texts, determine the accuracy of his interpretations. This activity is followed by one in which students are to figure out the time period depicted in his work, citing evidence to support or reject their hypotheses.

Another activity in a unit focusing on early America calls for students to read a text or an encyclopedic account of Paul Revere's ride and compare it with the more romanticized, less accurate version in Longfellow's poem. Besides being a natural and useful incorporation of poetry, this is a worthwhile activity for helping students to understand some of the ways in which historiography and fiction differ in goals, processes, and products.

Undesirable Integration

Integration is assumed to always be productive, but often it is not. Potential pitfalls in applying the concept are often masked by arguments related to the latest trend in curriculum, the goal of getting teachers to be collaborative, the desire to heighten interest, or the attempt to increase the amount of time that can be given to a particular subject. All of these arguments should give cause for pause. From our point of view, all integration of content, skills, or activities into social studies should tie directly to the subject and add meaningfulness to social education. If it does not, we urge you to delete it from the social studies curriculum (although you might want to include it as part of the curriculum for the other subject involved, if it promotes progress toward that subject's major goals). The following are examples of integration activities that we view as inappropriate for use in social studies.

Activities That Lack or Mask Social Education Goals

Most of the ill-conceived forms of integration that we have seen suggested for social studies classrooms involve activities that draw on content or skills from other subjects (Brophy & Alleman, 1991). Often these activities lack significant value in any subject and are just pointless busywork (alphabetizing state capitals, counting the number of states included in each of several geographical regions). Others may have value as language arts activities but do not belong in the social studies curriculum (exercises that make use of social studies content but focus on pluralizing singular nouns, finding the main idea in a paragraph, matching synonyms, using the dictionary, etc.). Others are potentially useful as vehicles for pursuing significant social education goals but are structured with so much emphasis on the language arts aspects that the social education purpose is unclear. We believe that these activities are not cost-effective uses of social studies time.

One fourth-grade social studies manual suggested assigning students to write research papers on coal. The instructions emphasized teaching the mechanics of doing the investigation and writing the paper. There was little mention of social education goals or major social studies understandings such as "humans have unlimited wants but limited resources," or policy issues such as conservation of natural resources or development of energy alternatives. With the task conceived narrowly and the focus on research and report writing, it is unlikely that the twenty-five or so individual reports would yield enough variety to allow students to benefit from one another's work. Consequently, the social education value of this assignment would be minimal and its cost-effectiveness would be diluted further because of the considerable time required to obtain and read content sources, copy or paraphrase data, and make presentations to the class.

Cost-Effectiveness Problems

Similar masking of social education goals and ignoring the time factor were seen in a unit on families in which students were asked to recreate their families by portraying each member using a paper plate decorated with construction paper, crayons, and yarn. The plates were to be used to "introduce" family members to the class and then later combined to make murals. This activity not only is time consuming but also is structured to emphasize the artistic dimensions rather than the social studies dimensions. We doubt that art teachers would support this activity as appropriate for art classes either.

In a unit on shelter, students were asked to construct examples of homes in tropical areas of the world. Again, such an activity would take a great deal of time, especially if authentic building materials were used. We fear that the emphasis would focus on accomplishing constructions instead of understanding and appreciating the impact of climate and local geography on living conditions.

Besides time-consuming art and construction projects, role-play is another frequent basis for activities that are either inherently limited in social education value or too time consuming to be cost effective. For example, a unit on families called for students to dress in costumes, play musical instruments, and participate in a parade as a means of illustrating how families celebrate. On the following day, they were to write about the event. This series of activities offers tie-ins with humanities and physical education and provides a stimulus for language arts work, but it lacks a significant social education content base. Students already know that families celebrate holidays, and despite the extensive hands-on features of this activity series, it fails to elaborate usefully on the big ideas associated with family celebrations. Instead, the emphasis is on participating in the parade.

Cost-effectiveness problems are also embedded in collage and scrapbook activities that call for a lot of cutting and pasting of pictures but not much thinking or writing about ideas linked to major social education goals. Instructions for such activities are often given in ways that focus students on the processes involved in carrying out the activities rather than on the ideas that the activities are supposed to develop, and the final products often are evaluated on the basis of criteria such as artistic appeal. For example, one activity called for students to cut out pictures of clothing and paste them under categories such as wool, linen, cotton, and polyester. Students could spend a substantial amount of time on this "hands-on" activity without learning anything important about the different fabrics.

We believe that the time spent on activities must be assessed against the time quotas allocated to the subject in ways that reflect the cost-effectiveness of the activities as a means of accomplishing the subject's major goals. Ask yourself, "Is this activity the best choice given the limited time allocated for social studies?" Also keep in mind that cognitive/affective engagement need not be "hands-on"—in fact, hands-on doing can sometimes be a hindrance to "minds-on" learning.

Content Distortion

Attempts at integration sometimes distort the ways that social studies is represented or developed. For example, a unit on clothing included a lesson on uniforms that called for students to make puppets of people dressed in uniforms. The teacher was to set up situations where two puppets would meet and tell each other about the uniforms they were wearing. This activity is problematic because it is time consuming, emphasizes art activities instead of social studies content, and calls for knowledge not developed in the lesson (which provided only brief information about the uniforms worn by firefighters and astronauts). Most fundamentally, however, it is problematic because it results in a great deal of social studies time being spent on uniforms, a topic that at best deserves only passing mention in a good unit on clothing as a basic human need.

Content distortion was also observed in a unit on pioneer life that included a sequencing-skills exercise linked to an illustration of five steps involved in building log cabins. The last three steps in the sequence were arbitrarily imposed rather than logically necessary, and in any case, they did not correspond to what was shown in the illustration. It appeared that the text authors wanted to include an exercise in sequential ordering somewhere in the curriculum and chose this lesson as the place to include it, rather than seeing the exercise as important for developing key knowledge about pioneer life.

Difficult or Impossible Tasks

Ill-conceived integration attempts sometimes require students to do things that are difficult, if not impossible, to accomplish. In a fifth-grade unit focusing on the U.S. economy, students were asked to demonstrate their understanding of the joint-stock company by diagramming its structure to show relationships and flow among the company, stocks, stockholders, and profits. Besides being a distraction from the main ideas of the unit, this activity seems ill considered because the operations of a joint-stock company, although relatively easy to explain verbally, are difficult to depict unambiguously in a diagram.

Other examples of strange, difficult, or even impossible integration tasks that we have observed include asking students to use pantomime to communicate one of the six reasons for the U.S. Constitution as stated in the Preamble; asking students to draw "hungry" and "curious" faces as part of a unit on feelings; and role-playing life in the White House as part of a unit on famous places. None of these activities reflect the key social education understandings of the units, and each will probably leave students confused or frustrated because it is difficult if not impossible to accomplish unambiguously.

Feasibility Problems

Activities that call for integration should also be feasible within the constraints under which the teacher must work. Certain activities are not feasible because they are too expensive, require space or equipment that is unavailable, involve unacceptably noisy construction work, or pose risks to the physical safety or emotional security of students. For example, an activity attempting to integrate geography, physical education, and music called for the teacher to post the cardinal directions appropriately, then have the students line up and march around the room to music as the teacher called out "March north," "March east," and so on. Implementation of this activity in a classroom full of desks and other furniture would invite chaos and potential injury.

Conclusion

We acknowledge the value of productive forms of integration in social studies, but we suggest two caveats. First, content, skills, and activities included in the name of integration should be educationally significant and desirable even if they do not involve the across-subjects feature. Second, such content, skills, and activities should foster rather than disrupt or nullify the accomplishment of major social studies goals.

Successful integration comes in many forms. Sometimes the nature of the topic makes integration natural or even necessary. Other worthwhile integration results when the teacher selects learning experiences that fit the established social education goals by allowing students to apply skills learned elsewhere in ways that promote social studies understanding or application or by adding useful affective dimensions that make learning more interesting or personalized.

Teachers cannot depend on the manuals supplied with social studies textbook series to suggest activities that meet the criteria we have outlined (Alleman & Brophy, 1993). Consequently, you will need to learn to assess suggested learning activities, not just for whether your students are likely to enjoy them but also for whether they offer sufficient educational value to merit inclusion in the curriculum. For judging activities that purport to integrate across subjects, we suggest that you consider the following questions:

- Does the activity have a significant social education goal as its primary focus?
- Would this be a desirable activity for the social studies unit even if it did not feature across-subjects integration?
- Would an "outsider" clearly recognize the activity as social studies?
- Does the activity allow students to meaningfully develop or authentically apply important social education content?
- Does it involve authentic application of skills from other disciplines?
- Do students have the necessary prerequisite knowledge and skills?
- If the activity is structured properly, will students understand and be able to explain its social education purposes?
- If they engage in the activity with those purposes in mind, will they be likely to accomplish the purposes as a result?

Summary

Curriculum integration should not be considered an end in itself but a means of accomplishing significant instructional goals. Activities that feature integration across subjects should not be used anywhere in the curriculum if they lack one or more of the essential characteristics of goal relevance, appropriate level of difficulty, feasibility, and cost-effectiveness. Furthermore, many integrating activities that do meet these criteria should not be included in the social studies curriculum because they do not support progress toward major social education goals (such activities might be appropriate for inclusion in the curriculum for literacy or some other subject). Some topics addressed in social studies are naturally integrative, and others can benefit from integrated activities that involve using skills taught elsewhere to process or apply social studies content, to help make that content more concrete or personalized, or to add an important affective dimension. We believe that most issues surrounding curricular integration will take care of themselves if social studies teaching is organized around major social education goals and big ideas because this will naturally lead to activities and assignments calling for students to use skills such as critical thinking, data collection, and articulating and supporting arguments.

Reflective Questions

1. Suppose your mentor or principal has indicated that, because of time constraints, you need to find opportunities to integrate social studies with other school subjects. How will you respond? Be ready to provide reasons and to give examples to illustrate your points.
2. Recent research on literacy learning suggests that acquiring skills in the use of informational texts results in better-informed citizens and higher scores on standardized literacy measures. Select one of the social studies units you have observed or taught and think of at least three "spaces" where informational texts would be useful. What could you expect as additional student outcomes?
3. Revisit a familiar social studies unit, preferably one you are observing or currently teaching. Which of its activities clearly match the goals and enhance meaningfulness? Should certain activities be excluded because they detract, distort the content, are not cost effective, or for another reason?
4. Imagine that the art or music teacher in your school is interested in planning opportunities for integration with your social studies curriculum. How will you respond to the request? Select an upcoming social studies unit. Identify the overarching goals and describe opportunities for meaningful integration with the arts.
5. Suppose you are planning a unit with an activity that calls for integration, but after reading this chapter, you realize it simply is not cost effective and even though it is topic-relevant, it will take time away from the development of big ideas. Describe how you could reconfigure it as an out-of-school assignment and have the students share the results in a future lesson. Prepare a short note to families explaining the activity and its purpose. Encourage family participation.

Your Turn:
Integrating Social Studies within the Total Curriculum

Use the following exercise focusing on a shelter unit to assess your level of understanding regarding the perspective on integration contained in this chapter. Study the goals carefully, then read each of the activities. Using the guiding principles for productive integration and the questions for making decisions about social studies integration, label each activity "good," "bad," or "conditional." Be prepared to give reasons for your decisions.

UNIT GOALS

- To build on children's understanding that shelter is a basic need and that different forms of shelter exist
- To help children understand and appreciate the reasons for different forms of shelter. Shelter needs are determined in large part by local climate and geographical features. Most housing is constructed using materials adapted from natural resources that are plentiful in the local area. Certain forms of housing reflect cultural, economic, or geographic conditions: Tipis and tents are easily movable shelters used by nomadic societies; stilt houses are an adaptation to periodic flooding; high-rises are an adaptation to land scarcity in urban areas.
- To help children understand and appreciate how inventions, discoveries, new knowledge, and development of new materials have enabled many people today to live in housing that offers durability, better waterproofing, insulation, and temperature control, with fewer requirements for maintenance and labor
- To help children understand how the development of modern industries and transportation make it possible to construct almost any kind of shelter almost anywhere on earth. It is now possible for those who can afford it to live comfortably in very hot or very cold climates.
- To help children appreciate the energy efficiency now possible in modern homes due to the developments of technology
- To help children acquire sensitivity toward the range of factors that contribute to the type of home (shelter) that a family can afford (This includes consciousness-raising regarding the homeless.)
- To engender in children an appreciation for their current and future opportunities to make decisions about and exercise some control over aspects of their lives related to their shelter needs (choice making, life applications)
- To help children acquire an appreciation for the range of structures that have been created for shelters over time

POSSIBLE ACTIVITY SELECTIONS

ACTIVITY	RATING	REASONS
1. Students read about various forms of shelter, view pictures of these forms, and then discuss reasons why people might select each form.		
2. Students read about a range of workers, their expertise needed in constructing a house, and the order in which their work would be completed. Then they make puppets to represent these workers talking to one another. The focal		

point of the discussion should be the role each plays in the completion of the shelter and the sequence in which each job would be done.

3. Students prepare a collage that illustrates all the ways in which people satisfy their shelter needs.

4. Provide the class with a mural illustrating the range of shelters that exist in your area. Have the students study the mural carefully and count the number of shelters depicted.

5. After describing (using pictures) inventions, new knowledge, and the development of new materials used in shelters, ask each student to share with the class the ones he or she thinks are most significant and why.

6. Students interview members of their households to find out if and how their homes are energy efficient. (A brief interview schedule will be developed for use in retrieving the data.) A guided class discussion will follow.

7. Give students an opportunity to study a collection of pictures that illustrate how forms of housing reflect cultural, economic, and geographic conditions. Then lead a discussion that addresses these issues. At the conclusion of the discussion, each student will be asked to identify the most important thing he or she learned.

8. Provide pictures to show changes in shelters over time. Have students work in groups to arrange the pictures in chronological order. Each group will be asked to provide reasons for its response.

9. Students will bring in pictures of shelters from around the world, make a class mural, create lyrics for a song about shelters, and then make a presentation to parents.

10. Lead students on a walk around the neighborhood. Focus on the types of shelters that exist and the types of construction materials that are used. Analyze the findings in a follow-up discussion.

11. Using an outline map of one or two neighborhood blocks, plan a walk with the class to determine the locale of each shelter. Plot each shelter. Upon return, have students make a 3-D model representing the area visited.

12. Read a story about the White House. Then have groups of students plan puppet shows representing the following scenarios: the day nobody visited, the day a visitor got lost, the day the presidential family moved in, and the day the electricity went off.

CHAPTER 12

HOW CAN
I ASSESS STUDENT
LEARNING?

Stephanie Lampi, Third-Year Teacher

As educators, we are continually trying to improve and enhance our lessons to better meet our students' needs. Many times, we focus on our daily lessons and change activities and delivery methods but forget to look at our assessments. This chapter has encouraged and challenged me to consider putting just as much energy into my assessments as I do on the rest of the lesson/unit plan.

A good assessment shows how well an individual has mastered the unit goals. We need to use different types of well-written assessments to get a clear picture. I find that sometimes I get in a rut and use the same method over and over because it has been successful in the past. I plan on keeping a copy of this chapter in my planning book, so I can revisit it daily and make sure I vary my methods and give my students a better opportunity to be successful.

Believe it or not, multiple-choice and true-false tests, if written well, can be useful. We need to look at our current assessments and also make sure that we include assessment tools that our students encounter on standardized tests. I used to think that if students mastered the unit goals, they could be successful on any method of assessment. Now I know that I need to make sure the assessment tool matches the goals, and I realize that more than one type of tool may be appropriate.

I appreciate the many examples provided in this chapter. I learn by doing and seeing, and it helps me to have something concrete to hold on to and serve as a springboard for my planning for assessment. The examples were motivating because they challenged me to think out of the box and provided me with new ideas to expand on. We all need to be reminded of the importance of assessment as a vital part of curricular design and development.

The Present:
A Broader View of Assessment and Evaluation

Recognizing the need for accountability but concerned about the narrowing effect on the curriculum that current versions of high-stakes testing might have, the National Council for the Social Studies (NCSS) and leading scholars who have focused on assessment methods have been arguing for social studies assessment that is well aligned with major social studies goals, more complete in the range of objectives addressed, and more authentic in the kinds of tasks included. NCSS guidelines call for systematic and vigorous evaluation of social studies instruction that (1) bases the criteria for effectiveness primarily on the school's own statement of objectives; (2) includes assessment of progress not only in knowledge but in thinking skills, valuing, and social participation; (3) includes data from many sources, not just paper-pencil tests; and (4) is used for assessing student progress in learning and for planning curriculum improvements, not just for grading (NCSS, 1990).

We believe that standardized testing has a legitimate role within the larger social studies picture, but it is foolhardy to plan a full social studies curriculum around a few hours of testing. Instead, standards and assessment programs need to be kept in appropriate perspective within larger systematic efforts to accomplish major citizenship education goals. We encourage teachers and curriculum leaders to consider the intentions of national and state standards and benchmarks in relation to local social studies needs, reflect on what it means to experience powerful social studies teaching, resist the tendencies for standards and high-stakes testing to narrow the curriculum counterproductively, and develop local assessment plans that align with locally established social studies program goals and are not overly dependent on state or national instruments.

Authentic Assessment

The key to keeping standards and high-stakes testing in perspective is viewing assessment as an integral part of the curriculum and not just an add-on. This view expands the notion of assessment beyond the paper-and-pencil test, an expansion that is needed in order to address the range of curricular goals. Newmann (1997), Wiggins (1989a, 1989b), and other scholars refer to this expanded notion as *authentic assessment* and note that authentic tasks have the following attributes:

- Tasks go to the heart of essential learning (i.e., they ask for exhibitions of understandings and abilities that matter).
- Tasks resemble interdisciplinary real-life challenges, not schoolish busywork that is artificially neat, fragmented, and easy to grade.
- Tasks are standard setting; they point students toward higher, richer levels of knowing.

- Tasks are worth striving toward and practicing.
- Tasks are known to students well in advance.
- Tasks strike teachers as worth the trouble.
- Tasks generally involve a higher-order challenge that requires students to go beyond the routine use of previously learned information.
- All tasks are attempted by all students.

These attributes add up to an "exhibition of mastery" (Parker, 1991).

Authentic assessment should always reflect the full range of curricular goals, so multiple-choice, true-false, or essay tests sometimes will be appropriate. Other times, however, will require measures such as observation checklists, self-assessment checklists, open-ended "I learned" statements, "open-closed" windows, reflective journal entries, laboratory-type performance assessments, portfolios, or observation measures such as graphs for evaluating discussions. All of these tools can help students and the teacher to get a reading of how learning is progressing.

Since assessment is considered ongoing, frequently cast as preliminary, formative, and summative, *many instructional activities can also be used as assessment tools*. Different forms and times for assessment will be determined by the purpose of the learning situation, the kind of information acquired, and how it will be used to accomplish the social studies goals. Learning activities are both curriculum components that need to be assessed as such and mechanisms for eliciting indicators of students' learning.

At the end of this chapter, an exercise is provided to help you become familiar with NCSS strands and performance indicators and learn to judge activities as assessments. Assessment tools should be viewed as opportunities to take multiple snapshots of student performance and progress. It is most critical that the assessment tool matches the goals. Other considerations include its level of difficulty, its appropriateness in terms of time and trouble, and its feasibility. More than one assessment tool often is appropriate to provide variety and balance, so reading, writing, speaking, and drawing opportunities, among others, also merit consideration.

Preliminary Assessment

Prior to formal instruction, eliciting students' prior knowledge (including both valid ideas and misconceptions) about the upcoming content is a good way to determine where you need to start. The *preliminary assessment* may be as simple as a TWL exercise (listing "What I think I know" and "What I want to learn"—with later attention to "What I learned"), collection of wonders (each student verbalizes what s/he wonders about the content of the upcoming unit), or group or individual interviews focusing on student thinking associated with the content. A pretest is another form of preliminary assessment. Whatever form is selected, it should focus on the goals and its results should be used to inform the planning of instruction. Later, the results should be revisited at the conclusion of the unit to document student growth.

Formative and Summative Assessment

Formative assessment refers to the assessments that are made during the unit, and *summative assessment* refers to those implemented at the end of the unit or marking period. The tools we describe in the following pages can be used in or adapted to either situation. Typically, however, we think of formative assessments as taking less time and focusing on a lesson or two but summative measures as reflecting an accumulation of knowledge, understanding, applications, and so on.

The important things are that the tools or instruments you select should match your goals, reflect your instruction, and communicate the idea that every learner is accountable. The results should be scrutinized to detect weaknesses in the assessment practices themselves as well as to detect special learner needs, misunderstandings, misconceptions, and so on. Analysis of results should include considering whether there is any need to adjust plans for future versions of current lessons or activities.

Assessment Tools

Multiple-Choice Items

The multiple-choice format is probably the most versatile form of objective test item. Every item has two parts: the stem, which represents the problem or question; and three or more response choices, of which one is the correct answer and the others are distracters, or plausible alternatives for students who do not know the answer (Good & Brophy, 1995). Consider the following illustration built around a unit on media with the goal being for students to recognize and understand various kinds of media and their purposes:

1. Which of these inventions is of *least* help to a disc jockey?
   a. record
   b. microphone
   <u>c.</u> camera
   d. studio

2. A person whose main job is to find out news is a _____.
   <u>a.</u> reporter
   b. printer
   c. typist
   d. proofreader

3. If you wanted to purchase a pet, which part of the newspaper would you check?
   a. letters to the editor
   b. movie section
   <u>c.</u> classified section
   d. comics

4. If you wanted to find out quickly how you could locate an unusual coin to add to your collection, which source would you check?
   <u>a.</u> eBay
   b. local newspaper
   c. radio
   d. telephone directory

It is challenging to build good multiple-choice items. Writing a stem that provides sufficient pertinent information but is not too wordy is very important, especially if some of your students have reading difficulties. Hints for writing good items include: first write the stem and correct answer simultaneously; next, carefully analyze both question and answer to ensure accuracy and clarity; finally, write your distracters. Are they worded to flow from the stem? Are they believable but incorrect or not as good as the correct alternatives? Are any of the distracters weird, odd-ball alternatives that students are likely to recognize as incorrect? If so, get rid of them. Are the distracters roughly the same length? If not, edit them or write new ones.

The advantages of multiple-choice items—if they match your goals—are that they can be scored objectively, and some of the effects of guessing are mitigated. Selecting this format, at least once in awhile, also prepares students for a format that is typically used on standardized tests.

True-False and Yes-No Items

True-false and yes-no items can be constructed much more quickly than multiple-choice items. However, a major limitation of this type of question is that much content built around big ideas is difficult to express in this format. Also, students will be correct 50 percent of the time by guessing, because they are choosing between only two alternatives rather than four or five. Consequently, this type of question can be used successfully when only a general estimate of performance is needed.

There are strategic ways of building higher-order thinking into this type of assessment. One is to ask students to make false items true. Another is to ask them to explain the reasoning for their responses. Still another is to include a short text selection followed by a series of yes-no or true-false questions.

Here is an example based on the goal of developing strategies for being a wise consumer and applying them to real-life situations.

GRAND OPENING
42-inch TV sets
Beautiful picture, fine piece of furniture
Hurry! They won't last at this price!
$999.95
JEFF'S TV SHOP

After reading this ad, Mark and his dad hurried over to Jeff's TV shop. "You don't really want this TV," the salesperson pleaded. "It's two years old and doesn't have a factory warranty. But if you insist on buying it and it causes you problems within

30 days, I'll try to get it fixed for you." Pointing to another TV, the salesperson said, "This brand new set with a five-year warranty is a steal for $1,499.95."
Directions: Circle "yes" if the answer to the question is yes. Circle "no" if the answer to the question is no.

Yes   No   1. Was Jeff's TV shop using bait-and-switch advertising?
Yes   No   2. By using such words as "beautiful picture" and "fine piece of furniture," was Jeff puffing the TV set?
Yes   No   3. Was the salesperson's offer to "try and repair the set" a binding contract?
Yes   No   4. If Marks' dad bought the used TV and it broke in a few days, would the manufacturer be likely to repair the set free of charge?

Reluctant readers and the time factor need to be considered when deciding whether to use a short text with yes-no or true-false items. Another consideration is that narrative followed by a series of items is a format frequently found on standardized measures. Often students are stressed not by the questions being asked but by the form in which they are presented; therefore, it is a good idea to take advantage of opportunities to prepare students for new encounters when they match the goal.

Short-Answer and Completion Items

Short-answer and completion items require students to finish a statement from recall rather than just recognize the correct answer. In a short-answer format, students provide their own responses. Suppose you were teaching a lesson on hunger and the goals were to (1) develop an understanding that in extreme cases, people are unable to pay for the food they need; and (2) help students acquire sensitivity for people in need and practice citizenship as it relates to other people. You explained to your students what soup kitchens were, plotted the locations of soup kitchens on a local map, and discussed reasons why people come to soup kitchens. Finally, you read the story of *Uncle Willie and the Soup Kitchen* (DiSalvo-Ryan, 1991). You provided some background information and set the stage for "minds-on" listening by posing a couple of questions. After the debriefing and a large-group activity that had the students write an editorial for the local newspaper explaining the class's ideas for helping local people who are in need of food, you prepared an open-ended assessment as follows (see Alleman and Brophy [2001]):

    1. A soup kitchen is _____.
    2. People go to soup kitchens because _____.
    3. Uncle Willie is a good citizen because _____.
    4. People in need can _____.
    5. Being a volunteer is _____.
    6. Places in our community where people can go to get free food or food at a lower price include _____, _____, and _____.

Responses would be shared and discussed in a follow-up to the assessment.

Matching Items

Matching tests present two lists and require students to pair up items from one list with items from the other. These tests lack the flexibility of multiple-choice tests because they require items with common properties, such as names, processes, events, or objects. A well-constructed matching test, however, contains a range of options from which the student chooses in attempting to match terms and definitions, important persons and their contributions, events and dates, and so on.

Imagine that one of the goals of your fourth-grade unit on regions was for students to develop an understanding of energy sources and be able to explain how they are produced. A set of matching items might be used as part of the assessment:

<u>Directions</u>: Match each source of energy in Column 1 with the way in which it is produced in Column 2. Write the letter on the line in front of the question number. Some of the sources are produced in more than one way.

	Column 1	Column 2
a, c, d	1. oil	a. drilling
a, c, d	2. gas	b. digging
b	3. coal	c. manufacturing
c	4. gasoline	d. collecting
d	5. solar heat	
c	6. kerosene	
b	7. peat	
c	8. steam	
c	9. water power	
c	10. electricity	

To avoid cuing answers, it is helpful to have more response alternatives than items, or as is the case in this example, to include response alternatives that may be used more than once.

Essay Questions

Essay questions provide students with the greatest latitude to construct their own responses. Students are required to produce their own answers. They have the freedom to decide how to organize their response and the conclusions they will draw. Essay questions are most useful for assessing higher cognitive processes. The main limitations are the amount of time needed for writing and reading the responses and the ability to assess only a limited amount of student learning.

Providing students with multiple key words or phrases they might use in formulating their responses can "jump-start" even the most reluctant writer/speller. This tactic is often referred to as a modified word wall. It can also be used as a stimulus for "table talk" prior to responding individually to the essay questions.

Many types of essay questions might be asked. Imagine that you have just completed a unit on government and your overarching goal was for students to develop an understanding and appreciation for the influence of government and the legal system on our daily lives. We have listed ten types of essay questions and an example of each. It would be unlikely, however, that you would use all of these types in a single unit test.

1. Comparison of two things:
   In what ways are rules and laws alike and different?
2. Decision (for and against):
   Suppose that there is a law in your state that you cannot ride a motorcycle until you are 16 years old. Is this a fair law? Explain your answer.
3. Cause and effect:
   Why do stores have signs posted that read: "Shoplifters will be prosecuted"?
4. Explanation of the use or meaning of some phrase or statement in a passage:
   A sign in front of a store reads: "Parking reserved for handicappers." Explain what the sign means.
5. Analysis:
   It is dark and you are riding your bike without any lights. Why is this dangerous?
6. Statement of relationships:
   Why are older students instead of younger ones on your school's safety patrol? Explain your reasons.
7. Discussion:
   Explain what a lawyer and a judge do in the courtroom.
8. Reorganization of facts:
   Tell the steps you would follow if your bicycle were stolen.
9. Formulation of new question (problems and questions raised):
   Suppose that there were no laws against smoking. How would this affect the health of the people?
10. Criticism (as to the adequacy, correctness, or relevancy of a pointed statement):
    "Students can come to school only when they want to." Explain what is good and bad about that idea.

Before giving the essay test, write down what you would regard as the best answers to each of your essay questions. Doing this can disclose some inherent deficiencies to the questions, but more importantly, the answers can serve as standards for evaluating your students' responses. If you decide to use rubrics, consider engaging your students in the conversation for creating them. For example, if you were to ask students to write a journal entry focusing on the reasons for taxes or comparing the Vietnam War to the war in Iraq, talk about how many ideas should be included, the role of examples for adding credibility to the response, and the importance of spelling and grammar. Consider modeling (using a different example) what a strong journal entry would look like. Co-constructing rubrics can build ownership and enlist students as partners in designing and using them. Make sure you start with a sharply focused vision of a good response (Stiggins, 2001).

Essay tests are most appropriate in classrooms that are literacy rich. Students will be most successful if they have had many in-class opportunities to be verbally active in both large- and small-group settings. Primary-grade students who are still mastering the basics of writing are not yet ready to compose written responses to essay questions, but they can respond orally during interview assessments.

Informal Assessment

Assessment should be an integral part of the curriculum rather than an "add-on" or "afterthought," and the way it is carried out sets the tone for expectations and conveys to students what is valued. In the previous sections of this chapter, we have emphasized traditional approaches to knowledge and skills and described student achievement associated with goals for knowing, understanding, and applying within the context of local, state, and national frameworks. Participation, engagement, online understanding, values, attitudes, dispositions, and empathy are equally important within a comprehensive social studies program. The assessment of these is best addressed at the local level.

Participation in Discussions

The kind of assessment implied by constructivism flows from the belief that students develop new knowledge and make it their own through an active process of "meaning making." Constructivists differ in their philosophical beliefs regarding the nature of knowledge, but they all favor moving from transmission models of teaching toward models that involve crafting reflective discussions scaffolded around networks of powerful ideas.

Social constructivists emphasize that the teaching–learning process works best in social settings in which individuals engage in discourse about a topic. Participants advance their own thinking through exposure to the views and insights of others. Communicating their own beliefs and understandings forces them to articulate their ideas more clearly, which sharpens their conceptions and frequently helps them make new connections.

As the teacher, you need to determine what behaviors are expected of students during discussions, create a set of norms, and over time, determine if they are being realized. The following three examples illustrate the kinds of tools you can create to help students get clearer about what is expected and to monitor one another as well as themselves (see Tables 12.1, 12.2, and 12.3).

Engagement and Online Understanding

As a teacher, you will want to acquire a broad range of assessment tools in order to develop a comprehensive profile of each student in your classroom. The most important consideration in selecting an assessment instrument is to make sure it matches your goal. Sometimes you will want to assess formally

TABLE 12.1

Teacher's Evaluation of Individual Contributions to Discussion

Select a few students each day for observation and feedback. Use checkmarks to indicate meeting the standards and zeroes to indicate failure to do so.

Student Names _____ _____ _____ _____

Student Behaviors

Helps define the issues	_____	_____	_____	_____
Sticks to the topic	_____	_____	_____	_____
Is an interested and willing listener	_____	_____	_____	_____
Considers ideas contrary to own	_____	_____	_____	_____
Synthesizes information presented by peers	_____	_____	_____	_____
Generalizes when appropriate	_____	_____	_____	_____
Arrives at conclusions that produce new meaning	_____	_____	_____	_____

TABLE 12.2

Group Evaluation of Discussion

	Always	*Usually*	*Sometimes*	*Never*
We checked to make sure everyone understood what to do.	_____	_____	_____	_____
We responded to questions, giving explanations where needed.	_____	_____	_____	_____
We clarified what we did not understand.	_____	_____	_____	_____
We helped one another and made sure we all understood and could apply what we learned.	_____	_____	_____	_____

TABLE 12.3

Individual's Self-Assessment of Contributions to Discussion

How well do I work with my peers?	*Always*	*Usually*	*Sometimes*	*Never*
I cooperate with others as we work toward our group's goals.	_____	_____	_____	_____
I keep on task.	_____	_____	_____	_____
I contribute new ideas.	_____	_____	_____	_____
I make constructive suggestions when asked for help.	_____	_____	_____	_____
I give others encouragement.	_____	_____	_____	_____

using one or more of the more traditional tools previously described. Other times you will use more informal measures, such as anecdotal records, open-closed windows, or "I learned" statements.

Anecdotal records enable you to record specific incidents of student behavior over a period of time. Interpersonal relations; the development of language, geographic or problem-solving skills; contributions to class discussions; and changes in interest or attitudinal patterns are among the many types of information about students that can be described in anecdotal records. Such records should portray the specifics of student behavior at a given time and place. Your interpretations and suggestions for improvement should be recorded separately.

Open-closed windows are another useful tool to gauge where students are in their learning. Provide students with a piece of lined paper. Have them fold the paper in half (vertically), write "Open" at the top of the left-hand side, and write "Closed" at the top of the right-hand side. Then ask them to think about what they have learned and list those things under the open category. Most students will probably have a long list. Then ask them to think about what things from the lesson (or series of lessons) they still are unclear or confused about. Ask them to list these on the closed side. Then ask them to share in pairs. This tool is particularly useful when you want to encourage students to discuss among themselves what they have been learning. Closed windows can be opened by peer conversations, and those that remain closed can be addressed in subsequent instruction.

"I learned" statements are simple, but they can reveal a lot over time. At the end of an activity or lesson, ask students to write down or share verbally what they learned. This provides each student with an opportunity to reflect on the experience. The responses will give you a measure of what students thought was important.

Assessing Attitudes, Values, and Dispositions

Techniques for assessing attitudes, values, and dispositions are especially useful when attempting to determine students' previous experience with a specific issue or topic. The results can inform your planning, which should incorporate experiences and life applications whenever possible.

Imagine you are planning a unit on government and one of your goals is to develop an appreciation for rules and laws and why we have them. You might design a Likert scale to generate a preliminary "reading" of students' attitudes about rules and laws. A *Likert scale* asks students to express the extent to which they agree or disagree with a series of statements. Usually a 5–7 point scale is used, with the most positive response being the highest number. Below are two examples relating to rules and laws.

<u>Directions:</u> Make an X on the line that best represents your feelings about these statements.

	1 Strongly Disagree	2 Disagree	3 Undecided	4 Agree	5 Strongly Agree
1. If you don't like a law, you should follow it anyway.	_____	_____	_____	_____	_____
2. If you see kids breaking windows in the school, you should tell the principal.	_____	_____	_____	_____	_____

A *semantic differential* is another useful tool. Below are examples of semantic differential terms that might be used in evaluating students' beliefs, values, and dispositions about government. Ideally, this instrument would be administered prior to teaching the unit and again at the end to determine if and how their attitudes have changed.

<u>Directions:</u> Make an X in the space that best shows what government means to you.

Good	_____ _____ _____ _____ _____	Bad
Democratic	_____ _____ _____ _____ _____	Authoritarian
Closed	_____ _____ _____ _____ _____	Open
Valuable	_____ _____ _____ _____ _____	Worthless
Strong	_____ _____ _____ _____ _____	Weak
Impersonal	_____ _____ _____ _____ _____	Personal
Necessary	_____ _____ _____ _____ _____	Unnecessary
Responsive	_____ _____ _____ _____ _____	Unresponsive
Greedy	_____ _____ _____ _____ _____	Generous
Considerate	_____ _____ _____ _____ _____	Inconsiderate
Wasteful	_____ _____ _____ _____ _____	Saving

Performance Assessment:
The Laboratory Model

The "laboratory" model is another useful tool. This form is usually implemented at the end of a unit. You probably have experienced it in high school or college science classes. On "test" day, stations are located at desks, bulletin boards, whiteboards, murals, wall charts, computer screens, or other appropriate places. Each station displays material such as a chart, artifacts, or an open book with a marked passage. Students visit the stations with clipboards, answer sheets, and pencils in hand. When instructed to do so, they move to the next station. Some time should be allowed for returning to stations where questions have been left unanswered. When all the students have finished, answers are checked.

This model can work very successfully as a means of fostering authentic performance assessment in elementary social studies. Of course, like every type of assessment considered, it must be driven by the social studies goals. If one of the goals of a unit on community is to develop understandings related to transportation systems, students might learn about how to read and interpret bus schedules, locate bike paths, or find the most direct routes for reaching certain sites. Later, they might be asked to resolve transportation dilemmas using a city map, bus schedules, and other pertinent artifacts at one or more testing stations.

Given the goals for the community unit, it is likely that charts, murals, passages from books, slides, flat pictures, newspaper ads, student projects, and so on would be used to develop major understandings. These could easily be placed at individual stations, accompanied by a series of questions that address the big ideas and draw upon skills such as location, decision making, advertising techniques, and so on.

Here are some helpful hints to consider when planning laboratory-type assessments:

- Try to make the exercises similar in length.
- Begin each sequence with an easy question and build toward the most challenging one.
- Consider providing optional questions at some of the stations.
- For younger students, arrange for adults or older students to help with reading items or manipulating materials.
- If you are concerned about having a station for each student, divide the number in half. You can have half of the class take the test while the other half works on a project in the library, then switch roles. Students can later work in pairs to correct their responses. For younger students, invite upper-grade mentor-partners to do the reading and writing.
- Plan a "dry run" of the model before you use it.
- After administering several lab tests in social studies successfully, gradually add student projects at stations. More advanced students can design questions around their individual and group projects based on the goals of the unit. Provide them with whatever guidelines needed to ensure that they include questions that address higher-order thinking.
- Be open. There are no hard and fast rules for this model except that the items must be based on your goals and matched to your teaching modalities.

To stimulate your thinking regarding the use of authentic assessments, we have provided sample station plans from two units. (See Figures 12.1 and 12.2.)

The number of questions per station and the amount of time to allocate for each station will depend on your goals and the age and abilities of your students. As you complete your final preparations for trying this model, we suggest you go through the Lab Test Checklist (see Figure 12.3). You should be able to answer "yes" to each question.

FIGURE 12.1

Sample Stations for a Laboratory Assessment in Geography

STATION 1. Questions about the Globe

Turn the globe slowly. Find the country marked with an X.

1. What is the name of this country?
   _____

2. In which hemispheres is it located? (Circle two of these.)

   Eastern   Western   Northern   Southern

3. Is the time of day earlier or later in this place than here?
   _____

4. Approximately how many miles is it from this country to here?
   _____

5. What would be the fastest mode of transportation to take from here to this place?
   _____

6. If you were to travel southwest from here, would you reach this country or the Hawaiian Islands first? _____

STATION 2. The Kyoto Billboard

(A student project of a billboard advertising Kyoto is displayed at this station.)

1. Is Kyoto an old or a young place? _____

2. Is it a country, province, or city? _____

3. If you were a gardener, would you expect to find work here? _____
   Why or why not? _____

4. If you were a deep sea fisherman, would you find work here? _____
   Why or why not? _____

5. According to the billboard, what is the most unique characteristic of Kyoto?
   _____

6. According to the billboard, what is one thing a tourist could do for entertainment?
   _____

7. (Optional) According to the billboard, what is one thing that Kyoto and (a city near you) have in common?
   _____
   _____

Another sample of a performance lab test follows in Figure 12.2. This one was designed for a group of third-graders learning about their community and world, with a heavy emphasis on maps:

FIGURE 12.2

Performance Lab Test for Third-Grade Unit

STATION 1. Pictures of People in Our School Community Who Help Our School Run Smoothly

1. What do these people have in common?
2. What is the purpose of a school community?
3. Which member of the school community is of the most interest to you? Please explain.

STATION 2. Pictures of School Community Members Cooperating

1. Why do community members need to cooperate?
2. What kinds of problems can school community members solve?
3. How are the school and the community alike?

STATION 3. Map of the School

1. When you enter the front door of our school and turn to your right, whose office do you come to first?
2. Give the directions to the principal's office from the front door entrance.
3. How would you get to the library from the principal's office?
4. Explain how you would get to the computer lab from the principal's office.

STATION 4. Map of North America

1. What is the largest country in North America?
2. Is Mexico or Canada the larger country?
3. Where is Central America in relation to Greenland?
4. Which country do you think would have the coldest temperatures in winter? Why?

STATION 5. Regional Map of the United States

1. What is the northernmost state in our region?
2. If you were flying from North Carolina to Mexico, how many major rivers would you cross? What are their names?
3. Which ocean is closest to New Mexico?
4. If you are planning a winter vacation and want to experience warm weather, where would you go and why?

STATION 6. Five States, Five Great Lakes

1. What is the purpose of the compass rose?
2. Where is Michigan in relation to the Ohio River?
3. Which Great Lake separates us from Illinois?
4. Where is Lake Superior in relation to the Mississippi River?
5. Would you cross any of the Great Lakes if you were flying from Lansing, Michigan, to Anchorage, Alaska? Explain.

STATION 7. Michigan County Map

1. What county do we live in?
2. What county is in the southwest corner of our state?
3. In what direction would you travel (from where you live) to get to Cheboygan? To Allegan?

STATION 8. Road Map of Michigan

1. What is the best way to go from Dansville to Mason?
2. What is the best way to go from Dansville to Stockbridge?
3. Approximately how many miles is it from Dansville to Leslie?
4. How would you get from Dansville to the state capitol?

FIGURE 12.3

Lab Test Checklist

Did you . . .

_____ acquire clipboards for students to use?

_____ match test items to objectives (subsets of goals)?

_____ match test items to concepts and skills?

_____ design test items that include higher-order thinking?

_____ use the wide variety of instructional materials that you used in teaching?

_____ use student-made materials? (Gradually infuse these after several successful lab experiences.)

_____ provide optional test items for diverse learners at some of the stations?

_____ make provisions for students to catch up in their writing as they progress through the test?

_____ attempt to make items at each station similar in length, or make necessary accommodations?

_____ provide answer sheets that are easily interpreted?

_____ plan for students who complete the test in minimum time?

_____ prepare an effective feedback strategy?

_____ plan a strategy for reteaching (if necessary)?

_____ plan a strategy for collecting and recording student results?

Portfolio Assessment

Authentic assessments might include having students submit portfolios representing their work. While most teachers would have students develop a composite of work samples from across the subject areas for portfolios, we will focus on the social studies section. Examples of work types we have observed on visits to classrooms include research projects on such topics as "Customs from Our Heritage That We Observe in Our Home," "Rosa Parks, A Native of Michigan Who Championed Civil Rights," and "Life in the Swiss Alps"; and essays such as "Why I Would Prefer to Live in the City versus the Country," "Some of the Hidden Advantages of Cold Climates," and "What I Can Do to Save Our Country Environmentally." Charts, graphs, maps, photos, letters from pen pals across the globe, interview data and analysis, and drawings are among the other work samples we have observed. Often students are asked to include copies of their tests, home assignments, notes taken while on field trips—any artifact that helps explain themselves as learners. Frequently, teachers ask students to include narrative in response to certain questions, such as "Which piece(s) of work are you most proud of and why?" "What would you add or do differently next time?" "Which social studies unit was most meaningful to you and why?" "What do the portfolio entries say about you as a learner?"

Potential portfolio contents should reflect the diversity of reading, writing, questioning, analyzing, and experiences that are incorporated with the social studies units. They also should reveal students' continuing development. The social studies section should represent the important things learned in that subject. It should serve as a powerful stimulus for students to use as they articulate the major understandings in the units of study and evaluate their own work.

Periodically, students should be expected to confer about their work with their peers, with you as their teacher, and with their parents. One teacher we observed also has her students confer with the teacher they will have next year, explaining what they have learned across the year and what knowledge, skills, understandings, appreciations, applications, and curiosities they will bring to the next grade. We also have witnessed students, beginning in the early grades, conducting conferences with their parents regarding their social studies goals and showing work samples to represent where they are in their development, what aspects they need to work on more diligently, and what types of assistance and support they think they need from the family. We view this approach as extraordinary in building a sense of self-efficacy in the domain of social education.

Student-Led Parent Conferences

Student-led conferences provide an opportunity to talk about what has been learned, using the contents of the portfolio as the springboard for discussion. These conferences between the student and the teacher are often arranged on an informal, ongoing basis. Ideally, they include one or two sessions during the year with students and their families. The combination of students' work collected over time with their own explanations of what they did and why provides a powerful venue for students to begin assessing their own progress. Often students simply do not know what they know, so when they verbalize it, it is as informative to the student as it is to his/her audience. Although conferences vary in purpose, they share the intent of raising students' interest in their own learning, helping them to be more reflective about it and as a result, take more responsibility for it. They begin to see connections between reading, writing, speaking, and thinking, as well as across content areas, and both they and their families begin to realize that learning is a continuous and ongoing process.

Student-led parent conferences are motivating because they incorporate elements of choice (of what work to include) and create authentic audiences and venues for assessment. They also reveal levels of learning and openly certify that additional work is needed in certain areas.

Conclusion

Because powerful social studies teaching and learning are goal-oriented and integrative, value-based, challenging, meaningful, and active, the evaluation component should reflect these same features. In the past, teachers and administrators who preferred to deemphasize assessment in social studies, or to treat it serendipitously, could do so without high-stakes consequences. Now, however, this benign-neglect approach risks adverse consequences. Even if the movement toward national tests fails in social studies, the pressures exerted on other school subjects could result in the reduction of curriculum time allocated to social studies or the importance assigned to social studies courses by students and community members. We therefore suggest that it is essential for social studies teachers to develop goal-oriented classes and programs, and in the process, develop assessment systems that support accomplishment of these goals and solidify social studies as the flagship for citizenship education.

Summary

Assessment should be treated as an ongoing and integral part of each social studies unit. The results should be scrutinized to detect weaknesses in the assessment practices themselves, as well as to detect special-learner needs, misunderstandings, or misconceptions. The results of the ongoing analysis should be carefully considered when reviewing, and if necessary, adjusting plans for future versions of currently taught units.

The assessment should address the full range of goals pursued in the unit, including attitudes, values, and dispositions along with knowledge and skills. Different assessment tools might be more or less appropriate at the different stages of assessment (preliminary, formative, summative), but the unit's assessment components should build toward authentic applications at the ends of lesson sequences and the unit itself. In addition to traditional formats such as multiple-choice, short-answer, and essay questions, we recommend a variety of informal assessments, the laboratory model and other performance assessments, and portfolio assessments. An especially powerful form of portfolio assessment is the student-led conference in which students assemble portfolios illustrating their work and present them not only to the teacher but also to parents or other family members who attend the conference.

Reflective Questions

1. How do you view the relationship between ongoing assessment and academic achievement?
2. How do you view social studies assessment in the early grades?
3. What do you view as the major challenges of social studies assessment for the classroom teacher?
4. How do you view the relationships among assessment, expectations, and accountability? What are some scenarios that would illustrate these relationships?
5. Why do you think assessment and evaluation are sometimes seen as negatives by teachers?

Your Turn:
Evaluation

Your unit assessment. Select a social studies unit that you have designed and taught, or one that you have observed being taught. Collect the evaluation materials that were used as preliminary, formative, and summative assessment. Examine them in terms of the following criteria:

- Do the written items reflect the major understandings that were developed?
- Are the items reflective of the unit goals?
- Does student work show a balance between knowledge and skills on the one hand, and values and dispositions on the other?
- If standardized, norm-referenced tests or publisher-supplied criterion-referenced tests are used, do the items closely match the values, goals, and major understandings defined in the local social studies curriculum?
- How authentic was the assessment? (Formal strategies? Informal strategies?)
- What evidence is there that performance assessment is being woven into the social studies curriculum?
- Is social studies finding its way into portfolio assessment?
- Are teachers at least talking about student-led conferences and the role they can play in engendering student responsibility and a sense of self-efficacy?

After you reflect on the responses from this exercise, write a paragraph characterizing what you have observed about the evaluation component of the unit. Write a second paragraph describing what you would retain and what you would modify and/or add to make the evaluation reflect ideal learner outcomes more clearly.

Using the laboratory model. The laboratory model for social studies performance assessment probably is the one with which you have had the least experience in the elementary school classroom. We urge you to incorporate it into one of your upcoming units. Start small, with just a few stations. One might consist of a wall map accompanied by a series of questions; another might be a chart; another an open book with a marked passage; and another might include a hand slide projector, slides, and questions. As students become more acclimated to the lab-like process and as they become more adept at engaging in higher-order thinking, you can expand the number and nature of the stations. At some point, at least by fourth grade, you can include their finished products and their questions as a part of the lab test. Our experiences suggest that students are stimulated by this type of assessment and find it more challenging than fearful.

OR

Your Turn:
Using NCSS Strands and Performance Indicators

Use the following exercise focusing on the ten NCSS Content Strands and some performance indicators to assess your level of understanding regarding the use of activities as assessments (providing they match the goals and are the appropriate level of difficulty, feasible, and cost effective in terms of time and trouble).

Early Elementary, Strand I. Culture

Performance Expectation d	Compare ways in which people from different cultures think about and deal with their physical environment.
Assessment	The teacher has prepared a bulletin board that depicts a range of physical features. Each student is asked to select a picture from the photo box and explain where it fits on the bulletin board. (Each picture represents a different culture, and the student is expected to explain how, for example, the Swiss people might use their mountainous environment.)
Rate the Assessment	Good Bad Conditional

Early Elementary Strand II. Time, Continuity, Change

Performance Expectation b	Construct simple timelines identifying examples of change.
Assessment	Each student is asked to construct a timeline depicting the changes that have occurred in his/her family and verbally describe these changes to the class.
Rate the Assessment	Good Bad Conditional

Early Elementary Strand III. People, Places, Environment

Performance Expectation k	Consider existing uses and propose and evaluate alternate uses of resources and land in home, school, community, the region, and beyond.
Assessment	Each student is given a physical map of the community and asked to locate three sites where the land might be used differently, visually depict possibilities, and be able to explain the reasoning to the class.
Rate the Assessment	Good Bad Conditional

Early Elementary, Strand IV. Individual Development and Identity

Performance Expectation c	Describe the unique features of one's nuclear and extended families.
Assessment	Each student is asked to bring in pictures and words to describe his/her nuclear and extended families. These will be assembled and put in individual book form. If students wish to draw pictures, they will be encouraged to do this during "down time" or at home. Students will share their family books with the class and describe the unique features of their nuclear and extended families.
Rate the Assessment	Good Bad Conditional

Early Elementary, Strand V, Individuals, Groups, and Institutions

Performance Expectation g	Show how groups and institutions work to meet individual needs and promote the common good, and identify examples where they fail to do so.
Assessment	Each student will be given a list of institutions that promote the common good and asked to explain why each might be considered negative.
Rate the Assessment	Good Bad Conditional

Middle Grades, Strand VI. Power, Authority, and Governance

Performance Expectation e	Identify and describe the basic features of the political system in the United States, and identify representative leaders from various levels and branches of government.
Assessment	Students will be asked to list at least seven basic features of the political system of the United States. They then will be given a set of pictures depicting leaders from various levels and branches of government and asked to identify each individual.
Rate the Assessment	Good Bad Conditional

Middle Grades, Strand VII. Production, Distribution, and Consumption

Performance Expectation g	Differentiate among various forms of exchange and money.
Assessment	Students will be provided with a display of forms of exchange and money, with each item given a number. They will be asked to select at least seven of the twelve items and explain what they are, when they are used most appropriately, and what their negatives and positives are. Finally, they will write a paragraph explaining why we have more than one form.
Rate the Assessment	Good Bad Conditional

Middle Grades, Strand VIII. Science, Technology, and Society

Performance Expectation b	Show through specific examples how science and technology have changed people's perceptions of the social and natural world, such as in their relationships to the land; animal life; family life; and economic needs, wants, and security.
Assessment	Students will read about the Seven Wonders and design a structure of their own that is worth being called an Eighth Wonder. They will describe the technology needed to build their Wonder and consider its costs and benefits to society. Each student's project includes a written component that is evaluated on two criteria: analysis of the relationship between technology and building structure, and the description of the potential impact of the technology on the environment.
Rate the Assessment	Good Bad Conditional

Middle Grades, Strand IX. Global Connections

Performance Expectation b	Analyze examples of conflict, cooperation, and interdependence among groups, societies, and nations.
Assessment	Students are given a series of articles written during the Gulf War. Each student is to select three examples and describe how conflict, cooperation, and interdependence were incorporated into each of the situations.
Rate the Assessment	Good Bad Conditional

Middle Grades, Strand X. Civic Ideals and Practices

Performance Expectation b	Identify and interpret sources and examples of the rights and responsibilities of citizens.
Assessment	Students are asked (during a two-day period) to develop an essay with pictures collected in advance to explain what rights and responsibilities of the local citizenry have come to mean. Examples should be included.
Rate the Assessment	Good Bad Conditional

HOW CAN THE CURRICULUM BE EXPANDED AND MADE MORE MEANINGFUL THROUGH HOME–SCHOOL CONNECTIONS?

Amy Emerine, Teacher Intern

Home assignments provide opportunities for students to think and reflect critically on how what they are learning in school relates to their everyday lives. Out-of-school activities tend to answer the question, "Why should I care about learning this?" When students understand that what they are learning really does matter and apply to life, motivation to put in the effort seems to come on its own. This chapter stresses how to incorporate out-of-school learning in meaningful ways that will enrich not only the classroom learning but also the lives of the students as they learn more about themselves, their families, and others in their communities.

This chapter offers ideas on how to incorporate and invite families and the community into classroom learning in a nonintimidating manner. Home assignments that require learning about family history or conducting interviews with community members are noninvasive, appealing, and meaningful and do not make participants feel like they are wasting their own time. When children include their family and the community in their education, it fosters diversity naturally and serves the notion that it takes a village to raise a child. The more people who are actively involved in a child's education, the richer and fuller it is likely to be.

In preparing for my internship in a fourth-grade class, I was informed by the teacher that the social studies textbook was the only source we were required to use during the year. My plans to use out-of-school learning activities as a means of extending learning beyond the textbook will create an opportunity to intersect the disconnected facts and ideas that frequent textbooks. To prepare the families, I plan to send home a letter explaining the importance of the home assignments and how they will connect to what is going on in the classroom.

Learning should not end each day with the final bell at school. Instead, teachers can find ways to incorporate what is being learned in the classroom into the everyday lives of children in noninvasive and meaningful ways.

The focus of this chapter is out-of-school learning opportunities aligned with in-school social studies units, in which students interact with family and community members to enhance the meaningfulness of big ideas introduced and discussed in the classroom. We will provide a rationale for out-of-school learning, identify and use specific examples to illustrate several potential purposes and functions, and explain how powerful social studies teaching that emphasizes authentic out-of-school learning opportunities (home assignments) can provide life applications, engender students' sense of self-efficacy, and create natural opportunities to construct understandings beyond what can be realized in a regular classroom (given the diversity of students, the time constraints imposed for meeting standards, and the range of school subjects to be taught). Finally, we will provide guidelines for framing out-of-school learning opportunities and ensuring that data from these experiences are linked back to the classroom and shared with classmates.

Given the age-grading system, the high student-to-teacher ratio, the ambiguity and risk involved in academic work (Doyle, 1983), and the other features built into mass education systems, students' learning opportunities in classrooms necessarily are limited and somewhat artificial compared to what is possible under more natural and unconstrained conditions. One way for teachers to compensate for this is to use the community as a living laboratory for social studies learning, and in the process, use the diversity of student backgrounds represented in the class as a resource for promoting social studies understandings.

By *out-of-school learning opportunities,* we do not mean conventional homework, which traditionally has focused on practice exercises designed to reinforce in-class teaching (Cooper, 1989). Instead, we refer to opportunities to expand and enrich the curriculum by causing students to think and collect information about how social studies concepts learned at school apply to their home and family situations and their community, and then feed their findings back into subsequent class discussions. This can make social studies learning more meaningful and personally relevant than it would have been otherwise.

Out-of-school learning opportunities in social studies complement what goes on in school by exploiting home and community resources and environments. Many involve activities that are unfeasible or even impossible to do in classrooms yet are vital components of a well-rounded social studies education.

Principles for Designing and Implementing Out-of-School Learning Activities

We will consider out-of-school learning opportunities within the context of the principles for planning and implementing social studies learning activities that we described in Chapter 9. These principles include four primary criteria that all learning activities must meet: (1) goal relevance, (2) appropriate level of difficulty, (3) feasibility, and (4) cost. Secondary criteria to consider when choosing from among activities that meet all the primary criteria include activities that allow students to accomplish several goals simultaneously; are viewed as enjoyable, or at least as meaningful and worthwhile; involve natural, holistic, or authentic applications of learning rather than isolated skills practice or artificial exercises; engage students in higher-order thinking; and are adaptable to accommodate individual differences in interests or abilities. Activities should be structured and scaffolded by teachers in ways that help students to engage in them with awareness of their goals and metacognitive control of their learning strategies.

These principles also apply to out-of-school activities, with some minor modifications. First, out-of-school learning can use the students' total environment to provide data or learning resources. This makes certain activities feasible that would not be feasible in the classroom. Also, cost-effectiveness does not need to be assigned as high a priority. Class time is limited and needs to be concentrated on lessons and structuring of assignments, but once students are clear about what they need to do, they can work on assignments outside of class. They also can work on individually negotiated or time-consuming projects that complement the group lessons and activities that occur during class time.

Out-of-school learning opportunities provide a natural mechanism for nurturing intergenerational communication by encouraging students to share and discuss with their families what they are learning in school. The idea is to use home assignments to provide a forum for interaction, not to suggest that families are to "teach" what was not accomplished in school. The assignments should encourage students to talk about what they are learning with their families, to take more responsibility for their learning, and to appreciate that learning is continuous and lifelong (Alleman & Brophy, 1994a).

Purposes and Functions of Home Assignments

Coupling these principles and assumptions with our ideas about some of the advantages of using the students' total environment as a data source, as a learning laboratory, as a forum for expanded learning opportunities, and as a means of extending social studies to the home and community, we have identified several potential purposes or functions of out-of-school learning opportunities. We have not presented them in any particular order because their relative value will depend on the teacher's hierarchy of social education goals.

Provide for Expanded Meaningfulness and Life Application of School Learning

Home assignments offer daily opportunities to use what is learned in school in out-of-school settings. For example, goals for a government unit might include helping students to (1) understand and appreciate the value and importance of government regulations in their lives; and (2) become more aware of the written and unwritten rules and laws that are part of their environment. Students could be encouraged to read a journal entry that the class had compiled about governmental regulations to one or more family members and then discuss and look for examples of rules and laws that are part of the household. A Means and Functions of Government chart with examples could be sent home as a resource for use in completing the assignment. Examples of means of governing us might include traffic lights, clothing labels, money (government manufactures the coins and bills we use), driver's license, seat belts, tax statements, meat or restaurant inspection notices, and so on. (Alleman & Brophy, 2003b)

Another example for expanding meaningfulness comes from a unit on shelter. Typical goals might include developing understanding and appreciation of the types of homes that have been created over time, the changes they have undergone, and the reasons for these changes. As a follow-up to lessons comparing homes of the distant past, the recent past, and today, students could be asked to identify ways that their homes differ from the homes of earlier time periods, seek help from parents in writing their responses, and bring to school a list of differences accompanied by a paragraph explaining which type of home they would most like to live in and why (e.g., cave or stone hut, log cabin, modern frame house). In one of our classroom observations, we found that students were divided on their home preferences. About half favored the modern home because of the conveniences, but most of the others preferred the log cabin due to the adventure and curiosity associated with it. In addition, two students and their families preferred caves due to simplicity and mystery.

Constructing Meaning in Natural Ways and Engendering a Sense of Self-Efficacy

Out-of-school learning opportunities that focus on the unit goals provide a natural mechanism for situated learning and the social construction of knowledge, as students share and discuss with their families what they are learning in school. This challenges them to use higher-order thinking as they apply the learning to real-world settings. For example, in a unit on clothing, one of the goals might focus on economic decision making (e.g., what constitutes a "good buy"). An out-of-school learning activity might call for a family discussion about establishing a clothing budget, addressing associated issues such as how families decide when it is time to consider larger sizes for a growing child, and what the implications of that decision are. During one of our classroom observations, a child explained to the class that if he were willing to wear the coat his older brother had outgrown, he could save his family some money. Another child proclaimed that he was wearing a "new" shirt that his mother had purchased at a garage sale for 25 cents. He proudly rationalized that he was growing quickly and the shirt was silk—an expensive fabric if purchased brand new. These examples illustrate how home assignments can provide natural opportunities for students to contribute ideas— and sometimes even educate their families—as they examine choices and trade- offs that influence and regulate their social experiences and decisions (Alleman & Brophy, 2000).

Self-efficacy is a sense of empowerment, of being able to make a difference using what has been learned (Bandura, 1989; Bandura & Schunk, 1981; Schunk, 1991). It is a confident state of mind that says, "I can do it. I can contribute. I can decide. I can figure it out." Teachers and families can provide information and opportunities for students to make intelligent decisions in the real world—as well as begin to understand and explain why things are as they are and how they came to be. These experiences contribute to the students' development of self-efficacy perceptions concerning their knowledge and self-regulation potential in the social domain.

Extending Social Studies Education to the Home and Community by Involving Adults in Interesting and Responsible Ways

Parents usually value becoming involved with their children's learning in mean- ingful ways. While baking cookies for a special party is helpful and volun- teering to help in the classroom is important, there are more authentic ways for parents to become involved with their children and the social studies curriculum. These serve to keep families informed about what is happening in the classroom and at the same time enhance their children's skill development and ability to apply content learned in school in meaningful ways that relate directly to their lives outside of school.

For example, despite at least three U.S. history courses included in K–12 educa- tion and at least four curricular opportunities to learn about the states and capitals, students often do not know where the largest state is located, what states border their own, when the U.S. declared its independence, and so on. It is suspected that the root of the problem lies in the isolated "book-learning," "do-school" manner in which the material is covered. One way to overcome this hurdle may be to provide families with simple maps, timelines, and simulations/games to be used at home. By providing some of these resources, accompanied by instructions for activities, teach- ers can build learning opportunities into family discussions that include locating in time and space local places and events as well as those seen on television. Timelines could also be used to anchor family discussions about how old family members are, when their ancestors were born, or what significant historical events occurred during their lifetimes.

Similarly, activities such as planning vacations or discussing news events could be focused around appropriate maps to enhance in-class current-events discus- sions. Students can begin to see that the world is dynamic and changing, that things that impact our lives occur every day, and that significant events often happen around the world simultaneously.

Social studies is also rich with opportunities for involving students with fam- ily members and the community in collaborations that can be mutually satisfying and stimulating. Parents, older siblings, babysitters, family friends, neighbors, business owners, and politicians can be great collaborators for learning—and without special preparation. The key to success is careful selection of out-of-school learning experiences that reflect the goals of the teacher's lesson or unit.

For example, in a class studying communities, one of the goals might be to become aware of what is being done by local citizens to ensure that the community is safe and clean. Another goal might be to pave the way for students' participation in purposeful citizen action projects. Students could survey family members or other local people to determine what they personally are doing—or would be willing to do—to have a safe and clean community. The results could be shared in class, and students could follow up by developing a plan of action for themselves. The plan could include a map of the community with a legend depicting unsafe/unclean areas and using designated symbols to indicate particular problems. Students could use the data to inform the community of current conditions. They might elect to conduct an after-school campaign to encourage people to take positive action. Some might volunteer to work with adult community leaders on projects to ensure that the area becomes a more healthy and safe place to reside.

In another class, one of the goals might be to develop appreciation of the importance of community and home safety, especially in an age when many children spend considerable time alone. A powerful out-of-school activity could call for students, with assistance from available people in the household, to conduct home safety surveys. Using the data, follow-up in-class structured discourse could provide guidance for how students themselves might respond to their home safety needs and alert family members about areas needing attention. Students could decide to collect literature to assist in guiding the proposed changes.

When studying other regions or states, students could talk with their families about connections that they have with these parts of the country through family or business contacts, use of goods from places being studied, or vacations proposed or taken in those locations. Using the Internet to access data and/or to communicate with pen-pal students or relatives who live in those places could be encouraged.

During the study of the history of the United States, students could gather a wealth of information regarding the history of their locale—how it came to be; why it developed where it did; who explored and settled the place; and when it became recognized as a town, city, or part of the state. Local newspapers, graveyards, historical societies, and retirement facilities are invaluable resources for bringing history to life. These could be listed as potentials for "family outings" supported by teacher-provided questions that could be used during observations and interviews. The retrieved information could be invaluable input to subsequent in-class discussions.

In a unit on physical regions of the United States, the goals might include understanding the relationship of natural phenomena to industries and appreciating the pros and cons of humans manipulating the environment. Here, the teacher could encourage students to allocate some out-of-school time to discuss with family members how they have experienced human manipulation of the environment, such as during a vacation at a mountain resort or through employment (e.g., living in a variety of places so a parent could continue to work in highway construction). Students would be encouraged to bring in photographs, postcards, or newspaper articles as validation of these experiences.

All of these learning opportunities and a host of others that could be generated can effectively bring to life goals focusing on personalizing history, expanding understanding and appreciation for the past, helping students position themselves in time and space, and acquiring a greater sensitivity toward the environment and the ways that humans have manipulated it.

The collaborative learning that occurs outside the classroom has the potential for improving in-class participation by more enlightened learners and for creating a more informed cadre of human resources sprinkled throughout the community. Students can have opportunities to become involved with their parents and other adults in positive and productive relationships, and as a bonus, these adults will have opportunities to enjoy nonthreatening and personally rewarding involvement in their children's education.

Taking Advantage of the Students' Diversity by Using It as a Learning Resource

Too often, differences among students are viewed as problems. However, these differences can be used as opportunities for students to begin with what they know best and link their knowledge to the experiences of others. For example, one of the goals of a food unit might be to develop an understanding and appreciation of the role that culture plays in determining the way food is prepared. As a home assignment, family members could be encouraged to discuss the foods the family enjoys for special occasions. Families could be asked to share their recipes for these foods so that a recipe book could be compiled with help from volunteers.

Goals for a unit on family might include helping students to understand and appreciate the contributions of their ancestors, including some of their family's customs and traditions. For the home assignment, students could interview an older family member about their ancestors, make a family tree, talk about special things learned from the individuals represented on the family tree, and describe a family custom or tradition that has been passed down from one generation to another that is still enjoyed regularly or on special occasions. This activity would elicit an impressive and useful range of information for students to share with the class.

One of the goals of a shelter unit might be to develop an appreciation for the opportunities that people may have to exercise choice in meeting their shelter needs and wants. Students can be encouraged to discuss with their families the choices they have made regarding where to live and why. In one classroom we observed, this activity stimulated a lot of in- and out-of-class discourse, and on follow-up surveys, family members indicated that the exercise got their children to think more broadly about why they live where they do, where they would like to live and why, and the trade-offs associated with renting versus buying. Parents also indicated that they had never before thought of explaining their choices to their children. One said, "The assignment gave me a forum for giving reasons for my actions. In fact, I could remove what I'd formerly called guilt" (Alleman & Brophy, 1998).

Another goal in a shelter unit might be for students to understand and appreciate the range of homes that have been created over time, the changes they have undergone, and the reasons for these changes. Students could take home copies of a chart comparing the distant past, the recent past, and today, and identify differences between modern homes and those in earlier time periods. Older family members could be asked to help the students write responses in the appropriate spaces on the chart.

Other goals of a shelter unit might be for students to understand and appreciate how technology, inventions, and discoveries have enabled people today to live in controlled environments and for students to begin to grasp how these conveniences "work." As a home assignment, parents could be asked to assist their child in touring their home looking for ways that the family has taken advantage of modern conveniences such as heating, cooling, water, and lighting. They also could be encouraged to show their children how utilities are made available to the home and routed and controlled through pipes, faucets, thermostats, fuses, circuit breakers, switches, and so on. The drawings, photos, and explanations that this assignment yielded during our observations indicated enthusiasm and newfound knowledge. For example, one student shared his drawing and explanation of the furnace and said, "Ours is always broken. I sat down with the furnace guy on his last call to our house and said, 'Now tell me how this thing is supposed to work'" (Alleman & Brophy, 1998).

Having students gather data about their own families to share with peers can create immediate interest in an often bland, repetitive topic. For example, if students live within extended family arrangements, they might develop responses to a list of questions: What role does Grandmother play when Mother works nights? How is her role different from what it would be if she lived out of state? What are the gains in your home as a result of the extended family arrangement? What are the potential problems that need to be worked out? How is your living arrangement similar or dissimilar from the one you read about describing a family in Japan? These attributes of extended families can be compared to those of nuclear families in our culture and to those of extended families in other cultures, noting similarities as well as differences.

Data gathered from family members can also enhance students' appreciation of diverse perspectives on social studies content and engender the realization that social studies is broadly focused and frequently open to debate. For example, suppose one of the goals of a social studies unit is for the students to understand and appreciate the global connections between their community and East Asia. Typically, students would be asked to read textbook material, discuss it in class, and list connections on the chalkboard. This lesson would have more impact if students were asked first to interview the adults in their households and/or neighborhoods about their views of global connections with East Asia. For example, a parent or neighbor who is presently laid off from an automobile plant might feel quite differently from a parent or neighbor who sells Japanese-made audio/video equipment at an appliance store. Interviewing could be coupled with an investigation of the home to determine the number and nature of goods from East Asia that are found there. Homes with access to the Internet could provide still another rich resource and serve to illustrate the nearness of places formerly considered remote. These data then would be funneled back into the classroom to aid students in achieving the "documented" realization that there is a range of beliefs and values about globalness in the community that is directly tied to people's life experiences.

These out-of-school learning experiences can be rewarding for all of the individuals involved, and the data that are "harvested" during follow-up discussions can be provocative, insightful, and rich in diverse examples. It is helpful if the teacher provides snapshots into his/her personal life as well, to model sharing and add human interest elements to activities.

Personalizing the Curriculum and Reflecting on the Here and Now

Home assignments can enhance students' awareness and understanding of the contexts of their daily lives and the lives of their families. For example, goals of a unit on money might be to develop an understanding and appreciation for budgeting as a tool for managing money, an understanding of opportunity cost, and the ability to apply these concepts to life outside of school. The teacher might use a hypothetical child's budget and his/her own budget to illustrate major understandings and facilitate discussion. As a home assignment, students could talk with their families about budgeting and bring to school examples of how opportunity cost plays out in their households.

In a unit on communication, a viable goal might be to develop students' awareness of how they spend their out-of-school time and in particular, how much of it is spent with mass communication during a week. Class members, with the assistance of family members, could be asked to account for their television viewing, using a standard form provided for easy recording. The data could be returned to school and used to inform construction of a graph of students' television viewing and a subsequent discussion of the results (Alleman & Brophy, 2003b).

Another goal of the communication unit might be to develop an understanding and appreciation of the variety of ways in which television influences its viewers. After learning about commercials and advertising techniques, students could write letters to their families describing the important things they learned about television viewing and identify at least one recommendation they would like their families to consider during future viewing (e.g., "Don't believe everything the commercials tell you," "Some sports shoes cost a lot more than other brands because the companies pay popular sports figures to advertise their product. Check to make sure those shoes are worth the extra dollars," etc.). Families would be asked to discuss how commercials had influenced them and what new questions they might want to ask before they purchase advertised products.

Exploiting Learning Opportunities That Are Not Cost Effective on School Time

Students' homes and the surrounding community are filled with learning resources that might not be cost effective for exploitation during an organized field trip but could be explored by one or more individuals who might be asked to visit a particular site and report back to class. Suppose, for example, that an intermediate-grade class was going to study local government. Because of the expenses of bus rental and the complications involved in rescheduling classes, it may not be feasible for the whole class to attend a city council meeting. However, a few students and their families could volunteer to attend such a meeting, where they could serve as observers, data gatherers, and primary sources for a follow-up in-class discussion. The entire class would be involved in the initial reading and planning. The active student participants would go to the session armed with questions from their peers and return having fulfilled a class mission. The follow-up discussion could address the preliminary peer questions and the participants' observations. Such an out-of-school opportunity should serve to whet the appetite of others and provide the class with another avenue for becoming informed and involved citizens of the community. Students would be expected to take turns taking on special assignments with their parents so that their classmates could benefit from a range of field trips that would not be feasible within the parameters of most school budgets.

Suppose a class was studying government with special attention to rules and laws. Taking the whole class on a walking tour of the community looking for signs of unwritten and written rules and laws might be too time consuming; however, this task could be a very productive and challenging use of after-school time. Students could easily combine this assignment with the regular school bus ride or walk home. For best results, the teacher should provide a data-retrieval form so that the next day's discussion is not based simply on memory.

Other examples of out-of-school learning opportunities that are not cost effective if done during school time, yet could be useful when structured appropriately and tied to in-school goals, include watching a specific television show with an eye toward gender roles or to acquire knowledge and appreciation about a particular place or group of people (e.g., a special program on women in Islamic countries). These out-of-school learning opportunities expand students' learning horizons, serve as validity checks for book learning, and provide authentic connections that extend beyond the school day.

Keeping the Curriculum Up to Date

Social education courses based on textbooks as their chief data sources are often years behind on world events. In such cases, it is important to supplement the text with out-of-school learning opportunities involving newspapers, magazines, television broadcasts, and Internet linkages. The additional information can be used to inform discussions of the changes occurring and the challenges created by a new set of conditions. Instead of only reading outdated material regarding U.S. leadership and our country's affairs, students learn at the cutting edge of national and world developments. For example, discussion could be focused on the effects of the events of 9/11/01. How has our country changed since that historical event? Engagement of adults in the students' households or neighborhoods in discussion of such questions may cause them to view their children in a new light and create a cross-generational dialogue about a topic of real interest.

Teacher and Parent Involvement

Home assignments are one way to model and establish the norm that everybody has the capacity and the opportunity to learn out of school. We observed one student exclaim to the teacher, "You are doing the homework too!" The teacher explained that she also was learning new things about her community. On another occasion, a student with a rather puzzled look said, "I thought you just cooked up things to keep us busy. Look, you are doing them too!" Soon students came to realize that if the teacher participates in home assignments—and actually brings data back to the class to share—it must be important.

Having the teacher model returning home assignments is a good way to overcome one of the teacher's major concerns. Another concern relates to family willingness to participate in home learning opportunities. Many think that helping their child is cheating, that "I may not know the right answer," that "I simply don't have the time needed to help," or that "It's the teacher's job to educate my child." Overcoming these obstacles does not happen overnight. It requires ongoing education about the power of authentic learning out of school and the role families can play in enhancing student interest in curriculum content as well as potentially influencing student achievement. It requires explaining to parents through letters, conferences, and public presentations how parents can help their children and the thinking behind home assignments in social studies.

It is helpful if you as the teacher model what is being asked in home assignments to ensure that students understand the goals and directions for accomplishing the tasks. Establish the mindset that the home assignments are vital to learning because they add meaningfulness and new perspectives. Use the results in subsequent lessons. Create the expectation that students will return their completed homework assignments. When students fall short of this expectation, a friendly reminder note or call is in order. Asking students to recall what was on the paper left on the kitchen counter or using the student data when it does arrive are other subtle ways of indicating the importance of the assignments and their authentic connections to the in-school curriculum.

Guidelines for Framing Out-of-School Learning Opportunities

- Make sure that every assignment relates to the social education goals for the lesson/unit.
- Make sure students can clearly articulate the purpose of the out-of-school learning opportunity (home assignment).
- Educate families about the nature and purposes of the assignments.
- Provide students with letters to parents describing the assignments as well as materials such as charts, tables, worksheets, interview schedules, and so on for retrieving data. These materials make it easier for families to do the assignments and usually result in a higher return of information to inform future class discussions.
- Establish time frames appropriate for the tasks.
- Expect all students to complete the assignments, and make sure you acknowledge the returned data in subsequent lessons.

Summary

We have described different functions of out-of-school learning opportunities as a means of enhancing the social education curriculum and expanding the conception of homework. Out-of-school learning activities, if explained properly to students, parents, and community, will enhance the meaningfulness of the traditional social education curriculum, begin paving the way for a mentality of lifelong learning, and enhance the authenticity of what is learned in school.

Although we have suggested many different ways in which out-of-school learning opportunities can enhance the curriculum, most of these are elaborations on a few key ideas. One is that out-of-school assignments can provide opportunities for students to think critically about how some of the ideas learned in school apply to their lives out of school and, in the process, make personal decisions about issues that they raise. In theory, much of what is in the social studies curriculum is there because it is thought to be important as a means to prepare students to cope with the demands of modern living and to function as responsible citizens in our society. Unless students are encouraged and given opportunities to apply what they are learning to their lives outside of school, however, they may not see or appreciate these connections and thus may not get the intended citizen-preparation benefits. In a time when so much attention is given to standards and high-stakes testing, it is important to ensure that what we expect students to learn can be understood, appreciated, and readily applied to their lives.

A second key idea is that diversity in students' family, ethnic, and socioeconomic backgrounds and life experiences can provide valuable case material for the application of concepts and principles learned in school. With diversity as a recurring theme in social studies curricula, authentically addressing it through home assignments provides a context of respect and appreciation for students' home backgrounds.

A third key idea is that out-of-school assignments provide opportunities to involve parents and other family members in the school's agenda in nonthreatening and personally rewarding ways. Parents may feel irritated or threatened if asked to help with homework that they do not understand themselves, but they are likely to be pleased to be asked to serve as resources by answering their children's questions about what life was like when they were younger, how they reacted to a major news event in the past, the details of what they do at work, or the trade-offs involved in their jobs as lifetime occupations.

The payoffs of incorporating out-of-school opportunities into social studies lessons seem obvious. These experiences should encourage students to respect their families in new ways, reinforce familial bonds, make them more enthusiastic learners (with higher achievement levels as an anticipated by-product), and support their development of self-efficacy perceptions in the social domain.

Reflective Questions

1. Imagine that one of your district's highest priorities this year is to promote more meaningful learning through home–school connections. For many families, this will be unfamiliar and take some convincing in order to realize positive results. How will you approach the challenge? Explain.

2. You have been asked to speak to a parent group in your school community (or write an article for the school newsletter). The topic is "Family Participation for Promoting Powerful Social Studies." What will you include in your presentation?

3. Imagine that diversity has been identified as one of the top priorities at your school. Teachers have been asked to share proposals for addressing it. Yours centers around home–school learning opportunities in social studies. What points will you make to convince your colleagues that a systematic approach involving families with the curriculum can be powerful?

4. What do you view as the most challenging aspects of expanding the curriculum and making it more meaningful through home–school connections? How will you overcome them?

5. Research indicates that student achievement is often impacted by family involvement in school-related matters. How can home–school assignments in social studies promote this? How might you monitor this practice to determine its influence on student learning?

6. The authors of this text have observed special-needs students reaping enormous benefits from social studies assignments that include home–school connections. How would you explain this? What might you do to accelerate this practice in your classroom?

Your Turn:
Incorporating Out-of-School Learning

Select an upcoming social studies unit. Review the goals and big ideas that you are intending to feature. Then ask yourself: "What out-of-school learning opportunities could be designed to expand meaningfulness and enrich the overall social studies experience?" Prepare and implement at least three home assignments for the unit (see Figure 13.1 for an example planning format).

Be sure to inform families well in advance and clearly state your purposes for the assignments. A sample letter has been provided (see Figure 13.2). Modify it to meet your specific needs. You might also consider having a note accompany each home assignment, at least until students and families get into the habit of good practice. Keep a reflective journal as your unit unfolds.

For more examples of home assignments aligned with goals and big ideas, review the units published in Alleman and Brophy (2001, 2002, 2003b).

FIGURE 13.1

Planning Home Assignments around Goals and Big Ideas

Goal for the Unit	Big Ideas for the Unit	Appropriate Home Assignment That Aligns with the Big Idea(s) and Goals
To develop an understanding and an appreciation for what citizenship means and how it can be practiced within the community.	Example 1. Good citizens tend to be respectful, to think and act for the good of the community, and to be open to ideas of others that may be different from their own. 2. _____ _____ _____ 3. _____ _____ _____ 4. _____ _____ _____	Example 1. Have students discuss with their families what citizenship means to them and how they practice it in their community. Provide a good-citizen worksheet with a couple of examples as starters. 2. _____ _____ _____ 3. _____ _____ _____ 4. _____ _____ _____

Source: See Alleman & Brophy, 2003b.

FIGURE 13.2

Sample Letter to Families

Dear Family Members:

This year we are taking part in a new, exciting way to learn social studies. Our units of study will include _____. In each of the units, we will emphasize the connections between what is learned in school and their lives out of school. Our hope is to have students who are more excited and motivated to learn about the world within their reach and far away.

As family members, you will be asked to contribute your knowledge and experiences in this area as well. Some home assignments might include such things as collecting pictures, watching the news or a specified television program with your child and discussing some particular questions, responding to questions regarding your experience of an event in history, or facilitating the gathering of objects or observable examples that reflect a key idea.

The intent is that your family responses will be returned to school so that our class conversations can be expanded and that social studies will be more memorable overall.

CHAPTER 14

WHAT SOCIAL STUDIES PLANNING TOOLS ARE AVAILABLE?

Sarah Shooltz, Teacher Intern

Schools are beginning to change the way they look at assessing students, and sometimes instruction must also change. The authors are ahead of the game by providing a framework for planning units that promote memorable learning and incorporate these assessment strategies. They emphasize looking at the "bigger picture" and long-term goals as well as short-term goals within units. Educators often lose sight of long-range goals and get tied up in everyday activities.

The authors highlight the important components to planning meaningful units and lessons. By focusing on big ideas and goals, I can much more easily decide what information is important to share with my students and in turn, what activities will help further their learning. When I share these ideas, my students have a clear expectation of what they need to take from the lesson and know what they can expect on an assessment later.

Many districts struggle with social studies because the texts ask students to recall meaningless pieces of information that they eventually will forget. The authors demonstrate several ways to make the learning meaningful, so students will internalize it and can later demonstrate a working knowledge of the subject.

As I have prepared my unit on the Mayans, the Aztecs, and the Incas, I realized that the textbook was insufficient in the knowledge it provided, so I would have to supplement it with technology and other modes of learning. I used the planning guide along with the information in the text as a starting point and asked the students to think of questions that the book left them with. What more did they want to know? It took a little prompting at first, but once the ideas started flowing, they didn't stop! The students began to personalize their learning to make it more meaningful to them, and I was able to design lessons that interested and engaged them.

The aims that we profess for social studies often are invisible within our practices. "Aims talk is not a luxury in which only outside 'experts' and ivory-tower academics—who have time on their hands—engage, but it is essential for thoughtful classroom teaching" (Thornton, 2005, p. 47). Our textbook in general and this chapter in particular are intended to stimulate conversations with colleagues and be used as you chart your course for social studies instruction. Our goal is that you will develop a vision for what social studies can be in your classroom, enact it accordingly, and do so in ways that make your aims and goals transparent to your students.

Planning as Goal Oriented

Throughout our book, we emphasize that powerful teaching begins with clarifying goals and developing big ideas. Planning with these as a priority is an essential component in social studies teaching. You are responsible for selecting and designing social studies–based learning experiences that reflect your school's curriculum and community learning goals. You also need to be able to respond to your students' needs and interests, as well as be ready to make the most of unanticipated learning opportunities that surface during instructional interactions. To do all this, you need to be prepared.

Planning and preparation have been the objects of educational theory and research since the early 1950s, but dominant conceptions of teaching have shifted over the years. Today, with the increased pressures of standards and testing, there is heavy debate about whether planning is part of teachers' professional practice or has been co-opted by district or school administrators. We strongly support the professional approach. After you read this text and reflect on the key teaching/learning principles that we offer, we hope you too will adopt it as your standard of practice.

Long-Range Planning

One of the most difficult but most rewarding types of planning is the long-range version. It takes desire, tenacity, resourcefulness, and lots of time at first. It typically gets easier as you become more familiar with the nature of students at a particular age level, the specific content, and available tools such as standards and assessment expectations. Some of the advantages of long-range planning include your ability to (1) use student test data in diagnostic ways; (2) use the skills and formats from standardized tests in natural ways as the yearlong plan unfolds; (3) look for natural ways to integrate across subjects; (4) look for optimal places across the year to introduce new content and skills, places to practice them, and places to apply them to new situations; and (5) determine the most appropriate places for large-group, small-group, and individual instruction, realizing that all students are assessed on standardized tests individually. While preparing social studies students for life is your ultimate goal, you want them to be comfortable and confident in testing situations as well as feel efficacious as they work on their own in and out of the classroom.

During long-range planning, you will need to revisit the social studies aim adopted by NCSS. It states, "The primary purpose of social studies is to help young people develop the ability to make informed and reasoned decisions for the public good as citizens of a culturally diverse, democratic society in an interdependent world" (NCSS, 1994). As you think deeply about the year and familiarize yourself with the content designated for your grade level, *make a list of yearlong social studies goals that support the overall social studies aim.* Also, create a "portrait" that describes what your ideal social studies learner will look like at the end of the year.

Your yearlong goals and portrait of ideal student progress are likely to feature relatively generic knowledge and skill developments, and especially, growth in attitudes, beliefs, values, and dispositions to action, that transcend the content taught in individual lessons and even units. You need to plan to give these yearlong goals consistent attention if you expect your students to make consistent progress as the school year unfolds.

Revisit your list of goals and ideal-student image often. They have the potential to serve as powerful self-monitoring tools as you plan, implement, and assess instruction. Finally, consider engaging your students in these exercises. Talking about your goals and ideals and setting high expectations go a long way toward realizing them.

Unit Planning

Unit plans are the major subsets of the yearlong plan. From each unit plan, you will develop lesson plans that are at the most refined level of specificity. Research indicates that educational policymakers, textbook publishers, and teachers often become so focused on the content coverage or learning activities that they lose sight of the larger purposes and goals that are supposed to guide curriculum planning. This level of planning is typically ignored in elementary social studies textbook series, which provides one more reason why unit planning is necessary—and requires resources beyond the text.

Goals aligned with big ideas drawn from selected content are needed to guide each step in curriculum planning and implementation. Goals are most likely to be attained if all the curriculum components (content clusters, instructional methods, learning activities, and assessment tools—all topics of chapters in this text) are aligned and designed as means of helping students accomplish them. This involves planning curriculum and instruction to develop capabilities that students can use in their lives inside and outside school, both now and in the future. In this regard, it is important to emphasize goals of understanding, appreciation, and life application.

Ideally, each unit builds on the preceding ones so that there is a continuous revisiting and applying of big ideas. The net results are depth of understanding and memorable learning. Research indicates that networks of connected knowledge structured around powerful ideas can be acquired with understanding and retained in forms that make them accessible for application. In contrast, disconnected bits of information are likely to be learned only through low-level processes such as rote memorization, and most of these bits either are soon forgotten or retained in ways that limit their accessibility (Bransford, Brown, & Cocking, 1999).

Weekly and Daily Planning

Goals and big ideas should guide weekly and daily social studies planning. Unfortunately, due to the complexity of the classroom and the multiple challenges you face in your role as a decision maker (Doyle, 1986), they are often ignored as attention focuses on the planning of activities. This is how social studies becomes piecemeal, combining a flurry of disconnected bits of information with a worksheet, a fun hands-on activity, or a discussion of a fanciful piece of children's literature that only topically matches the original goal.

Generally speaking, all of the unit components, such as goals, big ideas, instructional strategies, activities, and so on, should remain in place as you prepare your weekly and daily lessons. Often, there are learning sequences that develop over several days, so your plans should reflect that. Coherent content linking prior knowledge to new material should be a daily priority along with scaffolding students' task engagement. Research on learning tasks suggests that activities and assignments should be sufficiently varied and interesting enough to motivate student engagement, and sufficiently new and challenging enough to constitute learning experiences rather than needless repetition, yet easy enough to allow students to achieve high rates of success if they invest reasonable time and effort.

You also need to plan appropriate opportunities for modeling and instructing students in learning and self-regulation strategies. This requires comprehension instruction that includes attention to propositional knowledge (what to do), procedural knowledge (how to do it), and conditional knowledge (when and why to do it). Strategy teaching is especially important for less able students who otherwise might not come to understand the value of consciously monitoring, self-regulating, and reflecting on their learning processes.

Introduction to Planning Tools

The host of tools that are available for you to use in your planning—especially those mandated by your district, such as content standards, pacing guides, and textbooks—often leave the impression that you simply "do" social studies. Teachers who are new to the field, not particularly passionate about social studies, or obsessed with facts might secretly feel a sense of relief: "At last, they have told me what to do." We, on the other hand, view all of the tools available to you, including the social studies standards, simply as resources to guide your planning.

NCSS Standards

The National Council for the Social Studies (1994) published standards that address overall curriculum design and comprehensive student performance expectations. Associations devoted to disciplines such as economics, government, history, and geography also have published standards that feature the priorities of their respective disciplines (see Chapters 5–7).

We encourage you and your colleagues to first establish your program framework using the social studies standards as a guide and then supplement it with standards from the single disciplines where relevant. The NCSS (1994) standards statement entitled *Expectations of Excellence: Curriculum Standards for Social Studies* has been designed to serve three purposes:

1. Serve as a framework for social studies program design from kindergarten through Grade 12
2. Function as a guide for curriculum decisions by providing student performance expectations in the areas of knowledge, processes, and attitudes
3. Provide examples of classroom activities that will guide teachers as they design instruction to help students meet performance expectations

The content standards consist of ten themes incorporating fields of study that roughly correspond to the major social studies disciplines and process skills. The ten themes are provided in Figure 14.1. See also www.socialstudies.org.

NCSS Guidelines for Social Studies Teaching and Learning

The National Council for the Social Studies (1994) document also provides guidelines for teaching and learning. It is an outgrowth of the position statement emphasizing the Five Elements of Powerful Teaching referred to in Chapter 9.

FIGURE 14.1

Ten Thematic Strands for Social Studies Curriculum

Ten themes serve as organizing strands for the social studies curriculum at every school level (early, middle, and high school); they are interrelated and draw from all of the social science disciplines and other related disciplines and fields of scholarly study to build a framework for social studies curriculum.

I. Culture
Human beings create, learn, and adapt culture. Human cultures are dynamic systems of beliefs, values, and traditions that exhibit both commonalities and differences. Understanding culture helps us understand ourselves and others.

II. Time, Continuity, and Change
Human beings seek to understand their historic roots and to locate themselves in time. Such understanding involves knowing what things were like in the past and how things change and develop—allowing us to develop historic perspective and answer important questions about our current condition.

III. People, Places, and Environment
Technical advancements have ensured that students are aware of the world beyond their personal locations. As students study content related to this theme, they create their spatial views and geographical perspectives of the world; social, cultural, economic, and civic demands mean that students will need such knowledge, skills, and understandings to make informed and critical decisions about the relationship between human beings and their environment.

IV. Individual Development and Identity

Personal identity is shaped by one's culture, by groups, and by institutional influences. Examination of various forms of human behavior enhances understandings of the relationship between social norms and emerging personal identities, the social processes that influence identity formation, and the ethical principles underlying individual action.

V. Individuals, Groups, and Institutions

Institutions exert enormous influence over us. Institutions are organizational embodiments to further the core social values of those who comprise them. It is important for students to know how institutions are formed, what controls and influences them, how they control and influence individuals and culture, and how institutions can be maintained or changed.

VI. Power, Authority, and Governance

Understanding of the historic development of structures of power, authority, and governance and their evolving functions in contemporary society is essential for emergence of civic competence.

VII. Production, Distribution, and Consumption

Decisions about exchange, trade, and economic policy and well-being are global in scope, and the role of government in policymaking varies over time and from place to place. The systematic study of an interdependent world economy and the role of technology in economic decision making is essential.

VIII. Science, Technology, and Society

Technology is as old as the first crude tool invented by prehistoric humans, and modern life as we know it would be impossible without technology and the science that supports it. Today's technology forms the basis for some of our most difficult social choices.

IX. Global Connections

The realities of global interdependence require understanding of the increasingly important and diverse global connections among world societies before there can be analysis leading to the development of possible solutions to persisting and emerging global issues.

X. Civic Ideals and Practices

All people have a stake in examining civic ideals and practices across time, in diverse societies, as well as in determining how to close the gap between present practices and the ideals upon which our democracy is based. An understanding of civic ideals and practices of citizenship is critical to full participation in society.

Data from National Council for the Social Studies. (1994). *Curriculum standards for social studies: Expectations of excellence* (Bulletin No. 89). Washington, DC: Author.

1. Meaningful

The social studies program should relate to the age, maturity, and concerns of students and help them connect social studies content to their lives. It should:

1.1. Provide students with a social studies experience at all grade levels, K–12

1.2. Involve students in the formulation of goals, the selection of activities and instructional strategies, and the assessment of curricular outcomes

1.3. Be based on the developmental and psychological needs of the students

1.4. Focus on the social world as it is: its flaws, its strengths, its dangers, and its promise

1.5. Include the study not only of human achievements but also of human failures

1.6. Emphasize pervasive and enduring social issues and connect them to the lives of students

1.7. Demonstrate the relationships among local, regional, national, and global issues

1.8. Include analysis of and attempts to formulate potential resolutions of present and controversial global problems

1.9. Provide intensive and recurring cross-cultural study of groups

1.10. Offer opportunities for students to interact with members of other racial, ethnic, and cultural groups

1.11. Provide opportunities for students to examine potential future conditions and problems

1.12. Provide a connection to the world of work

2. Integrated

The social studies program should draw from currently valid knowledge representative of human experience, culture, and beliefs in all areas of the social studies. Strategies of instruction and learning activities should rely on a broad range of learning resources. The program should:

2.1. Integrate current valid social studies concepts, principles, and theories in anthropology, archaeology, economics, geography, history, law, philosophy, political science, psychology, religion, and sociology

2.2. Develop proficiency in methods of inquiry and analyzing, organizing, and using data

2.3. Balance the immediate social environment of students and the larger social world, examining multiple viewpoints

2.4. Use a variety of primary and secondary sources that accommodate a wide range of reading abilities and interests

2.5. Promote critical, creative, and ethical thinking on problems faced by citizens and leaders

2.6. Use the expertise and experiences of a variety of community resource people

2.7. Foster lifelong learning

3. Value-Based

The social studies program should consider the ethical dimensions of topics and address controversial issues while providing an arena for reflective development of concern for the common good and the application of democratic values. It should:

3.1. Help students understand the role that values play in decision making

3.2. Give students the opportunity to think critically and make value-based decisions

3.3. Support different points of view, respect for well-supported positions, and sensitivity to cultural similarities and differences

3.4. Encourage students to develop a commitment to social responsibility, justice, and action

3.5. Encourage students to examine and evaluate policy and its implications

3.6. Give students the opportunity to think critically and make value-based decisions about related social issues

4. Challenging

The social studies program should provide students with challenging content, activities, and assessments. It should:

4.1. Provide students with the opportunity to engage in reflective discussion as they listen carefully and respond thoughtfully to one another's ideas

4.2. Expose students to sources of information that include conflicting perspectives on controversial issues

4.3. Provide students with the opportunity to formulate oral and written responses to content-based questions and issues

4.4. Promote critical, creative, and ethical thinking on problems faced by citizens and leaders

4.5. Include in the evaluation process an assessment of progress not only in knowledge but also in skills and abilities, including thinking, valuing, and social participation

4.6. Include evaluation data for planning curricular improvements and ensure a challenging curriculum

4.7. Be evaluated using data from traditional and alternative assessments

5. Active

The social studies program should engage the student directly and actively in the learning process. It should:

5.1. Provide a wide and rich range of learning activities

5.2. Offer students opportunities to formulate hypotheses and test them by gathering and analyzing data

5.3. Encourage students to be involved in service-learning projects

5.4. Be sufficiently varied and flexible to engage all types of learners

5.5. Include activities that contribute to the students' perception of teachers as fellow inquirers

5.6. Create a climate that supports students' self-respect and respect for others

5.7. Stimulate students to investigate and respond to the human condition in the contemporary world

5.8. Encourage students to participate in a variety of individual, small-group, and whole-class activities

5.9. Utilize many kinds of work spaces to facilitate variation in the size of groups, the use of several kinds of media technology, and a diversity of tasks

5.10. Encourage students to function as a learning community

State Social Studies Standards

Most states have developed their own social studies standards. If you teach in one of these states, you will be expected to incorporate its standards into your planning. Typically, the state standards or strands are a more specific version of the national guidelines and usually are tied to the state's testing program. For example, Standard III (People, Places, and Environments) is the most obvious geographic standard in the NCSS document. Other standards, including I, VII, and IX, incorporate geographic components. In the state of Michigan, geography is one of seven major strands in the state standards. It has five standards associated with it, including diversity of people, places, and cultures; human/environment interaction; location, movement, and connections; regions, patterns, and processes; and global issues and events. If your state has standards, they probably will align with national standards in similar ways.

Local Curriculum Guides

If you and your colleagues are being asked to revise your existing social studies curriculum to meet a designated set of standards or create local ones, we encourage you to begin with what you have and use it as a framework for decision making. You might address the following questions as you engage in this process.

- How many of the standards clearly connect to my current curricular plan?
- Are there elements in my current social studies program that need to be expanded in order to align with the standards?
- How can the standards enhance my current social studies curriculum?

- How can I use the standards to guide my planning for depth of understanding and, if necessary, reduce the breadth of topic coverage?
- How can I use the standards accompanied by the performance expectations to guide my selection of instructional activities?
- How can I use the standards to align my assessment practices?
- How can I use the standards to guide my resource selections? (Brophy & Alleman, 1995).

Typically, the documents generated for social studies at the local level are designed by teachers serving on a curriculum committee whose primary task is to take national and state guidelines, localize them, and make them "user friendly" for teachers. These guidelines usually are helpful in determining what should be taught at a given grade level but if taken literally, may result in a litany of disjointed facts that in the grand scheme of things are meaningless.

Textbooks

Despite the criticisms rendered against social studies textbooks, they remain a favored resource. One reason is teachers' lack of time to create their own units. Another is textbook companies' claims to align to national and state social studies standards and testing programs. Finally, many educators still believe that by covering the specific topics in the text, often through an overreliance on a read/discuss model, their work is done. In contrast, we emphasize the Five Elements of Powerful Teaching, adopted in a vision statement published by the National Council for the Social Studies (1993) (see Figure 14.2 and www.socialstudies.org). Throughout this text, these elements are blended with content in an attempt to create meaningfulness.

FIGURE 14.2

Five Key Features of Powerful Social Studies Learning

Meaningful
The content selected for emphasis is worth learning because it promotes progress toward important social understanding and civic efficacy goals, and it is taught in ways that help students to see how it is related to these goals. As a result, students' learning efforts are motivated by appreciation and interest, not just by accountability and grading systems. Instruction emphasizes depth of development of important ideas within appropriate breadth of content coverage.

Integrative
Powerful social studies cuts across discipline boundaries, spans time and space, and integrates knowledge, beliefs, values, and dispositions to action. It also provides opportunities for students to connect to the arts and sciences through inquiry and reflection.

Value-Based
Powerful social studies teaching considers the ethical dimensions of topics, so that it provides an arena for reflective development of concern for the common good and application of social values. The teacher includes diverse points of view, demonstrates respect for well-supported positions, and shows sensitivity and commitment to social responsibility and action.

Challenging
Students are encouraged to function as a learning community, using reflective discussion to work collaboratively to deepen understandings of the meanings and implications of content. They also are expected to come to grips with controversial issues, to participate assertively but respectfully in group discussions, and to work productively with peers in cooperative learning activities.

Active

Powerful social studies is rewarding but demanding. It demands thoughtful preparation and instruction by the teacher, and sustained effort by the students to make sense of and apply what they are learning. Teachers do not mechanically follow rigid guidelines in planning, implementing, and assessing instruction. Instead, they work with the national standards and with state and local guidelines, adapting and supplementing these guidelines and their instructional materials in ways that support their students' social education needs.

The teacher uses a variety of instructional materials, plans field trips and visits by resource people, develops current or local examples to relate to students' lives, plans reflective discussions, and scaffolds students' work in ways that encourage them to gradually take on more responsibility for managing their own learning independently and with their peers. Accountability and grading systems are compatible with these goals and methods.

Students develop new understandings through a process of active construction. They develop a network of connections that link the new content to preexisting knowledge and beliefs anchored in their prior experience. The construction of meaning required to develop important social understanding takes time and is facilitated by interactive discourse. Clear explanations and modeling from the teacher are important, but so are opportunities to answer questions, discuss or debate the meaning and implications of content, or use the content in activities that call for tackling problems or making decisions.

Data from National Council for the Social Studies. (1993). "A vision of powerful teaching and learning in the social studies: Building social understanding and civic efficacy. *Social Education, 57,* 213–22.

New teachers often have high expectations for textbook series because they are packaged attractively and presented to suggest that they are carefully developed and revised to meet the needs of students at each grade level. Even experienced teachers may suppress their misgivings about these textbook series because they think, "These texts are written by experts who know what they are doing, so who am I to question their work?" In fact, textbooks are written by people who work for the publishers (mostly English majors) in response to multiple and conflicting pressures. Consequently, we urge you to view each textbook as a tool, not as "the curriculum." We have provided a checklist for you to use as you determine a textbook's function (see Figure 14.3) and to help you leverage your plea for additional resources.

If you are expected or mandated to use district-adopted social studies textbooks, be aware of the following:

- Typically, the activities found in the teacher's manual were written by outside vendors, so you should always ask whether each activity matches the goal and promotes understanding of the big idea(s). Other questions to ask relate to level of difficulty, feasibility, and cost-effectiveness (see Chapter 9 for additional principles).

- Social studies time should not be used as a venue for engaging students in round-robin reading (this is likely to make your students hate the subject). View the textbook as one of multiple information sources promoting silent or paired reading to gather data to be discussed later and expanded through interactive narrative and perhaps the use of an appropriate literary source, video, or other resource that promotes depth of understanding.

- The supplements that often accompany the textbook series may be effective for a learner who needs practice on a particular set of skills or who faces comprehension issues. However, they are unlikely to be useful as activities for the class as a whole.

FIGURE 14.3

Textbook Assessment

CIRCLE YOUR RESPONSES:

Goal-Oriented Approach

Yes _____ No _____ Are the goals clearly spelled out?

Yes _____ No _____ Do they represent understanding, appreciation, and life application?

Yes _____ No _____ Do they focus on the big ideas?

Content Selection

Yes _____ No _____ Is the content adequate?

Yes _____ No _____ Where appropriate, are multiple perspectives provided to alleviate bias?

Yes _____ No _____ Does the content connect to important social education goals?

Coverage

Yes _____ No _____ Does the sequence of ideas or events make sense?

Yes _____ No _____ Are relationships between the big ideas apparent?

Yes _____ No _____ Are prior knowledge and/or experience issues recognized?

Skills

Yes _____ No _____ Is what is promised as front matter in the teacher's guide delivered in the student text?

Yes _____ No _____ Are the skills linked to the knowledge content?

Yes _____ No _____ Is a range of skills included (i.e., map and globe skills, information gathering, report writing, critical thinking, decision making, value analysis, etc.?)

Teacher–Student Relationships and Classroom Discourse

Yes _____ No _____ Are there planned discussions of key ideas?

Yes _____ No _____ Would the plans yield sustained, critical, and reflective dialogue?

Yes _____ No _____ Are there opportunities for student–student discourse?

Activities and Assignments

Yes _____ No _____ Are the activities and assignments goal-oriented?

Yes _____ No _____ Are they at the appropriate level of difficulty?

Yes _____ No _____ Do they focus on concepts, generalizations, and applications?

Yes _____ No _____ Do they tie in to current events?

Yes _____ No _____ Do they apply to life outside of school?

Yes _____ No _____ Are they properly scaffolded?

Yes _____ No _____ Are the suggested learning processes well suited to the content?

Yes _____	No _____	Are integration activities clearly social studies driven?
Yes _____	No _____	Are the activities and assignments cost effective?

Assessment and Evaluation

Yes _____	No _____	Do assessment items and activities clearly reflect the social education goals?
Yes _____	No _____	Do they focus on major social studies understandings instead of trite facts?
Yes _____	No _____	Do they incorporate skills meshed with the content?
Yes _____	No _____	Is there an absence of memorization and regurgitation of miscellaneous facts?
Yes _____	No _____	Do the assessment and evaluation measures, as a whole, reflect the big picture of the unit?

Technology

Social studies–related websites offer a broad selection of lesson plans, instructional resources, and activities. Our advice is "Teacher, beware!" Do not assume that an activity is appropriate just because it exists in cyberspace or calls for students to use computer or other technology. We suggest the same guidelines for making decisions about technology that we offer for selecting other activities. The litmus test it must pass is, "Does the technology-based lesson plan or activity match your goals?" Simple relevance to the topic is not enough.

Social Studies on the Internet (Berson, Cruz, Duplass, & Johnston, 2004) is an annotated collection of websites to consider as you plan your units. One of its features is a series of chapters organized according to content topics aligned with the NCSS strands. Another is its listing of professional organizations related to social studies that maintain their own websites. Online journals such as *Reading On Line* (ROL) (1997–2005) (www.reading.org) also offer information regarding the use of technology to enhance learning in the content areas.

Children's Literature

Authentic children's literature selections can be desirable components of social studies units. Often these are nonfictional selections because social studies is about real human activities and experiences. Fanciful stories or folklore selections usually belong in language arts rather than social studies, even if they have some relevance to the social studies unit topic. For example, if you were planning a series of lessons about the executive branch of our federal government, including where our president lives, *The Story of the White House* (Waters, 1991) would be a much better choice than *Woodrow, the White House Mouse* (Barnes & Barnes, 1998). After students have developed a realistic perspective on the presidency, you might want to share the Barnes and Barnes text during literacy and ask students to distinguish fact from fantasy. At that point, you might even want to talk about the possible motivation behind the authors' decision for presenting playful/fanciful characters.

In several other places in this text, we have discussed the pitfalls to avoid when seeking to accomplish curricular integration. Remember, wise integration demands much more than simply selecting literature that connects to the topic under study.

Throughout this text, we offer you guiding principles to assist in your planning. For example, in Chapter 9 we elaborate on activity selection, and in Chapter 12 we provide guidelines for assessment. The planning tool on government introduced in Appendix C and the unit on shelter underscore the importance of a goals-oriented approach. We encourage you to consider these templates and the tools offered in this chapter as you plan your year to ensure a solid social studies program.

Frequently Asked Questions

While there is general agreement that planning is one of the most important responsibilities of a classroom teacher, it also is one of the most difficult. If you are beginning teaching, shifting grade levels, or changing curricula, planning can become overwhelming. Over the past several years, we have collected questions posed by professionals faced with planning issues. Following are our responses to those most frequently asked. We know that you will identify with many of them, and we hope our thoughts will stimulate your thinking. We encourage you to engage in conversation with your colleagues about these and other planning matters. Planning issues are ongoing due to changes in national and state standards, new testing requirements, changes in local school board policies, and so on. Getting planning changes on the table is the first step in maintaining a powerful social studies program in your classroom.

How can I avoid becoming simply a textbook teacher? Adopt the high road! The sooner you realize that if you are a true professional who will never be replaced by technology or textbooks, the happier you will be. Spend a major portion of your mental energy on goals and big ideas—even when you simply don't have time to create comprehensive units of your own. Don't hesitate to borrow units from others to get you started. The secret is to internalize and personalize the content. You need to reconstruct it for yourself, so you can model these practices for your students.

Accept the fact that the textbook is a single source developed for the full range of instructional situations. Help your students to realize its limitations. Engender curiosity and develop a realization that there is so much to learn outside the boundaries of a single source. Once students experience that for themselves, they will amaze you. A teacher recently remarked, "I cannot possibly teach everything my students need to know even at my grade level. It has been calculated that there are over 300 standards and benchmarks. My challenge is to open their heads and their hearts to the world. There are unlimited resources we can tap. I could get overwhelmed if I did not pay close attention to the goal and big idea pieces. They rein in my responsibility and help me maintain integrity when it comes to instruction and accountability."

How can I incorporate the state and national standards and yet not be overwhelmed by them? Familiarize yourself with them. Start with your existing curriculum and the units you have developed. Use the standards as a filter to determine what you need to add to align your plans more closely with them. (See the set of questions on pages 285–286 of this chapter.)

Suppose you were developing a unit on state government. In reviewing the state standards, you realize you have not included the core democratic values, such as common good. That observation can lead you to adding material on core values to your lesson focusing on elected officials and the role and function they play in deciding what is best for their constituency.

If you start with a blank slate and try to plan a yearlong program around standards, you probably will feel deflated and frustrated. The standards were never intended to be taught in sequence or as separate entities. They are guidelines for assessing the comprehensiveness of unit plans structured around topic-specific goals and big ideas.

What do I do if I'm handed a pacing guide and told, "This is what you need to follow"? First of all, don't panic! All of the pacing guides we have examined set minimal expectations, and none of them dictate how you will teach. Generally speaking, they contain skills such as finding absolute locations, using longitude and latitude, reading timelines, and recalling factual information. Some call for writing opportunities, such as taking a position and defending it or applying the core democratic values to a situation.

Take a deep breath. Step back. Then ask, "How can I build the specified elements in my upcoming social studies unit in meaningful ways within the designated time frame (because a quarterly assessment typically follows)?"

When it is all said and done, the pacing guide establishes minimal conditions. That is the good news. Your challenge remains the creation of robust instructional plans that far exceed what you are required to include. If you fail to exploit the degree of autonomy that you have and simply "drill and grill," neither you nor your students will get excited during social studies time.

How can I avoid getting so stressed about standardized testing? Find out what content and skills are expected at your grade level. For example, if students in fifth grade are expected to write a persuasive essay, understand cause and effect, or use longitude and latitude to locate specific places, find appropriate and natural places within your units for acquiring and practicing these skills. Being knowledgeable about test content serves as one more informant for developing a robust social studies program.

Consider preparing a matrix and plotting where you can naturally embed potentially testable content and skills. Periodically administer assessments in standardized testing formats, making sure students work independently. These strategic moves will promote efficacy and a realization that taking a test is "not such a big deal."

How do I figure out what my goals are? The academic disciplines are means of generating and systematizing knowledge. The school subjects that draw from them are means of preparing students for life in our society by equipping them with essential knowledge, skills, values, and dispositions. We want students not just to remember what we teach them in school but also to access and use it in appropriate application situations. These goals will not be met if students simply memorize disconnected bits of information.

It is important to emphasize goals of understanding, appreciation, and life application. *Understanding* means the students learn both the individual elements in a network of related content and the connections among them, so they can explain the content in their own words. For example, if they have been engaged in a unit on Mexico, they ought to be able to explain the idea that factors contributing to the types of work people do include geographic location, education, local needs, personal choice, and so on.

Appreciation means that students value what they are learning because they understand that there are good reasons for learning it. During the unit on Mexico, we would hope students would come to appreciate the range of ways families celebrate (and might even adopt similar practices for their own special events) or value and respect the range of shelter types that exist in Mexico because of the climate, available economic resources, personal choices, and so on.

Life application goals are accomplished to the extent students retain their learning in a form that makes it useable when needed in other contexts. For example, if students have been learning about opportunity cost in the context of virtual shopping at open-air markets in Mexico, they should be able to apply the decision-making model in their own lives. They can be encouraged to discuss with their families how they decide what to buy when they go to the city market or grocery store. They will soon realize that whenever anyone goes shopping, there are some things s/he needs to give up and that decisions involve choices.

How do I go about developing big ideas for my units? While it might sound boring—or perhaps even slightly simplistic, we suggest you begin by reading the section in a current encyclopedia that focuses on your specific topics. Continue by reading supplemental texts on the subject. Your social science college textbooks, along with your class notes, can be other useful references. For example, if you took an introductory course in political science, it could serve you well if you were planning a unit on government. The NCSS strands referenced earlier, along with the chapters in this text focusing on disciplinary knowledge, can be very useful. Grade-level social studies textbooks and authentic children's literature related to the topic are other possibilities for helping you formulate your ideas.

For our unit on government, we used all of the aforementioned resources. Our planning tool illustrating government provides examples of the big ideas we included. The other big ideas are listed here.

Focus on *selected* understandings from the following list:

Main Ideas to Develop

- A community is a place where people live, work, play, and share special times.
- People in a community work together, accomplish tasks, and achieve goals through cooperation.
- Members of communities are called citizens.

- Good citizens tend to be respectful, to be responsible, to think and act for the good of the community, and to be open to ideas of others that may be different from their own.
- Rules are designed to remind people of their rights and responsibilities. They help people get along, keep things fair, protect individual and public property, and keep people safe.
- A community (township, town, suburb, city) is a place where people live and usually have many common needs and wants. Among them are community services.
- Many people work for the community to make it a better place to live.
- Different communities have different needs based on their location and size.
- Families pay money to the community. This money is called taxes. Tax money pays for the community services.
- People living in a community also need rules and laws.
- Laws are rules made by the government leaders of the community that everyone in the community must follow.
- Leaders are elected by the people (of voting age) to make and enforce the laws.
- In some communities, the mayor is the chief leader. In other communities, there are township boards. Other leaders help the mayor, manager, or board watch over the community.
- A state is made up of many communities.
- Citizens of voting age have the opportunity to elect leaders for the state.
- Our state government focuses on services such as higher education, recreation, state highways, a system of justice, licensing regulations, and so on. The state government handles matters that affect people throughout the state.
- The United States government is defined as people running the country.
- The lawmaking branch of our United States government is made up of men and women elected by the people from the state that they represent. They are called senators and representatives. They are also called legislators. Together they are known as the U.S. Congress.
- The leader of our government is elected by the people of our country who are of voting age. The leader is known as the president.
- Our current president is George W. Bush. He lives and works in the White House. The president is elected by the voters in the United States to serve as the leader of our country. The president's position is voted on by the people every four years, and the same person cannot serve more than eight years.
- The power of the presidency goes with the office. When George W. Bush leaves the office, the new president will have the power and Mr. Bush will be an ordinary citizen.
- In the United States, we have two major political parties—Democrats, who tend to want more services and more taxes to pay for them; and Republicans, who tend to want fewer services and fewer taxes.
- Any U.S. citizen can run for office when s/he becomes an adult. The person running for office is called a candidate.

- The candidate has a platform—a list of ideas that s/he supports. In speeches and printed campaign materials, the candidate explains what s/he wants government to do and why. On election day, voters decide whom they want to represent them and why. Candidates who receive the most votes win.
- The United States government makes the rules and laws that affect everyone in the United States.
- The United States government does many useful things that keep our country running smoothly.
- A lot of people work for the United States in an effort to make life better for its citizens.
- Voting is a method by which people choose among several alternatives.
- A democracy is a form of government in which people take an active role in the decision making.
- A ballot is the list of names and offices (and sometimes ideas about certain issues) on which voters make their choices.
- It would be difficult and confusing for people to try to live and work together with no rules or laws—no government.
- The earliest societies were small ones ruled by tribal leaders. Later, societies grew to become nations ruled by kings or queens.
- People came to America long ago because they were unhappy with their home countries. They came seeking liberties and happiness.
- At first, they lived in colonies [Show map of colonial United States] that were controlled by the King of England. But they wanted to govern themselves, so they declared their independence and fought a war against England to gain their freedom. They won the war and became a new country called the United States.
- The Declaration of Independence and the U.S. Constitution are important governmental documents that guarantee rights and freedoms to the people.
- Governments can be classified as democracies or dictatorships.
- Customs and beliefs (part of culture) are reflected in governments around the world.
- Government services are needed to do the things that the people cannot do by themselves.
- All governments in the United States (e.g., community, township, city, state, and federal) provide some services for people.
- To pay for the services, the government collects money from the people. The money is referred to as taxes.
- Regulations (rules and laws) are designed to help people get along, keep things fair, protect individual and public property, and keep people safe.
- Government cannot be expected to do everything for its people.
- Volunteering is the act of giving time and sometimes money to promote a cause, provide a service, or work to solve a problem without making new laws.
- Volunteering is one way to practice responsible citizenship.
- When enough people volunteer to solve a problem, the need for making more laws or raising taxes to pay for the additional service is lessened.
- Individuals can personally contribute time and money to help solve problems that affect members of the community.

How do I address multicultural education (often referred to as diversity) in planning my social studies units? Diversity comes in many forms. If it is truly respected and integrated into children's lives, it needs to be affirmed early and be threaded throughout the K–12 curriculum, both formally and informally. We have embedded it throughout our text rather than treated it in a separate chapter. Social studies is one subject where diversity provides obvious benefits.

In our chapter on learning communities, we suggest a unit on childhood as the springboard for discussing the uniqueness of every individual as well as the importance of differences. In the chapter on home–school connections, we promote the learning of all students. The backgrounds and cultures of students in your classroom are not simply ethnic additives but contributors to everyone's learning, as when you create expanded social studies lessons using family response data.

We also suggest the importance of promoting empathy and avoiding stereotypes when selecting children's literature. Instructional materials such as textbooks, videos, pictures, artifacts, and websites often contain such stereotypes, so you will need to bring up differences. We encourage you to promote multiple perspectives throughout your units, partly because this creates natural ways of instilling diversity.

We view multicultural education as a way of looking at the world. We promote social and cultural capital by giving all students access to depth of social knowledge. The classroom teacher can make enormous positive differences for all children, and social studies is a natural venue for living multiculturally.

We find it ironic that pull-out programs often call for diverse students to be excused from social studies lessons and assigned to ESL sessions, speech therapy, special reading groups, and so on. We encourage you to schedule social studies when all of your students can be in attendance. Other classroom guidelines include the following:

- Demand that students be respectful and thoughtful of one another.
- Hold appropriately high expectations for all children, and build in strategies that help them succeed at their grade level.
- Model "Teacher as Learner." Share the pleasures of learning about new places, unfamiliar customs, beliefs, and values. Be matter-of-fact when dealing with differences. Model and discuss how to encounter and deal with unfamiliar people and situations.
- Initiate frequent and open communication with all families.
- Get to know families, so you can draw on them as resources that can enhance specific aspects of the curriculum.
- Plan in-school activities that include families with an eye toward inclusiveness.

When do I integrate? The short answer is, "When it makes sense." Start with your primary content focus. For example, don't allow your social studies time to turn into an extended literacy period. Using round-robin reading to cover the social studies text is a poor instructional choice for either subject.

Ask yourself questions such as "Would an outsider clearly recognize the lesson as social studies? Is the content drawn from other subjects authentic? Enriching? Is it obvious that if I use skills from math or literacy, students are being asked to apply them in social studies settings to bring more meaning to both the content and the skills?'

Integration certainly should not be adopted as a shortcut. Rather, the content, skills, and activities included should be educationally significant and desirable even if they did not involve the cross-subjects feature. Secondly, the content, skills, and activities should foster rather than disrupt or nullify the accomplishment of major social studies goals.

How do I select appropriate instructional strategies and activities? The possibilities are endless. The key to their effectiveness is their cognitive engagement potential—the degree to which they get students actively thinking about and applying content, preferably with conscious awareness of their goals and development of the big ideas.

All sorts of diversity exist within any classroom, so make room for variety. Often the content or skills lend themselves naturally to certain strategies or activities. For example, content associated with a faraway place unfamiliar to your students would be well suited to a virtual field trip; the study of local community officials would lend itself well to an on-site visit by the mayor or member of the city council; and the history of shelter might best be developed through the use of an interactive timeline. Other topics lend themselves to debate, case studies, role-plays, or simulations. Typically, we think of instructional strategies as means of introducing and developing new content with the whole class, and activities as means of processing and applying the learning (as a whole class, in small groups, or individually).

With all the emphasis on literacy, how do I spend a lot of time on it yet teach powerful social studies units? There are lots of natural connections. Reading, writing, speaking, and listening need to be about something; some literacy time ought to incorporate social studies content; and you are always using literacy when teaching social studies. However, guard against teaching new skills and new content simultaneously.

For example, if you are teaching the skill of selecting the main idea during literacy time, use familiar text. Then, during an upcoming social studies unit, design questions that focus on gleaning the big ideas from social studies sources. Increased use of informational text can motivate many students who prefer that kind of reading as well as those who have a strong interest in the social studies topic. It also can expand opportunities for home–school connections (e.g., use of newspapers, magazines, reference materials, sets of directions for cooking/fixing things, the Internet) that support both social studies and literacy (Duke & Bennett-Armistead, 2003).

Writing opportunities in social studies can allow students to construct and communicate understandings regarding the content and realize what they know or remain unclear about. Consider using independent brainstorming, table talk, or verbal pair share as opportunities for students to develop ideas to write about. Scaffold verbal collaboration by using modified word walls or other visual prompts as tools to jumpstart students' thinking, so they can focus on ideas they want to express rather than on spelling. Students' writing vocabularies are far smaller than their speaking ones.

Similar cases for using literacy in the development of social studies understandings could be made for speaking and listening. Sharing ideas publicly through planned debate, reports, class discussions, and so on promotes social studies learning. So does asking students to listen for specific things and then think about and respond to questions.

What is the rule of thumb regarding time allocations for large-group, small-group, and individual work? The short answer is, "It depends on your goals." Generally speaking, we would encourage you to provide a balance. Typically, when you are presenting new material, there will be more large-group time. Then, as students engage in processing the information, they will work more in small groups or individually.

Large-group time can be well spent for demonstration, delivery of new content through interactive discussion, storytelling, reading a piece of children's literature, and so on, as well as for review and debriefing. Small-group time should be spent on processing new information. If it is allocated for research, the information needs to be fed back to the large group in ways that show connections to big ideas. Concept webs and data-retrieval charts are examples of organizers that can be effective for this process.

Individual work time provides students with opportunities to "test" their understanding and application of the key ideas and skills. We have observed a paucity of independent work time, especially work calling for real writing (not just filling in blanks). It is very important in order to assess individual understanding and ability to apply what is learned. It can also contribute to a student's confidence level when faced with a standardized test.

Out-of-school learning opportunities allow students to communicate about what they have learned in school by engaging family members in real-life application activities. This "co-construction" of expanded learning takes the meaning to a more sophisticated level and promotes a sense of efficacy. It encourages students to "explain" their world.

How often do I need to assess? In one sense, you are always assessing. Before you launch a new unit, you want to find out what conceptions or misconceptions students have. During the unit, you want to find out what they are learning. At the end, you want to find out what they have retained and are applying. It does not stop there either because using what they have learned in new ways across units is the true test of retention.

Assessments are important even in the early grades. They send the message to students that content and skills are important and that they are expected to engage in the learning process. Recently, a second-grade teacher aptly stated, "I want my students to realize early on that they are not tourists in my classroom. They are there to learn. I assess large groups, small groups, and individuals in a host of ways. Frequently, I ask them to assess themselves and each other using guidelines we establish together. We are kidding ourselves if we ignore the connection between high expectations and student achievement."

How do I get families excited about participating in home assignments? Begin the year with a newsletter that includes your vision regarding home–school connections, and use other venues, such as weekly communications to families, parent conferences, PTA meetings, and so on to elaborate on this practice. Explain that the social studies home assignments are viewed as occasions for discussing and applying what has been learned in school in authentic situations. Underscore the importance of collaboration—repeating over and over that family members, including babysitters, neighbors, and other familiar adults, are encouraged to participate. Explain also that the diversity of responses will be used in extended social studies lessons. The responses will not be viewed as right or wrong but as opinions or reports of experiences. Sometimes the data will be tallied, graphed, or charted, but the underlying goal is to increase the meaningfulness of the social studies content.

When you assign home activities, make sure you use the responses as an integral part of subsequent lessons—and in a timely fashion. For students who seemingly have no family support, offer adult volunteers to assist before school or during other appropriate times. Do not get discouraged if at the beginning of the year only a small percentage of students and their families respond. Keep working to build "habits" of good practice.

Summary

Planning around goals and big ideas sets the stage for powerful social studies teaching. It begins with attention to your yearlong social studies goals—not just learning of knowledge and skills prescribed for your grade level but also development of related attitudes, beliefs, values, and dispositions to action. This agenda needs consistent attention throughout the year. Within this framework, unit planning begins with identification of the most powerful ideas associated with the unit topic. These ideas then become the content base for your lessons, activities, and assessments. Weekly and daily planning then are needed to fit your planned lessons, activities, and assessments into your weekly and daily schedules.

Many tools are available to assist you in your planning, including national, state, and local social studies standards and curriculum guides, college textbooks, your elementary social studies textbook series, Internet websites, guides to children's literature that relates to social studies topics, and your teaching colleagues. Standards statements are most useful as checklists for assessing existing plans and identifying ways to improve them, and curriculum guides specify the content (topics and skills) you are expected to teach at your grade level. It all begins, however, with goal-oriented specification of big ideas around which to structure the unit in general and each of its component lessons and activities. If you have done this correctly, both you and your students will know why the content base of each lesson and activity is important and how it can be applied to life outside of school.

Reflective Questions

1. Imagine that your school district decided to pilot an initiative that would provide social studies teachers with a three-hour block of time each week to work on planning. How would you spend the time, and what effects do you think it would have on your teaching?

2. What are some creative ways of making more time for planning? What do you think would be the results?

3. Goal-oriented planning is viewed as a major challenge by many teachers. Why do you think this perception exists? What could be done to address it?

4. Imagine you are a teacher in a setting where literacy and math are the top priorities. Your background is heavily weighted toward social studies—and you believe you should be able to satisfy both. You are also committed to actualizing the NCSS aim that states, "The primary purpose of social studies is to help young people develop the ability to make informed and reasoned decisions for the public good as citizens of a culturally diverse, democratic society in an interdependent world." What steps will you take in your planning to ensure that you satisfy the priorities of your institution and at the same time prepare a powerful social studies program at your grade level?

5. The NCSS Guidelines for Social Studies Teaching and Learning, an outgrowth of the position statement emphasizing the Five Elements of Powerful Teaching, are sometimes viewed as overwhelming. Imagine that you have been asked to serve as the "point person" for using them during the upcoming year. How will you incorporate them into your plans? How will you monitor their impact?

Your Turn:
Planning Your Social Studies Program for the Year

Locate your district's social studies curriculum documents and other available planning tools (e.g., NCSS and state social studies standards, textbooks, maps, globe, technology resources, copies of old standardized tests) that your building administrator, mentor teacher, and other colleagues have referenced. Add your notes from your college social science classes; instructional units you have designed; artifacts you have collected, including objects, photos, pamphlets; and so on.

Set aside several hours for doing some overall social studies planning. If possible, pair up with your mentor or a peer teaching at the same grade level. Pose the question, "What do I want social studies to look like in my classroom this year?" List your ideas on large chart paper. You might consider adding pictures or photos. Visual representations can serve as powerful self-monitoring tools throughout the year.

Think deeply about the NCSS aim for social studies: "The primary purpose of social studies is to help young people develop the ability to make informed and reasoned decisions for the public good as citizens of a culturally diverse, democratic society in an interdependent world." List possible ways that you might do this during the year. Revisit the NCSS statement as you plan each of your units.

Draw a "portrait" of your ideal social studies learner and what s/he would look like by the end of the year. Revisit it before and after each unit. It too can serve you as a self-monitoring tool. Then, answer the following questions to get you started.

1. What are my overall social studies goals for the year?
2. Imagine that you are writing a letter to your students' families describing your social studies program for the year. What would you include?

Think specifically about one unit.

3. What is the topic?
4. What are the overall goals for the unit?
5. What are the big ideas I want to address?

(We have included a sample list for a unit on government. If it fits your curriculum, use parts of it. Feel free to add others. Refer to other chapters for other lists (e.g., shelter, mountainous regions) or develop your own for your selected topic.

6. What resources do I have available?
7. How will I preassess?
8. How will I introduce my unit so that it is engaging and interesting to my students?
9. What strategies do I plan to use during the unit to develop the big ideas?
10. What sorts of authentic home assignments do I have in mind?
11. What do I have planned for a culminating activity?
12. What are my plans for an end-of-unit assessment?

CHAPTER 15

WHAT IS THE RESEARCH BASE THAT INFORMS IDEAS ABOUT POWERFUL SOCIAL STUDIES TEACHING?

Jessica Holen, Teacher Intern

I found this chapter very informational and useful in thinking about my future as a teacher. It is filled with ideas on how to meet the challenges that the school systems and the U.S. Department of Education have placed in the middle of our school days. We have to remember that our first responsibility as educators is to educate every child who walks into our classroom.

The authors discuss the limitations placed on social studies due to testing and the math and literacy block timeframes. They also provide ideas on how to incorporate social studies into the literacy curriculum to keep social studies units powerful and meaningful to students. There are demands placed on teachers, but the good news is that they usually do not tell teachers how to teach, only what they must cover. As future and beginning teachers, we must remember that it is not bad to be held accountable for what you are supposed to be doing.

The synthesis of good teaching principles in this chapter is an effective way to close the book. It reflects the foundation for this textbook and provides the "secret" of powerful teaching. The easy-to-read manner makes it a great reference when you get discouraged, stumped about where to go next, or simply in a rut. The synthesis is a recipe for powerful social studies teaching. It outlines the necessities and complexities, yet allows for the educator's personal touch.

This book began with an overview of social studies as a strand within the larger school curriculum. In the preface and first chapter, we delineated the nature of social studies as a pandisciplinary subject emphasizing citizen education goals and delineated the major approaches that different groups of social studies educators have developed. The idea was to create a context within which to situate our own approach as developed throughout the rest of the book.

In this final chapter, we want to reconnect to the big picture, this time situating the contents of the book within an even larger context: theory and research on curriculum and instruction in general (not just in social studies). A great deal of good research on teaching has accumulated over the last 40 years, most notably research on teaching school subjects for understanding, appreciation, and life application. The major findings of this research are reflected in our approach to elementary social studies education, as developed in previous chapters.

We conclude the book with a brief synthesis of these findings, for two major reasons. First, the synthesis provides you with a higher-level organizer—a cognitive structure within which to organize and assimilate the many concepts and principles you have studied. The synthesis features twelve principles around which to structure your learning in a network of connected knowledge. Structuring your knowledge this way will make it easier for you to remember it and access it in application situations.

Second, it is important to know about and implement research-based principles of effective teaching. These principles have enduring validity and applicability, not just for social studies but for all school subjects.

The Current High-Stakes Testing Environment

Education will always be partly an art but also should be partly applied science in which an established base of validated procedures is gradually expanded and refined in response to gradual advances in its scientific knowledge base. Unfortunately, education in this country has not featured a history of slow but steady and highly consensual development in response to advances in the knowledge base. Instead, it has featured strongly advocated and often hotly contested calls for relatively extreme measures, typically based on educational or political ideology rather than reputable research. Some of the "reforms" have been ill conceived and impractical, but essentially harmless. Others have been counterproductive—doing more harm than good.

In our view, the recent and ongoing high-stakes testing era has been one of the most counterproductive periods in our educational history. At a time when more and more of society's burdens and responsibilities have been shifted from the family and other social institutions to the school, politicians have been emphasizing "reforms" that feature unrealistic demands and punitive responses to failures to meet them. Initially in many states, and later at the federal level through the No Child Left Behind (NCLB) legislation, schools have been forced to administer more and more tests, with higher and higher stakes attached to students' test scores.

Although contrary to the spirit of many educational purposes and goals, high-stakes testing policies would be difficult for informed educators to contest if the policies were based on solid research or demonstrably successful. They are neither. These policies do little, if any, good and a lot of harm. It is true that mobilizing to prepare students to take high-stakes tests will raise their test scores, but the raised test scores do not mean much when the tests are mostly confined to memory for discrete information or disconnected subskills, and the improved scores mostly reflect specific test preparation rather than improved learning across the curriculum as a whole. In Texas, for example, a focus on preparing students to take the state's achievement test did in fact succeed in raising students' scores on those tests, but the students' scores on national assessments, college entrance exams, and the like remained unchanged (Amrein & Berliner, 2003). In high-stakes testing environments, improved test scores no longer have the meaning they might have had before the stakes were raised.

The benefits of mobilizing to raise test scores are dubious, but the costs are not. Thomas (2005) identified and documented quite a list of what he called "collateral damage" from high-stakes testing: narrowing of the curriculum, both in the sense of cutting back on teaching other subjects to focus on teaching the subjects tested and in the sense of focusing instruction in the subjects tested on the material likely to be included in the test, at the expense of a richer coverage; the high costs of implementing testing and its consequences (paying for the tests themselves, test administration and scoring, test preparation materials, follow-up tutoring and other remediation materials and activities, etc. eats up a lot of budget and often leads to reduction or elimination of art and music programs, sports teams, and other nonacademic functions of schooling); both teachers and students get bored and frustrated with the heavy focus on test preparation in lieu of a richer curriculum; lower achieving students face the possibility of being retained in their grade for another year in the short run, which markedly increases the likelihood that they will drop out of school in the long run; and a combination of poor fit between the curriculum and the tests, unrealistic expectations, and punitive policies toward schools and students that fail to meet them create unnecessary anxiety and frustration for all concerned.

Most of the reform movements that have come and gone in the past were fads supported by ideological rationales but not kept in place by legal mandates. However, even legal mandates will be reversed when they become political liabilities to their sponsors. Because they are so unrealistic and counterproductive, the NCLB legislation and other mandates sustaining the current high-stakes testing overkill are likely to disappear before long, or at least to be reshaped into something more sensible. Perhaps at that point, the nation will be ready for research-based guidance on curriculum and instruction.

So What Can You Do in the Meantime?

In the meantime, you will have to negotiate some kind of compromise between focusing exclusively on teaching for understanding and focusing exclusively on preparing students for high-stakes tests. You cannot ignore the standards, the tests, and the pressures associated with them, but there is no need to view them as the complete curriculum or to buy into the "grill and drill" mentality that focuses narrowly on test preparation. We suggest the following guidelines to help you act responsibly to include appropriate efforts to prepare your students for achievement tests, yet embed these efforts within a powerful social studies program.

Content

- Accept the fact that the state standards identify content and skills to be taught at your grade level.
- Familiarize yourself with these standards, including the content and skills specified for other grade levels. This will help you to do appropriate foreshadowing and reviewing at your grade.
- Go beyond the content and skills allocated to your grade level in an effort to provide meaningful context and enrichment to your units and lessons. Remember, the standards only specify minimum expectations.
- As you plan your lessons and units, keep aware of standards and benchmarks not only for social studies but also for literacy. Review these standards periodically so you can fill in the gaps. When you actively look for them, you will find many opportunities to address standards naturally in the process of developing social studies content, as well as opportunities for adding standards-related content or skills in ways that make sense.

Time Allocation

- Work within local mandates for allocating instructional time to different subjects. If you lack sufficient time to teach social studies because inordinate time is allocated to literacy, use social studies texts and literature selections as the content base for some of the literacy activities. This is likely to improve test scores in both subjects.
- Along with primarily oral whole-class and small-group activities, include frequent opportunities for students to work independently on written assignments, especially assignments that call for formulating and writing extended text in response to questions calling for higher-order thinking. If your district is obsessed with test preparation, your students probably will get more than enough practice responding to multiple-choice tests in literacy and mathematics but not enough opportunities to develop and apply higher-order thinking skills.

Testing

- To minimize scoring costs and complications, the tests used in high-stakes testing programs typically follow multiple-choice formats and emphasize memory for specific information rather than higher-order thinking skills. Consequently, see that your students receive sufficient experience with these standardized test formats so that they are not unnecessarily stressed when they take the high-stakes tests.

- However, make sure that your teacher-made assessment tools reflect the full range of your instructional goals. Include questions calling for higher-order thinking as part of your larger effort to go beyond minimal requirements.
- In general, provide all students with sufficient experience working independently on assignments and tests to ensure individual accountability, communicate high expectations, and build test readiness.

Quality of Curriculum and Instruction

- Assume responsibility for designing a powerful social studies program that reflects the five elements of powerful teaching emphasized in the NCSS standards statement, as well as the twelve principles outlined later in this chapter.
- Recognize that although standards identify expected content and skill learning, they do not delineate the curriculum as a whole, and especially not the quality of the classroom discourse and the learning activities. The *how* of teaching is up to you! As the teacher, you are the key to the depth and quality of your students' learning.

How Some Teachers Have Coped

Case studies reported by Wills (in press) illustrate both the challenges and some of the potential coping strategies brought on by high-stakes testing pressures on the social studies curriculum. Wills observed in middle-grade classrooms in an elementary school located in a poor neighborhood in California, during the school year immediately following mandated increases in the instructional time allocated to literacy and mathematics (the focus of the state's high-stakes testing program). The school's principal left it up to individual teachers to decide how they would restructure their weekly schedules to accommodate this mandate. One teacher did so by eliminating physical education, reasoning that her students had greater needs for a rich science and social studies curriculum. The changes made by most teachers, though, had the effect of reducing the time allocated to science and social studies to less than half of what it had been before. The teachers were still expected to cover the same material, however (in social studies, national and state history through the Civil War).

Teachers who taught a barren social studies curriculum with little or no emphasis on thoughtfulness in classroom discourse simply persisted with this approach, except that now they required their students to read and answer questions about textbook chapters at home, so they could spend most class time going over the answers. Meanwhile, teachers who understood the value of thoughtful discourse scrambled to find ways to retain this emphasis while still addressing the full range of prescribed content in less than half the time. One teacher's strategies were only partially successful. To save as much time as possible for class discussion, she cut back on less essential content and instituted shortcuts such as dividing students into small groups and jigsawing a textbook lesson in order to "get through it more quickly," directing students to specific pages to look for answers to questions on study sheets, requiring them to read their textbooks at home rather than during class, and substituting short films for some textbook sections. Despite these adjustments, she fell increasingly behind schedule as the year progressed so that planned discussions increasingly were cut short or omitted in order to push on through the content. Classes became more and more recitation, less and less discussion. Even so, she never got to the last several chapters of the book.

The most successful teacher also covered less content. However, this was because she eliminated or reduced coverage of content she deemed less important, not because she ran out of time. Each of her social studies units included discussions, activities, and other projects that asked students to analyze, interpret, or apply their learning to address challenging problems or issues. She made time for this by skipping certain chapters of the textbooks and eliminating the need to work systematically through the other chapters by providing her students with succinct summaries of key facts and main ideas. Although she expected her students to read relevant chapters for background and occasionally exposed them to videos or other input sources, her classroom discussions were focused on the material contained in her handouts. The difference could be seen in her unit on European exploration, settlement, and establishment of the mission system in California. Instead of basing it on the 45-page textbook chapter, she based it on 28 pages (including maps and illustrations) that briefly and clearly covered the important information she thought her students needed to know.

She also made time for student thinking in social studies by incorporating social studies content into language arts lessons. The afternoon language arts period typically included 25 minutes of either silent reading or writing instruction. The teacher frequently used this time for students to read social studies information and work on writing assignments calling for them to analyze or apply this information. Her solution was not completely satisfactory, but it did enable her to sustain a focus on big ideas and thoughtful classroom discourse in social studies, despite the mandated increases in time allocated to literacy and mathematics.

A Synthesis of Generic Principles of Good Teaching

The following twelve principles of good teaching have served as the informal underpinning to our text. We include them here to support your efforts to move beyond the current standards and rhetoric with confidence. Implementing these principles will help you teach all subjects effectively and in particular, offer your students a robust social studies program.

For much of the 20th century, basing curriculum and instruction theories and reform ideas on ideology rather than research was not only possible but also necessary because there was not very much research available to inform the enterprise. Over the last 40 years, however, a great deal of relevant, useful, and mostly mutually supportive research has accumulated. It is now possible to make confident, research-based statements about many aspects of teaching. Some of this research-based information is specific to particular grade levels, subject areas, and so on, but some of it is relatively generic, applicable to most aspects of teaching in typical classrooms.

One of us was asked to develop a brief synthesis of these research findings for a booklet in a series sponsored by the International Academy of Education (Brophy, 1999). The charge was to focus on generic aspects of good teaching, rooted in principles that reflect aspects of classrooms that are much more similar than different across countries and cultures: Most subject-matter teaching involves whole-class lessons in which content is developed during teacher–student interaction, followed by practice and application activities that students work on individually or in pairs or small groups. The student/teacher ratio and other constraints cause most instruction to be directed primarily to the class as a whole, with the teacher seeking to individualize around the margins. This description fits the situation of most teachers who teach social studies to elementary students, so much of the content of this book can be subsumed within the twelve principles that anchor the synthesis.

Introduction to the Twelve Principles

There is broad agreement among educators associated with all school subjects that students should learn each subject with understanding of its big ideas, appreciation of its value, and the capability and disposition to apply it in their lives outside of school. Analyses of research done in the different subject areas have identified some commonalities in conclusions drawn about curricular, instructional, and assessment practices that foster this kind of learning. If phrased as general principles rather than specific behavioral rules, these emerging guidelines can be seen as mutually supportive components of a coherent approach to teaching that applies across subjects and situations. Thus, it is possible to identify generic features of good teaching, although not to outline a specific instructional model to be implemented step-by-step.

Much of the research support for these principles comes from studies of relationships between classroom processes and student outcomes. However, some principles are rooted in the logic of instructional design (e.g., the need for alignment among a curriculum's goals, content, instructional methods, and assessment measures). In addition, attention was paid to emergent theories of teaching and learning (e.g., sociocultural, social constructivist) and to the standards statements circulated by organizations representing the major school subjects. Priority was given to principles that have been shown to be applicable under ordinary classroom conditions and associated with progress toward desired student outcomes.

These principles rest on a few fundamental assumptions about optimizing curriculum and instruction. First, school curricula subsume different types of learning that call for somewhat different types of teaching, so no single teaching method (e.g., direct instruction, social construction of meaning) can be the method of choice for all occasions. An optimal program will feature a mixture of instructional methods and learning activities.

Second, within any school subject or learning domain, students' instructional needs change as their expertise develops. Consequently, what constitutes an optimal mixture of instructional methods and learning activities will evolve as school years, instructional units, and even individual lessons progress.

Third, students should learn at high levels of mastery yet progress through the curriculum steadily. This implies that, at any given time, curriculum content and learning activities need to be difficult enough to provide some challenge and extend learning but not so difficult as to leave many students confused or frustrated. Instruction should focus on the zone of proximal development, which is the range of knowledge and skills that students are not yet ready to learn on their own but can learn with help from the teacher.

Fourth, although twelve principles are highlighted for emphasis and discussed individually, each principle should be applied within the context of its relationships with the others. That is, the principles are meant to be understood as mutually supportive components of a coherent approach to teaching in which the teacher's plans and expectations, the classroom learning environment and management system, the curriculum content and instructional materials, and the learning activities and assessment methods are all aligned as means to help students attain intended outcomes.

The Twelve Principles

1. Supportive Classroom Climate

Students learn best within cohesive and caring learning communities.

Research findings. Productive contexts for learning feature an ethic of caring that pervades teacher–student and student–student interactions and honors the individuality and diversity among students who differ in gender, race, ethnicity, culture, socioeconomic status, handicapping conditions, or other personal characteristics. Students are expected to assume individual and group responsibilities for managing instructional materials and activities and for supporting the personal, social, and academic well-being of all members of the classroom community (Good & Brophy, 2003; Sergiovanni, 1994).

In the classroom. To create a climate for molding their students into a cohesive and supportive learning community, teachers need to display personal attributes that will make them effective as models and socializers: a cheerful disposition, friendliness, emotional maturity, sincerity, and caring about students as individuals as well as learners. The teacher displays concern and affection for students, is attentive to their needs and emotions, and socializes them to display these same characteristics in their interactions with one another.

In creating classroom displays and in developing content during lessons, the teacher connects with and builds on the students' prior knowledge and experiences, including their home cultures. The teacher addresses diversity proactively, honoring the full range of individualities and family backgrounds represented in the class in ways that validate students' personal identities. Extending the learning community from the school to the home, the teacher establishes and maintains collaborative relationships with parents and encourages their active involvement in their children's learning.

The teacher promotes a learning orientation by introducing activities with emphasis on what students will learn from them, treating mistakes as natural parts of the learning process, and encouraging students to work collaboratively and help one another. Students are taught to ask questions without embarrassment, to contribute to lessons without fear of ridicule of their ideas, and to collaborate in pairs or small groups on many of their learning activities.

2. Opportunity to Learn

Students learn more when most of the available time is allocated to curriculum-related activities and the classroom-management system emphasizes maintaining students' engagement in those activities.

Research findings. A major determinant of students' learning in any academic domain is their degree of exposure to the domain at school through participation in lessons and learning activities. The lengths of the school day and the school year create upper limits on these opportunities to learn. Within these limits, the learning opportunities actually experienced by students depend on how much of the available time they spend participating in lessons and learning activities. Effective teachers allocate most of the available time to activities designed to accomplish instructional goals.

Research indicates that teachers who approach management as a process of establishing an effective learning environment tend to be more successful than teachers who emphasize their roles as disciplinarians. Effective teachers do not need to spend much time responding to behavior problems because they use management techniques that elicit student cooperation and engagement in activities and thus minimize the frequency of such problems. Working within the positive classroom climate implied by the principle of learning community, the teacher articulates clear expectations concerning classroom behavior in general and participation in lessons and learning activities in particular, follows through with any needed cues or reminders, and ensures that students learn procedures and routines that foster productive engagement during activities and smooth transitions between them (Brophy, 1983; Denham & Lieberman, 1980; Doyle, 1986).

In the classroom. There are more things worth learning than there is time available to teach them, so it is essential that limited classroom time be used efficiently. Effective teachers allocate most of this time to lessons and learning activities rather than to pastimes that do not support progress toward learning goals. Their students spend many more hours each year on curriculum-related activities than do students of teachers who are less focused on instructional goals.

Effective teachers convey a sense of the purposefulness of schooling and the importance of getting the most out of the available time. They begin and end lessons on time, keep transitions short, and teach their students how to get started quickly and maintain focus when working on assignments. Good planning and preparation enable them to proceed through lessons smoothly without having to stop to consult a manual or locate an item needed for display or demonstration. Their activities and assignments feature stimulating variety and optimal challenge, which helps students to sustain their task engagement and minimizes disruptions due to boredom or distraction.

Successful teachers are clear and consistent in articulating their expectations. At the beginning of the year they model or provide direct instruction in desired procedures if necessary, and subsequently they cue or remind their students when these procedures are needed. They monitor the classroom continually, which enables them to respond to emerging problems before they become disruptive. When possible, they intervene in ways that do not disrupt lesson momentum or distract students who are working on assignments. They teach students strategies and procedures for carrying out recurring activities, such as participating in whole-class lessons, engaging in productive discourse with classmates, making smooth transitions between activities, collaborating in pairs or small groups, storing and handling equipment and personal belongings, managing learning and completing assignments on time, and knowing when and how to get help. The teachers' emphasis is not on imposing situational control but on building students' capacity for managing their own learning, so that expectations are adjusted and cues, reminders, and other managerial moves are faded out as the school year progresses.

These teachers do not merely maximize "time on task" but spend a great deal of time actively instructing their students during interactive lessons, in which the teachers elaborate the content for students and help them to interpret and respond to it. Their classrooms feature more time spent in interactive discourse and less time spent in independent seatwork. Most of their instruction occurs during interactive discourse with students rather than during extended lecture presentations.

The principle of maximizing opportunity to learn is not meant to imply emphasizing broad coverage at the expense of depth of development of powerful ideas. The breadth/depth dilemma must be addressed in curriculum planning. The point of the opportunity-to-learn principle is that, however the breadth/depth dilemma is addressed and whatever the resultant curriculum may be, students will make the most progress toward intended outcomes if most of the available classroom time is allocated to curriculum-related activities.

3. Curricular Alignment

All components of the curriculum are aligned to create a cohesive program for accomplishing instructional purposes and goals.

Research findings. Research indicates that educational policymakers, textbook publishers, and teachers often become so focused on content coverage or learning activities that they lose sight of the larger purposes and goals that are supposed to guide curriculum planning. Teachers typically plan by concentrating on the content they intend to cover and the steps involved in the activities their students will do, without giving much thought to the goals or intended outcomes of the instruction. Textbook publishers, in response to pressure from special-interest groups, tend to keep expanding their content coverage. As a result, too many topics are covered in not enough depth; content exposition often lacks coherence and is cluttered with insertions; skills are taught separately from knowledge content rather than integrated with it; and in general, neither the students' texts nor the questions and activities suggested in the teachers' manuals are structured around powerful ideas connected to important goals.

Students taught using such textbooks may be asked to memorize parades of disconnected facts or to practice disconnected subskills in isolation instead of learning coherent networks of connected content structured around powerful ideas. These problems are often exacerbated by externally imposed assessment programs that emphasize recognition of isolated bits of knowledge or performance of isolated subskills. Such problems can be minimized through goal-oriented curriculum development, in which the overall purposes and goals of the instruction, not miscellaneous content coverage pressures or test items, guide curricular planning and decision making (Beck & McKeown, 1988; Clark & Peterson, 1986; Wang, Haertel, & Walberg, 1993).

References to attitudes, values, dispositions, and appreciations are intended to underscore the fact that instructional purposes and goals include not only knowledge and skills but also aesthetic experiences, positive attitudes toward the subject, efficacy perceptions, and other affective and motivational outcomes. Curricula should include activities that have important personal meanings for students and induce aesthetic and dispositional experiences, such as appreciating the beauty of a poem, the elegant simplicity and symmetry of mathematics, the excitement and generative power of science, or the value of privileging the common good in delineating the rights and responsibilities of citizens. The curricular alignment principle implies not only including such aesthetic and affective outcomes in the overall set of purposes and goals that guide curriculum planning but also teaching the knowledge and skill components of the curriculum in ways that support progress toward desired attitudes, values, dispositions, and appreciations.

In the classroom. A curriculum is not an end in itself but a means, a tool for helping students to learn what is considered essential as preparation for fulfilling adult roles in society and realizing their potential as individuals. Its goals are learner outcomes—the knowledge, skills, attitudes, values, and dispositions to action that the society wishes to develop in its citizens. The goals are the reason for the existence of the curriculum, so that beliefs about what is needed to accomplish them should guide each step in curriculum planning and implementation. Goals are most likely to be attained if all of the curriculum's components (content clusters, instructional methods, learning activities, and assessment tools) are selected because they are believed to be needed as means for helping students to accomplish the overall purposes and goals. This involves planning curriculum and instruction not just to cover content but to accomplish important student outcomes—capabilities and dispositions to be developed in students and used in their lives inside and outside of school, both now and in the future. In this regard, it is important to emphasize goals of understanding, appreciation, and life application. Understanding means that students learn both the individual elements in a network of related content and the connections among them so that they can explain the content in their own words and connect it to their prior knowledge. Appreciation means that students value what they are learning because they understand that there are good reasons for learning it. Life application means students retain their learning in a form that makes it useable when needed in other contexts.

Content developed with these goals in mind is likely to be retained as meaningful learning that is internally coherent, well connected with other meaningful learning, and accessible for application. This is most likely to occur when the content itself is structured around powerful ideas and the development of this content through classroom lessons and learning activities focuses on these ideas and their connections.

4. Establishing Learning Orientations

Teachers can prepare students for learning by providing an initial structure to clarify intended outcomes and cue desired learning strategies.

Research findings. Research indicates the value of establishing a learning orientation by beginning lessons and activities with advance organizers or previews. These introductions facilitate students' learning by communicating the nature and purpose of the activity, connecting it to prior knowledge, and cueing the kinds of student responses that the activity requires. This helps students to remain goal oriented and strategic as they process information and respond to the questions or tasks embodied in the activity. Good lesson orientations also stimulate students' motivation to learn by communicating enthusiasm for the learning or helping students to appreciate its value or application potential (Ausubel, 1968; Brophy, 2004; Meichenbaum & Biemiller, 1998).

In the classroom. Advance organizers tell students what they will be learning before the instruction begins. They characterize the general nature of the activity and give students a structure within which to understand and connect the specifics that will be presented by a teacher or text. Such knowledge of the nature of the activity and the structure of the content will help students to focus on the main ideas and order their thoughts effectively. Therefore, before beginning any lesson or activity, the teacher should see that students know what they will be learning and why it is important for them to learn it.

Other ways to help students learn with a sense of purpose and direction include calling attention to the activity's goals, overviewing main ideas or major steps to be elaborated, administering pretests that sensitize students to main points to learn, and posing prequestions that stimulate student thinking about the topic.

Although it always is important to identify the purposes of activities as part of introducing them in ways that support optimal student engagement, teachers sometimes might want to withhold formal statements of key ideas or detailed elaboration of learning strategies until after students have had opportunities to explore an issue or problem, communicate their ideas about it, and negotiate understandings on their own. For example, a teacher might want to use inductive, guided-discovery, experiential, or problem-based approaches that initially engage students in inquiry or problem solving and only later move to negotiation and synthesis of what was learned (including "bridging" from students' natural language to more formal terminology).

5. Coherent Content

To facilitate meaningful learning and retention, content is explained clearly and developed with emphasis on its structure and connections.

Research findings. Research indicates that networks of connected knowledge structured around powerful ideas can be learned with understanding and retained in forms that make them accessible for application. In contrast, disconnected bits of information are likely to be learned only through low-level processes such as rote memorization, and most of these bits either are soon forgotten or are retained in ways that limit their accessibility. Similarly, skills are likely to be learned and used effectively if taught as strategies adapted to particular purposes and situations, with attention to when and how to apply them, but students may not be able to integrate and use skills that are learned only by rote and practiced only in isolation from the rest of the curriculum (Beck & McKeown, 1988; Good & Brophy, 2003; Rosenshine, 1968).

In the classroom. Whether in textbooks or in teacher-led instruction, information is easier to learn to the extent that it is coherent—the sequence of ideas or events makes sense and the relationships among them are made apparent. Content is most likely to be organized coherently when it is selected in a principled way, guided by ideas about what students should learn from studying the topic.

When making presentations, providing explanations, or giving demonstrations, effective teachers project enthusiasm for the content and organize and sequence it so as to maximize its clarity and "learner friendliness." The teacher presents new information with reference to what students already know about the topic; proceeds in small steps sequenced in ways that are easy to follow; uses pacing, gestures, and other oral communication skills to support comprehension; avoids vague or ambiguous language and digressions that disrupt continuity; elicits students' responses regularly to stimulate active learning and ensure that each step is mastered before moving to the next; finishes with a review of main points, stressing general integrative concepts; and follows up with questions or assignments that require students to encode the material in their own words and apply or extend it to new contexts.

Other ways to help students establish and maintain productive learning sets include using outlines or graphic organizers that illustrate the structure of the content, study guides that call attention to key ideas, or task organizers that help students keep track of the steps involved and the strategies they use to complete these steps.

In combination, the principles calling for curricular alignment and for coherent content imply that to enable students to construct meaningful knowledge that they can access and use in their lives outside of school, teachers need to (1) retreat from breadth of coverage in order to allow time to develop the most important content in greater depth, (2) represent this important content as networks of connected information structured around powerful ideas, (3) develop the content with a focus on explaining these important ideas and the connections among them, and (4) follow up with learning activities and assessment measures that feature authentic tasks that provide students with opportunities to develop and display learning that reflects the intended outcomes of the instruction.

Clear explanations of coherent content structured around powerful ideas do not always have to be transmitted from the teacher to the students at the beginnings of lessons. Often, they can be elicited from students or developed in the course of carrying out inquiry or problem-solving activities. Also, some activities do not require much content explanation because they are designed primarily to address process goals (e.g., to develop connoisseurship through discussion of artistic or literary works, or to develop desired citizenship dispositions through productive discussion of controversial issues). However, teachers should conclude inquiry, problem-solving, and process-learning activities with reflection on what has been learned, including providing or eliciting clear statements of key concepts and principles.

6. Thoughtful Discourse

Questions are planned to engage students in sustained discourse structured around powerful ideas.

Research findings. Besides presenting information and modeling application of skills, effective teachers structure a great deal of content-based discourse. They use questions to stimulate students to process and reflect on the content, recognize relationships among and implications of its key ideas, think critically about it, and use it in problem solving, decision making, or other higher-order applications. Such discourse is not limited to factual review or recitation featuring rapid pacing and short answers to miscellaneous questions but instead features sustained and thoughtful development of key ideas. Through participation in this discourse, students construct and communicate content-related ideas. In the process, they abandon naïve ideas or misconceptions and adopt the more sophisticated and valid ideas embedded in the instructional goals (Good & Brophy, 2003; Newmann, 1990; Rowe, 1986).

In the classroom. In the early stages of units when new content is introduced and developed, more time is spent in interactive lessons featuring teacher–student discourse than in independent work on assignments. The teacher plans sequences of questions designed to develop the content systematically and help students to construct understandings of it by relating it to their prior knowledge and collaborating in dialogue about it.

The forms and cognitive levels of these questions need to be suited to the instructional goals. Some primarily closed-ended and factual questions might be appropriate when teachers are assessing prior knowledge or reviewing new learning, but accomplishing the most significant instructional goals requires open-ended questions that call for students to apply, analyze, synthesize, or evaluate what they are learning. Some questions will admit to a range of possible correct answers, and some will invite discussion or debate (e.g., concerning the relative merits of alternative suggestions for solving problems).

Because questions are intended to engage students in cognitive processing and construction of knowledge, they ordinarily should be addressed to the class as a whole. This encourages all students, not just the one eventually called on, to listen carefully and respond thoughtfully to each question. After posing a question, the teacher needs to pause to allow students enough time to process it and at least begin to formulate responses, especially if the question is complicated or requires students to engage in higher-order thinking.

Thoughtful discourse features sustained examination of a small number of related topics, in which students are invited to develop explanations, make predictions, debate alternative approaches to problems, or otherwise consider the content's implications or applications. The teacher presses students to clarify or justify their assertions, rather than accepting them indiscriminately. In addition to providing feedback, the teacher encourages students to explain or elaborate on their answers or to comment on classmates' answers. Frequently, discourse that begins in a question-and-answer format evolves into an exchange of views in which students respond to one another as well as to the teacher and respond to statements as well as to questions.

Teachers structure discussions by engaging students with problems that are open to different solutions or issues that allow different positions to be taken and defended. As the discourse develops, they intervene as needed to ask for clarifications, revoice and elaborate on students' ideas, summarize progress, and move the discussion forward. In using such techniques to steer discourse in productive directions, however, teachers should do so in ways that support learning-community principles, thus helping students to develop ownership over their ideas and confidence in their abilities to make sense of content and contribute to developing conversations.

Students need to develop coherent networks of knowledge structured around powerful ideas. The degree to which these understandings are transmitted by the teacher versus constructed by the students themselves will vary with the ages of the students, their prior knowledge of the topic, and other factors. Overreliance on transmission encourages learner passivity and can lead to boredom and emphasis on rote learning methods. Overreliance on inquiry or other constructivist methods can lead to lessons that stray from their intended goals or content and expose students to misconceptions rather than elegantly structured knowledge representations.

7. Practice and Application Activities

Students need sufficient opportunities to practice and apply what they are learning, and to receive improvement-oriented feedback.

Research findings. Teachers help their students to learn in three main ways. First, they present information, explain concepts, and model skills. Second, they lead their students in review, recitation, discussion, and other forms of discourse surrounding the content. Third, they engage students in activities or assignments that provide them with opportunities to practice or apply what they are learning. Research indicates that skills practiced to a peak of smoothness and automaticity tend to be retained indefinitely, whereas skills that are mastered only partially tend to deteriorate. Most skills included in school curricula are learned best when practice is distributed across time and embedded within a variety of tasks. Thus, it is important to follow up thorough initial teaching with occasional review activities and with opportunities for students to use what they are learning in a variety of application contexts (Brophy & Alleman, 1991; Cooper, 1994; Dempster, 1991; Knapp, 1995).

In the classroom. Practice is one of the most important yet least appreciated aspects of learning in classrooms. Little or no practice may be needed for simple behaviors like pronouncing words, but practice becomes more important as learning becomes complex. Successful practice involves polishing skills that already are established at rudimentary levels to make them smoother, more efficient, and more automatic, not trying to establish such skills through trial and error.

Much practice that involves revisiting core ideas and skills can be embedded in problem-solving activities, games, or other application situations. Fill-in-the-blank worksheets, pages of mathematical computation problems, and related tasks that engage students in memorizing facts or practicing subskills in isolation from the rest of the curriculum should be minimized. Instead, most practice should be embedded within application contexts that feature conceptual understanding of knowledge and self-regulated application of skills. Thus, most practice of reading skills is embedded within lessons involving reading and interpreting extended text, most practice of writing skills is embedded within activities calling for authentic writing, and most practice of mathematics skills is embedded within problem-solving applications.

Opportunity to learn in school can be extended through homework assignments that are realistic in length and difficulty given the students' abilities to work independently. To ensure that students know what to do, the teacher can go over the instructions and get them started in class, then have them finish the work at home. An accountability system should be in place to ensure that students complete their homework assignments, and the work should be reviewed in class the next day.

To be useful, practice must involve opportunities not only to apply skills but also to receive timely feedback. Feedback should be informative rather than evaluative, helping students to assess their progress with respect to major goals and to understand and correct errors or misconceptions. At times when teachers are unable to circulate to monitor progress and provide feedback to individuals, pairs, or groups working on assignments, they should arrange for students to get feedback by consulting posted study guides or answer sheets or by asking peers designated to act as tutors or resource persons.

8. Scaffolding Students' Task Engagement

The teacher provides whatever assistance students need to enable them to engage in learning activities productively.

Research findings. Research on learning tasks suggests that activities and assignments should be sufficiently varied and interesting to motivate student engagement, sufficiently new or challenging to constitute meaningful learning experiences rather than needless repetition, and yet sufficiently easy to allow students to achieve high rates of success if they invest reasonable time and effort. The effectiveness of assignments is enhanced when teachers first explain the work and go over practice examples with students before releasing them to work independently, then circulate to monitor progress and provide help when needed. The principle of teaching within the students' zones of proximal development implies that students will need explanation, modeling, coaching, and other forms of assistance from their teachers but also that this teacher structuring and scaffolding of students' task engagement will fade as the students' expertise develops. Eventually, students should become able to autonomously use what they are learning and regulate their own productive task engagement (Brophy & Alleman, 1991; Rosenshine & Meister, 1992; Shuell, 1996; Tharp & Gallimore, 1988).

In the classroom. Besides being well chosen, activities need to be effectively presented, monitored, and followed up if they are to have their full impact. This means preparing students for an activity in advance, providing guidance and feedback during the activity, and leading the class in post-activity reflection afterwards. In introducing activities, teachers should stress their purposes in ways that will help students to engage in them with clear ideas about the goals to be accomplished. Then they might call students' attention to relevant background knowledge, model strategies for responding to the task, or scaffold by providing information concerning how to go about completing task requirements. If reading is involved, for example, teachers might summarize the main ideas, remind students about strategies for developing and monitoring their comprehension as they read (paraphrasing, summarizing, taking notes, asking themselves questions to check understanding), distribute study guides that call attention to key ideas and structural elements, or provide task organizers that help students to keep track of the steps involved and the strategies that they are using.

Once students begin working on activities or assignments, teachers should circulate to monitor their progress and provide assistance if necessary. Assuming that students have a general understanding of what to do and how to do it, these interventions can be kept brief and confined to minimal and indirect forms of help. If teacher assistance is too direct or extensive, teachers will end up doing tasks for students instead of helping them learn to do the tasks themselves.

Teachers also need to assess performance for completion and accuracy. When performance is poor, they will need to provide reteaching and follow-up assignments designed to ensure that content is understood and skills are mastered.

Most tasks will not have their full effects unless they are followed by reflection or debriefing activities in which the teacher reviews the task with the students, provides general feedback about performance, and reinforces main ideas as they relate to overall goals. Reflection activities should also include opportunities for students to ask follow-up questions, share task-related observations or experiences, compare opinions, or in other ways deepen their appreciation of what they have learned and how it relates to their lives outside of school.

9. Strategy Teaching

The teacher models and instructs students in learning and self-regulation strategies.

Research findings. General learning and study skills as well as domain-specific skills (such as constructing meaning from text, solving mathematical problems, or reasoning scientifically) are most likely to be learned thoroughly and become accessible for application if they are taught as strategies to be brought to bear purposefully and implemented with metacognitive awareness and self-regulation. This requires comprehensive instruction that includes attention to propositional knowledge (what to do), procedural knowledge (how to do it), and conditional knowledge (when and why to do it). Strategy teaching is especially important for less-able students who otherwise might not come to understand the value of consciously monitoring, self-regulating, and reflecting upon their learning processes (Meichenbaum & Biemiller, 1998; Pressley & Beard El-Dinary, 1993; Weinstein & Mayer, 1986).

In the classroom. Many students do not develop effective learning and problem-solving strategies on their own but can acquire them through modeling and explicit instruction from their teachers. Poor readers, for example, can be taught reading comprehension strategies such as keeping the purpose of an assignment in mind when reading; activating relevant background knowledge; identifying major points in attending to the outline and flow of content; monitoring understanding by generating and trying to answer questions about the content; or drawing and testing inferences by making interpretations, predictions, and conclusions. Instruction should include not only demonstrations of and opportunities to apply the skill itself but also explanations of the purpose of the skill (what it does for the learner) and the occasions in which it would be used.

Strategy teaching is likely to be most effective when it includes cognitive modeling: The teacher thinks out loud while modeling use of the strategy. This makes overt for learners the otherwise covert thought processes that guide use of the strategy in a variety of contexts. Cognitive modeling provides learners with first-person language ("self talk") that they can adapt directly when using the strategy themselves. This eliminates the need for translation that is created when instruction is presented in the impersonal third-person language of explanation or even the second-person language of coaching.

In addition to strategies for use in particular domains or types of assignments, teachers can model and instruct their students in general study skills and learning strategies such as rehearsal (repeating material to remember it more effectively), elaboration (putting material into one's own words and relating it to prior knowledge), organization (outlining material to highlight its structure and remember it), comprehension monitoring (keeping track of the strategies used and the degree of success achieved with them, and adjusting strategies accordingly), and affect monitoring (maintaining concentration and task focus, minimizing performance anxiety and fear of failure).

When providing feedback as students work on assignments and when leading subsequent reflection activities, teachers can ask questions or make comments that help students to monitor and reflect on their learning. Such monitoring and reflection should focus not only on the content being learned but also on the strategies that the students are using to process the content and solve problems. This will help the students to refine their strategies and regulate their learning more systematically.

Teachers' questions and cognitive modeling also can be used to support students' self-regulation of attitudinal, value, and dispositional learning, including aesthetic appreciations. With such support, students who have not already learned to do so on their own can learn to look for and experience the personal satisfactions and aesthetic pleasures of the learning experiences in which they are engaged, as well as to think about ways in which what they are learning might improve the quality of their lives outside of school or help them to accomplish personal goals.

10. Cooperative Learning

Students often benefit from working in pairs or small groups to construct understandings or help one another master skills.

Research findings. Research indicates that there is often much to be gained by arranging for students to collaborate in pairs or small groups as they work on activities and assignments. Cooperative learning promotes affective and social benefits, such as increased student interest in and valuing of subject matter and increases in positive attitudes and social interactions among students who differ in gender, race, ethnicity, achievement levels, and other characteristics.

Cooperative learning also creates the potential for cognitive and metacognitive benefits by engaging students in discourse that requires them to make their task-related information-processing and problem-solving strategies explicit (and thus available for discussion and reflection). Students are likely to show improved achievement outcomes when they engage in certain forms of cooperative learning as an alternative to completing assignments on their own (Bennett & Dunne, 1992; Johnson & Johnson, 1994; Slavin, 1990).

In the classroom. Traditional approaches to instruction feature whole-class lessons followed by independent seatwork time during which students work alone (and usually silently) on assignments. Cooperative learning approaches retain the whole-class lessons but replace part of the individual seatwork time with opportunities for students to work together in pairs or small groups on follow-up practice and application activities. Cooperative learning can be used with activities ranging from drill and practice to learning facts and concepts, discussion, and problem solving. It is perhaps most valuable as a way to engage students in meaningful learning with authentic tasks in a social setting. Students have more chances to talk in pairs or small groups than in whole-class activities, and shy students are more likely to feel comfortable expressing ideas in these more intimate settings.

Some forms of cooperative learning call for students to help one another accomplish individual learning goals, such as by discussing how to respond to assignments, checking work, or providing feedback or tutorial assistance. Other forms of cooperative learning call for students to work together to accomplish a group goal by pooling their resources and sharing the work. For example, the group might paint a mural, assemble a collage, or prepare a research report to be presented to the rest of the class. Cooperative learning models that call for students to work together to produce a group product often feature a division of labor among group participants (e.g., to prepare a biographical report, one group member will assume responsibility for studying the person's early life, another for the person's major accomplishments, another for the effects of these on society, and so on).

Cooperative learning in pairs or small groups should be viewed as a supplement to, not a substitute for, clarification of key concepts and principles in whole-class lessons. If students are asked to assume too much of the responsibility for managing their learning while operating independently of the teacher, they may fail to develop key ideas or develop distorted versions of them. Also, if students are asked to divide responsibilities so that each works on a separate part of a larger task, many of them may never develop a coherent grasp of the big picture.

Cooperative learning methods are most likely to enhance learning if they combine group goals with individual accountability. That is, each group member has clear objectives for which he or she will be held accountable (students know that any member of the group may be called on to answer any one of the group's questions or that they will be tested individually on what they are learning).

Activities used in cooperative learning formats should be well suited to those formats. Some activities are most naturally done by individuals working alone, others by students working in pairs, and still others by small groups of three to six students.

Students should receive whatever instruction and scaffolding they may need to prepare them for productive engagement in cooperative learning activities. For example, teachers may need to show their students how to share, listen, integrate the ideas of others, and handle disagreements constructively. During times when students are working in pairs or small groups, the teacher should circulate to monitor progress, make sure that groups are working productively on the assigned tasks, and provide any needed assistance.

11. Goal-Oriented Assessment

The teacher uses a variety of formal and informal assessment methods to monitor progress toward learning goals.

Research findings. Well-developed curricula include strong and functional assessment components. These assessment components are aligned with the curriculum's major purposes and goals, so they are integrated with the curriculum's content, instructional methods, and learning activities, and are designed to evaluate progress toward major intended outcomes.

Comprehensive assessment does not just document students' ability to supply acceptable answers to questions or problems; it also examines the students' reasoning and problem-solving processes. Effective teachers routinely monitor their students' progress in this fashion, using both formal tests or performance evaluations and informal assessment of students' contributions to lessons and work on assignments (Dempster, 1991; Stiggins, 1997; Wiggins, 1993).

In the classroom. Effective teachers use assessment for evaluating students' progress in learning and for planning curriculum improvements, not just for generating grades. Good assessment includes data from many sources besides paper-and-pencil tests. Its forms and content address the full range of goals or intended outcomes (knowledge and skills at a variety of levels, attitudes, values, dispositions). Standardized, norm-referenced tests might comprise part of the assessment program (these tests are useful to the extent that what they measure is congruent with the intended outcomes of the curriculum and attention is paid to students' performance on each individual item, not just total scores). However, standardized tests ordinarily should be supplemented with publisher-supplied curriculum-embedded tests (when these appear useful) and with teacher-made tests that focus on learning goals emphasized in instruction but not in external testing sources.

In addition, learning activities and sources of data other than tests should be used for assessment purposes. Everyday lessons and activities provide opportunities to monitor the progress of the class as a whole and of individual students, and tests can be augmented with performance evaluations using tools such as laboratory tasks and observation checklists, portfolios of student papers and projects, and essays or other assignments that call for higher-order thinking and application. Finally, holistic and broad-ranged methods may be needed to assess progress toward aesthetic, affective, motivational, and other dispositional outcomes. A broad view of assessment helps to ensure that the assessment component includes authentic activities that provide students with opportunities to synthesize and reflect on what they are learning, think critically and creatively about it, and apply it in problem-solving and decision-making contexts.

In general, assessment should be treated as an ongoing and integral part of each instructional unit. Results should be scrutinized to detect weaknesses in the assessment practices themselves; to identify learner needs, misunderstandings, or misconceptions that may need attention; and to suggest potential adjustments in curriculum goals, instructional materials, or teaching plans.

12. Achievement Expectations

The teacher establishes and follows through on appropriate expectations for learning outcomes.

Research findings. Research indicates that effective schools feature strong academic leadership that produces consensus on goal priorities and commitment to instructional excellence, as well as positive teacher attitudes toward students and expectations regarding their abilities to master the curriculum. Teacher-effects research indicates that teachers who elicit strong achievement gains accept responsibility for doing so. They believe that their students are capable of learning and that they (the teachers) are capable of and responsible for teaching them successfully. If students do not learn something the first time, they teach it again, and if the regular curriculum materials do not do the job, they find or develop others that will (Brophy, 2004; Creemers & Scheerens, 1989; Good & Brophy, 2003; Shuell, 1996; Teddlie & Stringfield, 1993).

In the classroom. Teachers' expectations concerning what their students are capable of accomplishing (with teacher help) tend to shape both what teachers attempt to elicit from their students and what the students come to expect from themselves. Thus, teachers should form and project expectations that are as positive as they can be while still remaining realistic. Such expectations should represent genuine beliefs about what can be achieved and therefore should be taken seriously as goals toward which to work in instructing students.

It is helpful if teachers set goals for the class and for individuals in terms of floors (minimally acceptable standards), not ceilings. Then they can let group progress rates, rather than limits adopted arbitrarily in advance, determine how far the class can go within the time available. They can keep their expectations for individual students current by monitoring their progress closely and by stressing current performance over past history.

At minimum, teachers should expect all of their students to progress sufficiently to enable them to perform satisfactorily at the next level. This implies holding students accountable for participating in lessons and learning activities and turning in careful and completed work on assignments. It also implies that struggling students will receive the time, instruction, and encouragement needed to enable them to meet expectations.

When individualizing instruction and giving students feedback, teachers can emphasize the students' continuous progress relative to previous levels of mastery rather than how they compare with other students or with standardized test norms. Instead of merely evaluating relative levels of success, teachers can diagnose learning difficulties and provide students with whatever feedback or additional instruction they need to enable them to meet the goals. If students have not understood an explanation or demonstration, the teacher can follow through by reteaching (if necessary, in a different way rather than by merely repeating the original instruction).

In general, teachers are likely to be most successful when they think in terms of stretching students' minds by stimulating them and encouraging them to achieve as much as they can, not in terms of "protecting" them from failure or embarrassment.

Conclusion

Curriculum and instruction designed to promote understanding, appreciation, and life application of school subjects will reflect these twelve principles. Because such learning is built around big ideas developed through authentic applications, it is likely to be perceived by students as relevant and worthwhile and to be not only learned initially but also retained and used in situations where it is applicable. In contrast, curricula that feature mile-wide but inch-deep content and fill-in-the-blank activities are demotivating to students and yield mostly short-lived memorization of disconnected content. Such disconnected learning, especially if it occurs in the context of cramming to prepare for high-stakes tests, may succeed in boosting scores on those tests. However, much of what was learned will soon be forgotten, and little of what remains will be readily accessible or usable.

Comparison studies typically show that students taught for understanding, appreciation, and life application typically perform much better on assessments of higher-order outcomes than students confronted with memorizing a host of disconnected specifics. Furthermore, the former students tend to do as well or even better on lower-order knowledge retention tests (featuring the kinds of items typically emphasized in high-stakes testing programs). Consequently, even in the current high-stakes testing environment, both you and your students will be better off if you focus on teaching school subjects for understanding, appreciation, and life application.

Summary

Many of the principles for powerful social studies teaching emphasized in this text are social studies adaptations of more generic principles for teaching school subjects for understanding, appreciation, and life application. It has been challenging for American teachers to apply these principles in recent decades because of the mile-wide but inch-deep problem with the textbooks, as well as their failure to structure the content or the suggested learning activities around big ideas. Teaching for understanding, appreciation, and life application has become even more difficult recently because of pressures associated with high-stakes testing, primarily in literacy and mathematics. If you teach in states or districts where these pressures are particularly intense, you may have to make at least temporary compromises between doing what you view as best for your students and doing what appears necessary to prepare them for the tests. Some potential strategies for accomplishing this were suggested and illustrated early in the chapter.

The rest of the chapter presented and briefly elaborated on a list of twelve generic principles of good teaching distilled from the large body of research literature on the topic. Because so much of what is suggested in this text relates to these twelve principles, we have presented them at the end of the text as a way to synthesize much of its content. Both now and in the future, if you find yourself "losing the forest for the trees" as you learn more and more about the details of implementing particular teaching strategies or learning activities, you should find it helpful to revisit these principles as a way to reconnect with the big picture.

Appendix A

A Resource Unit for Fifth-Grade U.S. History: The American Revolution

Although conceived as part of a chronologically organized introduction to U.S. history for fifth-graders, this unit is designed to focus on a connected set of key ideas developed in depth rather than to offer broad coverage of the details of the revolutionary period. In support of the citizen education goals of social studies, it concentrates on the conflicts over governance issues that developed between England and the colonies, and the ways in which the colonists' views on these issues shaped the ideas expressed in the Declaration of Independence and the forms of government established through the Articles of Confederation and the U.S. Constitution. Many of these ideas about government are relatively abstract and new to fifth-graders, so unit plans concentrate on developing appreciation of the ideas themselves without getting into the history of philosophy that led up to those ideas. Nor do the unit plans call for detailed study of the war itself because we do not view this content as central to our major goals. However, teachers who wish to incorporate material on the war (because it is highly interesting to many students) can easily do so.

GOALS

1. Help students come to understand the conflicts that developed between England and the thirteen colonies, how these led to the Declaration of Independence, how independence was secured through the Revolutionary War, and how all this resulted in the establishment of a new nation (federation)
2. Help students come to appreciate the political values and governmental ideals that emerged during this crucial period as keystones of American political traditions, as expressed in the Declaration of Independence, the Articles of Confederation, and the U.S. Constitution

KEY IDEAS

Recommendations about key ideas to emphasize have been informed by the findings of McKeown and Beck (1990) and VanSledright, Brophy, and Bredin (1993) concerning the prior knowledge that needs to be in place and the primary storylines that need to be developed to enable students to construct coherent understandings of the nature and implications of the American Revolution. Suggestions about key historical events to emphasize in this unit were taken from Crabtree, Nash, Gagnon, and Waugh (1992) and McBee, Tate, and Wagner (1985).

The Colonies' Relationship to England Prior to 1763
Either in previous units or in the introduction to this unit, students will need to understand the following key ideas as context for their learning about the American Revolution:

1. More than 150 years elapsed between the founding of the first English colonies at Jamestown and Plymouth and the Declaration of Independence on July 4, 1776. During that time, the English colonies in America grew from a few isolated settlements to thirteen large and populous collections of communities that became the original thirteen states. Also, ties with England gradually weakened as the colonists developed identities as Americans.

2. Although they were located in America, the colonies were governed by England through governors and other officials appointed by the king.

3. Colonists were considered British subjects, so they enjoyed British protection but also were governed by British laws. They elected their own leaders and made some of their own laws at the local community level, but unlike British citizens living in England, they did not vote in Parliamentary elections. Thus, they were unable to send representatives to Parliament to specifically represent their interests.

4. Yet, they were subject to British laws and regulations. Like other colonial powers of the time (most notably France, Spain, and the Netherlands), England had built up an empire by claiming lands in other parts of the world, defending them militarily, and sending people to colonize and govern them. Colonies served as sources of raw materials for the mother country's factories, as well as markets for its manufactured exports.

5. Through a system of laws and taxes, England pressured the colonies to trade only with or through England. The colonists were supposed to buy things only from England (even if they could get them cheaper from somewhere else) and sell their crops or raw materials only to England (even though they might have sold them elsewhere perhaps at greater profit).

Tensions Build after 1763

1. England fought wars against France and other European nations that competed with them in their efforts to build empires around the world. British conflict with the French over land in North America (what we call the French and Indian War) was part of this competition. Between 1740 and 1763, the British were too busy fighting these wars to enforce their economic restrictions on the colonies, and colonists began to trade more freely than the British wanted.

2. However, the Treaty of Paris in 1763 established peace for a while, so England began to pay closer attention to the colonies. It also needed money to pay off war debts, including debts accumulated fighting the French and their Indian allies in North America. Between 1763 and 1770, England imposed a series of taxes on the colonies, viewing this as a way to get the colonists to pay a reasonable share of the war debts (after all, British-paid soldiers had fought the French and Indian War partly on their behalf and were continuing to protect their borders). However, the colonists resented these taxes, not only because of the financial burden but because they were imposed by a Parliament in which they were not represented. This was expressed in the phrase "no taxation without representation," which became a rallying cry against British policies. The British position was that members of Parliament represented not just the people who voted them into office but all British citizens everywhere, including in the colonies, but many American colonists did not accept this.

3. Besides imposing taxes, the British did several other things that angered the colonists: trying colonists accused of certain crimes in British courts (thus depriving them of the right to a trail by a jury of their peers); forbidding them to settle west of the Appalachian Mountains (in an attempt to keep the colonists separated from the Indians, and thus to reduce the need for soldiers to prevent frontier conflicts); forbidding them to print their own money; and where necessary, requiring them to provide living quarters for British troops.

Resistance and Punishment, 1770–1774

1. Anger and political protests built up as the British kept imposing new taxes and restrictions, sometimes leading to attacks on tax collectors or other government officials. Tensions were greatest in Boston, where England sent troops in 1768 to protect government officials. Local citizens sometimes harassed the troops by yelling and throwing things at them. One such incident in 1770 got out of hand and became the Boston Massacre.

2. Following the Boston Massacre, England sought to reduce tensions by removing the troops to an island in Boston Harbor and by repealing all taxes except the tax on tea. Much of the anger dissipated, and things settled down between 1770 and 1772.

3. However, the tea tax stood as a symbol of imposed British restrictions, and many colonists continued to oppose the notion of taxation without representation. Tensions flared up again in 1773 when the British East India Company was given a monopoly over the tea trade in the colonies. Colonists resisted this by refusing entry of "monopoly" ships into colonial ports, and they destroyed the cargo of one such ship that had docked at Boston by staging the Boston Tea Party in 1773.

4. Angered at these developments, the British passed a series of Acts of Parliament (called the Intolerable Acts by the colonists) designed to punish Boston and the Massachusetts colony. These included revoking self-government, closing the port of Boston, and forcibly quartering troops in people's homes. In effect, Boston was occupied and put under martial law, and steps were taken to reorganize the Massachusetts government.

5. In turn, the British actions alarmed the colonists, leading them to establish the First Continental Congress in 1774 to discuss how to respond to the developing crisis and to arrange for the thirteen colonies to act as a united group. Talks continued at the Second Continental Congress held in 1775, culminating in decisions to organize resistance to Parliament's actions and to petition the king for repeal of measures viewed as tyrannical, especially the "Intolerable Acts" directed against Boston and Massachusetts.

Revolution and Independence

1. Attempts to work out a peaceful settlement failed. The king ignored the colonists' petition, sent more troops, and announced further restrictions. In the colonies, verbal resistance spilled over into armed conflicts, including battles at Lexington, Concord, and Bunker Hill.

2. Giving up on attempts to compromise, the Congress accepted a motion to declare independence on July 2, 1776, and issued the Declaration of Independence two days later. In the process of listing grievances against England that justified the declaration, the document put forth some important basic principles concerning human rights that governments ought to respect and identified actions that governments ought not to take. Many of these reflected the colonists' recent experiences with the king and the Parliament.

3. The declaration meant war with England. The colonies established themselves as a federation through the Articles of Confederation, recruited George Washington to command the army, and began raising money to recruit, equip, and train soldiers.

4. The colonists were fighting the world's foremost military power, but several factors worked in their favor that enabled them to prevail in the end. England was involved in empire building and armed conflict all over the world, so it could allocate only limited resources to the conflict in America. England had to ship soldiers thousands of miles away to the colonies, but the colonists were fighting on their home ground. England's enemies, most notably France, helped the colonies by sending needed materials and in some cases military assistance. Finally, there was considerable division of opinion in England about the war against the colonies so that governmental leaders were less eager to pursue it and more willing to conclude a peace agreement than they might have been otherwise.

5. For the most part, the war involved relatively small battles between relatively small armies, nothing like what occurred later in the Civil War. Early battles were mostly in New England and New York, and were mostly inconclusive or won by the

British. Later battles were mostly fought farther south and more often won by the colonists. Hostilities climaxed with a major American victory at Yorktown in 1781, and the war ended after a long period of peace negotiations concluded in 1783.

6. The united colonies were now an independent nation. The new nation still operated under the Articles of Confederation at first, but this form of federal government proved too weak to be effective and was soon replaced by the U.S. Constitution (these events will be the focus of the next unit).

POSSIBLE ACTIVITIES

The nature of the content (past history) and the students' lack of much background knowledge limits opportunities for experiential learning or independent inquiry (except for research assignments based on textbook or encyclopedia accounts of the Revolution or biographies of Revolutionary figures). However, students can use teacher-provided summaries of key information items or historically based children's literature selections as a basis for dramatic reenactments, debates, simulations, or writing assignments that involve taking the role of an individual who was involved in some way in the Revolution. Representative activities include the following:

1. Have students pretend to be journalists or pamphleteers writing about the Boston Massacre or the Boston Tea Party. Have some individuals or groups pretend to be Sam Adams or another colonist seeking to foment rebellion, others pretend to be a news-paper reporter seeking to write a neutral or balanced account, and still others pretend to be a Tory dismayed by unjustified defiance of legitimate authority.

2. Have the class simulate a town meeting (or a Continental Congress meeting) called to decide whether, and if so how, the group should support the people of Boston in resisting the Intolerable Acts.

3. Simulate a debate or trial concerning whether or not the American Revolution was justified. Include arguments or testimony by King George and other defenders of the view that British actions prior to the Revolution were not only consistent with established laws and customs but also reasonable and respectful of the colonists' concerns, as well as arguments or testimony by Tom Paine and other defenders of the view that the colonists were justified in breaking away from England to form an independent nation.

4. Have small groups of students simulate family discussions of whether or not the father or one of the sons should join the Continental Army. Assign different geographical locations and life circumstances to different groups (a Boston shop owner, a Massachusetts farmer, a farmer in rural Pennsylvania, a plantation owner in Georgia, a former slave now living in New York City).

5. Have students pretend to be citizens of Boston beginning to get caught up in the events preceding the Revolution, discussing among family members or writing to friends elsewhere about their experiences and how they might respond to them (a family forced to quarter British troops, a family whose son threw a rock at British troops and barely escaped when they gave chase, a Tory family trying to decide what they will do if conflict with England continues to escalate, formerly close friends who find that disagreement over political issues is ruining their friendship).

Other possible activities for this unit include the following:

1. Map activities highlighting key items of information, such as the role of the Appalachians as a barrier to westward expansion of the colonies, the long distances and travel times between the colonies and England and between the northern and southern colonies (which created delays of weeks or months in communications), and the locations of major cities and battle sites

2. Essays or class presentations on why we celebrate the Fourth of July

3. Discussions or class presentations focusing on comparison and contrast between the issues that led the colonies to declare independence from England and the issues involved in more recent struggles for independence (satellite nations versus the USSR prior to its break up, former component nations within the USSR versus Russia since the break up, Quebec)

PRINT RESOURCES FOR POTENTIAL USE IN THIS UNIT

Avi: *The Fighting Ground*

James Lincoln Collier and Christopher Collier: *War Comes to Willy Freeman*

Ingri and Edgar Peres D'Aulaire: *George Washington*

S. Edwards: *When the World's on Fire*

Esther Forbes: *Johnny Tremain*

Jean Fritz: *Where Was Patrick Henry on May 29th*; *Can't You Make Them Behave, King George?*; *Will You Sign Here, John Hancock?*; *Why Don't You Get a Horse, Sam Adams?*; *And Then What Happened, Paul Revere?*; *What's the Big Idea, Ben Franklin?*; *Shh! We're Writing the Constitution*

Robert Lawson: *Ben & Me*; *Mr. Revere & I*

Elizabeth Levy: *If You Were There When They Signed the Constitution*

Ann McGovern: *If You Lived in Colonial Times*

Scott O'Dell: *Sarah Bishop*

Edwin Tunis: *Colonial Living*

Cobblestone magazine (issues dealing with the Revolutionary period)

REFERENCES USED IN DEVELOPMENT OF THE UNIT

Crabtree, C., Nash, B., Gagnon, P., & Waugh, S. (Eds.). (1992). *Lessons from history: Essential understandings and historical perspectives students should acquire.* Los Angles: National Center for History in the Schools, University of California, Los Angeles.

McBee, T., Tate, D., & Wagner, L. (1985). *U.S. history. Book 1: Beginnings to 1865.* Dubuque, IA: William C. Brown.

McKeown, M., & Beck, I. (1990). The assessment and characterization of young learners' knowledge of a topic in history. *American Educational Research Journal, 27,* 688–726.

VanSledright, B., Brophy, J., & Bredin, N. (1993). *Fifth-graders' ideas about the American Revolution expressed before and after studying it within a U.S. history course.* (Elementary Subjects Center Series No. 81). East Lansing: Center for the Learning and Teaching of Elementary Subjects, Michigan State University.

Appendix B

A Resource Unit on Mountains

GOALS

1. Help students to understand the nature of mountains, the physical environments that they create, and the advantages and limitations that these environments pose for human activities
2. Help students to learn about mountain regions in the United States, especially those in which they live or that have noteworthy connections to the region in which they live
3. Engage students in personal and civic decision making related to the nation's mountain regions

KEY IDEAS TO BE DEVELOPED

The Physical Geography of Mountain Regions

1. Mountains are not just hills but very high elevations of land. Define mountains in terms of distance from sea level and compare them with plains that are mostly within a few hundred feet of sea level. (Show and explain relief maps and schematic diagrams that name and illustrate the land forms found between sea level and the highest mountains.)
2. Mountains have not "just always been there." They were formed by movements of the earth's surface plates or by volcanic activity erupting from below the surface. Three major causal mechanisms have been identified: (1) Two surface plates clash directly and force each other upwards at the point of contact (as when you push two clay pancakes together on a tabletop). This process created most of the major mountain ranges that feature high and sharp peaks. (2) Two plates come together, but instead of a direct clash, the edge of one plate slips over the edge of the other, which slips under. This creates more rounded ranges, high enough to be considered mountains but not among the highest peaks on earth. (3) Volcanoes cause upward bulging of the earth while they are still underground, and once they begin erupting above the ground, they expel lava (sometimes millions of tons) that can build up to mountainous proportions over the centuries.
3. Although there are isolated peaks (mostly volcanoes), most mountains are parts of ranges (study the globe or sets of maps to locate and discuss the world's major mountain ranges, especially those that form the "spine" of the Americas).
4. Physical environments (and the ecologies that they are capable of supporting) change as one moves from sea level toward higher elevations. In general, as one continues to move higher, the climate becomes colder and there is less variety in plants and animals. Most plants and animals (and people) are found at low elevations that feature relatively warm climates, flat land, and rich soil. As one begins to move up into mountain elevations, the climate cools, the land is mostly sloped, and the soil becomes rockier. It becomes harder for people to grow crops and for animals to find food. If the mountain is high enough, one eventually will reach a tree line beyond which trees no longer grow. These elevations still support bushes and wildflowers that can survive without rich soil or a warm climate, and animals such as bears, mountain lions, marmots, and mountain goats that are adapted to the rough terrain and forbidding climate. Still higher up, there is only rock, sometimes

covered in part by snow (or even glaciers). Only species such as lichen and insects, and perhaps a few wildflowers and marmots, can survive in this environment.

5. Prevailing winds blowing into a mountain range create weather patterns that may affect entire regions. The mountain range interrupts the flow of clouds and moist air, turning it back on itself and building up the air's moisture content until it forms precipitation. As a result, there is frequent rain or snow on the windward side of the mountain range but dry, even desert, conditions on the leeward side (illustrate using diagrams taken from textbooks). This is why the northwest coast of the United States has a wet climate but the Great Basin east of the mountains is very dry (refer to a globe or maps to elaborate on this and other examples of mountains' effects on weather and climate, especially effects on the local region).

People and Mountains

1. In the past, people who did not live in mountain areas tended to view them as forbidding and unpleasant places to be avoided if possible. Prior to modern paved roads and motor-driven vehicles, mountain ranges were significant barriers to trade and travel, as well as significant protection against invasion. Heavy snows often meant that even passes through the mountains were open only during the warmer months. Even then, they were difficult to negotiate because the roads were often sloped. In many places, one could easily slip off the road and either tumble down a steep slope and get hurt or fall off a cliff and get killed. Mountain ranges were significant barriers to westward migration during the pioneer days when people used horses and wagons to cross over the Appalachians into the Midwest, and later, to cross the Rockies and the Sierras in the West.

2. Even then, though, some people lived in the mountains. Usually they lived not on the peaks but in valleys between ranges or in flat areas such as Jackson Hole that lay between surrounding mountains. Some forms of farming and animal grazing were possible in these areas, supplemented by hunting and fishing in the mountains (perhaps embellish here with books or videos on 19th-century "mountain men" or other people who managed to live in mountain areas without benefit of modern housing and transportation).

3. Most mountain regions were (and still are) sparsely populated. However, towns developed in a few places because they became centers for local industry (typically mining or lumbering operations) or transportation hubs (they were located at a key crossroads or served as the point of departure into a major mountain pass).

4. Today, mountain regions are much less isolated than they used to be, and people can drive through them, using modern roads that snake their way around mountains (and sometimes tunnels that go through them). People in our country have good access by car or train to the Appalachians, the Ozarks, the Rockies, and the Sierra Nevada ranges. They also can fly to these areas and to remote areas in Alaska and Hawaii. Many people take advantage of these opportunities: Instead of thinking of mountain regions as unpleasant places to be avoided, most modern people think of them as attractive places to visit to enjoy scenic vistas, hike in national parks, fish in mountain streams, go skiing or mountain climbing, or visit art colonies, historic places, or other tourist attractions. Europeans enjoy visiting the Alps for similar reasons.

5. Even today, however, certain mountain regions are still formidable barriers to travel by land, and certain mountain communities are still quite isolated. This is especially true of the Himalayan range and the nations of Nepal and Tibet, as well as various mountain regions in Indonesia and South America.

6. Even in our country and in the Alps, heavy snows and bitter cold make it impossible (or even if possible, economically unfeasible) to keep certain roads or mountain

passes open in the winter. Except for ski resorts, mountain communities and national parks that host a great many visitors in the warmer months do not see many outsiders in the colder months.

7. Mountain regions are not heavily populated even today. A major exception is Mexico City—the largest city in the world—that is located in a "bowl" high in the mountains of central Mexico. There are also a few large cities in mountains areas of the United States that have grown because they are regional marketing and service centers, most notably Denver. However, even the cities in mountain areas tend to be small, and most mountain communities exist for the same economic reasons as in the past (principally mining, lumbering, and cattle or sheep ranching). The major recent addition is tourism, notable in ski resorts (Aspen, Park City, etc.) or in towns located near national parks or other places of natural beauty (Jackson Hole, Lake Tahoe).

8. Large cities in mountain regions often suffer from cost-of-living and quality-of-life problems. Food and manufactured items often cost more because they have to be shipped greater distances to remote mountain locations. Local geographic factors sometimes create air inversions or other conditions that limit air flow and thus magnify air pollution problems. Mexico City has a terrible air-quality problem, and Denver is developing one.

9. Even though they are sparsely populated, mountain regions make important contributions to our national productivity and quality of life. In some areas, runoff from mountain rain and snow is collected in reservoirs and used to provide vital water supplies—not only for drinking but also for irrigation of lands that otherwise would not support farming. The rich central valley of California is irrigated in this way. Mountain regions also supply significant proportions of the nation's lumber and minerals, including some vital minerals that are not found anywhere else in the nation.

ADDITIONAL IDEAS SUGGESTED FOR OPTIONAL INCLUSION

1. Humans accustomed to living at lower elevations need to adapt when they visit or move to mountain areas (shortness of breath accompanies physical exertion at high elevations; dry air on the lee side of mountains can lead to dehydration and skin irritation problems; daytime and nighttime temperatures may be much more variable).

2. Along with people who exploit the natural resources found in mountain regions, some people make a living in these regions through occupations that require specialized skills more than abundant raw materials. Many people living in villages in the Swiss Alps make watches or cuckoo clocks. In our country, some people living in mountain communities are artists or crafts workers who make specialized creations.

3. In many parts of the world, farmers cope with sloped land by reshaping it into series of steplike terraces so that soil and water are prevented from running down the slope.

4. People in mountain areas have learned to construct houses to maximize exposure to the sun, minimize exposure to wind, and cause snow to slide off of their roofs and pile up against the house so as to provide insulation.

5. Mountain climbers using special equipment have scaled many of the world's highest peaks, including Mount Everest.

6. There are active volcanoes in our country, including many in Hawaii and Mount St. Helens in Washington (you might wish to develop a lesson on volcanoes if your curriculum treats this topic as part of social studies rather than science).

7. Many of our highest mountain regions have been reserved as national parks (perhaps show photos or videos from some of these).

8. Some mountain ranges stretch along coast lines (most notably in western North and South America). Often this creates favorable conditions for the development of communities along the coast. Travel between coastal communities is usually easy by land or water, but these communities may be isolated from inland communities on the other side of the mountain range. Some communities in places like Alaska and Chile are accessible only by air or sea.

POSSIBLE ACTIVITIES

1. Start the unit with a story from children's literature about mountain living or with brainstorming about what it is like to live in the mountains.
2. Read children's books or show videos about mountain life in the past and perhaps today in Switzerland or Nepal.
3. Engage students in a research project on how the local area is affected by mountains or is interdependent with mountain regions. Even if located at a great distance from a mountain range, your area probably has some connections via climate and weather patterns, importing of raw materials, visiting of national parks or ski resorts, and so on.
4. Study changes over time in the economy/population of a particular mountain region or community (especially if local).
5. Study and discuss travel brochures or videos that feature tourist options in mountain regions. Invite students to show and tell about vacation trips or other family experiences in mountain regions.
6. Discuss policy issues relating to mountain regions (air and water quality, land and water use, etc.).
7. Have students discuss or write about the trade-offs involved in living in mountain regions, then explain why they would or would not want to live there (or, alternatively, why they would want to visit or move to Denver, Aspen, Lake Tahoe, the Blue Ridge, or some other specific location).

Appendix C

Planning Tool

This textbook is intended to impart understanding and appreciation for the most salient elements of a strong social studies curriculum. The authors have selected Government as the exemplary unit. Each of the chapter topics will be illustrated by using government-related examples. The planning tool is intended to reveal the steps in developing a meaningful unit that leads toward memorable learning with an eye toward high student achievement.

We deliberately set the tool apart from the text in this appendix to provide a cohesive depiction of how a goals-oriented approach built around big ideas drives meaningful practice. The thematic example is intended to serve as a "minds-on" thread woven throughout the chapters to show how theory is applied to daily practice.

CHAPTER 3—WHAT DOES GOAL-ORIENTED INSTRUCTION ENTAIL?

Sample Unit Goal: To help students to develop understanding and appreciation for government as a cultural universal

Sample Lesson Goal: To help students understand and appreciate (1) the value of government services and (2) how the funding of these services is supported (taxes)

CHAPTER 4—WHAT DO SELECTING AND REPRESENTING CONTENT ENTAIL?

Selecting Content Knowledge

The focus for this lesson (or series of lessons, depending on the age level and the amount of depth you want to develop) is on functions and services provided by governments to local communities, individual states, and all citizens of the United States. Governments are needed to do things that people cannot do by themselves.

Main Ideas to Develop

- Government services are needed to do things that the people cannot do by themselves.
- All governments in the United States (e.g., community, township, city, state, and federal) provide some services for people.

To pay for the services, the governments collect money from the people. The money is referred to as taxes. (See Chapter 14 for a complete list of main ideas for the Government unit, pp. 292 to 294.)

CHAPTER 7—HOW CAN I TEACH OTHER SOCIAL SCIENCE CONTENT MORE MEANINGFULLY?

Content is drawn from political science (the study of how people create and change structures of power, authority, and governance) and economics (the study of how people organize the production, distribution, and consumption of goods and services) for this lesson. Government at all levels serves as the power/authority structure for determining the services needed in a given community that individuals/families cannot pay for themselves. The government figures out how these services will be provided and how much they will cost the taxpayers. Oftentimes, people are asked to vote on issues related to taxes. The economics aspects of the lesson relate to the consumption of services—in this case services the government provides, using the individual tax dollars to pay for them.

CHAPTER 8—HOW CAN I STRUCTURE CLASSROOM DISCOURSE TO HELP STUDENTS
DEVELOP SOCIAL STUDIES UNDERSTANDINGS?

For this lesson, we recommend using interactive narrative. Its main function is to gather, review, and connect information from previous lessons and to expand on ideas students bring up by using the artifacts, charts, and pictures from previous lessons and input students have acquired from their families about governmental services and the taxes they pay to support them.

Begin by reviewing responses to the home assignment. Diversity within the classroom will be revealed through the range of family responses. The responses will contribute to students' expanded understanding of the big ideas. Then introduce the new lesson with a role-play or skit depicting a family member paying taxes to the government. (See Chapter 7.)

After the debriefing of the role-play, use a graphic to show where the money goes. Create a data retrieval chart to organize the information gleaned about taxes and services. Use the following as an interactive narrative/class discussion focusing on the big ideas.

Suggested Lesson Discussion

Every community provides certain kinds of services. Think about some of the services you and your family depend on every day. You need good streets to walk or ride on to school. You need police officers and firefighters to protect you and help you in times of emergency. You need teachers to help you learn in school. You need the garbage collector to pick up your rubbish so that your community will be clean. You may get your water from a water company run by your community. Your community has traffic lights and traffic signs to help people travel safely. These are all services provided by the community.

Different communities have different needs, so the services they provide might be different too. Location may make a difference in the services that a community provides. For example, clearing the streets after a snowstorm is an important service in northern communities, but snow removal is not needed in Orlando, Florida. The size of the community also makes a difference. Large communities need more services than small communities do. For example, most communities do not have a subway system like New York or Chicago because they do not have enough people to support it. Instead, most people drive to work. Some services are common to all communities (e.g., teachers, police officers, firefighters). Larger communities need more workers to provide more services.

Communities need money to provide the services that people need and to pay the workers who provide them. Schools need money to pay for teachers, building repairs, heating, electricity, buses, and drivers. Firefighters and police officers need to be paid, and their vehicles need to be maintained. Parks have to be taken care of, and roads need to be maintained. Everyone in the community helps pay for these things.

Every level of government in the United States provides some services. The state government handles matters that affect all of the people who live in the state, and the federal government handles matters that affect all of the people who live in the United States. To pay for these services, people pay taxes. We all pay because we all are helped by these services.

CHAPTER 9—HOW CAN I DESIGN, IMPLEMENT, AND EVALUATE INSTRUCTIONAL
ACTIVITIES?

Activity

Provide each table with illustrations or photographs depicting community services. These might include: traffic lights, good streets, police officers, firefighters, teachers, city librarians, postal workers, and so on. Also provide each table with a description of a community (rural, large city in winter, suburb in summer, etc.). Using large sheets of white paper, crayons, paste, and so on, have each group create a mural illustrating the services that the government provides based on the needs of a particular kind of community. Have each group write a short summary that includes how the government pays for the services. Share the results.

CHAPTER 10—WHAT ARE SOME OTHER STRATEGIES FOR TEACHING SOCIAL STUDIES?

Role-play can be a very useful strategy for introducing a new lesson because it is engaging and because if the teacher orchestrates it carefully, it can set the stage for the big ideas that will be introduced and developed.

The scene shows Mom, Dad, or another adult family member at the table paying bills, including checks to local, state, and federal government for taxes. The individual paying the taxes is grumbling a bit, and a child observing this activity asks such questions as "Who gets the money?" "Why do you have to pay the money?" "How is the money used?" "Why can't the family simply keep the money?" You as the teacher provide a brief overview of the lesson by introducing the big ideas as they relate to the questions posed by the child.

After the class debriefing, use a graphic to show where the money goes and to underscore that tax money pays for the services that families cannot afford individually. Also, different communities have different needs, so the services that they provide may be different too.

CHAPTER 11—WHAT IS THE ROLE OF CURRICULAR INTEGRATION?

The literature sources selected for this lesson are supplemental but intended to match the goals and expand on the big ideas. They should be placed in the social studies corner and be made available during literacy choice time and for home sign-out.

Examples of sources for this lesson include:

Killoran, J., Zimmer, J., & Jarrett, M. (1997). *Michigan and Its People.* Ronkonkona, NY: Jarrett Publishing. [Note: Look for similar sources focusing on your state.]

Marsh, C. (1998). *Michigan Government for Kids.* Peach Tree City, GA: Gallopade Publishing. [Note: Look for similar sources focusing on your state.]

Sobel, S. (1999). *How the U.S. Government Works.* Hauppauge, NY: Barton's Educational Series.

*Make sure the literature sources you select are authentic.

CHAPTER 12—HOW CAN I ASSESS STUDENT LEARNING?

Ask each student to complete an open-ended statement and illustrate it with a picture. For example:

It is important that our families pay taxes to our government because _____

_____

_____

If upper-grade mentors are available, they could assist in this writing assignment. Compile the responses into a class booklet and title it: "Why Our Families Pay Taxes to the Government." Duplicate. Have each student take a copy home to share with family members.

CHAPTER 13—HOW CAN THE CURRICULUM BE EXPANDED AND MADE MORE MEANINGFUL THROUGH HOME–SCHOOL CONNECTIONS?

Home Assignment

Encourage each student to read the class booklet entitled "Why Our Families Pay Taxes to the Government" to family members. Discuss work roles of people who work for the government, noting especially family and friends. Discuss what they do to help members of the community. Interviewing people who work for the government would be very beneficial.

Who do we know who works for the government to provide services to the community? State? Nation?	*What does s/he do and how does s/he help members of our community?*

Dear Parents,

We have been learning about the functions and services provided by the government. We encourage you to ask your child to share the class booklet entitled "Why Our Families Pay Taxes to the Government." Then, identify people you know who work for the government. If possible, interview them. Discuss the kinds of services they provide to the community. Please send your response back to school so that we can include it in our next class discussion.

Sincerely,

CHAPTER 14—WHAT SOCIAL STUDIES PLANNING TOOLS ARE AVAILABLE?

The National Council for the Social Studies (1994) published standards that address overall curriculum design and comprehensive performance expectations. We encourage you to establish your program framework using these, along with those identified by your state and local school district.

NCSS Standards

VI. Power, Authority, Governance

   The study of how people create and change structures of power, authority, and governance.

VII. Production, Distribution, and Consumption

   The study of how people organize for the production, distribution, and consumption of goods and *services*.

FIGURE A.1

Proposed Planning Checklist

We encourage you to use the following checklist as a self-monitoring tool as you engage in planning. If you can answer "yes" to all of the questions, we think you are well on your way to developing a powerful social studies program in your classroom.

_____ Do I have adequate data about my students that can inform my content and process plans?

_____ Is there evidence in my long-range plans that I am seriously considering what an ideal social studies learner will look like at the end of the school year?

_____ Do my long-range plans show evidence of using skills and formats from standardized tests in natural ways?

_____ Do my long-range plans show evidence of incorporating designated content standards in meaningful ways?

_____ Do my long-range plans show evidence of integrating across subjects in natural ways?

_____ Do my long-range plans show evidence of a thoughtful pattern of introducing new content and skills, places for practicing them, and places for applying them in new situations?

_____ Do my long-range plans show evidence of my strategic decisions for using large-group, small-group, and individual instruction, realizing that all students are assessed individually?

_____ Do my long-range plans reflect the primary purpose of social studies: to help young people develop the ability to make informed and reasoned decisions for the public good as citizens of a culturally diverse, democratic society in an interdependent world?

_____ Have I made a list of yearlong social studies goals that support the overall social studies aim?

Unit Planning

_____ Are all the curriculum components aligned (e.g., content clusters, instructional activities, learning activities, assessment tools, and home assignments)?

_____ Do my units include goals that focus on understanding, appreciation, and application?

_____ Do my goals align with the big ideas drawn from selected content needed to guide my planning, teaching, and evaluating?

_____ Does each unit build on the preceding ones so that there is a continuous revisiting and applying of big ideas?

Weekly and Daily Planning

_____ Do I focus on the goals and big ideas in every lesson?

_____ Are my daily priorities focused on coherent content linking prior knowledge to new material and scaffolding students' task engagement?

_____ Are my activities and assignments sufficiently varied and interesting enough to motivate student engagement?

_____ Are my activities and assignments sufficiently new and challenging enough to constitute learning experiences rather than pointless repetition and yet easy enough to allow students to achieve high rates of success if they invest reasonable time and effort?

_____ Am I planning adequate opportunities for modeling and instructing students in learning and self-regulation strategies?

_____ Is my instruction comprehensive, with adequate attention to propositional knowledge (what to do), procedural knowledge (how to do it), and conditional knowledge (when and why to do it)?

_____ Am I considering the less able students by making sure my teaching is strategic—that is, doing lots of modeling; explaining the what, how, when, and why of instruction; and expecting and looking for success?

References

Abramovitch, R., Freedman, J., & Pliner, P. (1991). Children and money: Getting an allowance, credit versus cash, and knowledge of pricing. *Journal of Economic Psychology, 12,* 27–45.

Ajmera, M., & Ivanko, J. (1999). *To be a kid.* Watertown, MA: Charlesbridge.

Akenson, J. E. (1989). The expanding environments and elementary education: A critical perspective. *Theory and Research in Social Education, 17*(1), 33–52.

Alleman, J., & Brophy, J. (1992). Analysis of the activities in a social studies curriculum. In J. Brophy (Ed.), *Advances in research on teaching. Planning and managing learning tasks and activities* (Vol. 3, pp. 47–80). Greenwich, CT: JAI Press.

Alleman, J., & Brophy, J. (1993). Is curriculum integration a boon or a threat to social studies? *Social Education, 57*(6), 289–91.

Alleman, J., & Brophy, J. (1993–1994). Teaching that lasts: College students' reports of learning activities experienced in elementary school social studies. *Social Science Record, 30*(2), 36–48, *31*(1), 42–46.

Alleman, J., & Brophy, J. (1994a). Taking advantage of out-of-school opportunities for meaningful social studies learning. *The Social Studies, 85*(6), 262–67.

Alleman, J., & Brophy, J. (1994b). Trade-offs embedded in the literary approach to early elementary social studies. *Social Studies and the Young Learner, 6*(3), 6–8.

Alleman, J., & Brophy, J. (1998). Strategic opportunities during out-of-school hours. *Social Studies and the Young Learner, 10*(4), 10–13.

Alleman, J., & Brophy, J. (2000). On the menu: The growth of self-efficacy. *Social Studies and the Young Learner, 12*(3), 15–19.

Alleman, J., & Brophy, J. (2001). *Social studies excursions, K–3. Book one: Powerful units on food, clothing, and shelter.* Portsmouth, NH: Heinemann.

Alleman, J., & Brophy, J. (2002). *Social studies excursions, K–3. Book two: Powerful units on communication, transportation, and family living.* Portsmouth, NH: Heinemann.

Alleman, J., & Brophy, J. (2003a). History is alive: Teaching young children about changes over time. *The Social Studies, 94,* 107–10.

Alleman, J., & Brophy, J. (2003b). *Social studies excursions, K–3. Book three: Powerful units on childhood, money, and government.* Portsmouth, NH: Heinemann.

Alleman, J., & Brophy, J. (2004). Building a learning community and studying childhood. *Social Studies and the Young Learner, 17*(2), 16–18.

Alleman, J., Brophy, J., & Knighton, B. (2003). Co-constructing classroom resources. *Social Studies and the Young Learner, 16*(2), 5–8.

Almarza, D. (2001). Contexts shaping minority language students' perceptions of American history. *Journal of Social Studies Research, 25*(2), 4–22.

Amrein, A., & Berliner, D. (2003). The effects of high-stakes testing on student motivation and learning. *Educational Leadership, 60*(5), 32–38.

Armento, B. (1993). Reform revisited: The story of elementary social studies at the crest of the 21st century. In V. Wilson, J. Little, & G. Wilson (Eds.), *Teaching social studies: Handbook of trends, issues, and implications for the future* (pp. 25–44). Westport, CT: Greenwood Press.

Aronson, E., Blaney, N., Stephan, C., Sikes, J., & Snapp, M. (1978). *The Jigsaw classroom.* Beverly Hills, CA: Sage.

Ausubel, D. (1968). *Educational psychology: A cognitive view.* New York: Holt, Rinehart, & Winston.

Baker, J. (1998). The social context of school satisfaction among urban, low-income, African-American students. *School Psychology Quarterly, 13,* 25–44.

Bandura, A. (1989). Human agency in social cognitive theory. *American Psychologist, 44,* 1175–84.

Bandura, A., & Schunk, D. (1981). Cultivating competence, self-efficacy, and intrinsic interest through proximal self-motivation. *Journal of Personality and Social Psychology, 41,* 586–98.

Banks, J. (2005). *Cultural diversity and education: Foundations, curriculum, and teaching* (5th ed.). Boston: Allyn & Bacon.

Barnes, P., & Barnes, C. (1998). *Woodrow, the White House mouse* (2nd ed.). Alexandria, VA: VSP Books.

Barrett, M. (2005). Children's understanding of, and feelings about, countries and national groups. In. M. Barrett & E. Buchanan-Barrow (Eds.), *Children's understanding of society* (pp. 251–285). Hove, England: Psychology Press.

Barton, K. (1992, November). *"It seems a lot like a story": Narrative presentation of the American Revolution*. Paper presented at the annual meeting of the College and University Faculty Assembly of the National Council for the Social Studies, Detroit, MI.

Barton, K. (1996). Narrative simplifications in elementary students' historical thinking. In J. Brophy (Ed.), *Advances in research on teaching* (Vol. 6, pp. 51–83). Greenwich, CT: JAI Press.

Barton, K. (1997). History—it *can* be elementary: An overview of elementary students' understanding of history. *Social Education, 61,* 13–16.

Barton, K. (2001) A picture's worth: Analyzing historical photographs in the elementary grades. *Social Education, 65,* 278–83.

Barton, K. (2005). Primary sources in history: Breaking through the myths. *Phi Delta Kappan, 86*(10), 745–53.

Barton, K., & Levstik, L. (1996). "Back when God was around and everything": Elementary children's understanding of historical time. *American Educational Research Journal, 33,* 419–54.

Barton, K., & Levstik, L. (2003). Why don't more history teachers engage students in interpretation? *Social Education, 67,* 358–61.

Barton, K., & Levstik, L. (2004). *Teaching history for the common good.* Mahwah, NJ: Erlbaum.

Beck, I., & McKeown, M. (1988). Toward meaningful accounts in history texts for young learners. *Educational Researcher, 17*(6), 31–39.

Beck, I., McKeown, M., & Gromoll, E. (1989). Learning from social studies texts. *Cognition and Instruction, 6,* 99–158.

Beninati, A. (1991). History Teaching Alliance. *OAH Magazine of History, 6*(1), 46.

Bennett, N., & Dunne, E. (1992). Managing small groups. New York: Simon & Schuster.

Berman, S. (1990). Education for social responsibility. *Educational Leadership, 48*(3), 75–80.

Berman, S., & LeFarge, P. (Eds.). (1993). *Promising practices in teaching social responsibility.* Albany: State University of New York Press.

Berson, M., Cruz, B., Duplass, J., & Johnston, H. (2004). *Social studies on the Internet* (2nd ed.). Columbus, OH: Merrill Prentice-Hall.

Berti, A. (2002). Children's understanding of society: Psychological studies and their educational implications. In E. Nasman & A. Ross (Eds.), *Children's understanding in the new Europe* (pp. 89–107). Stoke on Trent, England: Trentham.

Berti, A. (2005). Children's understanding of politics. In M. Barrett & E. Buchanan-Barrow (Eds.), *Children's understanding of society* (pp. 69–103). Hove, England: Psychology Press.

Berti, A., & Bombi, A. (1988). *The child's construction of economics.* Cambridge, England: Cambridge University Press.

Berti, A., & Monaci, M. (1998). Third graders' acquisition of knowledge of banking: Restructuring or accretion? *British Journal of Educational Psychology, 68,* 357–71.

Blumenfeld, P., Mergendoller, J., & Swarthout, D. (1987). Task as a heuristic for understanding student learning and motivation. *Journal of Curriculum Studies, 19,* 135–48.

Boehm, R., & Petersen, J. (1994). An elaboration of the fundamental themes in geography. *Social Education, 58,* 211–18.

Bohan, C. (2005). Digging trenches: Nationalism and the first national report on the elementary history curriculum. *Theory and Research in Social Education, 33,* 266–91.

Booth, M. (1993). Students' historical thinking and the national history curriculum in England. *Theory and Research in Social Education, 21,* 105–27.

Bradley Commission on History in Schools. (1988). *Building a history curriculum: Guidelines for teaching history in schools.* Washington, DC: Educational Excellence Network.

Brandhorst, A. (1988). Historical fiction in the classroom: Useful tool or entertainment? *Southern Social Studies Quarterly, 14,* 19–30.

Bransford, J., Brown, A., & Cocking, R. (Eds.). (1999). *How people learn: Brain, mind, experiences, and school.* Washington, DC: National Academy Press.

Britt, M., Rouet, J., Georgi, M., & Perfetti, C. (1994). Learning from history texts: From causal analysis to argument models. In G. Leinhardt, I. Beck, & C. Stainton (Eds.), *Teaching and learning history* (pp. 47–84). Hillsdale, NJ: Erlbaum.

Brophy, J. (1983). Classroom organization and management. *Elementary School Journal, 83,* 265–85.

Brophy, J. (1992). The *de facto* national curriculum in U.S. elementary social studies: Critique of a representative example. *Journal of Curriculum Studies, 24,* 401–47.

Brophy, J. (Ed.). (1993). *Advances in research on teaching. Vol. 4. Case studies of teaching and learning in social studies.* Greenwich, CT: JAI Press.

Brophy, J. (1999). *Teaching* (Educational Practices Series No. 1). Geneva, Switzerland: International Bureau of Education.

Brophy, J. (2004). *Motivating students to learn* (2nd ed.). Mahwah, NJ: Erlbaum.

Brophy, J., & Alleman, J. (1991). Activities as instructional tools: A framework for analysis and evaluation. *Educational Researcher, 20,* 9–23.

Brophy, J., & Alleman, J. (1992). Planning and managing learning activities: Basic principles. In J. Brophy (Ed.), *Advances in research on teaching. Planning and managing learning tasks and activities* (Vol. 3, pp. 1–45). Greenwich, CT: JAI Press.

Brophy, J., & Alleman, J. (1995). NCSS social studies standards and the elementary teacher. *Social Studies and the Young Learner, 8*(1), 4–8.

Brophy, J., & Alleman, J. (2005). *Children's thinking about cultural universals.* Mahwah, NJ: Erlbaum.

Brophy, J., & VanSledright, B. (1997). *Teaching and learning history in elementary schools.* New York: Teachers College Press.

Bruner, J. (1990). *Acts of meaning.* Cambridge, MA: Harvard University Press.

Buchanan, C. (2001, Spring). *Faculty assess pros and cons of instructional technology @ library.edu.* Swarthmore College Libraries.

Bunting, E. (1991). *Fly away home.* New York: Clarion.

Byrnes, J. (1996). *Cognitive development and learning in instructional contexts.* Boston: Allyn & Bacon.

California State Department of Education. (1991). *Literature for history–social science. Kindergarten through grade eight.* Sacramento, CA: Author.

California Department of Education. (1997). *History-social science framework for California public schools: Kindergarten through grade 12.* Sacramento, CA: Author.

Carey, S. (1985). *Conceptual change in childhood.* Cambridge, MA: MIT Press.

Causey, V., & Armento, B. (2001). Strategies for increasing achievement in history. In R. Cole (Ed.), *More strategies for educating everybody's children* (pp. 101–18). Baltimore, MD: Association for Supervision and Curriculum Development.

Center for Civic Education. (1994). *National standards for civics and government.* Calabasas, CA: Author.

Chinn, C., & Brewer, W. (1993). The role of anomolous data in knowledge acquisition: A theoretical framework and implications for science instruction. *Review of Educational Research, 63,* 1–49.

Clark, C., & Peterson, P. (1986). Teachers' thought processes. In M.C. Wittrock (Ed.), *Handbook of research on teaching* (3rd ed., pp. 225–96). New York: Macmillan.

Cohen, E., Lotan, R., Scarloss, B., & Arellano, A. (1999). Complex instruction: Equity in cooperative learning classrooms. *Theory into Practice, 38,* 80–86.

Cooper, H. (1989). *Homework.* White Plains, NY: Longman.

Cooper, H. (1994). *The battle over homework: An administrator's guide to setting sound and effective policies.* Thousand Oaks, CA: Corwin.

Cornbleth, C., & Waugh, D. (1999). *The great speckled bird: Multicultural politics and education policymaking.* Mahwah, NJ: Erlbaum.

Crabtree, C. (1989). History is for children. *American Educator, 13*(4), 34–39.

Creemers, B. & Scheerens, J. (Guest Editors). (1989). Developments in school effectiveness research. *International Journal of Educational Research, 13,* 685–825.

Davis, Jr., O. L., Yeager, E., & Foster, S. (Eds.). (2001). *Historical empathy and perspective taking in the social studies.* New York: Rowman & Littlefield.

Delpit, L. (1992). Acquisition of literate discourse: Bowing before the master? *Theory into Practice, 31,* 296–302.

Demko, G. (1992). *Why in the world: Adventures in geography.* New York: Anchor Books.

Dempster, F. (1991). Synthesis of research on reviews and tests. *Educational Leadership, 48,* 71–76.

Denham, C., & Lieberman, A. (Eds.). (1980). *Time to learn.* Washington, DC: National Institute of Education.

Dewey, J. (1900/1956). *School and society.* Chicago: University of Chicago Press.

Dewey, J. (1902). *The child and the curriculum.* Chicago: University of Chicago Press.

Dewey, J. (1910). *How we think.* Boston: D.C. Heath.

Dewey, J. (1938). *Experience and education.* New York: Collier Books.

Dillon, J. (Ed.). (1988). *Questioning and teaching: A manual of practice.* London: Croom Helm.

Dillon, J. (Ed.). (1990). *The practice of questioning.* New York: Routledge.

DiSalvo-Ryan, D. (1991). *Uncle Willie and the soup kitchen.* New York: Morrow Junior.

Dorsett, C. (1993). Multicultural education. Why we need it and why we worry about it. *Network News and Views, 12,* 3–31.

Downey, M., & Levstik, L. (1991). Teaching and learning history. In J. Shaver (Ed.), *Handbook of research on social studies teaching and learning* (pp. 400–10). New York: Macmillan.

Doyle, W. (1983). Academic work. *Review of Educational Research, 53,* 159–99.

Doyle, W. (1986). Classroom organization and management. In M.C. Wittrock (Ed.), *Handbook of research on teaching* (3rd ed., pp. 392–431). New York: Macmillan.

Duke, N., & Bennett-Armistead, S. (2003). *Reading and writing informational text in the primary grades: Research based practices.* New York: Scholastic.

Durkin, K. (2005). Children's understanding of gender roles in society. In. M. Barrett & E. Buchanan-Barrow (Eds.), *Children's understanding of society* (pp. 135–68). Hove, England: Psychology Press.

Egan, K. (1986). *Teaching as storytelling: An alternative approach to teaching and curriculum in elementary school.* Chicago: University of Chicago Press.

Egan, K. (1988). *Primary understanding: Education in early childhood.* New York: Routledge.

Egan, K. (1990). *Romantic understanding: The development of rationality and imagination, ages 8–15.* New York: Routledge.

Emler, N., & Dickinson, J. (2005). Children's understanding of social class and occupational groupings. In. M. Barrett & E. Buchanan-Barrow (Eds.), *Children's understanding of society* (pp. 169–97). Hove, England: Psychology Press.

Engle, S., & Longstreet, W. (1972). *A design for social education in the open curriculum.* New York: Harper & Row.

Engle, S., & Ochoa, A. (1988). *Education for democratic citizenship: Decision making in the social studies.* New York: Teachers College Press.

Epstein, T. (2001). Racial identity and young people's perspectives on social education. *Theory into Practice, 40,* 42–47.

Evans, R. (2004). *The social studies wars: What should we teach the children?* New York: Teachers College Press.

Evans, R., & Saxe, D. (Eds.). (1996). *Handbook on teaching social issues.* Washington, DC: National Council for the Social Studies.

Farrell, R., & Cirrincione, J. (1989). The content of the geography curriculum—a teacher's perspective. *Social Education, 53,* 105–08.

Ferretti, R., MacArthur, C., & Okolo, C. (2001). Teaching for historical understanding in inclusive classrooms. *Learning Disability Quarterly, 24,* 59–71.

Fertig, G. (2005). Teaching elementary students how to interpret the past. *Social Studies, 96,* 2–8.

Field, R. (1991). The general store (poem). In B. Armento, G. Nash, C. Salter, & K. Wixon (Eds.), *The world I see* (p. 77). Wilmington, MA: Houghton Mifflin.

Field, S. (2003). Using children's literature and the universals of culture to teach about Mexico. *The Social Studies, 94,* 123–27.

Fraenkel, J. (1980). *Helping students think and value: Strategies for teaching the social studies* (2nd ed.). Englewod Cliffs, NJ: Prentice-Hall.

Fraenkel, J. (1992, November). *A comparison of elite and non-elite social studies classrooms.* Paper presented at the annual meeting of the National Council for the Social Studies, Detroit, MI.

Frazee, B., & Ayers, S. (2003). Garbage in, garbage out: Expanding environments, constructivism, and content knowledge in social studies. In J. Leming, L. Ellington, & K. Porter (Eds.), *Where did social studies go wrong?* (pp. 111–23). Washington, DC: Thomas Fordham Foundation.

Furnham, A. (1996). The economic socialization of children. In P. Lunt & A. Furnham (Eds.), *Economic socialization: The economic beliefs and behaviours of young people* (pp. 11–34). Cheltenham, England: Edward Elgar.

Galdone, P. (1991). *The little red hen.* Wilmington, MA: Houghton Mifflin.

Gardner, H., & Boix-Mansilla, V. (1994). Teaching for understanding—within and across the disciplines. *Educational Leadership, 51*(5), 14–18.

Geography Education National Implementation Project (GENIP)/ NGS. (1986). *Maps, the landscape, and the fundamental themes in geography.* Washington, DC: National Geographic Society.

Geography Education National Implementation Project (GENIP). (1987). *K–6 geography: Themes, key ideas, and learning opportunities.* Washington, DC: Author.

The Geography Education Standards Project (1994). *Geography for life: National geography standards 1994.* Washington, DC: National Geographic Research & Exploration, pp. 34–35.

Girod, M., & Wong, D. (2002). An aesthetic (Deweyan) perspective on science learning: Case studies of three fourth graders. *Elementary School Journal, 102,* 199–224.

Good, T., & Brophy, J. (1995). *Contemporary educational psychology.* White Plains, NY: Longman.

Good, T., & Brophy, J. (2003). *Looking in classrooms* (9th ed.). Boston: Allyn & Bacon.

Goodlad, J. (1984). *A place called school.* New York: McGraw-Hill.

Gregg, M., & Leinhardt, G. (1994). Mapping out geography: An example of epistemology and education. *Review of Educational Research, 64,* 311–61.

Haas, M. (1991). An analysis of the social science and history concepts in elementary social studies textbooks grades 1–4. *Theory and Research in Social Education, 19,* 211–20.

Haas, M. (2000). *A Street through Time* used with powerful instructional strategies. *Social Studies and the Young Learner, 13*(2), 20–23.

Haas, M. (2001). Strategies for increasing achievement in geography. In R. Cole (Ed.), *More strategies for educating everybody's children* (pp. 87–100). Baltimore, MD: Association for Supervision and Curriculum Development.

Haas, M. (2004). The presidency and presidential elections in the elementary classroom. *Social Education, 68,* 340–46.

Haas, M., & Laughlin, M. (2001). Elementary education: A profile of elementary social studies teachers and their classrooms. *Social Education, 65,* 122–26.

Hakim, J. (1993). *The history of us.* New York: Oxford University Press.

Hallden, O. (1994). On the paradox of understanding history in an educational setting. In G. Leinhardt, I. Beck, & C. Stainton (Eds.), *Teaching and learning in history* (pp 27–46). Hillsdale, NJ: Erlbaum.

Hamilton, M., & Weiss, M. (1990). *Children tell stories: A teaching guide.* Katona, NY: Richard C. Owen.

Hanna, P. (1963). Revising the social studies: What is needed? *Social Education, 27,* 190–96.

Hanna, P., Sabaroff, R., Davies, G., & Farrar, C. (1996). *Geography in the teaching of social studies: Concepts and skills.* Boston: Houghton Mifflin.

Harms, J., & Lettow, L. (1994). Criteria for selecting picture books with historical settings. *Social Education, 58,* 152–54.

Harwood, D., & McShane, J. (1996). Young children's understanding of nested hierarchies of place relationships. *International Research in Geographical and Environmental Education, 5,* 3–29.

Hess, D. (2001). *Teaching students to discuss controversial public issues.* Bloomington, IN: ERIC Clearinghouse for Social Studies/Social Science Education.

Hess, R., & Torney, J. (1967). *The development of political attitudes in children.* Chicago: Aldine.

Hickey, M. G. (1999). *Bringing history home: Local and family history projects for Grades K–6.* Boston: Allyn & Bacon.

Hidi, S., & Baird, W. (1988). Strategies for increasing text-based interest and students' recall of expository texts. *Reading Research Quarterly, 23,* 465–83.

Hirsch, Jr., E. D. (1987). *Cultural literacy: What every American needs to know.* New York: Houghton Mifflin.

Hirschfeld, L. (2005). Children's understanding of racial groups. In. M. Barrett & E. Buchanan-Barrow (Eds.), *Children's understanding of society* (pp.199–221). Hove, England: Psychology Press.

Hoge, J., & Crump, C. (1988). *Teaching history in the elementary school.* Bloomington, IN: Social Studies Development Center and ERIC Clearinghouse for Social Studies/Social Science Education.

Hoge, J., Foster, S., Nickell, P., & Field, S. (Eds.). (2004). *Real-world investigations for social studies: Inquiries for middle and high school students based on the ten NCSS standards.* Upper Saddle River, NJ: Pearson/Merrill Prentice-Hall.

Hollyer, B. (1989). *Wake up, world! A day in the life of children around the world.* New York: Henry Holt & Co.

Holt, T. (1990). *Thinking historically: Narrative, imagination, and understanding.* New York: College Entrance Examination Board.

Howard, R. (2003). The shrinking of social studies. *Social Education, 67,* 285–88.

Hunter, M. (1984). Knowing, teaching and supervising. In P. Hosford (Ed.), *Using what we know about reading.* Alexandria, VA: Association for Supervision and Curriculum Development.

Hynd, C., & Guzzetti, B. (1998). When knowledge contradicts intuition: Conceptual change. In C. Hynd (Ed.), *Learning from text: Across conceptual domains* (pp. 139–63). Mahwah, NJ: Erlbaum.

Ingalls-Wilder, L. (1935). *Little house on the prairie.* New York: Harper & Row.

International Reading Association, (1997–2005). *Reading Online (ROL).* Edited by Bridget Dalton and Dana L. Grisham, www.readingonline.org

James, M., & Zarrillo, J. (1989). Teaching history with children's literature: A concept-based, interdisciplinary approach. *Social Studies, 80,* 153–58.

John, D. (1999). Consumer socialization of children: A retrospective look at twenty-five years of research. *Journal of Consumer Research, 26,* 183–213.

Johnson, D., & Johnson, R. (1994). *Learning together and alone: Cooperative, competitive, and individualistic learning* (4th ed.). Boston: Allyn & Bacon.

Johnson, D., Johnson, R., & Holubec, E. (1998). *Cooperation in the classroom* (7th ed.). Edina, MN: Interaction Book Co.

Joint Committee on Geographic Education. (1984). *Guidelines for geographic education: Elementary and secondary schools.* Washington, DC: Association of American Geographers and the National Council for Geographic Education.

Joyce, W., & Beach, R. (1997). *Introducing Canada: Content backgrounds, strategies, and resources for educators* (Bulletin 94). Washington, DC: National Council for the Social Studies.

Kalman, B. (1994). *Homes around the world.* New York: Crabtree.

Kehler, A. (1998). Capturing the "economic imagination": A treasury of children's books to meet content standards. *Social Studies and the Young Learner, 11*(2), 26–29.

Kendeau, P. & van den Broek, P. (2005). The effects of readers' misconceptions on comprehension of scientific text. *Journal of Educational Psychology, 97*, 235–42.

Kindersley, B., & Kindersley, A. (1995). *Children just like me.* New York: D.K. Publishing, Inc.

Kliebard, H. (2004). *The struggle for the American curriculum 1893–1958* (3rd ed.). New York: Routledge.

Knapp, M. (1995). *Teaching for meaning in high-poverty classrooms.* New York: Teachers College Press.

Knight, P. (1993). *Primary geography, primary history.* London: David Fulton.

Kourilsky, M. (1983). *Mini-society: Experiencing real-world economics in the elementary school classroom.* Menlo Park, CA: Addison-Wesley.

Kourilsky, M. (1992). *KinderEconomy+: A multidisciplinary learning society for primary grades.* New York: Joint Council on Economic Education.

Krey, D. (1998). *Children's literature in social studies: Teaching to the standards* (Bulletin No. 95). Washington, DC: National Council for the Social Studies.

Lamme, L. (1994). Stories from our past: Making history come alive for children. *Social Education, 58*, 159–64.

Laney, J. (1997). Economics for elementary school students: Research-supported principles that guide classroom practice. In M. Haas & M. Laughlin (Eds.), *Meeting the standards: Social studies readings for K–6 educators* (pp. 176–79). Washington, DC: National Council for the Social Studies.

Laney, J. (2001). Enhancing economic education through improved teaching methods: Common sense made easy. In J. Brophy (Ed.), *Subject-specific instructional methods and activities* (pp. 411–35). New York: Elsevier Science.

Laney, J., & Schug, M. (1998). Teach kids economics and they will learn. *Social Studies and the Young Learner, 11*(2), 13–17.

Lawson, J., & Barnes, D. (1991). Learning about history through literature. *Social Studies Review, 30*(2), 41–47.

Levstik, L. (1986). The relationship between historical response and narrative in the classroom. *Theory and Research in Social Education, 14*, 1–15.

Levstik, L. (1989). Historical narrative and the young reader. *Theory into Practice, 28*, 114–19.

Levstik, L. (1993). Building a sense of history in a first-grade classroom. In J. Brophy (Ed.), *Advances in research on teaching. Case studies of teaching and learning in social studies* (Vol. 4, pp. 1–31). Greenwich, CT: JAI Press.

Levstik, L., & Barton, K. (2005). *Doing history: Investigating with children in elementary and middle schools* (3rd ed.). Mahwah, NJ: Erlbaum.

Libbee, M., & Stoltman, J. (1988). Geography within the social studies curriculum. In S. Natoli (Ed.), *Strengthening geography in the social studies* (Bulletin No. 81, pp. 22–41). Washington, DC: National Council for the Social Studies.

Lo Coco, A., Inguglia, C., & Pace, U. (2005). Children's understanding of ethnic belonging in the development of ethnic attitudes. In M. Barrett & E. Buchanan-Barrow (Eds.), *Children's understanding of society* (223–50). Hove, England: Psychology Press.

Lucey, T., & Grant, M. (2005, October). *Exploring effective technology use in economics instruction.* Paper presented at the annual meeting of the National Council of Economic Education, San Antonio, TX.

Ludwig, G., et al. (1991). *Directions in geography: A guide for teachers.* Washington, DC: National Geographic Society.

Marshall, B. (Ed.). (1991). *The real world: Understanding the modern world through the new geography.* Boston: Houghton Mifflin.

Martorella, P. (1994). *Social studies for elementary school children: Developing young citizens.* New York: Macmillan.

McCall, A., & Ristow, T. (2003). *Teaching state history: A guide to developing a multicultural curriculum.* Portsmouth, NH: Heinemann.

McDevitt, M., & Chaffee, S. (2000). Closing gaps in political communication and knowledge: Effects of a school intervention. *Communication Research, 27*, 259–92.

McGuire, M. (1997). *The presidential election.* Chicago: Everyday Learning.

McKeown, M., & Beck, I. (1990). The assessment and characterization of young learners' knowledge of a topic in history. *American Educational Research Journal, 27,* 688–726.

McKeown, M., & Beck, I. (1994). Making sense of accounts of history: Why young students don't and how they might. In G. Leinhardt, I. Beck, & C. Stainton (Eds.), *Teaching and learning in history* (pp. 1–26). Hillsdale, NJ: Erlbaum.

McKinney, C., McKinney, K., Larkins, A., Gilmore, A., & Ford, M. (1990). Preservice elementary education majors' knowledge of economics. *Journal of Social Studies Research, 14*(2), 26–38.

McNeal, J. (1992). *Kids as customers: A handbook of marketing to children.* New York: Lexington.

Meichenbaum, D., & Biemiller, A. (1998). *Nurturing independent learners: Helping students take charge of their learning.* Cambridge, MA: Brookline.

Merryfield, M. (2004). Engaging elementary students in substantive culture learning. *Social Education, 68,* 270–73.

Merryfield, M., & Wilson, A. (2005) *Social studies and the world: Teaching global perspectives* (Bulletin No. 103). Silver Spring, MD: National Council for the Social Studies.

Millard, A. (1998). *A street through time.* New York: DK Publishing.

Mitchell, M. (1993). Situational interest: Its multifaceted structure in the secondary school mathematics classroom. *Journal of Educational Psychology, 85,* 424–36.

Moll, L. (Ed.). (1990). *Vygotsky and education: Instructional implications and applications of sociohistorical psychology.* Cambridge, England: Cambridge University Press.

Moll, L. (1992). Bilingual classroom studies and community analysis. *Educational Researcher, 21,* 20–24.

Moore, S., Lare, J., & Wagner, K. (1985). *The child's political world: A longitudinal perspective.* New York: Praeger.

Morris, A. (1992). *Houses and homes.* New York: Lothrop, Lee & Shephard.

Morrison, G., Lowther, D., & Demuelle, L. (1999). *Integrating computer technology into the classroom.* Upper Saddle River, NJ: Prentice-Hall.

Muessig, R. (1987). An analysis of developments in geographic education. *Elementary School Journal, 87,* 519–30.

Nash, G., Crabtree, C., & Dunn, R. (1997). *History on trial: Culture wars and the teaching of the past.* New York: Knopf.

National Center for History in the Schools. (1996). *National standards for history: Basic education.* Los Angeles: Author.

National Council for the Social Studies (NCSS). (1990). *Social studies curriculum planning resources.* Dubuque, IA: Kendall/Hunt.

National Council for the Social Studies (NCSS). (1993). A vision of powerful teaching and learning in the social studies: Building social understanding and civic efficacy. *Social Education, 57,* 213–23.

National Council for the Social Studies (NCSS). (1994). *Curriculum standards for social studies: Expectations of excellence.* (Bulletin No. 89). Washington, DC: Author.

National Council on Economic Education. (2005). *Children in the marketplace: Lesson plans in economics for grades 3 and 4* (2nd ed.). Washington, DC: Author.

National Education Association. (1916). *Social studies in secondary education: A six-year program adapted to the 6–3–3 and the 8–4 plans of organization.* (Bulletin No. 28). Washington, DC: U.S Department of the Interior, Bureau of Education.

Naylor, D., & Diem, R. (1987). *Elementary and middle school social studies.* New York: Random House.

Newman, D., Griffin, P., & Cole, M. (1989). *The construction zone: Working for cognitive change in school.* Cambridge, England: Cambridge University Press.

Newmann, F. (1990). Qualities of thoughtful social studies classes: An empirical profile. *Journal of Curriculum Studies, 22,* 253–75.

Newmann, F. (1997). Authentic assessment in social studies: Standards and examples. In G. Phye (Ed.), *Handbook of classroom assessment* (pp. 359–80). San Diego, CA: Academic press.

Newmann, F., Secada, W., & Wehlage, G. (1995). *A guide to authentic instruction and assessment: Vision, standards, and scoring.* Madison, WI: Wisconsin Center for Education Research.

Nieto, S. (2004). *Affirming diversity: The sociopolitical context of multicultural education.* Boston: Pearson/Allyn & Bacon.

Ochoa, A. (1988). *Education for democratic citizenship: Decision making in the social studies.* New York: Teachers College Press.

Onosko, J. (1990). Comparing teachers' instruction to promote students' thinking. *Journal of Curriculum Studies, 22,* 443–61.

Palmer, J. (1994). *Geography in the early years.* New York: Routledge.

Parham, C. (1994). Ten views of the past: Software that brings history to life. *Technology and Learning, 14*(6), 36–39, 42–45.

Parker, W. (1991). *Reviewing the social studies curriculum.* Alexandria, VA: Association for Supervision and Curriculum Development.

Paxton, R. (2003). Don't know much about history—never did. *Phi Delta Kappan, 85,* 265–73.

Petersen, J., Natoli, S., & Boehm, R. (1994). The guidelines for geographic education: A 10-year retrospective. *Social Education, 58,* 206–10.

Pliner, P., Freedman, J., Abramovitch, R., & Darke, P. (1996). Children as consumers: In the laboratory and beyond. In P. Lunt & A. Furnham (Eds.), *Economic socialization: The economic beliefs and behaviours of young people* (pp. 35–46). Cheltenham, UK: Edward Elgar.

Pressley, M., & Beard El-Dinary, P. (Guest Eds.). (1993). Special issue on strategies instruction. *Elementary School Journal, 94,* 105–284.

Pugh, K. (2002). Teaching for transformative experiences in science: An investigation of the effectiveness of two instructional elements. *Teachers College Record, 104,* 1101–37.

Raths, J. (1971). Teaching without specific objectives. *Educational Leadership, 28,* 714–20.

Ravitch, D. (1987). Tot sociology or what happened to history in the grade schools. *American Scholar, 56,* 343–53.

Ravitch, D. (1989). The plight of history in American schools. In P. Gagnon & The Bradley Commission on History in Schools (Eds.), *Historical literacy: The case for history in American education* (pp. 51–68). New York: Macmillan.

Resnick, L., & Klopfer, L. (Eds.). (1989). *Toward the thinking curriculum: Current cognitive research: 1989 yearbook of the Association for Supervision and Curriculum Development.* Alexandria, VA: Association for Supervision and Curriculum Development.

Richgels, D., Tomlinson, C., & Tunnell, M. (1993). Comparison of elementary students' history textbooks and trade books. *Journal of Educational Research, 86,* 161–71.

Rogers, P. (1987). History—the past as a frame of reference. In C. Portal (Ed.), *The history curriculum for teachers* (pp. 3–21). New York: Falmer.

Rose, S. (2000). Fourth graders theorize prejudice in American history. *International Journal of Historical Learning, Teaching, and Research, 1*(1), 1–11.

Rosen, H. (1986). The importance of story. *Language Arts, 63,* 226–37.

Rosenshine, B. (1968). To explain: A review of research. *Educational Leadership, 26,* 275–80.

Rosenshine, B., & Meister, C. (1992). The use of scaffolds for teaching higher-level cognitive strategies. *Educational Leadership, 49,* 26–33.

Ross, E. (1998). *Pathways to thinking: Strategies for developing independent learners, K–8.* Norwood, MA: Christopher-Gordon.

Rowe, M. (1986). Wait time: Slowing down may be a way of speeding up! *Journal of Teacher Education, 37,* 43–50.

Rylant, C. (1982). *When I was young in the mountains.* New York: Dutton Children's Books.

Sansom, C. (1987). Concepts, skills and content: A developmental approach to the history syllabus. In C. Portal (Ed.). *The history curriculum for teachers* (pp. 116–41). London: Falmer.

Savage, T., & Armstrong, D. (2004). *Effective teaching in elementary social studies* (5th ed.). Upper Saddle River, NJ: Pearson.

Schlene, V. (1990). Computers in the social studies classroom: An ERIC/ChESS sample. *History Microcomputer Review, 6*(2), 45–47.

Schug, M., & Hartoonian, H. (1996). Issues and practices in the social studies curriculum. In M. Pugach & C. Warger (Eds.), *Curriculum trends, special education, and reform: Refocusing the conversation* (pp. 106–22). New York: Teachers College Press.

Schunk, D. (1991). Self-efficacy and academic motivation. *Educational Psychologist, 26,* 207–31.

Schwartz, S. (2000). My family's story: Discovering history at home. *Social Studies and the Young Learner,12*(3), 6–9.

Scoffham, S. (1998). Young geographers. In R. Carter (Ed.), *Handbook of primary geography* (pp. 19–28). Sheffield, England: The Geographical Association.

Scoffham, S. (2000). Europe matters. In C. Fisher & T. Binns (Eds.), *Issues in geography teaching* (pp. 219–33). London: RoutledgeFalmer.

Seiter, D. (1988). Resources for teaching with computers in history. *History Microcomputer Review, 4*(2), 37–38.

Seixas, P. (2001). Review of research on social studies. In V. Richardson (Ed.), *Handbook of research on teaching* (4th ed., pp. 545–65). Washington, DC: American Educational Research Association.

Selby, D., Pike, G., Mytebari, F., Llambiri, S., Dautaj, A., Gjkutaj, M., & Rexha, B. (2000). *Global education: Preparation of children to face up to the challenges of the 21st century.* Tirana, Albania: UNICEF.

Sergiovanni, T. (1994). *Building community in schools.* San Francisco: Jossey-Bass.

Shaftel, F., & Shaftel, G. (1982). *Role playing in the curriculum.* Englewood Cliffs, NJ: Prentice-Hall.

Sharan, S. (Ed. (1990). *Cooperative learning: Theory and research.* New York: Praeger.

Sharan, Y., & Sharan, S. (1992). *Group investigation: Expanding cooperative learning*. New York: Teachers College Press.

Shaver, J. (Ed.). (1991). *Handbook of research on social studies teaching and learning*. New York: Macmillan.

Shuell, T. (1996). Teaching and learning in a classroom context. In D. Berliner & R. Calfree (Eds.), *Handbook of educational psychology* (pp. 726–64). New York: Macmillan.

Siddle-Walker, E. (1992). Falling asleep and failure among African-American students: Rethinking assumptions about process teaching. *Theory into Practice, 31*, 321–27.

Siegler, R., & Thompson, D. (1998). "Hey, would you like a nice cold cup of lemonade on this hot day?" Children's understanding of economic causation. *Developmental Psychology, 43*(1), 146–60.

Skeel, D. (1988). *Small-size economics: Lessons for the primary grades*. Glenview, IL: Scott, Foresman.

Slavin, R. (1986). *Using student team learning* (3rd ed.). Baltimore, MD: Center for Research on Elementary and Middle Schools, The Johns Hopkins University.

Slavin, R. (1988). Cooperative learning and student achievement. *Educational Leadership, 46*(2), 31–33. New York: Longman.

Slavin, R. (1990). *Cooperative learning: theory, research, and practice*. Englewood Cliffs, NJ: Prentice-Hall.

Slavin, R. (1995). *Cooperative learning, theory, research, and practice* (2nd ed.). Boston: Allyn & Bacon.

Smith, F. (1988). *Understanding reading* (4th ed.). Hillsdale, NJ: Erlbaum.

Smith, J., & Girod, M. (2003). John Dewey and psychologizing the subject-matter: Big ideas, ambitious teaching, and teacher education. *Teaching and Teacher Education, 19*, 295–307.

Sonuga-Barke, E., & Webley, P. (1993). *Children's saving: A study in the development of economic behaviour*. Hillsdale, NJ: Erlbaum.

Sosniak, L., & Stodolsky, S. (1993). Making connections: Social studies education in an urban fourth-grade classroom. In J. Brophy (Ed.), *Advances in research on teaching. Case studies of teaching and learning in social studies* (Vol. 4, pp. 71–100). Greenwich, CT: JAI Press.

Stanger, T. (1997). Future debtors of America. *Consumer Reports, 62*(12), 16–19.

Stiggins, R. (1997). *Student-centered classroom assessment* (2nd ed.). Upper Saddle River, NJ: Prentice-Hall.

Stiggins, R. (2001). *Student-involved classroom assessment* (3rd ed.) Upper Saddle River, NJ: Prentice-Hall.

Stodolsky, S. (1988). *The subject matters*. Chicago: University of Chicago Press.

Stodolsky, S., Salk, S., & Glaessner, B. (1991). Student views about learning math and social studies. *American Educational Research Journal, 28*, 89–116.

Stoltman, J. (1990). *Geography education for citizenship*. Bloomington, IN: ERIC Clearinghouse for Social Studies/Social Science Education. (ED 322 081).

Stoltman, J. (1991). Research on geography teaching. In J. Shaver (Ed.), *Handbook of research on social studies teaching and learning* (pp. 437–47). New York: Macmillan.

Sunal, C., & Haas, M. (1993). *Social studies and the elementary/middle school student*. Fort Worth, TX: Harcourt Brace Jovanovich.

Symcox, L. (1991). *Selected teaching materials for the United States and world history: An annotated bibliography*. Los Angeles: National Center for History in the Schools, University of California, Los Angeles. (ERIC Document No. ED 350 249).

Symcox, L. (2002). *Whose history? The struggle for national standards in American classrooms*. New York: Teachers College Press.

Teddlie, C., & Stringfield, S. (1993). *Schools make a difference: Lessons learned from a 10-year study of school effects*. New York: Teachers College Press.

Tharp, R., & Gallimore, R. (1988). *Rousing minds to life: Teaching, learning, and schooling in social context*. Cambridge, England: Cambridge University Press.

Thomas, R. M. (2005). *High-stakes testing: Coping with collateral damage*. Mahwah, NJ: Erlbaum.

Thornton, S. (2005). *Teaching social studies that matters: Curriculum for active teaching*. New York: Teachers College Press.

Thornton, S., & Vukelich, R. (1988). Effects of children's understanding of time concepts on historical understanding. *Theory and Research in Social Education, 16*, 69–82.

Thornton, S., & Wenger, R. (1990). Geography curriculum and instruction in three fourth-grade classrooms. *Elementary School Journal, 90*, 515–31.

Tomlinson, C., Tunnell, M., & Richgels, D. (1993). The content and writing of history in textbooks and trade books. In M. Tunnell & R. Ammon (Eds.), *The story of ourselves: Teaching history through children's literature* (pp. 51–62). Portsmouth, NH: Heinemann.

Torney-Purta, J., Hahn, C., & Amadeo, J. (2001). Principles of subject-specific instruction in education for citizenship. In J. Brophy (Ed.), *Subject-specific instructional methods and activities* (pp. 373–410). New York: Elsevier Science.

Tucker, C., Zayco, R., Herman, K., Reinke, W., Trujillo, M., Carraway, K., Wallack, C., & Ivery, P. (2002). Teacher and child variables as predictors of academic engagement among low-income African American children. *Psychology in the Schools, 39,* 477–88.

Tunnell, M. (1993). Unmasking the fiction of history: Children's historical literature begins to come of age. In M. Tunnell & R. Ammon (Eds.), *The story of ourselves: Teaching history through children's literature* (pp. 79–90). Portsmouth, NH: Heinemann.

VanFossen, P. (2003). Best practice economic education for young children? It's elementary! *Social Education, 67,* 90–94.

VanFossen, P. (2005). Reading and math take so much of the time . . .: An overview of social studies instruction in elementary classrooms in Indiana. *Theory and Research in Social Education, 33*(3), 376–403.

VanSledright, B. (2002). *In search of America's past: Learning to read history in elementary school.* New York: Teachers College Press.

VanSledright, B., & Frankes, L. (1998). Literature's place in learning history and science. In C. Hynd (Ed.), *Learning from text: Across conceptual domains* (pp. 117–38). Mahwah, NJ: Erlbaum.

Vygotsky, L. (1962). *Thought and language.* Cambridge, MA: MIT Press.

Vygotsky, L. (1978). *Mind in society: The development of higher psychological processes.* Cambridge, MA: Harvard University Press.

Wade, R. (2001). Social action in the social studies: From the ideal to the real. *Theory into Practice, 40*(1), 23–28.

Wallace, R. (2004). A framework for understanding teaching with the Internet. *American Educational Research Journal, 41,* 447–88.

Wang, M., Haertel, G., & Walberg, H. (1993). Toward a knowledge base for school learning. *Review of Educational Research, 63,* 249–94.

Waters, K. (1989). *Sarah Morton's day: A day in the life of a Pilgrim girl.* New York: Scholastic.

Waters, K. (1991). *The story of the White House.* New York: Scholastic.

Weinstein, C., & Mayer, R. (1986). The teaching of learning strategies. In M.C. Wittrock (Ed.), *Handbook of research on teaching* (3rd ed., pp. 315–27). New York: Macmillan.

White, J. (1993). Teaching for understanding in a third-grade geography lesson. In. J. Brophy (Ed.), *Advances in research on teaching. Case studies of teaching and learning in social studies* (Vol. 4, pp. 33–69). Greenwich, CT: JAI Press.

Wiegand, P. (1993). *Children and primary geography.* New York: Cassell.

Wiggins, A. (1989a). A true test: Toward more authentic and equitable achievement. *Phi Delta Kappan, 70,* 203–13.

Wiggins, A. (1989b). Teaching to the (authentic) test. *Educational Leadership, 46*(7), 41–47.

Wiggins, G. (1993). *Assessing student performance: Exploring the purpose and limits of testing.* San Francisco: Jossey-Bass.

Willig, C. (1990). *Children's concepts and the primary curriculum.* London: Paul Chapman.

Wills, J. (in press). Putting the squeeze on social studies: Managing teaching dilemmas in subject areas excluded from state testing. *Teachers College Record.*

Winitzky, N. (1991). Classroom organization for social studies. In J. Shaver (Ed.), *Handbook of research on social studies teaching and learning* (pp. 530–39). New York: Macmillan.

Winston, B. (1986). Teaching and learning in geography. In S. Wronski & D. Bragaw (Eds.), *Social studies and social sciences: A 50-year perspective* (Bulletin No. 78, pp. 43–58). Washington, DC: National Council for the Social Studies.

Winston, L. (1997). *Keepsakes: Using family stories in elementary classrooms.* Portsmouth, NH: Heinemann.

Wyman, R. (1998) Using children's diaries to teach the Oregon Trail. *Social Studies and the Young Learner, 10*(3), M3–M5.

Yell, M., Scheurman, G., & Reynolds, K. (2004). *A link to the past: Engaging students in the study of history* (Bulletin No. 102). Silver Springs, MD: National Council for the Social Studies.

Zahorik, J. (1996). Elementary and secondary teachers' reports of how they make learning interesting. *Elementary School Journal, 96,* 551–64.

Zais, R. (1976). *Curriculum: Principles and foundations.* New York: Harper & Row.

Index

TO THE OWNER OF THIS BOOK:

I hope that you have found *Powerful Social Studies for Elementary Students*, Second Edition, useful. So that this book can be improved in a future edition, would you take the time to complete this sheet and return it? Thank you.

School and address:_____

Department:_____

Instructor's name:_____

1. What I like most about this book is:_____

_____

_____

2. What I like least about this book is:

_____

_____

3. My general reaction to this book is:

_____

_____

4. The name of the course in which I used this book is:

_____

5. Were all of the chapters of the book assigned for you to read?_____

   If not, which ones weren't?_____

6. In the space below, or on a separate sheet of paper, please write specific suggestions for improving this book and anything else you'd care to share about your experience in using this book.

_____

_____

_____

BUSINESS REPLY MAIL

FIRST-CLASS MAIL   PERMIT NO. 34   BELMONT CA

POSTAGE WILL BE PAID BY ADDRESSEE

Attn: *Dan Alpert, Education Editor*

Wadsworth/Thomson Learning
10 Davis Drive
Belmont, CA   94002-9801

IIıluıluıIIIııIIııııIılIIılıluIılIIıııııIIIııII

OPTIONAL:

Your name:_____ Date: _____

May we quote you, either in promotion for *Powerful Social Studies for Elementary Students*, Second Edition, or in future publishing ventures?

Yes: _____ No: _____

Sincerely yours,

Jere Brophy
Janet Alleman